Killer Clown is a fast-paced, suspenseful account of the pursuit and prosecution of America's most notorious mass murderer.

"Gripping study . . . for true-crime addicts."
—*Publishers Weekly*

"You will learn more in this book about the daily activities of a police department than you will from any number of Ed McBain novels or episodes of *Hill Street Blues*."
—*The Charleston News & Courier*

"As with a good mystery story, to the very end of *Killer Clown* we find ourselves still rooting for good to triumph over evil, yet fearing that the dice may be loaded the other way."
—*Chicago Tribune*

"For those who have nearly forgotten John Wayne Gacy—*Killer Clown* is a chilling reminder."
—*Nashville Banner*

KILLER CLOWN

Terry Sullivan with
Peter T. Maiken

PINNACLE BOOKS NEW YORK

KILLER CLOWN

Copyright © 1983 by Terry Sullivan and Peter T. Maiken

All rights reserved, including the right to reproduce this book or portions thereof in any form.

A Pinnacle Books edition, published by special arrangement with The Putnam Publishing Group.

Grosset & Dunlap edition/July 1983
Pinnacle edition/July 1984

ISBN: 0-523-42274-1

Can. ISBN: 0-523-43269-0

Cover photo by United Press International

Printed in the United States of America

PINNACLE BOOKS, INC.
1430 Broadway
New York, New York 10018

9   8   7   6   5   4   3   2   1

To Mom and Dad,
　　　with love and thanks

I am deeply indebted and most grateful to many people for their help on this manuscript. Any attempt to credit everyone would be futile. Nonetheless, with apologies to others, I thank my investigator Greg Bedoe; Sgt. Joe Hein; former Assistant State's Attorney Larry Finder; my writer (and his patience) Peter Maiken; my trial partner, Bill Kunkle; Officers Albrecht, Hachmeister, Robinson, Schultz, and Tovar; and my sister, Kathy Tully.

My thanks, finally and simply, to my faithful friends for their endurance through it all.

TERRY SULLIVAN

KILLER
CLOWN

INVESTIGATION

Monday
December 11, 1978

Kim Byers couldn't decide what to do with the photo receipt. Had it been a customer's order, she simply would have given that person the stub from the envelope. But these were her own photographs, which she could easily identify when they came back from the lab. They were prints she planned to give to her sister for Christmas, now just two weeks away.

It was 7:30 P.M. when Kim, one of several teenagers working at Nisson Pharmacy in Des Plaines, Illinois, had used a brief lull in customer traffic to process her order. Nisson's was in a nondescript, one-story building in a small shopping center. Its glass front was papered with signs advertising sale items. Among its neighbors were a 7-Eleven, a Gold Medal Restaurant, and a liquor store. Across busy Touhy Avenue lay the northern perimeter of Chicago's O'Hare International Airport. Inside Nisson's, you smelled the usual drugstore aroma of candies and scented notions, while your ears absorbed the recurring thunder of jets.

Kim logged the order number in the record book and tore off the receipt. After a moment's thought, she stuck it in a pocket of the parka she was wearing. While she was working at the cash register she had borrowed the coat to protect her from the drafts at the front door.

Rob Piest, whose parka Kim had on, was now midway through his after-school shift at Nisson's. Rob was a fifteen-year-old sophomore at Maine West High School, and he'd worked at the pharmacy since the previous summer. Although Kim was two years older, Rob and she had dated occasionally. Mature for his age, Rob usually went out with older girls, and Kim was attracted to the handsome boy with the trim athletic build, shaggy brown hair, and wide smile. Tonight, however, the smile was not in evidence as he stocked shelves in silence: Phil Torf, one of the owners of the pharmacy, had just turned down his request for a raise.

"I'm going to quit and find another job," Rob told Kim.

"Don't quit now," Kim advised him. "You'll probably get a Christmas bonus."

"Yeah," Rob answered, "but I need the money now."

Rob would turn sixteen in March, and he wanted to buy a Jeep. He had saved $900, but he knew he couldn't afford the payments on the $2.85 an hour he was earning at Nisson's.

Rob had just broken up with the first special girlfriend in his life, but he hoped for a reconciliation, and having his own wheels would help. He wanted a Jeep, too, because of his interest in camping and the wilderness. Three merit badges shy of Eagle rank, he was tiring of the Boy Scouts but not of the outdoors. He had become a skilled nature photographer, and with a tough vehicle he could explore country that roads never crossed.

A dedicated athlete, Rob was training for the sophomore gymnastics team, but on that Monday afternoon he'd left practice early: he wanted to stop at K-Mart to buy fish to feed his snakes. (Snakes were only some of the pets the Piests kept. Several years earlier, much to the delight of Rob and his brother and sister, the family had inherited a relative's menagerie of several dozen animals.)

As usual after school, Rob's mother, Elizabeth, was waiting in her car for him, and as usual they were both on a tight schedule. She had just come from her job as a telephone operator in a chemical company to drive him home for a quick meal. After that, she or Rob's father, Harold, would drive him to Nisson's shortly before 6 o'clock and pick him up after he finished work at 9. Tonight's routine was different only because of the stop at K-Mart (which was unsuccessful—the fish, Rob decided, were too expensive).

Tonight was special, though, because it was Elizabeth Piest's forty-sixth birthday. At home, she saw Rob looking at her birthday cake. "We'll have the party when you get home from work," she told him. Rob bent over to hug the family's two German shepherds, Caesar and Kelly, who had bounded into the kitchen to greet him.

"Here's your dinner," Rob's sister said as she scooped a hot ham and cheese sandwich off the grill.

"Thanks, Kerry," Rob said, taking his meal on the run.

He and his mother went out into the winter night and got in the car for the eight-block drive to Nisson Pharmacy. Rob remarked that once he bought his Jeep, his mother wouldn't have to bother driving him to work. She smiled and said she didn't mind the trip at all.

Now the family would wait for Rob's return to celebrate Elizabeth's birthday. The Piests were always together on occasions like this. They were an uncommonly close family, and Rob was the center of it.

When Phil Torf's brother, Larry, had remodeled the drugstore two years before, he had employed P.E. Systems, a firm specializing in pharmacy design and construction. The work had been done by a gregarious supervisor named John Gacy. Although Larry Torf thought Gacy's craftsmanship was merely passable, he was impressed with the man's knowledge of pharmaceutical marketing and his energy in getting the job done. Gacy, working with Phil and several youths, did all the remodeling after hours, allowing the store to remain open for business. During that time, Gacy and Phil Torf became passing friends.

Now Gacy was in business for himself, and Phil had asked him to come in to give advice on rearranging shelving. At 5:30 P.M. on Monday, as agreed, Gacy pulled up in front of Nisson's in a new 1979 four-door black Oldsmobile 98. The car was rigged for CB radio and carried two spotlights, a red one on the passenger side.

A heavyset man with a round face, Gacy, thirty-six, was considerably overweight at 195 pounds and five feet nine inches. His brown hair was graying at the temples and his knobby chin was well cushioned by sagging jowls; he wore a mustache. He was dressed in wash pants, an open-collar shirt, and a waist-length black leather jacket.

Gacy greeted Phil Torf warmly, and the two bantered about old times for more than an hour. He had his own firm now, he told Phil; it was called PDM, for Painting, Decorating, and Maintenance. He told Phil he also did snowplowing and sold Christmas trees.

"Looks like you've got pretty much of a new crew here," Gacy said, surveying the store. His eyes came to rest on Rob Piest, who was sitting in an aisle about ten feet away, stocking shelves.

"They're high school kids," Phil explained. "They go on to college or other jobs. There's always a turnover."

"I hire high school kids, too," Gacy said, turning to Linda Mertes, an employee he recognized from the remodeling days two years before. "You remember Dick, don't you?" Linda nodded. "I was paying him only three or four dollars an hour when he started, but now he's making four hundred dollars a week. Now I start everybody at a five-dollar-an-hour minimum."

"Wow," Linda said. "Hey, Rob. Do you want a job?" she asked, laughing. Rob continued stocking the shelves and didn't answer.

Gacy wandered through the store, inspecting the aisles, measuring shelves, and checking structural supports.

He told Torf that he estimated that the job would run about $1,600. The two talked a while longer, then Gacy left at 7:15, saying he would be in touch. A few minutes later, Torf noticed a brown appointment book, fastened with a thick strap, sitting on the pharmacy desk. It was Gacy's. Phil wondered about calling him, but decided not to. Gacy would probably return for it anyway.

"Hey, I need my coat," said Rob. "I've got to take out the garbage."

It was now 8 o'clock. Kim Byers slipped off Rob's parka and watched him put it on for his trip out the back of the store. As Rob walked into the alley with an armload of cartons and trash, a freshman girl from his high school spotted him. She threw a snowball at him, then retreated with her girlfriend, giggling in delight. When he came back inside, Rob tossed his coat on some cigarette cartons near the front register, which he was supposed to watch while he finished stocking shelves until the end of his shift at 9.

A black pickup truck with a snowplow attached glided to a halt in front of the store. Gacy came inside and walked back to the pharmacy.

"Forget something?" Torf asked.

Gacy smiled and nodded. For the next forty-five minutes he wandered through the store, chatting and once again inspecting the shelving.

At five minutes to 9, Elizabeth Piest arrived to pick up her son.

"Mom," Rob said, "I'm not done stocking. I'll be a few minutes."

"Take your time," she said. She spoke briefly with Kim Byers then wandered over to the card section.

At 8:58, Rob bounded up to Kim and asked her to watch the register. Then he called to his mother. "Some contractor wants to talk to me about a job," he said, grabbing his parka and rushing out the door.

Moments later, seeing Kim at the register, Torf asked her where Rob was.

"He's outside talking to that guy who was in here," Kim said. "Don't worry," she added offhandedly. "He's a big boy."

Several minutes later, Elizabeth Piest asked Kim if she'd seen Rob come back. Kim had not. Mrs. Piest had a strong feeling that she wanted to be with her son right now, but she didn't know why. She felt a sense of fear she couldn't explain. Nonetheless, she chatted briefly with Kim; then, showing mounting uneasiness, she said she was leaving and asked Kim to have Rob call her at home when he returned. She said she would come back and pick him up. It was 9:20.

A few moments later, Torf walked by the register.

"Who is that construction guy?" Kim asked him.

"You mean John Gacy?" Torf replied. "He's all right. He's a good guy."

Her family was perplexed when Elizabeth Piest walked into the kitchen at 9:25 without Rob. "He went off with some kind of contractor to see about a job," she explained. She went to the phone and called Nisson's. Kim Byers answered; still no Rob. "Do you have any idea," asked Mrs. Piest, "who Rob was going to talk to?" Kim told her that the man's name was John Gacy.

By now the family should have been cutting Elizabeth's birthday cake. This was not like Rob. He was thoroughly a creature of habit, and neither he nor his brother or sister, nor, for that matter, anyone in the family, ever went anywhere without letting the others know. Something was very wrong.

Fifteen minutes went by. The Piests' concern mounted. Kerry, six years older than Rob, and her brother Ken, a twenty-two-year-old premedical student, speculated on Rob's whereabouts. Elizabeth called Nisson's again, but Kim still hadn't seen Rob. She asked Elizabeth to wait a moment and put her on hold. The father and children watched anxiously.

"Phil wonders if you've already bought a Christmas tree," Kim finally said to Elizabeth.

"Why?" Elizabeth asked. She thought Torf was being flippant.

"Because John Gacy owns a Christmas tree lot, and Phil thinks that maybe Rob went there to buy a tree."

Meanwhile the others were checking the telephone listings for a John Gacy, but they weren't sure how to spell the name or which of the numerous suburban directories to consult. They found nothing close. They called several of Rob's friends, none of whom had seen him. Elizabeth called Nisson's one more time. Now she was becoming frantic, and she wished that Torf would show some concern.

Torf assured her that he would have someone check outside the store to see if Rob might have slipped on the ice and was lying unconscious. He said that although the store was now closed, he would be there for a while and gave Elizabeth the night number. "I'll call John and see if he knows anything about Rob," he said.

"What is his number?" Elizabeth Piest demanded.

"It's 457-1614," said Torf.

"Do you have his address?" she asked.

Torf hesitated, then said he didn't.

"Why would he want to be talking with a fifteen-year-old boy at this time of night?" asked Elizabeth.

"Hey, wait a minute," Torf replied. "This guy's no bum." Elizabeth hung up.

Harold Piest dialed Gacy's number and got the contractor's answering machine.

"We're going to the police," he said. Even though they didn't want to admit it to one another, by now they all feared the worst. They knew that if Rob were physically able to get home, he would be home. They knew him too well to think otherwise.

On the way to the Des Plaines police station, Harold and Elizabeth Piest stopped at the house of Rob's best friend, Todd Schludt. Todd had stayed away from home one night and Rob had admonished him for his behavior. Todd was surprised to hear of Rob's disappearance and was sure he wouldn't run away. Rob had been upset because Todd was moving from Des Plaines. They had both been to a farewell party the night before. Todd hadn't seen Rob since then.

Next, the Piests went to Nisson's, where they found Torf and a friend, Joe Hajkaluk, another pharmacist, standing at the door. Torf said he had called Gacy's number without success. He gave the Piests his own home number in Chicago.

Harold and Elizabeth continued on to the police station. The new Des Plaines shopping mall, on the southwest side of the train tracks, had emptied, and the sidewalks were mostly deserted. Two more yellow and green North Western commuter trains from downtown would yet come to a jerking halt, discharge passengers, then move on, like toys under a tree, through the array of street lights and Christmas decorations, to darker countryside and more distant suburbs. Soon the town would be silent.

The police station in Des Plaines is a modern two-story, brick, fortresslike box, mostly windowless on the ground floor, and is connected by an open walkway to the adjacent Civic Center. The complex was constructed in the early 1970s, long after Des Plaines had grown from the quiet little truck-garden and nursery suburb of its German origins into a congested hub of Chicago's suburban sprawl. The station lay at the northern end of the four-block downtown strip built along both sides of the railroad tracks.

The Piests walked up to the desk, manned by Watch Officer George Konieczny. Elizabeth explained what had happened. Konieczny said that he could only take the information for a missing-person report. The police would call if they learned of Rob's whereabouts, and a youth officer would be assigned to the case in the morning; there was nothing for the Piests to do but go home and wait. Suburban police stations are places of limited late-evening activity. Most of their people work during the day, and at night many specialized functions of the department cease entirely. Elizabeth sighed, then recited her son's vital statistics and recounted the events of the evening while Konieczny wrote: "Robert Jerome Piest, male/white, 15, wearing tan Levi pants and T-shirt, brown wedge-type suede shoes, and a light-blue down jacket . . ." Rob became Des Plaines police case No. 78-35203, one of the department's more than six dozen missing persons of 1978.

The Piests left the station. At 11:50 Konieczny completed his report. He called Phil Torf, who was still at Nisson's. Torf had no new information. Konieczny then took the report to his watch commander.

"The parents are really concerned," Konieczny said to him, "and the kid has never run away before. Still, you do crazy things at age fifteen." The watch commander signed his approval on the report, and Konieczny notified the radio room upstairs that he was sending along a "missing."

At 1:54 A.M. on Tuesday, five hours after the disappearance of Robert Piest, a dispatcher sent out a message from her LEADS (Law Enforcement Agencies Data System) terminal to all police jurisdictions in Illinois. The missing-person report, with a note appended by Officer Konieczny attesting to the Piest parents' genuine concern, was placed with other overnight reports on the desk of the commander of the Criminal Investigation Division, Lieutenant Joseph Kozenczak. Although the Youth Bureau, which would initially handle the case, had officers on duty until 1 A.M., they would not see the report until Kozenczak screened it after his arrival at 7:30 A.M. Missing-person cases were regarded as routine, and this was departmental policy.

The Piest family did as they were told and went home. But they didn't rest. They wanted action, and if the police department wouldn't give them much, they would make their own. They organized a search that took them over virtually every street and parking lot in Des Plaines. They theorized that Rob had been picked up by Gacy and then tried to jump out of the vehicle. They thought he might be hurt and trying to make his way home. They knew he would try as best he could.

Kerry took one shepherd in her Datsun, Ken the other in his van, each taking an article of clothing for the dogs to sniff. Harold went out in his car, and Elizabeth stayed home by the phone and waited. They patrolled the quiet streets and trudged over snowbanks that had been molded by plows after the seven-inch snowfall four days earlier. Periodically they rendezvoused with one another to coordinate their plans. They expanded their search to neighboring Mount Prospect, Park Ridge, and Rosemont. Several times they went back separately to Nisson's, Harold before midnight, Kerry about 12:30, and Ken shortly after 1 A.M. When they saw Phil Torf or his car, they wondered what he was doing. Torf told Ken that Hajkaluk knew where Gacy's house and tree lot were and that he would check them.

The three Piests searched all night to no avail. At daybreak they returned home, exhausted, to Elizabeth, who was still maintaining her vigil at the telephone. Distraught and sleepless, they went through the motions of preparing for the day. Ken had classes to go to, the other three had jobs. But before the parents and Kerry went to their offices, they would again visit the police station. In the kitchen, untouched, sat the cake Harold had bought for Elizabeth's birthday.

Tuesday
December 12, 1978

By 8:30 A.M., the day shift was on duty at the Des Plaines police station. Bedraggled from their search, Harold, Elizabeth, and Kerry Piest went to the front desk and asked to see the youth officer assigned to the case. Ronald Adams, twelve years on the force, six in the Youth Bureau, met them in a conference room. Adams got a copy of Konieczny's report and scanned it.

Mrs. Piest gave Adams her son's copy of *Dialtone*, the student telephone directory from Maine West High School, in which Rob had underlined the names of his friends. Then she recounted the events of the night before. Youth officers don't always believe parents who say, "My child would never run away." Every year tens of thousands of youths leave home, usually because they've quarreled with their parents, or they're unhappy in love, or they've had problems at school. Most of them return. But as he watched and listened to the Piests, Adams was sure from his years of experience that Rob was not another runaway. Here was a loving son disappearing from a close and caring family on the night of his mother's birthday. Adams was convinced there was foul play.

He asked the Piests to wait in the conference room and went to his office to call Nisson's. He spoke with Larry Torf, who said he had left the store early on Monday evening and that Adams should call his brother, Phil, who was still at home.

Phil Torf told Adams that Gacy had been in the pharmacy

13

twice on Monday night to discuss the remodeling. Gacy, he said, had mentioned hiring high school boys for construction work, and he thought Rob might have overheard that conversation. He added, however, that he had not seen the two of them together. After Mrs. Piest called, Torf said, he left a message on Gacy's answering device, but the contractor never called back. Torf said he thought that Gacy had a Christmas tree lot on Cumberland Avenue on the outskirts of Chicago, a few blocks from his house.

Next, Adams called Gacy. Yes, the contractor said, he had been in the pharmacy. He mentioned that he had asked Phil Torf if there were any fixtures in back of the store. No, he had not spoken with Rob Piest nor had any contact with him. Gacy was polite but firm.

Finally, Adams called Kim Byers. She confirmed that Rob had gone out about 9 P.M., saying, "That contractor guy wants to talk to me." She had not seen Rob talking with Gacy.

Adams went back to the conference room, although he had little to tell the family. He said he would continue checking but cautioned them not to intrude into the investigation. Despite their fears and anguish, he said, they must leave that to the police. The Piests thanked him and quietly left.

"This really stinks," Adams said, talking about the case to Kozenczak over lunch. The lieutenant had read the missing-person report and had passed it on through channels, but he hadn't been aware that the Piest family had come back to the station. Now, however, he saw from what Adams was telling him that the situation might be serious, and he told the youth officer to pursue the investigation without delay. He said he would have another detective, James Pickell, come in early to help.

Back at the station, Adams called the telephone company and was told there was no listing for John Gacy; the number that Mrs. Piest had given the police was listed as PDM Contractors Corporation, 8213 Summerdale Avenue, in Norwood Park Township, on the northwest outskirts of Chicago. Pickell was assigned to investigate the address on Summerdale and check the Christmas tree lot for any signs that Rob Piest had been held captive there. Adams would talk to Rob's school friends.

Pickell saw a tree lot near St. Joseph's Ukrainian Catholic Church on Cumberland Avenue. The man he talked to there said that no John Gacy worked at the lot and suggested that Pickell check another one on Cumberland just north of the expressway. There were two cars at the lot, and Pickell asked the station by radio for a registration check. Neither was Gacy's. At the other lot, the couple who ran it told Pickell they'd never heard of Gacy and referred him back to the church.

Pickell drove south about four blocks on Cumberland and turned east on Summerdale. Number 8213 was a small yellow-brick ranch-style house in a block of single-family dwellings. A four-door black 1979 Oldsmobile, license plate PDM 42, was parked in the semicircular driveway at the front of the house. Pickell went to the door and knocked. No one answered. He went to a rear door. No answer.

He then asked the next-door neighbor if she knew where Gacy was. She didn't, but she said that if his car was there, he was probably out in his truck. Nor did she know where his tree lot was. Pickell went back to the station.

Harold Piest had not followed Adams's advice to keep out of the investigation—and, together with Kerry, he was making almost as rapid progress as the Des Plaines police. After getting excused from work, he and his daughter went to Nisson's and asked directions to Gacy's tree lot.

As they approached the Ukrainian church, Piest wondered aloud whether he should go into the lot. Instead, he and Kerry decided to go to their own church, a little over a mile away, for help. He explained the situation to his pastor, who called the priest at St. Joseph's and arranged for Piest to meet him.

At the Ukrainian church, the priest told Harold and Kerry that he didn't know if a Gacy was involved in the lot, but he knew the man who ran it. He agreed to call him to see if he knew Gacy and also to try to get the contractor's address without explaining why he was asking. The priest quickly got the information: 8213 Summerdale Avenue. Harold pumped the priest's hand in gratitude.

He and Kerry drove the six or so blocks to Gacy's house and parked in front. They stared at the house, not sure what to do next. Maybe it *was* best to do as the police said, they finally decided. Don't interfere in the investigation. They turned around and drove home.

Meanwhile Adams had interviewed Kim Byers at school in the presence of the dean of girls. Kim recounted how Rob had asked her to take over the cash register, and she reviewed the events that had followed his disappearance. She had little to add to her previous account except to say that she thought Rob had no reason to leave home.

At the station, Adams received a call from a local Illinois Search and Rescue unit. The Piest family had asked them to use their dog teams to hunt through nearby forest preserves for any sign of Rob. Adams told the SAR member he would have to check with his superiors.

At 3 o'clock, Youth Bureau detective Mike Olsen reported for duty early. He and Adams began calling the schoolmates whose names Rob had underlined in his *Dialtone*. None had seen Rob, but the fact that they all regarded him highly confirmed that he was not the runaway kind. Kozenczak left for home at 3:45, the end of his shift, telling his men to inform him of any developments.

Pickell gave the license number of the black Oldsmobile to the radio room for a registration check with the State of Illinois. In addition, he ran the number through the Detective Bureau's own microfiche system, a compilation of all Illinois vehicle license numbers that lists owners' names, addresses, dates of birth, driver's license numbers, and vehicle identification numbers. He also called the credit bureau, several neighboring police departments, and Chicago police headquarters downtown. They told him that Gacy, date of birth 17 March 1942, had a parole record in Chicago and suggested he call the records section with Gacy's internal reference number, 273632.

When making a record check, Chicago police require the subject's address, date of birth, and Social Security number. Although Pickell didn't have the last item, he finally convinced the records officer of the urgency of his call and got him to check the IR number. Pickell waited ten minutes before the officer came back on the line. The rap sheet showed a John W. Gary paroled to Chicago on June 19, 1970. Gary, the officer said, was apparently a typographical error. All the other entries on the sheet were for John Wayne Gacy.

"What was the parole for?" Pickell asked.

"Sodomy," the officer said. "Waterloo, Iowa, May 20, 1968. Ten years, Iowa Men's Reformatory, Anamosa."

The last entry on Gacy's arrest record was a charge of battery, July 15, 1978, 16th District, Chicago Police Department, no disposition. The previous one was June 22, 1972, a charge of aggravated battery and reckless conduct in Northbrook, a suburb north of Des Plaines. This was listed as having been dismissed later that summer. The record showed no details of the sodomy conviction or the other arrests, but it was clear that Gacy had a background of both sexual deviance and violent behavior.

Day was now becoming night. In the windowless Detective Bureau, a ground-floor room to the rear of the waiting area and the watch commander's office, time changed imperceptibly. Only the fluorescent lights illuminated the bold sunflower walls, burgundy carpeting, and the half-dozen gray metal desks. In the ten days ahead, the distinction between daylight and darkness would become even more blurred for the detectives who labored longer and longer into the night.

Pickell called the Northbrook police, but their records section was closed for the day. However, a Northbrook detective said he would assemble their reports of Gacy's arrest from 1972, which included a fingerprint card and a mug shot. Before going to pick up the reports, Pickell called Kozenczak at home to tell him about Gacy's sodomy conviction and the other arrests.

Kozenczak knew then he had to hear John Gacy's story. The lieutenant had been a police officer in Des Plaines for sixteen years, most of them on patrol. He was a good, tough cop, but he had never run a major investigation. He had been promoted to commander of the Detective Bureau only six months before, and he was still feeling his way.

He called the felony review unit of the Cook County State's Attorney's Office for legal advice. In the post-Miranda climate of defendant's rights, police can't be too careful. Kozenczak explained the situation to an assistant state's attorney and added, "We don't know what we have, but we're going to talk to this guy and want to know how far we can push him."

"Don't push too hard," the assistant state's attorney told him. "If he says go screw yourself, back off and confer with the Third District assistants in the morning." The Third District, a suburban administrative unit of the State's Attorney's Office, is operated from the Des Plaines Civic Center, next to the police station.

Kozenczak got back to the station around 7 P.M., about the time Pickell returned from Northbrook with Gacy's arrest records. Adams had left for the day, and now Detective Dave Sommerschield was being briefed. The three men reviewed the Northbrook reports together.

The complainant, Jackie Dee, twenty-four, had told police he was offered a ride on June 7, 1972, at 3:40 A.M., by a stocky man in his mid-thirties wearing a Barnaby's Restaurant jacket. Dee was walking near the Lawson YMCA on Chicago's Near North Side at the time. When Dee saw that the man, who called himself John, was not taking him to his destination, he protested. The man took out a badge, identified himself as a "county police officer," and told Dee he was under arrest. He attempted, unsuccessfully, to handcuff the young man. Then he asked Dee what it was worth to get out of this. Dee said he had no money.

"Would you suck my dick?" the man asked. Fearing for his safety, Dee consented.

The two got out of the car at a Barnaby's in Northbrook, and "John" produced keys with which he unlocked the door to the building. Inside, Dee resisted, and the man clubbed him on the back of the neck, then kicked him as he lay on the floor. Dee ran outside, and the man pursued him in his car and struck him down. Dee finally reached a service station, where an attendant called the police.

The next day, police interviewed the night manager of the restaurant—John Gacy. He said he'd heard he had been implicated in the attack and welcomed the chance to exonerate himself. "I was home at 3 A.M.," he told police. "My wife will verify that." Two weeks went by, delaying the identification of Gacy. First, Dee said he was unable to appear because of his physical condition, then Gacy was transferred within, and finally separated from, the company. Police arrested Gacy on June 22.

In the end, charges were dismissed after Gacy complained to the police that Dee was making threatening phone calls attempting to extort money from him in return for dropping the charges. After a set-up drop, in which police caught Dee with $91 in marked currency passed by Gacy, they reviewed the arrest records of both men—sodomy for Gacy, and robbery, solicitation for prostitution, and disorderly conduct for Dee— and they left the two where they found them.

Despite the dismissal of the complaint, Dee's story, if true, presented a chilling picture of John Gacy—or, as the alias on his fingerprint card indicated, "Colonel."

By 9 P.M., the Des Plaines police had got responses from both their National Crime Information Center and LEADS computers: neither had any information on John Gacy. Now it was up to Kozenczak's men. The detectives drove the six miles to the house on Summerdale in two unmarked cars, Kozenczak and Pickell in one, Olsen and Sommerschield in another.

A brisk, warming wind from the south had brought temperatures up into the mid-thirties, leaving puddles of slush and water on the side streets. The warm air passing over cold ground had produced a haze that was illuminated by the lights of O'Hare and the multicolored glow of commercial signs along the expressway. To the west of Cumberland Avenue lay the many high-rise buildings under construction in a burgeoning new "airport city." To the east lay the modest bungalows, ranch houses, and duplexes of John Gacy's neighborhood in Norwood Park Township.

Kozenczak and Pickell walked past the black Oldsmobile in the driveway and knocked at the door. They got no response and knocked again. Still no answer. Peering through the diamond-shaped window in the door, they saw someone standing inside in the darkness. The officers were unsure what to do next.

A van came splashing down the street, slowed, and pulled into Gacy's driveway. The vehicle had a PDM sign on the door.

A young man got out. Kozenczak identified himself and asked the man who he was.

"Dick Walsh," he said (his name is changed here). "You looking for John? He won't answer the front door because he watches TV in the family room."

Sommerschield stepped out of the shadows from the rear of the house and confirmed Walsh's guess. Looking through a picture window, the detective had seen Gacy sitting in an easy chair, apparently watching TV and sipping a can of Diet Pepsi. Kozenczak and Pickell went to the rear of the house while Olsen and Sommerschield stayed with Walsh in the driveway.

"Is John in trouble?" Walsh asked.

"We just want to ask a few questions," Olsen told him.

"You guys got a warrant?" The detective ignored his question and asked him about his relationship with Gacy. Walsh said he worked for PDM, that the van was Gacy's. He talked about the remodeling jobs they worked on and said he was the supervisor in John's absence. Walsh seemed very curious about their presence, yet was not very specific in his replies to their questions. He volunteered that he and Gacy were going to a friend's Christmas tree lot that night. Olsen noted that Walsh seemed to make a point of mentioning his wife in their conversation.

"I heard you in front, but I had to go to the john," Gacy told Kozenczak and Pickell at the back door.

"We'd like some help about a missing juvenile," Kozenczak said, showing his badge.

"Come in," Gacy said, ushering the detectives into a large recreation room at the rear of the house. Gacy turned down the television and seated himself in a black recliner. Across from him was a large, well-stocked bar; next to it a refrigerator and the entrance to a powder room. "What can I do for you?"

Kozenczak went over the facts of Rob's disappearance and told Gacy that someone had seen him talking with the boy.

No, said Gacy, he had seen two boys working in the pharmacy, but he hadn't spoken to either one. Well, he might have asked one if there were any fixtures behind the store, but that was all. Gacy said that he left Nisson's between 8:45 and 9 o'clock. At home, he learned from his answering machine that his uncle was dying, so he went to Northwest Hospital in Chicago, where the man was a patient. When he got there he learned his uncle had died, so he went to his aunt's house.

"Did you talk with any Nisson employees about summer jobs?" Kozenczak asked. Gacy said no. "Well, since you were one of the last people to see Rob Piest, I'm going to have to ask you to come to the station and fill out a witness form."

No problem, said Gacy. He would cooperate fully. He couldn't come now, though, because he had to make funeral arrangements for his uncle and was waiting for his mother to call.

"Why don't you call her now?" Kozenczak asked. "We'll wait."

Gacy grumbled, then dialed her number. Several times he seemed to be stretching out the conversation. After about ten minutes, he hung up. His mood had changed.

"I can't go to the station now," he said brusquely. "I've got important things to do."

"How long?" Kozenczak asked. "An hour?"

"I don't know," Gacy said impatiently. "I'll try to be there in an hour. What's wrong with you guys, anyway? Don't you have any respect for the dead?"

Kozenczak gave Gacy his card. "I'll wait for you at the station," he said. Seeing a piece of notepaper next to the phone, Kozenczak picked it up. It had Phil Torf's name on it. Kozenczak pocketed it.

"Thief!" Gacy muttered.

When Kozenczak and Pickell came out of the house, Walsh went in. The detectives got in their cars, and Kozenczak pulled alongside Olsen. "I want you to sit on the house for ten minutes and see if he goes anywhere," the lieutenant said. "We're going to check Nisson's." As Olsen and Sommerschield moved to a stake-out position on the side street to the east, they debated whether they were supposed to give chase if Gacy drove off.

A few minutes later, Walsh came out of the house, got into the van, and pulled it further into the driveway, out of the detectives' view. The van then reappeared, stopped, and once again moved to the rear of the house. As it slowly backed up, Olsen looked underneath the high chassis and saw a pair of

feet. The van stopped again. Suddenly the Oldsmobile, which
had been blocked from the detectives' view, came roaring out
of the semicircular driveway and headed west down Summerdale. The van backed out and quickly fell in behind it.

Startled, Olsen tried to follow, but Gacy's head start was too
great and the driving conditions too hazardous. Gacy turned
left on a side street that curves west and comes out on
Cumberland. When the detectives got to that intersection, they
looked north and south. No sign of Gacy or the van.

At the first sign of activity, Sommerschield had radioed
Kozenczak that "somebody was moving" and then transmitted
several frantic bits of intelligence during the three-block chase.
Now, with chagrin, he had to tell the lieutenant, "We've lost
him."

"Then come on back to the station," Kozenczak radioed,
none too pleased.

About a mile away on the Kennedy Expressway, Sergeant
Wally Lang, commander of the tactical unit, was returning
from a drug investigation in Chicago. He had monitored the
radio traffic with great curiosity and no little amusement.

"All those guys," he said to his partner, "and they blow a
stake-out in twenty seconds!"

In the station, while waiting for Gacy, the officers discussed
what little they had learned. At 11 P.M., the time he was
expected, Gacy called and asked Kozenczak if he still wanted
him to come in. Yes, the lieutenant replied. It would be very
helpful to the investigation. I'll be there in an hour, Gacy said.
Kozenczak called the Piest family and told them that Gacy
would be coming in shortly. At 11:30 Olsen left. Midnight
came and still no Gacy. At 1 A.M., Kozenczak told Pickell and
Sommerschield to go home.

Kozenczak walked to the front desk and said to the watch
officer, "I've been expecting a John Gacy to come in. I've
waited a couple of hours, and I can't wait any longer. If Gacy
comes in, tell him to come back first thing in the morning."
Kozenczak left for the night.

At 2:29 on Wednesday morning, an Illinois state trooper was
making an entry in his daily log for disabled vehicles. A
highway truck patrolling the Tri-State Tollway, which girdles
the metropolitan area on the west, had called in a report of a

vehicle stuck in a ditch off the northbound lanes at milepost 29 South, near the suburb of Oak Brook, thirteen miles from Des Plaines. The driver had requested a tow. The vehicle was a 1979 Oldsmobile, license PDM 42.

At 3:20 A.M., the Des Plaines watch officer looked up from his desk and saw a man wearing a dark coat enter the station. His eyes were glassy and bloodshot, and he seemed apprehensive.

"My name is John Gacy. I'm looking for Lieutenant Kozenczak," he said. "The reason I'm late is because I was involved in a car accident."

The watch officer gave him Kozenczak's message.

"What does he want to see me about?" Gacy asked.

"Sir, I have no information at all. Just what I told you. You'll have to come back in the morning."

Gacy nodded and walked to the door. The watch officer saw that Gacy's shoes and trousers were covered with fresh mud.

Wednesday
December 13, 1978

My office phone rang at about 11 A.M. "This is Terry Sullivan," I said.

The caller was Lieutenant Joseph Kozenczak, who had asked to speak with the assistant state's attorney in charge. He said he needed some advice on a missing-person case. I told him to come over.

At the time, I was supervisor of the Cook County State's Attorney's Third District office, which comprises a territory of 200 square miles and a million people in Chicago's northwest suburbs. With twelve assistant state's attorneys on my staff, I was in charge of felonies and misdemeanors, as well as smoothing out problems involving local police departments and village officials.

Our offices in Des Plaines were spartan, just one small room, maybe fifteen by twenty feet, with a motley assortment of institutional furniture. I didn't even have my own desk. I just worked wherever I found the space, with my chief investigator not five feet away. We were hard pressed to find a chair for Kozenczak.

The lieutenant gave me a quick rundown of the facts, including Gacy's conviction for sodomy in Iowa. Because he thought Gacy might be holding Piest captive in his house, he wanted to get a search warrant. I looked over the arrest record. As usual, it was spare of details, but the sodomy listing was an ominous note.

"You draw up a search warrant," I told Kozenczak, "and I'll approve it. But you're going to have to call Waterloo and get more details on the sodomy conviction."

Kozenczak hesitated. "I've never drawn up a search warrant," he admitted.

"Greg," I said, "get over here."

My chief investigator, Greg Bedoe, was a sheriff's policeman detached for duty with the state's attorney's office. He had been assigned to me for about a year. I knew he was capable of writing a usable first draft for a search warrant, so I set him working with Kozenczak.

The lieutenant instructed his office to get more information on Gacy's sodomy conviction, then he and Bedoe sat down and hammered out a rough draft of the complaint we needed to get a judge's approval for a search warrant. At this stage I was thinking we had a possible kidnapping. But if the Piest boy had got into Gacy's vehicle voluntarily, I couldn't very well show that he had been abducted. We needed more information from Iowa. I left the two policemen, with Greg at the typewriter, and did some further checking of my own.

Rob Piest's parents, I learned, had been in the police station again that morning, and they had shown growing impatience over what they saw as police ineptitude. They were convinced that Rob was being held by Gacy, and Harold Piest wanted to storm the house and rescue his son. When they were told that Gacy had not shown up for his interview in the station, they were incensed that the police were treating him so gingerly.

Kozenczak had attempted to placate them by telling Piest he was a licensed lie-detector expert and that he would give Gacy a polygraph test.

Piest was angry and scoffed at Kozenczak's plans. He and his family, he said, were no longer content to sit and wait. The meeting ended when the police, hoping to forestall any rash actions, told the Piests that Gacy would be interrogated in the station that morning and that they would attempt to search his house for any sign of Rob.

I found that Jim Pickell and Ron Adams were not having total success ferreting information out of Waterloo, Iowa. Because of recent federal disclosure laws defining rights to privacy, authorities are cautious about divulging information and the checking procedures are burdensome. There is no way over regular telephones for a law enforcement agency to establish its identity and its right to the information. The statutes are very vague on the exchange of police data, and mostly you have to rely on the courtesy of the other agency.

Waterloo authorities were reluctant to say much about John Gacy, although there was no doubt they all knew about him. Finally, after a couple hours of digging, the officers emerged with a few more details of the sodomy arrest. Gacy had worked at a Kentucky Fried Chicken restaurant and got involved with some of his employees. He had bound and handcuffed his victims and had sex with one. They were teenage boys.

At 11:40 A.M., Pickell ushered John Gacy into a conference room at the police station. Gacy, dressed in sweatshirt, dark wash pants, and leather jacket, had called Kozenczak at 11 and asked if he still wanted to see him. The lieutenant said he did. Gacy said he was having car trouble but would be at the station in twenty minutes. Kozenczak detailed Pickell to conduct the interview and keep Gacy there until the lieutenant returned from my office.

Gacy told how he had come to Nisson's at Phil Torf's request and spent an hour talking about the occasion when Gacy previously remodeled the store. He said he was at the pharmacy Monday night from about 5:30 to 7:15, then he went home and learned from his message recorder that Torf had called, reminding him that he had left his appointment book at the store. (Torf had made it clear he had not called Gacy about the forgotten book.) Gacy said he returned to Nisson's at 8 o'clock, and left about 8:50. On the first trip, he said, he was driving his Oldsmobile, on the second his pickup truck. Aside from a conversation with Linda Mertes, Gacy said, he had spoken to only one other employee, and that was in regard to shelving units in back of the store. He said he told Torf he would be hiring additional help in the summer, but at no time did he discuss jobs with any Nisson employee.

After leaving the pharmacy, Gacy said, he went home, checked his machine, and learned that his uncle was dying. He drove to Northwest Hospital in Chicago and was told by nurses that the man had died and that his aunt had gone home. He went to her house in Chicago, found her next door at a relative's house, and stayed and had a beer with them while discussing funeral arrangements. He got home, he said, between 12:30 and 1 A.M.

Pickell asked Gacy about his business. Gacy said he had been involved in contracting for ten years, in several states, specializing in drugstore and shopping center work. He said that he had done more than a million dollars in business the year before. Previously he had worked as a cook. He was also a lighting commissioner in Norridge and involved in Democratic politics in Chicago: from his wallet, he produced a card billing him as a precinct captain in Norwood Park Township. He added that he was responsible for putting on the Polish Constitution Day Parade in Chicago and that he would be going soon to Washington to supervise the national event. He said he had been divorced twice and was now enjoying single life.

Pickell asked Gacy to make a written statement; the contractor said he would. The officer left for about a half hour, then came back and reviewed Gacy's two pages. He noticed there was no mention of the conversation about hiring summer help, just the closing statement: "I at no time offered any employee a job. Just joking with Phil since he stated that he wasn't making any money." Gacy said he would add the reference to summer hiring. He finished at 1:20, and Pickell asked him to wait in the Detective Bureau for Kozenczak's return. Gacy agreed. By now, his paging device had beeped several times, and he asked if he could make a call. Pickell said he could use the phones all he wanted.

By early afternoon, I was satisfied with the progress Bedoe had made on the complaint for a search warrant and, with the added information from Waterloo, I was ready to go with it. I had decided to specify unlawful restraint, which requires fewer elements of proof than kidnapping. I had the complaint and warrant retyped and prepared for the judge's signature.

Gacy was becoming increasingly restless and anxious to get back to his work. For a while he had been content to chat with Pickell and use the telephone. Now he was complaining about all the business he was losing and said he would wait for

Kozenczak no later than 2:30. Pickell came across to my office with a series of reports.

"He wants to leave," the detective said. Sit with him, I said. "He says he's going to call his lawyer." Fine, let him call. "His lawyer called." Fine, talk to him. "His lawyer called again."

"Tell his lawyer," I said, "if he wants to talk about it to call me."

"Yes, sir," Pickell said.

My phone rang moments later. The conversation went something like this:

"Mr. Sullivan? LeRoy Stevens here. I have a client, John Gacy."

"Yep."

"I understand you have him over there."

"I don't have him."

"Well, he's in custody of the police department, I think."

"Is that right?"

"Do you know that?"

"Well, I've been told that."

"Well, what are you going to do?"

"Well, I don't know." Pause. "Anything else, Mr. Stevens?"

"Are you going to let him go?"

"I don't have him."

"Well, he's over at the police station. I want to tell you something."

"Yes, sir?"

"Either charge him or release him."

"Okay. Anything else?"

"Well, what are you going to do?"

"I don't know. Anything more?"

"Well, no."

"Okay, goodbye."

Gacy, of course, was not under arrest. He was simply being treated as a witness in for questioning. He had come to the station on his own and was never told he couldn't leave. Had he said, "I'm walking out," I would have had to decide whether to detain him as a suspect: I could then hold him for up to forty-eight hours without charging him. As it was, Gacy was freely roaming the Detective Bureau, although he couldn't have got out without a key. Those who sat with him simply used an old police ploy of making a witness feel important. Gacy took the bait and seemed to enjoy telling the officers about himself and his business influence. He was "heavy" with the Democratic Party, he told Detective Rafael Tovar.

Kozenczak and I took the finished search warrant downstairs to the office of Marvin Peters, an associate judge of the Cook County Circuit Court. The judge read the complaint, drafted in Kozenczak's name, then swore the lieutenant to it. It was 3:10 when Peters signed the warrant.

I asked Kozenczak to bring the officers going on the search over to my office for instruction. A few minutes later, the lieutenant returned with Pickell, Tovar, and Detective Jim Kautz.

I explained what I had put into the warrant—an enumeration of Piest's clothing, hair and blood samples, and so forth—and told the officers they could look anywhere in Gacy's house those items might be found. In other words, if you're looking for a pink elephant or a television set, you can't legally look for them in someone's desk drawer because they obviously couldn't be there. Anything a policeman finds in the drawer, therefore, is inadmissible as evidence. But if you're in a place you have a right to be in, and you find something not specified in the warrant but of possible evidentiary value, the law does not require you to turn your back. That's why the descriptions in the warrant were as specific as possible, rather than just saying Robert Piest, or, God forbid, his body.

I also told the officers that if they had any doubt about seizing something, they should take it. At worst, the reviewing judge would order it returned and rule it inadmissible as evidence. Meanwhile, bring the item in and let the lawyers determine its importance. If you later decide you want something you left behind, you will need a new search warrant to get it, and chances are that by then it's gone.

It was twilight when we walked through the breezeway back to the police station. Kozenczak had sent Adams and Olsen to secure Gacy's premises, and a call had gone out to the county sheriff requesting the assistance of an evidence technician. The county maintains a well-equipped, expert staff of ETs, who willingly assist suburban police departments. An ET would meet the Des Plaines officers at the house on Summerdale.

From Kozenczak's office, I could see Gacy in his black leather jacket, watching all the action. I told Pickell to get his keys. The detective returned a moment later. Gacy wouldn't give them to him, so I went over.

"I'm a state's attorney," I told him, "and I'd like the keys to your house."

"What for?" he asked.

"I have a search warrant," I said, showing him the document. (You never show a person the complaint from which the warrant is drawn because it has information in it you don't want him to know you've got.)

"Well," Gacy said, "I'm not going to give them to you."

"Mr. Gacy," I said, "we're trying to be nice to you. You have a choice: either you give the police officers the keys, and they'll go into your house peaceably, or they'll have to break down the door. What do you want to do?"

Gacy said nothing, so I turned and walked away. "Big asshole," he muttered.

"Go *take* the keys," I told Kozenczak, back in his office. It wasn't necessary. Gacy had already given them to Pickell.

"Don't get the place all messed up," he grumbled as the officers filed out.

Gacy's one-story house had been built on a sixty-foot lot on the south side of Summerdale Avenue back in the 1950s. On the east side, the main driveway ran straight back, then turned west alongside a narrow shed attached to a new, brick double garage. Tall hedges lined both sides of the property. In the back yard, to the rear of a recreation room that was obviously a more recent addition, sat a large brick grill.

At the front of the house, near the semicircular driveway, stood an old municipal street lamp. The front door opened directly into what apparently had once been the living room, now divided by a temporary wall to the left of the doorway that blocked off a smaller room Gacy used as an office. The foreshortened living room had little furniture but was filled with plants. On the walls hung numerous pictures of clowns. The room was like a gallery.

Straight ahead, in the hallway, the walls were decorated with
a striking abstract pattern of bright yellow and brown. To the
left lay the kitchen, and to the right the bathroom and two
bedrooms, Gacy's in the front of the house. Off the kitchen was
a laundry/storeroom, and out in the new addition were a dining
room and the recreation room Kozenczak and Pickell had been
in the night before. In a closet off the front room, under a bag
of golf clubs, officers found a trap door leading to a crawl
space; the house had no basement. In the hallway ceiling, they
saw another trap door, with a pull-down ladder leading to the
unfinished attic. In all the rooms Gacy's housekeeping was
meticulous.

Adams and Olsen had waited outside the darkened house
about a half hour before they were joined by the other four Des
Plaines officers and Evidence Technician Karl Humbert of the
sheriff's police. Together they went inside, paired up, and
began the search. Kautz was assigned to write the inventory of
recovered evidence, noting its location before it was removed,
and Humbert took color photographs of all rooms in the house.

Kautz and Tovar started working the bedrooms. On Gacy's
dresser, underneath a Motorola portable television, Tovar
spotted a jewelry box containing dozens of trinkets and items
of jewelry, including a Maine West High School ring. The ring,
class of 1975, was inscribed with the initials J.A.S. At the
bottom of the jewelry box was an Illinois driver's license issued
to a Patrick J. Reilly. In the dresser he found seven erotic
Swedish films, a cigarette box containing plant material he
suspected was marijuana, and rolling papers.

In an armoire near Gacy's queen-size bed, Tovar found a
large and varied supply of pills, mostly pharmaceutical stock
as opposed to the low-grade stuff he had encountered on the
street. Also in the armoire were a switchblade knife, two sex
books, a bag containing starter pistol blanks, more of what
Tovar thought was marijuana, and a temporary Illinois driver's
license issued to a Matthew F. Cooper (both Cooper's name and
Patrick Reilly's have been changed).

In Gacy's closet were three suits, one a sort of cranberry;
another, a black one, had a long accumulation of dust on the
shoulders. Inside brown envelopes were eight more sex books.

The other bedroom, seemingly unused, had some personal

possessions of a Marion Gacy (his mother, the officers assumed), as well as a mail-order rendering of the Gacy family genealogy. In a dresser, they found a pair of handcuffs and keys and more pills. Behind the door was a two-by-four, about three feet long, with two holes drilled in each end.

In the office, the detectives saw color photographs on the wall of a clown in various stages of makeup. When they looked closely at the pudgy face, they saw it was John Gacy. Above the photos was a big picture of Bobby Vinton. In a file drawer they found business cards for John Gacy, Democratic Precinct Captain. A 6 mm. Italian starter pistol was in the top drawer of Gacy's desk.

On the pull-down stairway to the attic, Olsen noticed fresh splotches of spray paint, like a red primer, on some of the treads. He tried to see if the paint was covering darker stains, but he couldn't tell. In the attic under some insulation, officers found police badges and an eighteen-inch rubber dildo.

Elsewhere in the house, the searchers found a hypodermic syringe, a small brown bottle, a plastic card holder that had a reverse image of a library card on one sleeve, various items of clothing obviously too small for Gacy, and more books: *Tight Teenagers, Heads & Tails, Pederasty: Sex Between Men and Boys, The Rights of Gay People, The Great White Swallow, 21 Abnormal Sex Cases*. Gacy also had several dozen other books, mostly texts and self-help titles. Some of these had been checked out from the library of the Iowa Men's Reformatory at Anamosa.

Near the bathroom door in the hallway, Humbert cut out a section of carpeting that had been stained with what he suspected was blood. The state crime laboratory could determine its type and subgroups. Blood is not an absolute identifier, but analysts can be reasonably sure that a sample did or did not come from a particular person. Dried blood holds up for a long time; moist blood that's been isolated from the air decays rapidly and is useless for identification. The sample from Gacy's carpet was in good condition for examination.

In the kitchen, Kozenczak noticed a reddish-orange ticket sticking out of a bag of trash on the floor. A customer photo receipt, it had the name, address, and phone number of Nisson

Pharmacy and the serial number 36119. Kozenczak listed it on the inventory sheet and slipped it into an evidence bag.

Midway through the search, Olsen saw officers talking to a young man who had come to the house. The youth gave his name as Chris Gray (it has been changed here) and said that he worked for Gacy. He was returning Gacy's truck and asked if he could call a cab; he had to pick up his girlfriend at work. Olsen thought that Gray was making a point of mentioning the women in his life, just as Walsh had done.

"It smells really bad down there," Olsen said, nodding toward the open trap door in the closet. "Just like sewage."

Gray looked into the crawl space. "Yeah, John's been having trouble with seepage and stuff," he said.

Tovar and Humbert entered the room and said they were going into the crawl space. Humbert, somewhat shorter than Tovar, jumped down first. A single light bulb gave the only illumination. To the side of the entryway was a sump pump. Humbert went farther into the crawl space, and now Tovar jumped down. The men had less than three feet of headroom from the ground to the floor joists. In the dim light, the officers saw cobwebs and heating ducts overhead. Humbert shined a flashlight all around. The ground was covered with a damp mat of grayish yellow powder, probably lime.

From their search of house and attic, garage and shed, and the grounds outside, the officers had found some interesting things, but they had failed in the main mission. Now, in the crawl space, they thought they might at last find some clue as to the fate of Rob Piest, such as a mound of fresh earth or other signs of digging. They found nothing. The ground was intact.

The Des Plaines Police Department's tactical group, known as Delta Unit, was made up of four officers including their commander, Sergeant Wally Lang. These men were assigned to special investigations, usually drug related, and their job was to look seedy and blend into the surroundings. They drove jacked-up junkers with stereo speakers and tape decks and other favored teenage trappings; they wore jeans, T-shirts, scruffy tennis shoes, parkas; they grew long hair and beards. Now Delta Unit joined the Piest investigation.

When Delta officers Ron Robinson and Bob Schultz reported

for their shift at 5 P.M., Lang told them they all would search for Rob Piest in the large forest preserve between Des Plaines and the northwest outskirts of Chicago. Gacy, driving from Nisson's to his house, might have killed the boy and dumped his body in an isolated area.

A block east of Des Plaines River Road on Touhy Avenue, the officers spotted fresh tire tracks in the snow heading north down a bridle path. Schultz followed the tracks as far as he could but was soon stopped by muddy potholes. While he and Lang waited in the car, Robinson proceeded ahead on foot with a flashlight. Ten minutes later, he called them on his portable radio.

"I've found a campfire," he said. "It's still smoldering. There's a jacket lying close by."

"What color is the coat?" Lang radioed back.

"Red," Robinson replied.

"Wrong color," Lang said. "Come on back."

The officers continued to circle the forest preserve, looking for either fresh tire tracks or footprints leading in, but heavy traffic and darkness hindered their work. They decided to come back on Thursday during the day.

I was disappointed when Greg told me the results of the search of Gacy's house. "Boy, he sure is a kinky son of a bitch," Greg said over the phone when he described the items. But we were no closer to finding Rob Piest than before.

"I told Kozenczak we could charge him with contributing to the delinquency of a minor," Bedoe said, "but that's a real long shot."

I agreed.

"Gacy's still here, and I told Kozenczak we might as well have another go with him before we cut him loose. It can't hurt anything."

"Call me at home," I said.

During the execution of the search warrant, Officer Mike Albrecht was babysitting Gacy in the detective room. They chatted some, then Albrecht watched the contractor riffle through his appointment book and make phone calls. LeRoy Stevens had arrived, and at intervals Albrecht would go to the front waiting area to listen to the lawyer's threats of trouble if he didn't get to see his client right away. But Gacy had not requested to see his attorney and he was not being interrogated, so the stalling tactics were bona fide.

After the officers returned from the search and Gacy was informed that his car and pickup truck had been confiscated, he protested to anyone who would listen: "Okay, you've played your game. How am I going to get home? Why am I being treated this way?" He was moved to an interview room in the back of the station, near the lockup. Bedoe and Kozenczak joined him.

Greg did most of the questioning. Gacy continued his complaints: he had a heart condition, the room was too cold, and so forth. Just to be on the safe side, Bedoe handed the contractor a Miranda waiver and asked him to read it and sign it. By doing so, Gacy would be acknowledging that he had been informed that he had the right to remain silent, that anything he said could be used as evidence against him in court, and that he had the right to have an attorney present.

"I'm not signing anything," Gacy said, "until I talk to my lawyer." Kozenczak summoned Stevens. Bedoe explained the situation and told the lawyer of Gacy's request. Stevens read the statement and advised his client not to sign it.

"Fine," Bedoe said. "If you don't mind, counselor, I'm just going to note on the margin that Mr. Gacy refused to sign this Miranda, per your advice."

Refusal to sign a waiver, of course, is not admissible in a courtroom. If Gacy refused to sign it, he was free to walk out the door. In that case, however, we would have assumed that he was hiding something.

"John, do you know anything about this?" Stevens asked. "Did you have anything to do with this missing boy?"

"Of *course* not," said Gacy in a tone of exasperation.

"Then go ahead and sign it," Stevens told him.

That done, Bedoe asked Gacy to recount his activities of Monday night. Gacy said that he had spoken only briefly, about shelving, to one of the two boys who were stocking in Nisson's. He acknowledged, however, that Rob might have overheard him talking with Torf about summer hiring.

"Why didn't you come in to see Lieutenant Kozenczak on Tuesday night when he asked you to?" Bedoe said.

Gacy said he had business to attend to, and when he did start to come in, he got stuck.

"Where?" Bedoe asked.

At Summerdale and Cumberland, Gacy said. He had to pull to one side of the street to let another car pass, then got stuck. That was at about 1 o'clock. He'd rocked the car out, gone home, then come in to the police station.

Bedoe changed the subject. "You're divorced, aren't you?"

Gacy nodded.

"On what grounds?"

"That's it," Stevens said. There would be no more questions. It was 9:30 P.M. After almost ten hours, the policemen released John Gacy in the company of his lawyer.

In the security garage at the rear of the station, Evidence Technicians Humbert and William Dado were processing Gacy's car, which they had towed off the street near the station. They found miscellaneous papers, parking tickets, grape candy, and a 40-channel Realistic CB radio.

The ETs vacuumed the interior to pick up hair or clothing fibers they might be able to link to Rob Piest. People's hair is always falling out. Although hairs can't be matched, lab experts can find similarities between them by looking at the core, the color, the thickness, the texture, and the pattern of the spikes coming off them. With the proper three hairs and twelve fibers, an expert can establish that a certain person has definitely been in a car.

The men also dusted the doors, glass, seat belts, mirrors—any smooth surfaces on which a fingerprint of the missing boy might appear. But in northern winters people generally wear gloves, and cars are dirty with salt, road film, and dust, making it virtually impossible to get a usable print. Tonight's results were negative.

Bedoe and Kozenczak came in and inspected the car. The right rear wheel and quarter panel were impacted with wet mud and bits of sod. In the truck, the spare tire and jack base were similarly covered, as were the brake pedal and accelerator inside. Gacy hadn't mentioned using his spare.

"He's lying," Bedoe said. The two men walked back to
Kozenczak's office, where the lieutenant glanced at the reports
written that day: Adams had gone to Maine West and got Rob's
picture and personal possessions, and Olsen had picked up
Rob's hairbrush and cap, for hair samples, from the family.
Adams had also talked with the head nurse who had been on
duty Monday night on Gacy's uncle's floor at Northwest
Hospital. She didn't recall Gacy's visit. Pickell had arranged
for the Chicago Daily Bulletin, a brochure circulated to police
departments in the area, to publish a "wanted" listing for Rob
Piest. He had also checked the Cook County morgue. There
were no bodies fitting Rob's description.

Bedoe said they had to find Rob before they could go any
further with John Gacy, who obviously wouldn't say anything
more without a lawyer. Bedoe said that if the lieutenant didn't
mind, he'd like to work with Des Plaines on the case.
Kozenczak said he would welcome Bedoe's involvement.
"What's next?" he asked.

"Walsh and Gray," Bedoe replied.

One thing was sure. If Gacy was telling the truth about
getting stuck at Cumberland and Summerdale, there would be
no missing the crater he left behind.

Thursday
December 14, 1978

It seemed unlikely, although still possible, that Rob Piest was a runaway. But if Gacy had abducted Rob, what had he done with him?

By midmorning we knew that Gacy had lied to us about getting stuck. On his way to work, Bedoe had checked the intersection of Cumberland and Summerdale and found a paved crossing with curbs and gutters and no sign of muddy ruts. Still we could not afford to come down hard on John Gacy—he could slap us with a multimillion-dollar lawsuit for harassment. Our best bet at the moment was to focus the investigation on the evidence that the police had collected Wednesday night at 8213 Summerdale.

These items were displayed in the small interview room off the Detective Bureau in which Kozenczak had set up his polygraph. The ring with the initials J.A.S. was interesting because it was from Maine West High School. Did it have something to do with Rob Piest? I told Kozenczak to have his men find its owner.

I uncapped and sniffed the neck of the brown bottle. The inside smelled like something that could knock a person out. The bottle was empty, but it was possible that the state crime laboratory could determine its previous contents.

I was confounded by the items that were obviously not Gacy's, the drivers' licenses issued to Cooper and Reilly. Who were these people, and how did they fit into Gacy's life? At this point, the Robert Piest case was becoming the John Gacy case. I told Kozenczak I wanted Gacy put under twenty-four-hour surveillance.

At about 11 o'clock Kozenczak told me that Rob Piest's parents were once again in the station, and he asked what we should tell them. I wanted to bolster their confidence by showing them that the state's attorney's office was now involved and said I would see them. Kozenczak took Bedoe and me up to the second-floor conference room, introduced us to the parents, then left.

Elizabeth Piest seemed totally drained; she and her husband both looked as if they hadn't slept all week. Although I wanted to reassure them, I didn't want them to think we were miracle workers. On Wednesday, I had thought that Rob was being held captive; today, however, I was pessimistic. "Don't get your hopes up too high," I told the Piests, as gently as I could. "The chances of your son being found alive are very slim." I didn't know then that they had already abandoned hope.

They told us more about Rob, his good grades, his interest in math and science, his wanting to be an astronaut. He had money he'd earned: $900 in the bank, $80 in his dresser, and all of it was still there. They talked of his love for camping, the canoe trips he'd gone on with his father; once to Canada, once to an area southwest of Chicago where the Des Plaines and Kankakee rivers flow together and become the Illinois. Yes, he and his girlfriend, Carrie Gibbons, had parted. She had been special to him, and he had told his mother that much one day when they were chatting in his bedroom. Rob feared that Carrie was becoming more interested in a senior boy. "If you feel that way about her," Elizabeth had told her son, "you shouldn't give up. You'll never lose if you keep fighting." But even though Rob and Carrie had broken up weeks ago, they were still friends, still talking reconciliation. Rob certainly wouldn't run away because of girl trouble. He never ran away.

When we talked about what happened Monday night, the Piests focused their attention on Phil Torf. Elizabeth felt that he had been evasive and was trying to protect Gacy. Why was he so unhelpful about Gacy's address? What were Torf and his friend doing around Nisson's until 1 A.M.—three hours after closing?

I assured them that we knew Gacy's background and were dealing with him as aggressively as we could, but I did not describe him as the main suspect or disclose what we knew of his previous criminal activities. I didn't want them to take the law in their own hands. Finally, I told them that it was essential they not talk to reporters. We had learned nothing new from the Piests, but talking with them absolutely convinced Bedoe and me that Rob was not a runaway.

After the Piests left, we put together the chronology of Monday night's events at Nisson Pharmacy piece by piece, as we began interviewing witnesses and taking statements. Pickell talked to Linda Mertes and Carrie Gibbons; Adams and Pickell together interviewed Phil Torf and Tod Podgorny, the other Maine West High School boy who was working in the store that night; I saw Kim Byers. Officers interviewed half a dozen other youths, all of whom agreed that Rob was an unlikely runaway. But none of them had seen him since he had hurried out of Nisson's three days ago.

Early in the afternoon Kozenczak told me that Delta Unit of the Des Plaines police force would be able to handle the surveillance of Gacy. The three officers of the unit, Ron Robinson, Bob Schultz, and Dave Hachmeister would work twelve-hour shifts, and their sergeant, Wally Lang, would fill in where needed. Should Gacy be our man and decide to return to the scene of the crime, we would now have witnesses.

Lang assigned Robinson and Schultz to the first shift, from noon to midnight. Schultz would watch Gacy's house, and Robinson was to stake out the house of Gacy's newly widowed aunt.

The funeral of Gacy's uncle was to take place today. Robinson called the funeral director, one of his childhood friends, who told him there were no gatherings scheduled after the burial. The widow, and probably Gacy, would be returning to her house on Chicago's Northwest Side in the early afternoon. Robinson parked his car about a hundred yards down the street.

At about 3:30, he saw a car stop at the house. Several people got out and went inside. A short time later, a man and woman came out, got in the car, and drove off, the man at the wheel.

Robinson followed them. On the Kennedy Expressway, heading downtown, Robinson pulled abreast of them and looked across at the driver. He was thin and had no mustache. Recalling the mug shot from Northbrook, Robinson was sure the man was not Gacy. He dropped back, noted the license number, and returned to the aunt's house.

On Summerdale, all was quiet. Schultz and Lang were not sure what Gacy would be driving now that his car had been impounded. Lang decided to explore the Christmas tree lot at St. Joseph's, which by now he knew had been leased to a Ronald Rohde, an acquaintance of Gacy's. Lang went into the church and got permission to go up inside one of the towers. He was unable to get a good view of Rohde's operation, however, so he wandered about the tree lot instead. Seeing no sign of Gacy, he returned to Summerdale.

By early evening, as Robinson sat in his car, he was experiencing the discomforts—and boredom—of surveillance. The temperature was dropping, and Robinson periodically idled his engine to get heat. The Delta officers called his car the Batmobile. It was a 1973 Plymouth with a jacked-up front end. Schultz had rigged phony stereo speakers inside.

While changing his sitting position, Robinson accidentally poked his size thirteen shoe into some loose wiring under the dashboard. He heard an arcing snap and smelled smoke. Quickly he shut off the ignition. Peering under the dashboard, he saw some still-smoldering insulation. He radioed the station. "Don't worry," he reassured them. "I haven't burned to the ground yet." They decided to take no chances, however, and detailed Olsen to ferry another car to him, just in case.

Late in the afternoon Kozenczak sent Rafael Tovar and Sergeant Jim Ryan to bring Gacy's employee Richard Walsh into the station for questioning. Walsh lived with his wife and infant son on the second floor of a two-flat dwelling on Chicago's North Side. His wife told the officers that her husband wasn't home, but that she expected him shortly. She invited them in to wait.

Mrs. Walsh, a small, thin, attractive woman, asked if their questions were about John Gacy. The officers said they were.

Gacy was kind of weird, she offered. He was always trying

to get Dick to leave her, she said. He often called her, saying that when Dick "worked late" he was running around with other women.

"Have you ever been to Gacy's house?" Tovar asked.

She had and said that Dick had been living at Gacy's when she began dating him. Gacy had some odd things in his house, she added.

"Like what?" Tovar asked.

"A board with chains attached to it," she said.

"Can you describe it?" Tovar asked.

"It was like a two-by-four, about that long," she said, pointing to a carpenter's level propped against the wall.

Mrs. Walsh offered that her husband had been arrested in Cicero for beating Gacy and he was still on court supervision for the offense.

When Tovar asked if Gacy had ever made a play for her husband, she said she didn't know, but she'd heard that someone had once sent a friend over to Gacy's for some Valium, and the contractor had propositioned him. But on occasion she had seen Gacy in the company of a woman.

Walsh still hadn't arrived, and his wife suggested that the officers might find him at Coach's Corner, a nearby tavern where he often stopped after work.

The officers didn't know what Walsh looked like. "What kind of car does he drive?" Tovar asked.

"A white Plymouth Satellite," she told him.

Tovar and Ryan left and cruised the vicinity of the tavern. They didn't see Walsh's car, so they stopped for coffee. An hour later, they returned to Walsh's house. He still was not home. Mrs. Walsh again invited them in. She talked about herself and her child for a while, then Tovar gave her his card and asked her to have Walsh call him at the station.

As the officers were getting into their car, they saw a white Plymouth pull up to the curb. "Are you Dick Walsh?" Tovar asked the driver. He was.

"We'd like you to come to the police station," Tovar told him. "We want to talk to you."

"About the Gacy thing?" Walsh asked. Tovar nodded. "Okay. Do you mind if I go up and talk to my wife first?" The three men went inside, and the officers sat at the table while Walsh ate the dinner his wife had prepared.

On the way to the station, Walsh, a short, heavyset young man with long blond hair and a youthful face, said that Gacy was very upset about something. He had gone to a bank and withdrawn $4,000 in case he needed it for bond. He had asked Walsh not to "bad mouth" him in any way.

Walsh told the officers he had worked for Gacy for quite some time. When he started, Gacy had asked about his sexual preference, saying that he himself was quite "liberal." Walsh allowed as how he preferred women and that if there were any strings attached to the job, he wasn't interested. Gacy had dropped the subject.

Tovar and Ryan arrived at the station at about 8 o'clock and turned Walsh over to Kozenczak, who got nothing more out of him.

I now had no doubt that there was a connection between Rob Piest and John Gacy. If Gacy had hurriedly dumped, or even buried, Rob's body, an air search of the area fanning out from the route between Nisson's and Gacy's house seemed to be the quickest way of finding the site. There had been no fresh snowfall in a week, so any signs of digging or tire tracks should still be visible.

The Chicago Fire Department generally was very cooperative in making their helicopter available for criminal investigations such as this but, unfortunately, it was being used for an emergency job and wasn't available. Greg Bedoe suggested calling a colleague of his in the sheriff's police, Cliff Johnson, who flew, among other aircraft, search and rescue helicopters with the Air National Guard. "Don't worry," Greg said. "He won't leak anything."

Johnson agreed to search, but he couldn't work our target area during daylight because it lay in the terminal control area for two runways to O'Hare, just a couple of miles away. At night, when there was less airport traffic, the restrictions were somewhat relaxed. And, Johnson pointed out, it would be easier to spot something in the snow at night, using the powerful spotlight on the underside of the aircraft.

Early in the evening, Johnson came to Kozenczak's office

for a briefing. Because of government regulations, civilians were not allowed to go aloft with him, so Johnson would be given a police radio and two officers in a car would be assigned to follow him as ground coordinators. We defined the search area as a corridor on either side of Des Plaines River Road, starting with the high-rise apartment and commercial construction on Chicago's far Northwest Side and going through the forest preserves to the north.

I monitored the search from a radio in Kozenczak's office, where I had set up an easel and was beginning to diagram the key elements of the investigation. The controlled airspace on an approachway is like an inverted, tiered wedding cake. The closer Johnson got to the axis of the runway, the lower he was required to fly. For this reason, he couldn't cover the entire search area. Several times he reported being warned away by airport ground controllers—it was apparent that he was making O'Hare officials nervous.

Whenever Johnson spotted something unusual, the officers went in on foot to investigate. They found a jacket, but it was too old and rotten to be Piest's. The other findings were nothing more than logs or shadows. At 10:10, after an hour's search, they called it quits.

Although Pickell and Adams had interviewed Phil Torf earlier, I sent Bedoe and Kautz out that evening to question him in greater deatil. Torf confirmed that he had denied Rob's request for a raise, saying that no one would be getting one until after the first of the year. He told the officers that it was about 7:15 when he noticed that Gacy had left his appointment book at the pharmacy. Gacy, he said, supposedly had another appointment at 7 P.M., but he didn't know where. Again, he denied calling Gacy about the appointment book.

Torf mentioned that Joe Hajkaluk had come to the store about 11:30 P.M. to pick up Joe's brother's car, which they had used earlier in the day for a delivery. He added that, at his request, Hajkaluk had gone by the tree lot shortly after 1 A.M. and left a message with Torf's roommate that the lighs were out and everything was quiet.

"Why didn't you tell Mrs. Piest where Gacy lived the first time she asked you?" Greg asked.

"Because John Gacy is a nice guy," Torf responded.

"Is John Gacy gay?"

"I don't know."

One thing that stood out was Torf's observation that Gacy and Walsh were unusually close, and Walsh became that much more interesting. Walsh himself had given us leads: Why had Gacy told him he anticipated having to make bond? What did Walsh know about Gacy that he could "bad mouth" him? No answers yet, but some very interesting questions.

At about 11 P.M., Lang picked up Hachmeister at the station and, in the manner that had earned him the nickname "Powerslide," drove him to the house on Summerdale to relieve Schultz. Nearing the house, they heard Schultz report on the radio that a van had pulled into Gacy's driveway. Just as the two officers arrived, they saw the van leaving. It had a PDM sign. After it turned onto a side street, Lang stopped short of the intersection and told Hachmeister to run to the corner and see where it was going. Hachmeister looked, then rushed back to the car. The van, he reported, was out of sight. They circled the block and saw no sign of it.

While he waited at the house, Schultz inspected the back of Gacy's property. He saw nothing unusual. Coming back to the street, he slipped and fell in the snow. When Lang and Hachmeister returned, he told them that he didn't know who was driving the van, but whoever it was appeared to be male, about twenty, with blond hair. So at least they hadn't lost Gacy—but neither had they found him.

Robinson was doing no better at the home of Gacy's aunt. When her lights went out about 10 o'clock, he left and checked the houses of Gray and Walsh. No sign of Gacy. Lang told him to return to the station.

Schultz told Hachmeister that several times he had seen an old Chevy circle the block with its lights out. Before departing with Schultz, Lang told Hachmeister to radio the station if Gacy showed up, and they'd try to send another car.

Gacy's outside light burned brightly, but it did not shine on its owner's return. Hachmeister saw the car he thought Schultz was referring to slowly cruising on Summerdale, its lights out. He saw it stop in front of the duplexes west of Gacy's. Two men got out and looked into some cars parked on the street. He radioed this intelligence to the station, and a few minutes later a Chicago tactical car arrived. The officers frisked the men, then took them into custody. Hachmeister figured they'd made a drug bust.

Gacy's light burned on into the early morning. With nothing to do, nothing to report, Hachmeister spent the night listening to the sound of the wind, an occasional static pop on the radio, and, as he fought the battle of boredom, the electronic bleeps from his Mattel football game.

I was sure we were sitting on something big. But could we crack it with an essentially good though small and inexperienced suburban police department like Des Plaines's?

During the day, Tovar had taken pictures of various routes between Nisson's and Gacy's house. There was an awful lot of ground—parking lots, alleys, forest preserve trails—where a body could be dumped and at least temporarily hidden. Olsen and Sommerschield had spent three hours canvassing the neighborhood around Nisson's for anybody who might have seen a heavyset man in his thirties talking to a teenage boy on Monday night: results, nil. Evidence Technicians Karl Humbert and Daniel Genty had processed Gacy's pickup truck and had found nothing significant other than a broken hammer handle under the passenger's seat and a short piece of rope. And the four-man surveillance team hadn't even found Gacy.

As I drove home in the early hours of the morning, I was feeling nothing but fatigue and frustration.

Friday
December 15, 1978

We were stalled. The surveillance team still hadn't connected with Gacy, and in these crucial hours he was unobserved, free to do whatever he needed to do to cover up his tracks. What's more, we were told that his lawyers were preparing a harassment suit on their client's behalf, naming the City of Des Plaines, the police department, and various officers as defendants. This could be a serious threat to our investigation.

Two questions about Gacy still nagged at us: Why were Gacy and his car covered with mud? Why was he more than four hours late in reporting to the police station early Wednesday morning? We now suspected that if he had killed Rob Piest, he had disposed of the body before coming to the station—that would account for the mud. *But where was it from?*

Kautz called the soil chemistry testing laboratory at the University of Illinois. They could test samples from Gacy's car, they told him, but only for such things as farmers want to know—soil structure, acidity, and nutrient content. There was no way they could tell where the mud came from.

I wanted to continue searching uninhabited areas, such as the forest preserves and construction sites. Kozenczak had arranged to have the Search and Rescue Unit go out in the field with their dog teams. After they had sniffed an article of Rob's clothing, the dogs would react if they encountered a similar scent. The teams were scheduled to spend the weekend combing our target area.

Despite our lack of progress, the Piests, at least, were not prepared to see the investigation falter. Harold, Elizabeth, Ken, and Kerry came into the station again on Friday morning.

Although they conceded that the investigation was police business, they wanted to put out fliers showing Rob's picture, listing his description and the location he was last seen, and requesting that any information about him be given to the Des Plaines police. Friends, neighbors, schoolmates, and the Boy Scouts would photocopy and distribute them all over town. Kozenczak gave his approval.

Pickell asked the Piests if Rob had a Des Plaines library card. They said they thought he did and that he carried it with him.

After the Piests left, Pickell and Adams went to the library and confirmed that Rob did have a card. From looking at a sample, however, it was clear that it could not make the sort of impression left in the wallet card holder recovered from Gacy's house.

I became rather impatient with Kozenczak that morning and lost my temper. I asked if they had found out who owned the Maine West class ring, and he said his men were stymied, the manufacturer was out of business. I was dumbfounded. "How many people," I shouted, "have the initials J.A.S.?" I told him to check the school and find the owner right away.

If I seemed harsh, it was because I was totally wrapped up in the case. My assistants were now keeping the machinery of my district functioning as I focused on the Piest investigation. At first I had diplomatically suggested to Kozenczak what I thought needed doing. Now I was telling him. He had come to me for help, and I had given it to him. Now I could see he wanted continued guidance and was abdicating leadership of the investigation. The statutes are inconclusive on the relationship between the state's attorney's office and the police, but the prosecutor's office clearly has an investigatory responsibility, and I did not want to see a small and unsophisticated suburban police department mishandle what could be a very important case. That's why I moved in with my easel—and coffee machine, to boot.

We still had not picked up any Chicago Police Department records on Gacy, so Tovar and Ryan went downtown to get a current rap sheet. The Chicago department serves as a clearinghouse of information for law enforcement agencies in the metropolitan area. Their records would be more current and more complete than those we had from Northbrook.

Two items on the Chicago report were blacked out, indicating that they were FBI matters. Gacy's last arrest, on July 15, 1978, was for battery. The victim was Jeffrey D. Rignall of Winter Park, Florida. Rignall, a twenty-seven-year-old student, was walking on Chicago's Near North Side at 1:30 A.M. on March 22. A man driving a black car with spotlights pulled up and asked him if he wanted to split a joint of marijuana. Rignall got in the car. A short time later, the driver reached over and held a rag over his mouth. Rignall lost consciousness. He awoke behind a statue in Lincoln Park, on Chicago's lakefront, about 4:30 A.M. with burns on his face and rectal bleeding. He walked to the friend's apartment where he was staying and fell asleep.

In a supplementary report, Rignall told police he had later rented a car and set up a surveillance near the Kennedy Expressway on Chicago's Northwest Side, where he recalled the man had taken him. After three days, he spotted the black car and gave the license number to police. The car was Gacy's. Although there had been several court dates since July, the case was still pending. I knew we had to talk to Rignall, and I told Tovar to find him.

Meanwhile, Pickell and Olsen continued interviewing friends of Rob's and witnesses at Nisson's but turned up nothing new. Kozenczak called Gacy's former wife. She said she couldn't come in for questioning today, but would come in tomorrow. Did she know of any other associates of Gacy the police might interview? She mentioned a John Bukavitch, a former employee she had been particularly fond of, but said he might be hard to find: Gacy had told her the youth had run away.

An evidence technician went to the Piests' house and successfully lifted fingerprints of Rob from his 35 mm. Canon camera and other personal possessions. He also brought back a microscope slide containing what the parents thought was a smear of Rob's blood their son had used in an experiment.

Hachmeister had been watching Gacy's house in vain. By dawn on Friday, as other houses on the block were coming to life, it was evident that Gacy had spent the night elsewhere. Hachmeister's presence had now been noted by at least one of Gacy's neighbors, who kept peeking out at him from behind her living-room drapes.

At 8:45 a black and yellow Oldsmobile Cutlass pulled up to Gacy's house. Hachmeister radioed the station that there was activity. A man got out, looked around the front of the house, picked up the newspaper, then unlocked the door and went inside. The man was slim, probably in his fifties, and Hachmeister knew it wasn't Gacy. He asked the station for a license check. The car was registered to a Gordon Nebel of Norridge.

About an hour later, a black van with a PDM sign drove past Hachmeister. The youth driving did a double take when he spotted the officer, then the van pulled into Gacy's driveway. Twenty minutes later, a white Ford pickup and a silver Plymouth Volaré came down Summerdale. The truck made a U-turn at the end of the block and drove off, the Volaré pulled into Gacy's driveway. Hachmesiter saw a stocky man wearing a leather jacket and wash pants get out and go into the house. The man, he knew, was Gacy. And he had no doubt that the driver of the van was telling Gacy he was being watched.

Lang, Schultz, and Robinson arrived in two cars at about 11 o'clock. As Hachmeister sat in his car briefing Schultz, the PDM van pulled up to them. The same youth was driving.

"You guys cops?" he asked.

Hachmeister nodded.

"You scared the shit out of me last night. Why were you following me?"

"We're not following you," Hachmeister said. "It's no big thing. We're just watching a house." The officers thought, rightly, the youth must be Chris Gray.

Hachmeister turned the car over to Schultz and left with Lang to go back to the station. A couple of blocks away, they heard Schultz on the radio: "Gacy's leaving." Lang wheeled the car around and rushed back to Summerdale. Robinson had taken off after Gacy—Schultz had been facing the wrong way. A couple minutes later, Robinson radioed: "I lost him."

The score was now Gacy three, the coppers nothing. Gacy's driving habits and the weather weren't helping. It was alternately warming and freezing, and the streets were treacherous. The real question was whether the Delta Unit could keep their old beaters going against the Volaré Gacy had apparently rented.

In any case, the surveillance team was back where it started, much in the position of the jungle cook reading the recipe for tiger soup: first, catch the tiger.

After his interview with Dick Walsh on Thursday night, Kozenczak had concluded that he was dealing with a wise guy, and most of us would come to share that opinion. Given Walsh's attitude, we were surprised when he called the station just before 5 o'clock on Friday afternoon. Pickell talked to him while Kozenczak listened in.

Walsh said he had been thinking about the missing-person aspect of the case, and because Kozenczak had asked him to call back with any information he thought might be useful, he was now offering this: one of Gacy's former employees, a Gregory Godsick, had disappeared a couple of years ago, not even a week after he was hired. Walsh said Godsick was about seventeen or eighteen, lived near Gacy, and went to Taft High School in Chicago. To his knowledge, the youth had never been found. Gacy had told Walsh that the boy had got beaten in a fight over a girl and was too embarrassed to show his face. Walsh said there was another employee, Charles Itullo, who was found drowned in a river in a town about seventy miles south or southwest of Chicago. Walsh didn't remember the name of the town, but he thought Itullo's wife lived there. Furthermore, he wasn't sure of the spelling of either name. The officers thanked Walsh and told him to call back if he remembered anything else.

Pickell immediately called Chicago police and asked them to check their "active missing" file for a Gregory Godsick. The youth was in there: Gregory Godzik, five foot nine, 140 pounds, blond hair, gray eyes, seventeen years old, last seen

December 12, 1976. His address was in Chicago, about a mile from Gacy's.

Tovar, who had spent most of the day on the phone trying to track Jeffrey Rignall in Chicago and Florida, now started to pursue the Itullo lead. On a map he drew a circle with a seventy-five-mile radius from Chicago and sent LEADS messages to police jurisdictions near the southern portion of the arc. He requested information on victims, known or unidentified, whose bodieis had been found in rivers. He also began telephoning, making the same request, and got the same answer everywhere: "Our records section is shut down for the night."

Early closing hours weren't the only hindrance to the investigation. In the hall were camped a reporter and crew from Channel 7, Chicago's ABC station. I had warned the Piest family not to talk to the press, and they hadn't; but the reporter, Sylvia Cisneros, had interviewed some of the people at Nisson's and had some other information I was sure the police had leaked. She now wanted an official statement from me. I had to be careful. A television news report naming Gacy as our prime suspect would send his lawyers straight to Federal District Court for a temporary injunction. That would be the end of the investigation.

I took her a cup of coffee and tried to get her confidence. "Look," I told her, "just hold on. I'll let you know when you've got a story. You know, there really isn't a story yet, but when there is, I'll talk to you first." She didn't buy that—I saw by the way her eyes flashed through her television makeup that she didn't believe me. I decided to try to get her to let me see what she had on tape.

She didn't like it, but she finally agreed, on one condition: "I'll let you see the tape," she said, "if you talk to my assignment editor and tell him I've got a good story."

"First I've got to see it," I said. I looked at the tape through the viewfinder. The reporter had done her homework: she had a story that would have disclosed far more than we wanted. No way would I encourage her boss to run it.

"No," I said. "I won't tell him you have the story, because you don't."

Furious, she wheeled around and stalked out, camera crew in tow. I hoped I had bought some time.

I went back to the interrogation room where I'd set up my command post. I was looking at our flow chart when Bedoe came in. "We've got another missing," he said. "The kid who owned the Maine West class ring. Adams just talked to the mother."

My eyes went as wide as a couple of Eisenhower silver dollars. In less than an hour, we had learned of four youths, all linked with Gacy, who were missing or dead. John Bukavitch, Gregory Godzik, and Charles Itullo were all Gacy's former employees, and the Maine West boy's ring had been found at Gacy's house.

"What's his name?" I asked Greg.

"John Szyc," he said. "Adams and Kautz are going over to talk to his mother."

Mrs. Richard Szyc told the officers about the disappearance of her son John, who was last seen on January 20, 1977. At the time, he had been living on the North Side of Chicago and working as a repairman at an engineering firm in the Loop. He still had pay, including overtime, coming to him. When she and her husband went into his apartment, they found the bed unmade, his winter coat laid out, and incompleted tax forms on the kitchen table. Nothing was out of order, but several household items were missing: his twelve-inch black-and-white TV, a digital clock radio, a hair dryer, and an iron. There were no signs of a break-in.

Mrs. Szyc said that they had been told by Chicago police that John's car had been used by another youth in a robbery of a gas station in August, 1977; the youth had told police he had bought the car from John in February. John apparently had told the buyer he needed money to leave town.

Mrs. Szyc said that she and her husband were deeply distressed by what they thought was lack of either interest or competence on the part of the police and the fact that, after a dozen follow-up calls, they still had not found her son. She said that she and her husband had paid a month's rent on John's apartment, but moved his personal things to their own home when he failed to return by the end of February, 1977. She said she had a lot of his personal papers. Adams called the station asking what papers they should bring in. My reply was simple: Bring them all.

Bedoe, meanwhile, had asked Kozenczak to send someone downtown to get missing-person reports on Szyc, Godzik, and Bukavitch. When Ryan arrived at Chicago headquarters, he was told he couldn't get the records tonight. They were locked up in a basement.

Bedoe threw a tantrum and demanded that I call the top brass. This was our first argument. I didn't want to overreact, and I told him to settle down.

As it turned out, Ryan didn't need any help. He had worked as a cadet at headquarters for three years. Moreover, he came from an old Chicago police family, and that counts for something. He collared the supervisor of records, who agreed to go down personally and dig out the records as a favor.

After the embarrassment of losing Gacy again, the surveillance officers set out in different directions to find him. About 1 P.M., Lang alerted the other two that he had found Gacy's car at the office of his other attorney, Sam Amirante, in Park Ridge, a suburb southeast of Des Plaines. Schultz and Robinson joined Lang, and there they sat for the rest of the afternoon playing electronic football.

At 5:30, Gacy hurried out of the office, got into his car, and drove off. He was heading south on one of the main streets in the suburb when, apparently seeing that he was being followed, he made an abrupt U-turn and sped north. Robinson by now had had enough of Gacy's reckless driving. He turned his car sharply to the left, blocking the oncoming lanes of rush-hour traffic. This allowed Lang and Schultz to turn around, and Robinson fell in behind them. All three followed Gacy to an apartment on Lawrence Avenue in Norridge, which, from the license check that morning, they knew was the residence of Gordon Nebel. Gacy went into the building, and about five minutes later, Amirante arrived; the officers recognized him from his appearance as a public defender. About ten minutes later Amirante came out and walked up to Schultz's car.

"John knows he's being followed," Amirante said, "and we're aware of the situation. I just ask one thing: that if you do make an arrest of any type, please notify me." He handed Schultz his card.

"I'll be happy to cooperate," Schultz said, "but a lot depends on your client's driving habits."

Gacy next drove to a house nearby in Norridge and went inside. Ten minutes later, a light-colored Chevrolet Suburban pulled up, and the driver went into the house. The driver, Gacy, and a third man came out shortly, got into the Suburban, and drove to an address on Chicago's North Side. They were there about forty-five minutes, when Gacy's Norridge friend walked over to Robinson's car and told him they were going back to the house in Norridge.

The driver of the Suburban raced through the side streets of Chicago at more than fifty miles an hour. The streets were still packed with ice, and the narrow ones usually had just one set of deep ruts to drive in. At Lawrence Avenue, the Suburban made an abrupt right turn in front of a bus at the curb and got on the Kennedy Expressway. The driver accelerated his vehicle up to eighty miles an hour and began weaving in and out of traffic. He turned onto exit ramps, then at the last moment swerved back onto the highway. Lang had been ordered not to harass Gacy or arrest him for traffic violations unless his reckless driving got extreme. Even though Gacy was not at the wheel, Lang decided this was extreme. "Arrest him!" he barked into his radio.

The officers put their portable red lights up on their dashboards and maneuvered into position, one in front of the Suburban, one to the left, and one trailing. They began forcing the driver to the shoulder. The police in their battered vehicles obviously had less to lose than the driver of the Suburban. He stopped and the three men jumped out, both of Gacy's associates with their fists clenched. The driver, the younger man, stood about six foot two and weighed some 215 pounds. The man from Norridge was shorter but built like a bulldog. "You're under arrest for reckless driving," Lang told the driver.

Both the driver and the other man were furious. They shouted threats at the officers and accused them of harassing their buddy. Gacy tried to play peacemaker. When Lang threatened to have the Suburban towed into the station, however, the older man sided with the police and berated the driver.

The policemen identified the younger man as Donald Morrill, handcuffed him, and put him into Schultz's car. The other man, whom police identified as Ronald Rohde, owner of the tree lot, drove the Suburban, with Gacy as a passenger, to the Des Plaines police station. Lang and Robinson followed.

At the station, Gacy at first was reluctant to come in, then changed his mind. "Why are you doing this to me?" he demanded.

"The boss gives us a job to do," Robinson said, "and since he doesn't give us an explanation, I don't have one to give you."

Schultz booked Morrill, while Gacy and Rohde stood in the waiting area loudly complaining about the harassment. Morrill could not make bail, so Gacy and Rohde angrily went back to both their houses with police escort to get the necessary cash. At 11:40, two and a half hours after his arrest, Morrill was released. The officers followed the men back to Norridge.

Ryan had returned from Chicago with the missing-person reports on Szyc and Godzik. Headquarters had nothing on Bukavitch, but it was possible we had an incorrect spelling. The reports on Szyc's disappearance were mostly routine. The only exception was a notation from November 1977, that Szyc's brother, just home from the army, told his parents that friends had seen John at the beach some time the previous summer. When missing youths are "seen" by witnesses who should recognize them, investigators tend to regard the youths as no longer missing, and the case is given a lower priority. Perhaps this was why the Szycs detected a note of police disinterest.

"Look at this," Tovar said. "Szyc was driving a 1971 Plymouth Satellite."

"That sounds familiar," Ryan said.

"What kind of car did Walsh's wife say he had?" Tovar asked.

"A white Plymouth Satellite," said Ryan.

"What year would you figure?" Tovar asked.

"It was kind of old," Ryan replied.

Tovar called the radio room and gave them the 1976 plate number listed on Szyc's disappearance report. The answer came back: no information. The plate was too old. Tovar went over to the Sondex machine, the microfiche retrieval system listing Illinois drivers, dates of birth, addresses, license numbers, and vehicle identification numbers (in police jargon, "VIN numbers"). The list, which is updated every year, is used by local police departments for a variety of law enforcement purposes, especially to ensure that local motorists buy the village tax sticker they are supposed to.

Tovar checked for Dick Walsh's name and found he had a 1971 white Plymouth Satellite, plate number ZE 5523, VIN number RH23G1G739297.

"Didn't you say you got an auto registration card from Szyc's mom?" Bedoe asked Adams. He had. We looked at Szyc's VIN number: it was RH23G1G239297. We looked at Walsh's: RH23G1G739297. They were just one digit off! What was a 2 on Szyc's registration was a 7 on Walsh's.

We continued to run registration checks. When we fed in the license number from Szyc's 1977 application and Walsh's current plate numbers, the LEADS computer showed the same discrepancy in numbers. When we fed in Szyc's VIN number, the computer reported no record. No license or ownership assigned in 1978. Tovar showed me a booklet from the National Auto Theft Bureau explaining how VIN numbers are assigned. If both those VIN numbers were legitimate, Chrysler would have had to have made a half a million white Plymouth Satellites at the same plant. This *had* to be the same car. I told Kozenczak to have the radio room run a title check with the Secretary of State's office. This takes longer than a registration check, but from it we would be able to trace, step by step, the ownership of this mysterious Satellite. I no longer cared that it was past midnight.

As we continued going through Szyc's papers, Tovar was berating himself for having seen John's name on something at Gacy's house and not having brought it in. From Szyc's address book, we got the impression that the youth had homosexual ties. Many of the addresses were in a Mid-North gay neighborhood in Chicago, and he had a telephone number for a gay hotline. Also among the papers was a typed letter from a Chicago Police detective:

Mr. and Mrs. Szyc,
  I was unable to locate your son, but I did learn that he sold his auto in Feb of 77 and told the buyer that he needed the money to leave town.

Inv. Harry Belluomini
Area 5 GA 2138 N. Calif. Ave.

I took some time to go through the other reports Ryan had brought back. Gregory J. Godzik, seventeen, was last seen at 1:30 A.M. on December 12, 1976, by his girlfriend at her home. The girl had told police she thought Greg might have been going on to a party in suburban Niles. Godzik's car had been found, without the keys, in a Niles parking lot. Again, there were reports the youth had been seen since his disappearance.

Not until March 7 did the Chicago Police get around to talking with Godzik's last employer: PDM. Gacy had told them that Greg had a couple of days' pay coming and that he had sent the check to Greg's mother. Fifteen months went by before the next report was made. In June, 1978, the Godziks told police they had paid $5,000 to a private investigator to find their son.

Just before 2 A.M., the title check on Walsh's car came back from Springfield. The Satellite was registered to Walsh and showed his current address in Chicago. The previous owners were listed as Dick Walsh and John Grey. The next line showed "Grey's" address as 8213 Summerdale, Norridge. The second previous owner was John Szyc of Des Plaines.

After spending Thursday night and Friday morning alone at Gacy's house, Hachmeister decided he wanted company. And tonight he decided to carry two guns instead of the usual one. It wasn't the eerie sounds of dead leaves rattling in Gacy's bushes as much as the uncertainty of what he was up against. He was out of his own territory, where, at the threat of trouble, he could get on the radio and have four or five squad cars at his side in a couple of minutes. At Gacy's house, he was alone and not always reliably linked by radio with the station. Nor did he have anyone to spell him for a coffee and Twinkies run. The gnawing emptiness of his stomach the night before had taught him never to go on twelve-hour surveillance beyond the reach of food. Moreover, the Delta officers all were learning that Gacy's schedule paid little heed to their own bodily comforts. More than once they had to surreptitiously open their car doors and gently pour an old coffee cup of warm urine into the street.

Hachmeister was pleased when he was told that Mike Albrecht would be assigned as his surveillance partner. Albrecht already knew Gacy from babysitting with him two days before.

Before going to Gacy's house, Lang took Hachmeister to suburban Palatine to borrow that police department's night-scope, an infrared unit that illuminated objects in the dark. He thought it might be useful for spying on Gacy. Lang somberly warned Hachmeister not to let anyone else use it.

After their return to the station, Albrecht frowned when he saw Hachmeister move to the back seat of Lang's car, leaving the front for him. The officers were never sure if the sergeant noticed their silent jostling. No one, it seemed, wanted to ride shotgun when Wally Lang was driving.

As they approached Gacy's house, Robinson radioed that John was in Rohde's car out in front. Lang slowly cruised past the car; Gacy and Rohde watched the three of them intently. Lang turned and drove around the block.

"Let's screw around with them a little bit," Hachmeister said when they came out on Summerdale. He ducked down in the back seat as Lang drove by Rohde's car again. The two officers in front watched Gacy craning his neck, looking for Hachmeister.

"Looks like Gacy can count heads," Albrecht said, laughing. Moments later, Rohde jumped out of the car and walked to the back of Gacy's house. The officers chuckled. Gacy had obviously been convinced Hachmeister was going through his house and had detailed Rohde to check.

Rohde came back, and the two men drove off. They stopped briefly at Rohde's tree lot, then drove to his house and went inside. It was now 1 A.M. Hachmeister and Albrecht relieved

Schultz and Robinson, with whom Lang went back to the station.

For a while, Albrecht watched Rohde and Gacy talking, until they closed the drapes. Soon the lights went out. It looked as though Gacy was spending another night away from home. The officers played electronic football for a while, then Hachmeister decided to move to the street in back of Rohde's house, in case Gacy decided to leave.

Unfortunately, he didn't know he was too late. In the fog that shrouded the city early this Saturday morning, neither officer had seen the figure of a stocky man stealthily creeping through the snow and over back-yard fences in the direction of Summerdale Avenue.

Saturday
December 16, 1978

Although we had worked long past midnight, Bedoe and I were back in Des Plaines at 7 A.M. Saturday. We had learned too much Friday night to sleep on. Both John Szyc and Gregory Godzik had been gone about two years. The Bukavitch youth was another question, as was the mysterious drowning of Charles Itullo. If they all were dead, where were the bodies? If they still had not been found, would we have any chance of ever finding Rob Piest? Bedoe and I sat in my office, trying to pry our eyes and minds open with black coffee, asking each other these questions.

And Richard Walsh—why had he called, and why was he driving what in all likelihood was John Szyc's car? Perhaps he and Gacy were both involved in Szyc's disappearance. Had one of them forged the title application or altered the VIN number on the car itself? The questions were endless, and the most encompassing was: Do we now have multiple murders *and* multiple suspects?

In any case, we had to get Walsh back in for questioning, and we couldn't tell him what we knew about his car in the event he might be criminally involved. Furthermore, Chris Gray possibly knew some of what Walsh had told us—maybe even more. And what did Gacy's former wife, who had given us the Bukavitch name, have to say? Our confusions were now compounded, but at least we knew who might have some of the answers.

* * *

For the officers watching Rohde's house, Friday night passed without event. After several hours, Hachmeister came back to the street where Albrecht was parked, and the two amused themselves with the nightscope, peering at garages and shrubbery, which appeared strangely illuminated in a greenish glow. Mindful of Lang's warning, Hachmeister told his partner to go easy with the scope.

Albrecht had come to work twelve hours earlier and would be on duty at least nine more, so he decided to go eat while all was quiet. Police are accustomed to dining in restaurants for half price, courtesy of cooperating establishments. The uniform is the sole ticket for this form of petty graft. Albrecht was in plain clothes, but he hoped he could indicate his affiliation by laying his portable radio on the counter of the all-night restaurant. His signal was ignored. Breakfast cost him $5.

At about 9:30 A.M., Rohde came out of the house, jumped in his truck, and hurriedly drove off. The driver's side was obscured from the policemen's view.

"Damn it, Mike," Hachmeister said over the radio, "I think Gacy's in that truck."

"No," Albrecht replied, "I saw underneath it. There's no way he could be in there unless Rohde carried him waist-high."

Unconvinced, Hachmeister turned his car around and sped off after Rohde, who immediately eluded him. On the way back, Hachmeister swung past Gacy's house and saw no activity. Irritated, he returned to Rohde's house, in front of which Gacy's silver Volaré was still parked. Albrecht said he was sure Rohde had left alone.

Soon thereafter, a woman, presumably Mrs. Rohde, came out of the house with a young boy. As they were getting into their car, they looked at the two officers' cars and snickered. For the rest of their shift, until they were relieved at 1 P.M., the policemen speculated on whether Gacy was in the house or not. The discussion continued between Schultz and Robinson. Mrs. Rohde returned, then went out on a brief errand at 3:30; Rohde himself returned to the house. But as darkness fell, there was still no sign of Gacy.

At 6 o'clock, just after Robinson had left on a coffee run,

Gacy and Rohde came out of the house, got into Gacy's car, drove off, and quickly gained a six-car lead on Schultz, who was frantically radioing intercept directions to Robinson. Schultz saw Gacy make a right turn, then another on a side street. Looking down the street, Schultz saw no sign of the car. Then a pair of brake lights pierced the darkness. Schultz turned off his headlights. After going about a block, he suddenly saw a car coming at him out of the dark with no lights. As the two cars braked, both drivers turned on their headlights. In a rare miscalculation Gacy had driven into a cul de sac. He roared off and drove to the tree lot a few blocks away. There he dropped off Rohde and, as Robinson rejoined the surveillance, drove back to Summerdale.

A short time later, he came out of his house and said that he was going to visit some relatives in Chicago. The officers followed him at almost a hundred miles an hour on the Kennedy Expressway. At his destination, Gacy told them, "You guys sit here. There's my car—I'm not going anywhere." They watched him go into the house, and then Robinson got into Schultz's car for some football.

By now the surveillance policemen felt that the electronic football games were not only the best way of alleviating boredom, they were also the sole means of preserving their sanity. The surveillance had already drawn furtive peeks from behind curtains and windows. Now, at least in the daylight, it was undoubtedly generating outright bewilderment among the witnesses who saw the officers jiggling up and down under coats pulled over their heads. The officers had learned that lots of movement helped speed the play action and that it was easier to read the digital display in the relative darkness inside their coats. Schultz had devised his own shrewd strategy against the novice Robinson. Schultz played at the slower Pro I setting, but switched the game on Pro II when it was his partner's turn. Schultz won every time. When they were in separate cars, they celebrated touchdowns by pressing the radio microphone buttons, sending the electronics victory bleeps over the airwaves.

Schultz and Robinson were so engrossed in their game that they didn't notice the man who approached their car in the darkness. He rapped on the window.

"Are you guys about ready?" John Gacy asked. "I'm leaving."

Tovar's first asignment on Saturday was to follow up on the information from John Szyc's mother. He talked to Harry Belluomini, the Chicago investigator, about the gas station robbery in which Szyc's car had been used. In talking with neighbors at the time, Belluomini had been told that Szyc was gay and that he had possibly gone to Colorado. Belluomini told Tovar that he had not seen the car involved in the theft nor talked to the owner. Tovar checked with motor vehicle authorities in Colorado to see if they had issued a John A. Szyc either a driver's license or auto registration. They had not.

Tovar then called the police department in Cicero to learn more about the battery case Mrs. Walsh had said her husband was involved in. A Cicero policeman told Tovar that the only arrest record they showed for Walsh was for three traffic offenses, including reckless driving when he tried to elude the officers. Although the Cicero policeman told Tovar that Walsh's license had been suspended, Tovar, in checking the license number with the state, found it to be valid. Cicero was either careless with its record-keeping, or there was false information flowing into our investigation. It was time to hear Walsh's side of the story.

When Ryan and Tovar went to pick up Walsh at his apartment, they were met at the door by his wife. Dick, she said, had been out with his friends and got very drunk. She doubted if she could even wake him up. Glancing into the living room, the officers saw beer cans littered all over. They decided it would do no good to talk to him now and told Mrs. Walsh they would be back later.

Pickell and Adams, meanwhile, were having better luck interviewing a business associate of Gacy's, Richard Raphael, in a restaurant near a job site in Aurora. Raphael had started his own general contracting firm, Raphco, just a few months earlier, he told the officers. He employed Gacy, whom he had known as a subcontractor for nine years, as a superintendent. Gacy, he emphasized was not a partner: he paid Gacy $675 a week, plus labor and materials, out of which Gacy paid his own employees.

Raphael told the officers that on Monday Gacy had missed an important meeting at 7 P.M. with pharmacy clients. He said that Gacy had called him an hour or two before the meeting, saying he would be there. Raphael told Gacy he would order a pizza for him. While waiting for him, he called Gacy's number several times and got the answering machine. At 10:30 he got a busy signal. Five minutes later Gacy called back, saying that he had had a flat tire and that he was concerned about his uncle who was dying. He didn't feel up to conducting business. Raphael said he would talk to him in the morning.

On Tuesday, Raphael and Gacy met for breakfast, then went to one of their clients' pharmacies. Gacy told Raphael that he had forgotten his appointment book at Nisson's and admitted that he had not had a flat tire. He just had not wanted to talk on the phone. When they got to Gacy's house, Raphael said, Gordon Nebel, who worked half days doing Gacy's books, was in the office. They were interrupted, he said, by a phone call from the police. Afterwards, Gacy told Raphael that the officers wanted to speak with him as a character witness.

On Wednesday, according to Raphael, Gacy was supposed to be running errands and supervising a pharmacy remodeling on North Avenue. Raphael was surprised when he got a call at 2:30 from Gacy, who was then at the police station. He said Gacy sounded somewhat incoherent and asked Raphael, whose father is an attorney, to get him a lawyer. At about 10:30 that night, Raphael went to Gacy's house, where his associate was complaining that police had taken some gay magazines, pills, marijuana, and a hypodermic needle—which, Gacy said, was used by one of his boarders who had "plasma attacks." Gacy was also upset that a piece of his carpet had been cut out. Gacy told Raphael there had been a bloodstain on the carpet, left there by one of the installers, who had cut himself.

Raphael told the officers that Gacy had been acting irrational and scared since Wednesday. He didn't recall the names of any of Gacy's employees, other than Walsh, Gray, and an Ed Hefner: there were too many to remember. Walsh and Gray, he said, had lived with Gacy, as had other young men. Raphael added that his relationship with Gacy was 100 percent business. He said he didn't consider Gacy to be on the same social level as himself, that most of his associates were "more

professional." He characterized Gacy as a workaholic who
talked a big line.

Chris Gray was working on the Aurora job, and after their
interview with Raphael, Pickell and Adams talked to him in the
restaurant. When it became apparent that he was being
cooperative and had a lot to say, they asked him to come to the
station for a formal interview. The questioning began just about
2 P.M. in the second-floor conference room.

Gray was a twenty-one-year-old high school dropout who
had served a year in the army. He had gone to work for Gacy in
late 1976 after meeting him while hitchhiking. Gray moved in
with the contractor shortly thereafter, paying him $25 a week
rent.

The officers asked if he had noticed anything unusual about
Gacy's behavior.

"He came right out and said he was open-minded," Gray
told them. "I said I was, too, figuring that he was talking about
females. It turned out to be just the opposite. He sees nothing
wrong with bisexuality. He says that if God didn't intend for
one male to have sex with another, he wouldn't have put the
organs on, or something like that." But, Gray said, he knew of
no males with whom Gacy had engaged in sexual activity.

Gray described Gacy as hard-working and devoted to his
job, but occasionally happy-go-lucky. "Sometimes he's the
most easygoing person in the world," Gray said. "But
sometimes he's short-tempered. Sometimes he's patient, sometimes he's not." Gray said a lot of Gacy's employees quit because "they don't like the aggravation. John is so much of a
perfectionist, it gets to where he's nitpicking."

Now and then, Gray said, the two socialized, often at the
Good Luck Lounge in Chicago, where Gacy's employee Ed
Hefner tended bar. Once, on a trip to Missouri, Gray fixed up
Gacy, left him and the woman at a motel, "and from there on,
it's hearsay," he said. Gacy had dated other women, he said,
and talked, as guys always do, about his sexual activities with
them. Gray knew of the sodomy arrest—Gacy had told him
about it—and he had been led to believe "it had something to
do with dirty films and prostitution."

In the early part of the week, Gray told the officers, work at the job sites had proceeded routinely until Wednesday, when John failed to show up. That afternoon, when Gray went to the house to drop off the keys for the truck, he encountered the police and learned that Gacy was at the station. At about 11 P.M., while trying to find Walsh, he called Gacy's house and John answered. Gacy was upset and didn't want to talk on the phone, so he came and picked up Gray, and the two went out for cheeseburgers and coffee. Gacy told him what had happened.

"He felt insecure about staying alone at his house," Gray told the officers, "not knowing whether the police were there or whether they would come back. So I stayed for about an hour and straightened up a few things, listening to him complain about how things were wrecked."

"Did he indicate to you anything he found to be missing?" Pickell asked.

"Yeah," Gray said, "handcuffs, pills, dirty books, stuff like that."

"Did he say what the handcuffs were for?"

"Not at the time, but I'd seen them before. He uses them for charity benefits, clowning for hospitals, and stuff."

"Did he say what kind of pills were missing?"

"Preludins." Gray said he didn't know if they were prescribed or not. He thought that Gacy might have taken them for his weight problem.

"Did he walk through the house?" Adams asked.

"Yes," Gray replied.

"Then where did he go?"

"To the crawl space."

"Did you see him go down there?"

"Yes."

"What did he do?"

"Okay, he saw the mud on the floor. He complained about that. Then he went into the crawl space, crouched down, and went around in a complete circle with a flashlight. Just checked it out, then he came back up into the house."

After inspecting the attic, Gray said, Gacy drove him home about 2 A.M. On the way they went by the Des Plaines police station to see if Gacy's truck or car was in the parking lot. Gacy intended to pick them up, Gray said, but they weren't there.

On Thursday morning, Gacy picked up Gray in the van. Gacy said he couldn't get his vehicles back from the police, so he would have to rent a car. Gray took the van to the Aurora job site and returned to Gacy's house about 11 P.M. to unload some material. On Friday morning, he spoke with Gacy at the house. Gacy told him he had spent the night at his sister's house. He asked if the police had been in touch with Gray.

"Is there any reason for you to think that perhaps Mr. Gacy could be involved in this missing-person case?" Adams asked.

"Well," Gray said, "John is a funny person. He's a bit of a bragger, and he lives in a fantasy world. Now, how much is fact and how much is fiction is up to the individual to decide, but he claims that he does work for the syndicate. He's said he has set up people before."

"Did John make any statement to you about whether he was involved in this case?" Adams asked.

"He said, 'I swear to you, I had nothing to do with this guy' " Gray paused for a moment. "I don't know. I imagine an innocent man would get a little pissed off at the whole matter, rather than being shaken by it. I realize it is a serious charge, but why would he be upset, nervous, and drawn out, and go spend the night at his sister's house and be afraid of his own shadow? That's my personal opinion.

"Now, as far as violence goes with John," Gray continued, "we've wrestled around a few times. He's strong, but if this guy that is missing had a struggle with John, I think it could have been a fairly good fight if he was a halfway decent guy. John's physical appearance . . . well, he's not as strong as he looks."

Adams asked Gray if he had ever found anything suspicious around Gacy's home or property.

"He had a couple of wallets in the garage, with identification in them," Gray said. "One driver's license was still valid. I think it had a year left on it. I asked John if I could use it as an ID to go out drinking in bars because I was underage then. He said, 'No, you don't want those.' "

"Why?" Pickell asked.

"He said, 'Because they were some people that were deceased.'"

"Would you repeat that?" Pickell said.

"Deceased," Gray said. "No longer living."

"Did you ask him how he knew that?"

"No," Gray said, "because of that mysterious way he lives. One time when I was living there, my wallet was missing, with all my identification, pictures, and so on. Now, whether he wanted to create a psychological effect or something, I don't know."

"Has Mr. Gacy ever shown you any articles of jewelry?"

"Yeah, he gave me a couple of watches. I was late about three or four times that week, and after the ass-chewing he said, 'Come here.' He was digging through this box in his room. He had a lot of rings and stuff like that. 'Here,' he said. 'Now there's no excuse for you to be late,' and he handed me a watch. I said: 'Thanks a lot. Where'd you get this from?' and he goes, 'From a dead person.'"

Gray told the officers that the watch started losing time, and he buried it one day in concrete. Gacy gave him another one. This time Gray didn't ask about its origin.

Gray signed a release, authorizing a police search of the PDM van he had brought in, and turned over the keys to the officers.

Evidence Technician Daniel Genty was assigned to process the vehicle and caused a flurry of excitement when he brought into the station a tissue he had found in the van. It had a spot of fresh blood on it. Gray said the blood was his. While he was driving the van to the station, he said, he had popped a zit.

While Pickell and Adams were driving Gray home, he mentioned that Walsh had bought a Plymouth Satellite from Gacy for $300 and was paying it off in installments. It wasn't a very good car, Gray said. "Dick really got taken."

The best way to determine if Walsh's and Szyc's vehicles were the same car, I figured, was to find Walsh's car and read the VIN number on the driver's side of the dashboard. While Gray was in the station, I had asked him if Walsh was working that day. He said he thought he was remodeling a drugstore near North Avenue and Pulaski Road in Chicago. I jotted down Walsh's plate and VIN numbers and set out for the job site.

The Plymouth was parked halfway down the block from the store. From across the street, I couldn't see any activity in the store, so I crossed and looked through the window. Walsh was in the back, about thirty feet from where I stood, talking with Gacy.

Unwittingly, I had become Gacy's surveillance. I didn't know that Schultz and Robinson were still staking out Rohde's house, believing both men to be inside.

Seeing the PDM crew occupied in the drugstore, I went to Walsh's car to get the VIN number. I leaned over the hood and looked down through the windshield. The number certainly had not been tampered with. I jotted it down and went back to my car, where I compared it with the other VIN number. It was the same as Szyc's.

Now that there was no doubt the car was the same, we could concentrate on finding out how Gacy got the vehicle in the first place. The whole chain of transactions—from Szyc to Gacy/Walsh to Walsh—could have been totally legitimate. After all, it had been reported that Szyc had sold his car. If not for the different VIN numbers for Szyc and Walsh that our computer check had turned up, we might have dropped the matter there. But I had just established that the VIN number on Walsh's registration was not the same as that on the car itself—by one digit. Why? Had Gacy altered the number on the registration to cover his tracks? Was Walsh involved?

From a pay phone I called Bedoe at the station and told him what I'd learned. In turn, he reported that the interview with Gray was still going on, that Patrick Reilly, whose driver's license had been found at Gacy's house, would be brought in for questioning, and that Gacy's former wife was coming in with her new husband.

A few hours later, Bedoe and Kozenczak interviewed Gacy's former wife, now remarried. Cathy Hull Grawicz, whose name is changed here, was told that the police were investigating a missing boy and wanted some background information. Mrs. Grawicz told them that she and Gacy had been married from July, 1972, until February 11, 1975. She said they had had no children, although she had two daughters by a previous marriage.

Bedoe and Kozenczak asked where she and Gacy had vacationed, thinking that that might provide a clue as to the whereabouts of Rob Piest. Mrs. Grawicz mentioned that they had once gone on a trip to Las Vegas and that in fact John had worked there as a teenager. John had had a fight with his father, she said, and drove out there in his car. He had taken a job in a mortuary. Bedoe and Kozenczak asked her about that. She didn't know any of the details, but said that John had returned home several months later. Despite his earlier differences with his father, he was very depressed after the elder Gacy died on December 25 some years later, and ever after he became very saddened and sometimes cried on Christmas Day.

Mrs. Grawicz talked about her marriage and divorce from Gacy. About six months after they were married, Mrs. Grawicz said, she began to notice that Gacy was bringing young men to the garage late at night, sometimes spending hours with them. Looking in the garage once, after John had driven off with a boy, she found a mattress and a red light on the floor. Whenever she asked Gacy about his activities in the garage, he got angry and refused to answer.

Gacy had told her that he was bisexual, but early in their marriage she was convinced that he was turning more homosexual. Less than two years after they were married, Gacy announced to her—on Mother's Day—that this occasion would be their last sex together. It was. Mrs. Grawicz said she frequently found her bikini underpants in the garage. Often she found signs of Gacy's masturbation.

Mrs. Grawicz said that she had contemplated a divorce but initially did nothing because she worried about supporting her two daughters. Once, during an argument, Gacy called her a bitch, and she called him a jagoff. He exploded in rage and threw a candlestick at her. He threatened to strike her, but his sister restrained him. At other times he had thrown furniture in the house, sometimes over very little things.

In the last four months of their marriage, Gacy lived by himself locked behind a sliding door in the back of the house. There was no contact between them. Finally, she sought a divorce on grounds of mental cruelty; he countersued. She was bitter about Walsh's moving in after the divorce. "The minute I was gone," she said, "he was there."

Gacy continued to see his former wife after the divorce. By this time, he was quite open about his sexual preference. One night, in a tavern, a distraught Gacy had said, "I feel myself slipping the other way, and I can't do anything about it." He pointed out to her the sort of young blond men, with a certain shape of rear end, that sexually aroused him. Later, they went to bed and, despite all her efforts, she was unable to arouse him. "I'm sorry," he told her, crying. "I thought I had a chance, but I don't." "You should go for help," she said. "No, it's too late for that," he said. She was sorry she couldn't help John. She still had feelings for him because he had been a very good father to her daughters.

Mrs. Grawicz said that Gacy wanted to move up in the Democratic organization from precinct captain but feared that his arrest in Iowa for "prostitution" would hold him back. She knew how important his local political involvement was to him. She felt that he often had used it to buy his way out of trouble.

She knew of his Northbrook arrest in 1972, but she thought it was a case of mistaken identity. She also was aware of an incident involving a young man, Jack Pyssler, who had gone on a trip to Florida with Gacy. Back in Chicago, Pyssler had come over to the house and beaten Gacy, saying that he had been raped by him in Florida. She had heard that Gacy's employee Charles Itullo had been found dead in a river. She remembered that his relatives had asked for his last paycheck. She didn't know any details of Bukavitch's disappearance, just that John had said the police told him the youth had run away. That was about three years ago.

Cathy Hull Grawicz had contributed more to our knowledge of Gacy than we had expected. After more than four hours of interview, Bedoe aplogized to Grawicz for keeping his wife so long, and the couple left the station.

Schultz and Robinson were almost glad to see Gacy come out of his cousin's house at 11 P.M. Three hours of electronic football were enough. Without announcement this time, Gacy jumped into his car and drove off. After a brisk chase through the streets of Chicago's Northwest Side, Gacy stopped, parked, and entered the Good Luck Lounge.

Robinson parked across the street and Schultz in a nearby vacant lot. The neighborhood was lower middle class, bordering on light industrial. Several minutes after Gacy went in, a number of patrons came out, some pointing at the officers and making catcalls at them, while others stared sullenly.

Just before midnight, Gacy came out abruptly and got into his car. He made a quick U-turn, then sped toward downtown Chicago. For a while Gacy led the officers on an aimless journey, then he headed north on Pulaski Road at a fast clip. At one point, Pulaski ducks diagonally under a railroad viaduct in a ten-mile-an-hour S-curve. Going into the reverse S, Schultz lost control of his car and slid into the oncoming southbound lanes. Accelerating, he straightened out, but in the wrong lane. Now, at the top of the S, he was approaching a blind curve. Just as he was banking into a power slide to the right, he saw the lights of an oncoming car. The other vehicle lurched wildly and went bumping off to Schultz's left, onto the sidewalk and up the embankment. As the car swerved past him, Schultz saw that it bore a familiar slogan: "We serve and protect—Chicago Police." Looking in his mirror, he saw the car come to rest. It did not pursue him.

Shortly after midnight, the relief team picked up the chase on the Kennedy Expressway, and the three police cars followed Gacy to Des Plaines, where he stopped at the Moose Club. There, Albrecht and Hachmeister took over the surveillance cars and Lang shuttled the other two back to the station. Because Albrecht had connections in the club, the officers decided to follow Gacy inside.

Dressed in Levi's, they were challenged by the doorman: "You guys in the Moose?" Albrecht explained their mission and immediately enlisted the man's cooperation. He was an older man, a member of the police reserves. He showed the officers to a table near the door in the banquet and reception area.

Gacy was working the crowd with great ebullience, shaking hands, kissing the women, joking all the way. "It looks like he's the hit of the party," Hachmeister said. "The big shot has arrived." A Moose official came up to the officers' table and asked if they were concerned about the penny-ante card games going on at some tables. Albrecht said they were not. A waitress came to their table.

"What would you like to order?" she asked. "Mr. Gacy would like to buy you a drink." They looked over and saw Gacy nod in acknowledgment. They gave their order, then looked over at Gacy again. He now had a companion, a man who kept a fixed, angry stare on the officers. After Gacy and the man moved over to the bar, the officers motioned to the doorman.

"Don't look now," Hachmeister said, "but we know that short, fat guy over there. We don't know the other one. If you get a chance, see if you can BS them and get us a name."

The waitress brought their drinks, and the officers thanked her. "Mr. Gacy said he has to take care of his bodyguards," she said smiling. The officers followed Gacy into the lounge and stood near the bar.

Their friend at the door came up and told them that the man who was scowling at them was Ed Hefner. As they were thanking him, Gacy walked by. "I'm leaving now," he said.

The three men walked out to the parking lot. Gacy asked, "Do you know where we can get something to eat around here?"

Albrecht suggested a restaurant just a few blocks away. Gacy said fine, I'll meet you there. Before driving off, he asked what their names were.

So at 1:30 on Sunday morning, in the Pot and Pan Restaurant, Hachmeister and Albrecht had their first conversation with John Gacy. They sat at adjacent tables, but the three men were immediately on a first-name basis. After ordering breakfast, Gacy moved right in.

"Hey, are you guys with the feds?" he asked. The two shook their heads. "This is a lot of bullshit," Gacy continued. "Why are you following me? You know, I'll admit it, I'm in a lot of drugstores, and I get into a little drugs. Is that why you're following me?"

"No," Hachmeister said. "We're with the Des Plaines police on a missing-person investigation. They didn't tell us anything. They put us on the surveillance, told us to watch you, and that's all we're doing." Both officers felt that Gacy was trying to flatter them—and, by implication, himself—by making a federal case out of a small-time suburban surveillance.

"Well, there's no problem here at all," Gacy said indignantly. "My attorney and I have an appointment to take a lie detector test on Tuesday. I'm going to clear myself out of this thing.

"I don't know why you guys are following me," he continued, shrugging his heavy shoulders. "I'm a clown—a registered clown—by trade. I work with kids. I go to hospitals to entertain them. You guys are barking up the wrong tree." Gacy did most of the talking. His monologue turned to his bad health, and how difficult strenuous physcial activity was for him with his bad heart—as if to say he couldn't harm anyone if he tried.

"Jesus," the contractor said, "I even have leukemia. I only have four more years to live."

Albrecht and Hachmeister listened sympathetically, then began to delve. They asked Gacy where he traveled, where he spent his vacations. Gacy said he had some land near Spooner, Wisconsin, also some in Minnesota, Nevada, Florida, and Arizona.

Gacy was affable throughout the conversation, and when they finished their meal, he paid the check for all three. Outside, the officers suggested they continue chatting over a drink or two. Without a word, Gacy jumped in his car and drove off fast.

Now it was Hachmeister and Albrecht's turn to be introduced to the Good Luck Lounge. The two officers parked in opposite directions on the street; Hachmeister started following Gacy to the entrance. Suddenly, Gacy turned and hopped into a brown van that was idling in front of the tavern.

"Oh, shit," Hachmeister said, turning and running back to his car, about a hundred feet away. "He's going to get us now. He's in that van," he called out to Albrecht, who had just got out of his car.

But the van didn't move. After a brief time, Gacy emerged and went into the bar. Both officers followed him through a gauntlet of hostile stares, well aware that they were outside their jurisdiction in a young and rough bar crowd without their radios. The officers separated, and Gacy went to the back and struck up a conversation with several people. At 3 A.M., a bar girl came up to Albrecht and said it was closing time and he'd have to leave. Albrecht, who noticed Gacy had just been served a drink, pulled out his badge and said, "We're here, and we're not leaving."

Ten minutes later, Gacy left the bar, his destination unannounced. It was another rapid getaway. This time, Hachmeister, whose car was facing the wrong way, got left behind. Albrecht followed Gacy to PJ's, another Northwest Side bar, while radioing directions to his partner.

"Be careful in here," Gacy said after they got inside. "This is a real rough place."

Gacy went to a table occupied by two women. Albrecht stood by the bar, Hachmeister by the dance floor. Gacy sent each of them a drink. After a while, Hachmesiter saw a bouncer on the bandstand pointing him out to someone. Albrecht caught the signal and asked the bartender who the manager was. He then went over to the man and told him why they were there. The manager said there would be no problem and bought them a round of drinks. Gacy, meanwhile, had just sent them another round. The officers bought one for his table. At 4 A.M., just as the management was sending the officers more drinks, Gacy decided to leave.

By now Gacy was getting very jovial from the Scotch he had consumed; the officers were, too. Albrecht was heading for the men's room when Gacy beckoned him. "This is Jill Suck-a-lot-ski," Gacy said. "Give her a birthday kiss, Mike." As Albrecht was kissing the woman, Gacy left.

Outside, Hachmeister tried to occupy Gacy until Albrecht came out. Gacy was now making numerous comments on the physical endowments of women they had encountered. His assessments were usually exaggerated. At 4:30 A.M., they went on to the nearby Unforgetable Lounge, a neighborhood bar of older clientele. There Gacy introduced the officers to several acquaintances as bodyguards. At 5 A.M., Gacy said he knew of a great bar in Franklin Park, a western suburb.

He drove off, and soon the officers were clocking him at eighty-five miles an hour. Coming into Franklin Park, Gacy slowed down as he crossed the railroad tracks, then made a quick right. At the end of the block he braked and slid into a diagonal parking position on the wrong side of the street. Albrecht braked and swerved off to the right. After Hachmeister turned at the tracks, however, he lost control of his car, which spun around two full circles, skidding on the slick pavement, before coming to rest in front of a store window and less than a foot from Gacy's car.

The bar was closed. Gacy jumped back into his car and drove off at a notably slower speed. On a cross street, just a hundred feet from their near-collision, a Franklin Park squad car sat in full view. It's occupant did not stir as Gacy and his followers drove off; he had apparently slept through the entire incident.

With the dawn of Sunday morning little more than an hour away, Gacy pulled into a Golden Bear restaurant near his house.

"This is a lot of crap," Hachmeister told Gacy as all three got out of their cars. "Somebody's going to get hurt. If it isn't one of us, it's going to be some poor guy walking. You'd better watch your driving." Gacy made no comment.

Inside the restaurant, he began gossiping about the two Torf brothers. The officers sensed he was trying to turn the conversation away from himself. After a brief bit of light bantering, Gacy's mood turned serious.

He told the officers that although he was hard on his employees, he paid them well. He expected a lot out of them, he said. He was hung up on that, a real browbeater. Gacy said it took him two years to train Dick Walsh, but now he was paying him $400 a week. The youth was just like a son to him.

"I like to hire young kids," Gacy said, "so I can train them the way I want them to work. If I hire an older guy, he's already set in his ways." He added that he had given one kid a lot of training and a good salary, and the boy just up and took off. Gacy paused and looked at the officers, as if waiting for a reaction. He went on to say that Walsh had lived with him— he'd charged him $25 a week—as had other youths. Gacy said he had to stop this practice, however, because neighbors were starting to think he was homosexual.

He told the officers he was proud of how he had built his business, which at first involved remodeling nothing but bathrooms and kitchens; now his work was entirely commercial buildings. He discussed strategies of drugstore marketing: what items you want people to see first, what cigarette brands you put at eye level, how to route customers through the rest of the store to get to the pharmacy. Gacy said he owned seven companies and had a yearly income of $70,000. "If anything happened to me," he said, "I wouldn't lose anything. All my property is owned by my corporations. John Gacy is worth hardly anything, but John Gacy's companies are worth a lot."

It was now nearly 6 o'clock in the morning. If Gacy was tired, he didn't show it. If he was intoxicated after drinking most of the night away, his mental alertness seemed unimpaired. He appeared to be a man of boundless energy, both physical and mental, as he sat chatting over breakfast with Hachmeister and Albrecht.

Now his tone became more cocky. Are you guys sure, he asked, you're not with the feds, working on a drug bust?

"We're not with the feds," Hachmeister said. "We're here because a kid is missing. Somebody must suspect that you know something about him."

"Hey, look," Gacy replied, "I talked to the kid only once. If he walked into this place now, I wouldn't even recognize him." He, too, was concerned about the youth's safety, he said, but there was nothing more he could do and his lawyers were seeking an injuction against the surveillance.

"I know it's your job to follow me," Gacy said, "but I've got to do what I have to do, and I hired a bodyguard." He stared each officer in the eye in turn. "His name is Nick. All I can say is you guys better be careful because he carries a .357 magnum, and he wouldn't hesitate to waste one of you."

"How come we haven't seen him?" Albrecht asked.

"You haven't seen him," he answered, "because he knows how to tail people."

Gacy went on to say that he had clout in Norwood Park Township, where he was among the "heavies." His cousin, he added, was noted Chicago gangland figure Tony Accardo.

Hachmeister jumped into the game. "Hey, John," he said, "if you think Mike and I and Schultz and Robbie are the only guys tailing you, you're full of crap."

Gacy thought about that for a moment, then, pushing his

plate aside, turned the conversation to world affairs, the economy, and matters of morality.

"What burns me up more than anything," he said, "is people taking advantage of me. If I buy something for somebody, I expect him later to buy something for me. I don't like these kids who work for me to expect me to lay out all the money."

That morning the officers bought John Gacy's breakfast.

Sunday
December 17, 1978

"I want that goddamned Walsh in here today!" It was Greg Bedoe, roaring at me over the phone early Sunday morning. "Tell Kozenczak to get him in here. We've got to get to the bottom of this thing and find out how tight he is with Gacy."

Greg, of course, was right. We had to pursue the leads while they were hot. It was now just a week before Christmas Eve, and there would be no days off for anyone connected with the case until it was solved. With the harassment suit threatened and the press on our trail, we were running out of time. How much we had left was anybody's guess, but I knew that, if only for psychological reasons, we had to wrap up the investigation by Christmas.

As soon as I got to the office I went over the latest police reports. Tovar and Sommerschield had interviewed the youth here called Patrick Reilly. Had he ever had a valid driver's license that was lost or stolen? No. But when the officers showed him a photocopy of the license recovered at Gacy's house, Reilly admitted that he had lost his wallet, containing his license, in June, 1976. He had found the wallet, minus the license, two months later when it popped out of chair cushions while he was moving from his college dormitory. He could offer no reason the license was missing; he denied knowing anything about John Gacy. Reilly was ill at ease, and both officers thought he was lying. Asked if he would take a polygraph test, he said he would, then hedged. Sommerschield asked if he knew anyone in the gay community. Tovar asked Reilly if he was gay. Of course not, the young man responded angrily. The officers took him home.

Pickell and Adams had been able to find two nurses who confirmed that a man fitting Gacy's description had been at Northwest Hospital inquiring about the dead uncle at about 11 P.M. Monday night. This supported Gacy's story—and in no way contradicted our theory that he had disposed of Rob's body on the following night.

Lieutenant Kozenczak had made an interesting discovery that had been missed by the evidence technicians. While examining the trunk of Gacy's car, he found a clump of fibers that possibly were human hair. He turned it over to ET Genty for laboratory analysis.

Tovar was continuing the search for John Bukavitch. Looking in the Chicago telephone directory, he found only one name close to the spelling he had from Cathy Grawicz and called the number. The man who answered said there was no one named John in his family. Tovar called Chicago headquarters; again, their search of the missing-persons file was negative. About an hour later, however, Chicago called back: they did have a record of a John Butkovich, missing since July 21, 1975, and referred Tovar to the officer who had handled the case.

Tovar followed up and learned that Butkovich had been involved in some sort of disturbance at a friend's place the night before his disappearance. He was supposed to move into an apartment the next day but never got there. His car, with wallet and jacket inside, was found a block from where he lived. There had been rumors that Butkovich had gone to Puerto Rico to run drugs, and after he was reported missing his family had received a collect call from a girl in Puerto Rico who told them that John was there and well. The call had come from a pay phone and had proved impossible to trace. Butkovich's employer, PDM Construction Company, 8213 Summerdale Avenue, Norwood Park, said that the youth had been terminated.

Despite his all-night marathon with Hachmeister and Albrecht, Gacy was up and greeting a visitor at 9:10 Sunday morning. As he did, Gacy's little dog slipped out the front door, and the visitor went chasing down the street to retrieve him. The two men left in their own cars at 9:30. Gacy drove to the drugstore job site at North and Pulaski in Chicago, where he remained until early afternoon.

Schultz and Robinson were the surveillance team now. At about 2 o'clock, Robinson saw Gacy leave the drugstore and go into a nearby restaurant and lounge. The officers followed him inside and found him drinking beer and peppermint schnapps at the bar with Ed Hefner. They joined them and ordered coffee.

As Gacy had done with the other surveillance team, he struck up a conversation with Schultz and Robinson. He started buying them beers and quickly developed a rapport with Schultz, the more mechanically inclined of the two officers. Like Gacy, Schultz had a snowplowing business, and the contractor began describing his rig and complaining about the police department's seizure of his vehicles.

"You're not going to get your plow back," Schultz joked, "because I need it for spare parts." He laughed. "I'm going to use that sucker myself."

"Yeah, you probably will," Gacy said.

For the next hour and a half, Gacy kept up an animated and friendly conversation, all the while buying the officers more beers. He mentioned that he had been the chef for the Chicago Black Hawks. He named several of the hockey players, claiming them as personal friends.

At 3:30, the manager came over. He told Gacy he had a phone call and that he could take it in the office. After Gacy left the bar, Schultz strolled down the hallway to the office and looked in. Gacy was not there. Schultz ran back and got Robinson. They quickly searched the restaurant, then went outside. Gacy was back in the drugstore. They resumed the surveillance from one of their cars, parked in front of the store. More waiting, more football.

At 5:30, Gacy came out and said he had to go home and change clothes. He was due at a bowling alley in west suburban Schiller Park at 6 P.M.

"No way we're going to make it there by six," Schultz told him.

"Want to bet?" Gacy asked. He stopped at his house long enough to put on a flowery disco shirt and pick up his bowling ball, then drove off. He won the bet.

In light of what Chris Gray, Cathy Grawicz, and Phil Torf had told us, we felt that Dick Walsh knew a lot about Gacy he hadn't yet revealed. Just before 2 P.M., Bedoe and Pickell began questioning him in the second-floor conference room at the station.

Walsh told the officers that in 1976, after two years of high school, he had gone to work for a friend of Gacy's who was a plumber. Gacy offered him better pay, and Walsh signed on with him; now Gacy was paying him $10 an hour as a carpenter. Walsh had lived with the contractor for several months the winter before, then married and moved into a building owned by his new father-in-law. He said he once lived in Cicero, where his mother still ran a tavern.

Walsh characterized Gacy as a workhorse who liked to brag about things, especially money. He said his boss was a very lonely person, that he had admitted spending some time in jail for gambling and prostitution. Gacy had said to him that his father had died while he was in prison, but he had not been told until a month later; he was still very angry about that.

Bedoe asked Walsh to recount his activities with Gacy earlier in the week. Late Monday afternoon, Walsh said, he talked with Gacy on the phone, but he had no knowledge of his boss's appointment at Nisson's. On Tuesday, returning in the van about 9:30 P.M., he met the police at Gacy's house. After the officers left, Gacy had a telephone conversation with a Norridge lighting commissioner about having some checks signed. Gacy had promised to lend Walsh some of his tree ornaments, and when Walsh offered to go up to the attic to get them, Gacy emphatically told him to stay downstairs—he would hand them down to him. Walsh loaded the ornaments in the van. The two men had planned to get Christmas trees that night. Gacy told Walsh to go over to Rohde's lot, that he would meet Walsh there after running an errand. Walsh drove away right after Gacy did. He bought a tree from Rohde and waited at the lot until about 11 P.M. Gacy hadn't shown up.

Walsh returned to Summerdale and found Gacy standing in

the driveway. Gacy hopped in the van and suggested they go to a field just north of his house, where they had gone the year before to cut down a tree. Walsh said that on that occasion they had found seven trees, all cut and tied, all probably stolen. They had retrieved them and sold the trees themselves.

When they got to the field, Gacy said to Walsh, "It looks too messy to go out there. Let's go to Rohde's." There they saw that the lot was closed. Walsh dropped off Gacy at his house at about 11:30.

"Was Gacy hiding behind the van when you pulled out?" Bedoe asked.

"No," Walsh replied. "He just walked over to his car and left. He had nothing to hide."

"Did you mention to Rohde that the police were at Gacy's house?" Bedoe asked. Walsh hadn't. "Did you ask John Gacy about why the cops were there?"

"Well," Walsh said vaguely, "some bullshit over a missing kid. John didn't know anything about him."

Bedoe left the interview room and ran downstairs.

"Are the dog teams still out?" he asked Kozenczak.

"Yes," the lieutenant said. "They're searching the forest preserves."

"Can you see if they can take a sweep through a field near Gacy's?" Kozenczak nodded, and Bedoe returned to the interview.

Walsh was expressing concern to Pickell that he might lose his car in the wake of all the police interest in John Gacy. Pickell asked where he had got the car. Walsh said he had bought it from a friend of Gacy's name Szyc, who was moving to California and no longer wanted it. One morning, Gacy drove Walsh down to Chicago's Near North Side, where they found the vehicle parked on the street. Gacy handed Walsh the keys, saying, "Take it for a spin, see if you like it." Walsh said he'd buy it, whereupon Gacy told him he had paid the owner $300 for it. Gacy proposed that Walsh pay him $300 at $50 a week. Walsh, however, had to pay $200 of the debt before Gacy let him take the car. Walsh said Gacy got the first title, in both their names, then gave it to Walsh when the payments were complete. He told Walsh to buy new plates or he'd get into trouble.

"Do you know where Szyc is now?" Bedoe asked. Walsh shrugged. California? He didn't know, didn't seem to care. Walsh said he thought Szyc was kind of a jagoff anyway.

I had walked into the interview room for a moment and I saw that Bedoe was seething, convinced Walsh was still holding back.

"Do you know that John Gacy is a homosexual?" he said angrily to Walsh. "Do you?"

"No," Walsh said impatiently, "he's not homosexual."

"Are you sure?" Bedoe said, leaning over the table menacingly. "Are you sure?" He pointed at me. "Do you know who this guy is?" he exploded. "He's the state's attorney here, and if you don't start straightening up, this is the guy who will prosecute you."

Walsh was umoved. I sat in for a while and got the impression that Walsh was telling us, John Gacy's a jagoff, too, but, hey, I get paid by him. Walsh felt that he controlled Gacy, that if he wasn't around to supervise, Gacy wouldn't have anybody. He had a good thing going with Gacy, a good job for a guy his age and talent. Maybe that's why he was protecting him.

Kozenczak brought word that the dog teams would meet the investigators at a Rodeway Inn a few blocks from Summerdale. The police would take Walsh with them to the field where he and Gacy had been on Tuesday night. We all knew this might be it. Knowingly or not, Walsh might be taking us to Rob Piest's grave.

"You guys hungry?" Gacy asked.

It was 9:30 P.M. Gacy had just come out of Chris Gray's house, which Schultz and Robinson had been watching for the last hour. After more beer at the bowling alley earlier in the evening, the officers had worked up an appetite. Gacy had bowled with his league, all the while introducing Schultz and Robinson as either his bodyguards or as construction worker friends. The two officers had watched Gacy grab some of the women on his team, seat them on his lap, and feel them up. In asides to the policemen he had made repeated references to "nice ass and tits," pointing out who was an "easy lay."

"You're damned right we're hungry," Schultz said now.

"But we're tired of hot dogs and all this garbage food. Let's go someplace decent."

"I got just the spot," Gacy said. "They have the best steaks in town. Whatever you want, it's on me." Both officers were delighted to accept Gacy's offer.

The dinner crowd was thinning out as the three men were seated at a table in the Prime House on Chicago's Northwest Side. Looking at the menu, Schultz's eyes fixed on the fourteen-ounce prime filet; Robinson, too, was considering something substantial. Gacy commented on the menu from the point of view of a man with extensive experience in food service—after all, he had been the exclusive chef of the Chicago Black Hawks. He was also, he said, "a registered clown." He entertained at hospitals and orphanages and also did private parties and openings of restaurants and ice-cream parlors. The kids loved him. It was hard for as nice a guy as Gacy to believe that the police were after him.

"You guys think I did something bad, or something?" he asked. "Did the FBI put you on to me for drugs?"

No, the officers assured him. We're Des Plaines police, and we're following you in reference to a missing boy.

"I don't know," said Gacy, "you must be working on something bigger than just a missing kid. You know, I didn't even know that kid. I think I know who you're talking about, I remember seeing him, but I didn't talk to him. If he's the one I'm thinking about, I talked to him on another occasion, but he was too young to hire."

Gacy went on to say that he had retained his own private investigator to find the youth and resolve the whole matter. The surveillance had put a big crimp in his operation. The trunk of his car contained all the blueprints for the proposed remodeling of his house. The police had screwed up that job, and all his others, to the point where he could barely function. Couldn't they at least speak to Kozenczak and get his blueprints back for him? Incidentally, he asked, what size weapons do you guys carry?

Robinson said he had an automatic. Schultz, who wore his gun in an ankle holster under his bellbottom jeans, simply acknowledged that he had one but didn't describe it further.

"Well, my hit man carries a .357," Gacy said. "I don't

know if you've ever seen him, but all I have to do is snap my fingers, and he'll waste you. You guys are being followed all the time."

The officers never challenged Gacy's statements to his face, preferring to draw him out. But privately they brushed off his threat. Robinson said later, "The way Gacy was driving, there weren't nobody following us. We were damned sure of that."

Gacy switched tack. His creativity as a chef, he explained, enabled him to throw big theme parties at his house with four or five hundred guests. He held them around the Fourth of July and provided everything but the booze. In 1976 he hosted a Bicentennial party; subsequently he had chosen Southern and Italian themes. He invited neighbors, friends, and business associates, as well as politically well-positioned people. Gacy said that he knew every judge in Cook County except one. If he ever got into trouble, he intimated, he'd be in good hands.

In addition to being a Democratic precinct captain and a lighting commissioner, Gacy said, he had been an aide to Mayor Richard Daley, assigned to supervising parades. This had enabled him to become friends with important people, including President Carter's wife, Rosalynn. Before her appearance in Chicago at the Polish Constitution Day Parade, Gacy said, he had hired the sharpshooters who were posted in high-rise buildings for her security. For his trouble, she had sent him an autographed picture of the two of them together.

Parades, Gacy said to the two officers as they finished their meals, were especially fun for clowns. Nobody ever questions what clowns do. Hell, clowns can go up to broads on the sidelines and squeeze their tits, and all the women do is just giggle. "You know," Gacy said, looking at one officer and then the other, "clowns can get away with murder."

Pickell and Bedoe kept pumping Dick Walsh as they drove to their rendezvous with the dog teams. "Have you ever been arrested?" Bedoe asked.

Walsh said that he had been arrested for a traffic offense. He had tried to run away from the police and had been put on probation. He had also been involved in a gasoline theft the previous winter. One night, he explained, he was short of money, so he fished Szyc's license plates out of his trunk—the ones Gacy had told him to dispose of—and put them on his car. He went into a service station, got gas, and left without paying. The attendant saw his plate numbers and gave them to the police. The police traced the plates to John Szyc's family, who told the officers that their son and his vehicle were missing. The police then traced the title to Gacy. Gacy chewed Walsh out and took him to the police station to settle the gas theft. The police told Walsh to get rid of the former owner's plates. Walsh did.

And so the matter rested. The Chicago Police Department files held both John Gacy's arrest record and John Szyc's missing-person reports, but the only known link between Gacy and Szyc was the sale of the car, which the police had no reason to question. True, the sale had been made after Szyc's parents reported him missing, but this could indicate that the youth was alive and presumably well. The overworked detective on general assignment was interested in clearing a $10 gas theft, and he did.

For the last two days, six teams of dogs and their handlers had been combing the forest preserves for tire tracks, mud, and signs of Rob Piest. They had found just one clue of possible interest in the four inches of snow. A set of car tracks starting on Touhy Avenue ran north on an old work trail into the woods about three-quarters of a mile. The teams found two muddy spots, fifty feet apart, where the car had been stuck. The tracks then stopped near the Des Plaines River. Several footprints led from the road down to the river. The car apparently had turned around and gone out the same way it came in. There were tracks near the entrance that indicated that the car had briefly gone off the trail, nearly hitting a fence. This was the only discovery of any significance after two days in the field.

Now four teams and their dogs—Alexa, Guna, Willi, and Banjo—met the investigators near the Rodeway Inn and prepared to search the three-square-block field near Gacy's house. Walsh pointed out where he and Gacy had come late on Tuesday night, and the handlers prepared their dogs by letting them sniff "scent articles" of Rob Piest's clothing they had brought in plastic bags. The teams split up and the search began. The dogs worked methodically, now showing interest in a pile of brush, now moving on, at what seemed to the officers a very slow pace.

Bedoe left Walsh in the car with Pickell and joined Lang and Kautz in the field. They saw muddy tire tracks coming into it from a street that dead-ended on the north side of the field. It looked as though a car had got stuck. They began knocking on doors of the houses in the cul de sac and finally found a woman who remembered someone getting stuck there several nights ago. She didn't have a description of the vehicle. Was it Tuesday night, December 12, the car was there? Bedoe asked her. She thought for a moment. It was the night when there was all that racket from a helicopter. Thursday, Bedoe said, shaking his head. The officers thanked her and left.

For three hours the dog teams and policemen crisscrossed the field in the cold darkness. They found nothing of significance. Pickell, however, had learned some additional information while sitting with Walsh in the car. Earlier, Walsh had run down the list of former PDM employees he remembered. He had mentioned about fifteen names, including Gregory Godzik and Charles Itullo. Now he recalled that a friend of his named Peter had worked for Gacy, and the contractor had offered $100 to the youth if he would let Gacy blow him. Walsh added that he had found two wallets in Gacy's garage, one with a California driver's license, one with a license from Illinois. He said that Gray had seen the wallets, too.

Bedoe rode back to the station with Lang and Kozenczak, who announced he had told Pickell to drive Walsh home.

Furious, Bedoe burst into my office. "Kozenczak let Walsh go," he bellowed. "I could have got that little bastard to open up if I could have talked to him longer. You've got to get him back in here!"

I knew how he felt. He was in no position to tell Des Plaines how to run their investigation, but he was right.

"We'll get Walsh back tomorrow," I told him. "Let's go check on the dogs."

The police had parked sixteen vehicles, including Gacy's car and two trucks, in the station garage. All the doors and trunks were open. One of the dog team leaders explained that after giving each of the three dogs one of Rob Piest's boots as a scent article, the dogs would make their own unleashed search of the garage. The leader described the various ways that each of the dogs would react if Rob's scent was present anywhere.

The dogs slowly walked about the garage, sniffing all the vehicles, police as well as Gacy's. None responded to the PDM van, but they showed definite interest in the pickup and snowplow. Finally, one small German shepherd approached Gacy's black Oldsmobile.

I got a chill down my spine when she got in the passenger side and lay down on the seat. That, according to her handler, was the "death reaction"—and clear confirmation that John Gacy's car had been used to transport the body of Robert Piest.

Gacy had taken Schultz and Robinson for a good dinner; now Albrecht and Hachmeister thought they, too, were in for a good time. After settling the bill at the Prime House, Gacy had dropped off some plans at a Near North Side job site, then told Schultz and Robinson they were going to the Marriott Hotel on Chicago's Magnificent Mile for cocktails. The relieving ceremony had interfered, however, and Albrecht and Hachmeister assumed they would be the beneficiaries of Gacy's largesse.

Gacy didn't have a party in mind, after all. He wanted to inspect an airline ticket office that was going to occupy some of the hotel's commercial space fronting on Michigan Avenue. He told the officers that he liked to visit job sites at night, when there was less traffic and commotion. First, Gacy said that the construction project was his; later, he said he was merely bidding on the job. His mission on this Sunday midnight was unclear to the officers, who watched as he rattled doors and tried peeping between partitions. He found a security guard who was either without the proper key or unwilling to let him into the space. So much for cocktails at the Marriott.

Gacy then led the officers up the lake shore to the Little Sicily restaurant on the North Side, where, he said, the cook owed him $4,000. The place was closed. Continuing their tour, Gacy at one point slowed to a crawl.

"Look at that," Hachmeister radioed Albrecht. Gacy was craning his neck as he watched a young man walking on the sidewalk to his right. He circled the block, then continued his scrutiny of the man in the dimly lit street. Finally he resumed his usual pace. "Boy, I thought he was going to break his neck checking that guy out," Hachmeister said.

Now Gacy drove across town until he came to the Brickyard shopping center, then under construction. He pulled into the entrance, then slowly drove up a ramp to a parking area. The cars inched along among the construction trailers and large cylindrical pillars. The area was deserted, and the only illumination on the boarded-up store fronts came from the distant street lights near the entrance.

"This doesn't look good at all," Albrecht radioed Hachmeister. "Better back off a little." Albrecht made sure his gun was on the seat next to him, Hachmeister laid his on the console. If there was any truth to Gacy's story about "Nick" and his .357, this was the perfect setup. The officers took up stake-out positions and watched Gacy from a distance.

Gacy got out of his car and went up to one of the construction trailers. He was apparently trying to open the door when a man approached him. The two talked for a moment, then Gacy got back into his car. "Must be a security guard," Albrecht radioed. Gacy drove out of the mall and headed north.

The Brickyard shopping center was just another job he was checking out, Gacy explained to the officers over breakfast at a Golden Bear restaurant on Chicago's Northwest Side. It was now 1 A.M., and Gacy's mood was somewhat melancholy as he began talking about his previous marriages, neither of which, he said, was right for him. "Single life has its advantages," he said, and talked about a trip he and Walsh had taken to new York on which they had picked up "lots of broads." On the other hand, he added, "single life can be very lonely." Hachmeister thought Gacy was about to cry at this point.

Albrecht excused himself to go to the washroom, and Gacy began telling Hachmeister about doing a lot of magic tricks for children as a "registered clown." Once more, he mentioned the fun that clowns have at parades and, looking Hachmeister straight in the eye, he said: "You know, Dave, clowns can get away with murder."

When Albrecht came back, the officers turned the conversation to Gacy's Wisconsin property; they still thought this could be a possible place to look for Rob Piest's body. Gacy now said that it was not he, but Rohde, who had property near Spooner. His own land was in Rhinelander, he said, but he would not give a specific location. Albrecht said he had often vacationed in that area and asked Gacy about the nearby town of St. Germain. Gacy had never heard of it.

"I'll tell you where the ideal place is," Gacy said finally. "Where Raphael lives. He's only a couple minutes from downtown Glenview, but he's got five acres of land. Whenever I'm uptight, and I just want to get away, I go out there in back of his property. It's really secluded. The only bad part of it—I wish he'd put in some gravel—every time I go out there, I get stuck in the mud."

Monday
December 18, 1978

When I got to Des Plaines on Monday morning there was great excitement in the Detective Bureau and an intriguing diagram drawn on my easel in Kozenczak's office. The lieutenant had spoken the night before with an anonymous caller who had informed him that Gacy had killed five or six people, Robert Piest among them, and that she knew where the bodies were buried. Kozenczak already had sent some of his detectives out looking for the gravesites, and other officers in the station were making telephone queries. On the face of it, this seemed to be the most interesting lead we had yet encountered. I sat down with Bedoe and Kozenczak, who filled me in on the mysterious call.

Late Sunday night, when he was alone in the bureau reviewing reports, Kozenczak told us, a woman had called and given him the information. She had described certain landmarks around the gravesites: an incinerator, yellow and red construction equipment covered with plastic, a body of water, some wooded land, a red-brick building, and heavy cyclone fencing. From the descriptions she gave, Kozenczak had drawn a sketch on my easel with a blue marker pen, mapping the landmarks as well as six graves at the top of the plot. The grave on the right supposedly was Piest's.

Kozenczak went on to say that he thought the woman might be a friend in whom Gacy had confided. She knew that Gacy had a scar on one finger, a fact that the detectives had confirmed by checking the fingerprint card we had got from Northbrook.

I asked Kozenczak if there was any way to call her back. He said no, she would not give her name, but she had said she might call back. I was disappointed that he hadn't traced the call, although I knew this can be a difficult process because the Des Plaines phone system is an independent company. If the woman had telephoned from outside the suburb, it would have taken several calls and considerable time to effect a trace.

Bedoe asked why she hadn't given a specific location. Kozenczak said that she had told him that if she had done that, Gacy would know she had talked to the police. She wanted to help the investigators, but she had to be careful.

I wished we could talk to the woman; still, this seemed a credible lead and I was excited about pursuing it. The six graves she spoke of meshed with our developing theory that John Gacy might be a mass murderer. By mentioning the scar on his finger she seemed to be trying to let us know she knew what she was talking about.

Most important, she had mentioned Rob Piest—and at this point there had been no public disclosure connecting the two. She had to be someone close to Gacy, possibly a relative. I thought it might be Gacy's sister. We knew he had stayed with her on Thursday night. Perhaps he had confided in her, and she wanted him picked up because she feared for his physical safety. She wouldn't want him to know, of course, that she had turned him in. Possibly it was Gacy's former wife Cathy, although that seemed less likely.

In any case, we had to find the landmarks the anonymous caller had described, and they could be anywhere in the metropolitan area. I thought that a helicopter search would be the quickest way of spotting them, so I told Bedoe to see if Cliff Johnson could go up again. Bedoe, meanwhile, was calling the Environmental Protection Agency to get a fix on the incinerator the woman had mentioned, and other detectives checked on the locations of lots where construction equipment was parked.

Tovar and Sommerschield were sent out to Glenview to look at the property of Gacy's associate Richard Raphael; he might have heavy machinery on his premises. While listening to

Kozenczak's earlier briefing on the anonymous tip, Sommerschield had been greeted with stony silence when he said, "Gosh, Joe, that sounds like something a psychic would say." Now he had forgotten his indiscretion and was only too glad to be out in the field, away from his main responsibility, the flow chart.

Raphael was not home when the officers arrived, and his wife was just leaving on an errand. She said that although she was not very familiar with her husband's business, she didn't think he owned any construction equipment. She said that she did not like John Gacy very well. He was a kind of no-class person. She excused herself, but told the officers to feel free to look around.

After checking for landmarks on the property and part of the adjoining woods, the officers stopped at the barn, where they found Dick Walsh working. Tovar asked him if he knew any more about Charles Itullo, the young man who had drowned. Walsh said that he didn't think Itullo had any permanent address, that he just lived in his van. He added that another former PDM employee, who lived in Franklin Park, could probably tell the police more. He had been a drinking buddy of Itullo's, and his name was Bruce Borc.

Back at the station, Tovar reached Borc after several calls. Borc said that Itullo was about twenty-seven years old and drove a van with Texas plates. He did not get along very well with Gacy and had never returned to work. Borc said that he, too, was told by Gacy that Itullo had drowned. As far as he knew, Borc said, the name was spelled "Hattulo" and that his family lived in Houston.

Tovar started calling Houston authorities, as well as state agencies, for information on Itullos, Hattulos, and variants thereof. He continued his survey of downstate Illinois river towns for any information on unidentified bodies. The responses were discouraging: either nothing, or "We'll have to check."

"Every time I go out there, I get stuck in the mud." After hearing that, Hachmeister and Albrecht were certain that Rob Piest's body would be found somewhere on Raphael's property in Glenview. Before Gacy had said good night and gone home at 2:30 A.M., he had announced that he would be going out to Raphael's on Monday or Tuesday and stood back to observe Albrecht's reaction. Now the two officers talked it over as they sat in one of the surveillance cars dining on Twinkies and yogurt and decided they should share this information.

Albrecht went in search of a pay phone. He was unable to reach Lang, so he called Kozenczak at home. The lieutenant was not very interested in Albrecht's report; anyway, he thought Raphael's place had already been checked. He did, however, want Albrecht to take down some information. Albrecht went to his car and got a yellow pad. Kozenczak told him of the anonymous call and described some of the landmarks. He wanted Albrecht to investigate an old junk yard near Gacy's house.

Albrecht went to the scene and found several landmarks similar to those Kozenczak had mentioned. He diagramed what he saw, then called Kozenczak and described his findings. Kozenczak said it wasn't what he was looking for but promised to check Albrecht's diagram in the morning. Hachmeister, meanwhile, was trying to reach Albrecht on the radio, without success. He was irritated, thinking he was being left out of something important.

Albrecht finally returned an hour or so later. "Where the hell have you been?" Hachmeister asked him.

"I think Joe's been talking to a psychic," Albrecht said. He told Hachmeister where he had been and how Kozenczak had written off their theory. They spent the rest of the early hours of Monday morning talking about what they might find in the mud somewhere on Raphael's property in Glenview.

At 8:45 A.M., Gacy left his house and beat a fast track to the offices of his lawyer in Park Ridge, Sam Amirante. Hachmeister parked at the rear of the building and Albrecht pulled up in front, just as LeRoy Stevens, Gacy's other lawyer, was arriving. Stevens recognized Albrecht from Gacy's visit to the police station the previous Wednesday and came over to his car.

"Sullivan's going to take you guys off the surveillance," he said, "and if he doesn't, I'll have it done myself." Albrecht listened politely.

"Incidentally," Stevens said, "I just heard that the Piest boy called from Milwaukee, and he's all right." He paused while

Albrecht looked at him coldly. "By the way, did he have any juvenile delinquency problems?"

"No, he didn't," Albrecht said angrily as Stevens turned and walked to the building.

At 11 o'clock, Gacy drove home. Shortly after noon, the officers were relieved, and on the way back to the station Hachmeister asked Lang what they were going to do about investigating Raphael's property. Somebody had already been out there, Lang said, and they would let it go at that.

As it turned out, the surveillance team would get a look at the property sooner than they thought. Shortly after Schultz and Robinson came on duty, Gacy told them they were going to Raphael's. He seemed angry as well as nervous. A van had been broken into the night before, he explained, and he had to get some tools for his crew at a job site. On the way to Glenview, the officers discussed Gacy's agitation. They concluded that Walsh had informed him of Tovar and Sommerschield's visit to Raphael's that morning, and that he was upset about that. Schultz and Robinson were beginning to see a pattern in Gacy's meanderings: to find out what had happened, he always led his surveillance team to the place that Des Plaines investigators had just checked out.

After a hundred-mile-an-hour chase up the Tri-State Tollway, Gacy took a Glenview exit and drove to Raphael's. Walsh was still working in the barn. Gacy pulled him aside and spoke with him a short distance from the officers in hushed tones. As he was walking on an incline toward Walsh's car, Gacy slipped and fell on the ice. He lay there for a moment, moaning, then slowly got up. From Walsh's trunk, he took an impact gun and some blueprints.

It was 1:30 when he told the officers he was going to LeRoy Stevens's office, on the Northwest Side of Chicago. Gacy was now visiting his lawyers with increasing frequency. It was clear the strain of the surveillance was getting to him.

On the way into Chicago, Gacy stopped at the offices of the Polish National Alliance. By his own account, he was one of the organization's more important members. Schultz decided to go across the street for some coffee while Gacy was occupied at the Alliance. Just as he was ordering, Robinson's voice came over his portable radio: "Let's go. He's moving."

Gacy's next stop was his doctor's office to get a prescription. "My heart's been bothering me," he told the officers. "I've got this cardiac problem." He explained that he was getting some Valium to combat the stress he was under.

Then the officers sat in the waiting room of LeRoy Stevens's offices for almost three hours while Gacy met with his attorney. If there was going to be a harassment suit, it looked as if it would be coming quite soon.

At 5 o'clock Gacy came out. "Let's get going," he told the officers. "We've got someone to meet." In a few minutes, they arrived at Coach's Corner, where Gacy met Ed Hefner at the bar. After a brief conversation among the four of them, Gacy asked to see the electronic football game the officers had been entertaining themselves with. Schultz went to his car to get it. Meanwhile, Walsh came in and joined the party. For several minutes, he stood at the bar next to Gacy and Hefner, then the three moved over to the cigarette machine to talk privately. They stepped outside for a moment, then returned. Gacy seemed perturbed.

"You'd better not let me down, you fuckers," he told Walsh and Hefner. "You owe it to me." Schultz and Robinson strained to hear the rest of the conversation through the blare of the jukebox and the din of the after-work tavern crowd.

". . . and what?" they heard Walsh ask Gacy as the three turned to the bar. "Buried like the other five?"

After spending the morning with Lang looking in vain for landmarks fitting the anonymous tip, Bedoe returned to the station. Two LEADS messages reporting floating bodies found in the Des Plaines River had come over the wire in response to the queries sent out immediately after Rob Piest's parents had reported their son's disappearance. The reports had been awaiting follow-up for a couple of days. Bedoe noticed that the bodies had been discovered before Rob's disappearance, but he decided to investigate them anyway. We were now fairly sure that John Gacy might have had other victims.

A sheriff's policeman in Will County told Bedoe that they had recovered the body of a youth they had identified as a Frank Landingin on November 12. The body was nude and had been sexually molested. A rag was stuffed in his mouth. They had learned that Landingin was homosexual.

From Grundy County Coroner James Reeves, Bedoe found out that a body of a young man had been recovered from the river the previous summer. The corpse, nude and badly decomposed, had been spotted by a barge captain. Reeves said the man was in his twenties, possibly Oriental; he had very small hands and feet. There were no bullet wounds. The only identification mark was a tattoo on the left arm in three-quarter-inch block letters: "Tim Lee."

I was angry that no follow-up had been made on a piece of evidence we had recovered on the search of Gacy's house. The police had assumed the photo receipt that Kozenczak had picked out of the trash belonged to Gacy and had left it at that. I told Kozenczak to send somebody over to Nisson Pharmacy and find out for sure. From my own experience as a teenager working in a drugstore, I knew that stores keep photo logs to identify customers' orders. If the receipt was for Gacy's order, the log at Nisson's would tell us that. Besides, maybe the photos themselves would have some clue that might be useful.

Adams and Pickell went to Nisson's, where they were immediately rebuffed. "They don't want to give it to us," they reported to me. "They say they need it to check out the others."

"By God," I snapped, "bring it in and we'll Xerox a copy for them."

The crime laboratory of the Department of Law Enforcement had reported that because the brown bottle found in Gacy's house was empty, it was impossible to determine its previous contents. I asked the lab assistant if, judging by the smell, it could have been chloroform. Yes, she said. I told her it would be very helpful if she could put that in the laboratory report.

Sommerschield had found out that Matthew Cooper (not his real name), the other youth whose driving permit had been recovered in Gacy's house, was living with his parents. Despite the reluctance of the youth's father, Sommerschield and Tovar brought him into the station for questioning. They told the father they had found various drivers' licenses, including

Matthew's, in Gacy's possession, and they wanted to try to find a common denominator for the thefts.

At first, Cooper denied knowing anything about John Gacy, and he told the officers a highly unlikely story about losing his license. During a break in the questioning, Tovar talked with Bedoe, who told him, "Lean on him. Tell him we know better and he'll get in trouble if he doesn't open up."

Cooper finally admitted that Gacy had once offered him a ride. They drove around awhile, sharing a joint of marijuana, and ended up at Gacy's house. There, Cooper said, Gacy offered him money if he would let Gacy blow him. Cooper consented. Afterwards, Cooper took a shower, then Gacy drove him home. I know where you live now, Gacy had remarked on the way. Cooper assumed that Gacy had gone through his wallet while he was in the shower. Gacy apparently had taken Cooper's learner's permit, and the youth had not reported it missing because he was about to get his permanent license.

Over the weekend, Mrs. Szyc had sorted through more of her son John's possessions, and we had some property recovered from Chris Gray that we thought might be Szyc's also. Tovar and Adams went over to the Szyc residence late in the afternoon, taking with them photographs of a shirt and watch Gacy had given Gray. They asked Mrs. Szyc if she could identify them. She looked at the pictures for a moment, then said no, they were not her son's.

Mrs. Szyc gave the officers a brown bag containing some of John's papers. Among them was a warranty and service booklet for the television set and a manufacturer's brochure for the clock radio that was missing from John Szyc's apartment. Tovar thumbed through the pamphlets on the way back to the station.

"That's kind of odd," he said.

"What's that?" Adams replied.

"John Szyc had a black and white Motorola TV."

"Yeah, what about it?"

"John Gacy had a small Motorola in his bedroom."

Schultz and Robinson were still stunned by Walsh's remark about "buried like the other five" when Gacy compounded their surprise by inviting them to dinner at his house. He stopped at Hagen's fish market, bought several pounds of perch and shrimp, and the three drove back to Summerdale at about 6:30 P.M.

From the smell in Gacy's kitchen, the officers could tell immediately that his dog had relieved itself on the floor. Gacy let the animal outside through the back door, then gathered up the soiled newspapers. After putting the fish in his microwave oven, Gacy went over to the bar in the recreation room and asked the officers what they'd like to drink. He brought out albums of his photographs, pointing out shots in which he'd posed with Rosalynn Carter and Chicago mayor Michael Bilandic and pictures taken at his wedding and theme parties, lingering on those with politicians in them. He gave the officers a quick tour of his house, showing them his clown pictures, then he got out blueprints detailing the proposed second-story addition to his recreation room. As Gacy talked about the important politicians he knew, Schultz and Robinson hungrily wolfed down the major portion of the fish. How the hell can Gacy be so heavy, Schultz wondered, when he never seems to eat?

Gacy let the dog back into the kitchen and excused himself to play back his phone messages and make a few calls. The officers noticed that the animal would not venture from the kitchen into the rest of the house. Gacy returned and announced to the officers, "We're going back to Raphael's. I've got to work on the payroll."

On the way, Gacy stopped briefly at Walsh's, "to let him know where to report to work tomorrow," and-at another job site. They arrived at Raphael's at about 9 o'clock.

The officers played electronic football for about an hour, then decided they needed a coffee break. Robinson lost the coin toss and set out in search of a restaurant. He found one about a mile away. Although Robinson was dressed in blue jeans, the waitress apparently noticed his portable radio on the counter.

"We don't charge policemen for coffee," she said. Robinson thanked her and left a fifty-cent tip. Back in his car, he heard Schultz on the radio: "Shake your booty. He's going." Robinson accelerated and was at ninety miles an hour when he heard a siren. Looking into his rear-view mirror, he saw a flashing red light. A Glenview policeman had picked him up on radar. Robinson hurriedly braked and pulled over to the shoulder. He jumped out and flashed his badge at the headlights of the squad car that had pulled up behind him.

"Des Plaines police," Robinson yelled. "Official business. Just call my station." He jumped back into his car and roared off. The Glenview officer did not follow him.

"Ain't no justice!" Robinson snarled into his radio to Schultz. "Gacy drives like an animal, but the coppers stop *me*."

"He's heading home," Schultz replied.

Gacy's response to the surveillance teams was changing. Now he was trying to elude them whenever he could—and despite their best efforts, he had plenty of opportunities, not all of them due to coffee breaks. Because the officers gave their radios heavy usage, the batteries never got fully charged; more than once they had to stop to get new ones. If they were beyond the range of the Des Plaines transmitters, the radios were useless for communication with the station and they would have to find a telephone to call in. If the midnight team didn't get a chance to fill their tanks at the municipal garage, they had to find a gas station and fill up wherever and whenever they could. At least the accounting department was understanding. There wasn't always time to get a receipt, but the officers were reimbursed for whatever they said they had spent.

Robinson caught up by the time they got back to Summerdale. Gacy invited the officers in, but they declined. He told them that from now on they should park in his driveway—the neighbors were beginning to complain about their presence.

Schultz and Robinson began playing football and talking about Walsh's remark at Coach's Corner.

"Wouldn't it be something if Gacy had bodies buried under all those bushes?" Schultz said, nodding toward the dense hedge alongside Gacy's driveway.

"That's probably why they're growing so good," Robinson said.

Gacy came stomping out of the house and headed for his car.

"Hey, where are you going?" Schultz asked.

"Just follow me," Gacy replied angrily.

He went roaring off down Summerdale, then followed side streets that were still slick with standing water and melting ice. His car fishtailed from side to side as he tried to keep it under control at sixty miles an hour. Schultz and Robinson fell farther and farther behind. Finally, several blocks ahead of them, they saw his headlights sweeping wildly to the side and his car skating sideways for a few hundred feet. He plowed into a snowbank on the parkway. By the time they caught up, Gacy had extricated himself and was on his way. He drove to Resurrection Hospital in Chicago.

By the time Gacy came out, almost an hour later, he had calmed down. He told the officers he had visited Sam Amirante's kid, who was a patient. He was very concerned, he said, about the boy's health.

Gacy's anger before going to the hospital was, I imagine, brought on when he made a quick call from his house to Walsh's and learned that we had Dick back in the station. Bedoe was still irritated that he hadn't had another shot at Walsh on Sunday night, so he and Sergeant Joe Hein of the sheriff's police had gone out and brought him back in. Walsh was exasperated by all the attention the police had shown him, and he swore that he had told them all he knew. Bedoe, however, was convinced that there was something that was keeping him from telling all he knew about John Gacy.

With Hein, rather than someone from the Des Plaines force, Greg felt much more comfortable. He could raise his voice a little more to an uncooperative witness. The two policemen took Walsh into an interview room, took off their coats and ties, and picked up where Sunday's interview left off.

They asked Walsh if Gacy had any female friends. He knew of only one, a woman of about thirty who had a ten-year-old daughter. Walsh had seen them together several months before. He thought she lived somewhere near Gacy.

Next they asked about Gacy's house. Walsh said it was in Gacy's mother's name and that he still owed her $8,000 on it. The garage, he said, was mostly used for storage of business equipment and materials. Asked if he had ever been in the crawl space, Walsh said he had gone down there with Gacy to spread about ten bags of lime in the summer of 1977. The sump pump was not working right, and the whole house smelled.

Bedoe asked Walsh if he knew anything about Gacy's handcuffs and the two-by-four with holes drilled in it. Walsh said Gacy used the handcuffs for tricks: he would lock himself up in them, then get out. Walsh thought he worked them into his clown routine. The two-by-four, Walsh said, had some chains attached to, and Gacy kept it under his bed. He thought Gacy used it to spread a person's legs apart during anal sex. He added that he had never seen it used.

Bedoe thought he was getting somewhere with Walsh, so he went over and over the details of his previous statements. Walsh didn't budge any further, and he replied with his usual sarcasm and cockiness. Greg was fairly sure he wasn't lying, but he knew Walsh was holding back. Finally he stood over the young man and said: "Look, if you're involved in this thing, now's the time to tell us, not later. I want to know anything else that you and John Gacy may be involved in. If you don't tell us, and we nail Gacy, it's too late. There'll be no making deals then." Walsh was adamant: he knew nothing more.

While Walsh was being questioned, I was told that his mother was out in the waiting area, protesting loudly. I went out and saw a stocky woman with flaming red hair, attended by a tough-looking male companion. He said nothing but glared ominously. I introduced myself as an assistant state's attorney. She asked what we were doing. Was her son under arrest? I said we were conducting an investigation and that he was not under arrest. Then I'm taking him with me, she said, adding that her lawyer would sue. I decided to stall her and said I'd go check on the investigators' progress.

Greg was still hammering at Walsh, and through a window in the interview room I saw him give me a surreptitious wink that told me he was making progress.

"You know your problem, Dick?" he said. "Either you're involved in something Gacy is doing illegally and you don't want to admit it, or you're gay and you don't want that to come out because you're married. If that's your problem, it's not going to go past me or out this room. But get it off your chest."

Walsh would offer no more. Bedoe and Hein explained in detail the circumstances of Gacy's sodomy conviction in Iowa.

They did not, however, tell him what we had learned about the title to Szyc's car: we first had to know just how heavily Walsh was involved. Meanwhile, word came from the beleaguered watch officer that Mrs. Walsh was demanding to see her son. Since Dick wasn't cracking, Bedoe had her shown in.

He met her outside the interview room and explained to her that the police suspected Gacy was involved in the disappearance of the Piest boy, and that Dick could get into a lot of trouble if he was withholding information. Mrs. Walsh said that she was worried that Gacy might be threatening her son, because he had done it before. She obviously didn't like Gacy at all.

Dick, she said, had told Gacy the previous summer that if he didn't get a pay raise, he was going to report Gacy to the carpenters' union. Gacy told him not to do it, or he and his family might be harmed. Dick told his mother. Accompanied by a male friend, she went over to Gacy's house. The man pulled out a .38 and stuck it in Gacy's mouth. "If anything happens to my son or his family," Mrs. Walsh told Gacy, "*you* are dead!"

Bedoe took Mrs. Walsh into the interview room and left her alone with her son. She spent almost a half hour with him, and when she came out, Bedoe could see through the doorway that Dick had been crying.

"He says he had nothing to do with the boy's disappearance," Mrs. Walsh said, "and I believe him."

"Fine," Bedoe said. "You're his mother. Now we have a few more things to ask him." Mrs. Walsh said she would wait.

Bedoe and Hein reminded Walsh of what they had told him and asked if he wanted to say anything more. He didn't. "We'll be talking to you again," Bedoe said. "You think about it, Dick."

Before the day was over, we had our break. Pickell and Adams had managed to extract the photo log from Nisson Pharmacy. It was a single sheet, a form supplied by a Wisconsin firm called Sundance Photo, Inc., the lab that Nisson's used for processing. The sheet listed by serial number and customer's name the envelopes of film that Nisson's had sent in between December 2 and December 14. There were about thirty entries.

The serial number of the receipt found in Gacy's trash was 36119. The second to last entry in the log was dated December 11. The serial number was 36119. The customer's name was Kim Byers.

Tuesday
December 19, 1978

At 8:40 in the morning, Gordon Nebel arrived for work at Gacy's house, and Hachmeister absentmindedly logged the name "Johnson" on his notepad next to him. It wasn't that he didn't recognize Nebel. He simply had a case of morning grogginess after almost nine uneventful hours on stake-out.

A half hour later, Gacy came out the door scowling and walked quickly over to the police cars in what Albrecht by now recognized as his characteristic gait: almost no movement of his torso, just his legs trundling him along.

"You guys are really obnoxious," he said.

"What did we do now?" Albrecht asked.

"They're being very hostile," Gacy said.

"Who?" Albrecht asked.

"I don't want you guys parking on the street. I'm giving you permission to use my driveway because the neighbors are getting pissed off." The officers were reluctant to oblige Gacy on this because they worried about their own safety and, besides, they didn't want to be accused of impending his movements.

"Who's Vande Vusse, anyway?" Gacy continued.

"Vande Vusse?" Albrecht said. "He's a sergeant, the first watch commander at the station." The sergeant had been on duty last Wednesday when Gacy came in to give a statement.

"Well, you and Vande Vusse are going to be the first ones named in the suit," Gacy said, stuffing his hands in the pockets of his wash pants. He went on to say that he was missing tools from his garage, in a tone that intimated that the officers might know something about it. He complained that he was still waiting for his blueprints. Finally, Gacy turned away and said they were going somewhere, but first he had to empty his trunk.

"What's in there?" Albrecht asked.

Gacy wheeled around. "Two bottles of booze," he said with a leer, "and three bodies." He stalked back to the house.

A few minutes later Gacy came back out and walked over to Hachmeister's car. He said they would be going to Waukegan and gave him directions. Hachmeister saw him looking at the notepad on the seat.

"Oh, I see your other surveillance unit is here," Gacy said. "Johnson, huh?"

"No, John," Hachmeister said, "that's just a mistake," but Gacy did not believe him.

He jumped into his car and roared off. Driving north on the Tollway, Gacy weaved in and out of traffic at high speed, easing off a bit when he spotted cars with CB radio antennas. He appeared to be writing down their license numbers. As they approached the Waukegan exit, Gacy accelerated into the far left-hand lane. As soon as the officers fell in behind him, he swerved across the other lanes, just making the exit at Grand Avenue. The officers followed him off the toll road to his job site at a drugstore on the north side of town.

In the parking lot, Gacy walked toward Albrecht's car, then stopped about twenty feet away. "I know your car is bugged," he said, "and anything I say is going to be tapped, so get out. I want to talk to you. I saw your other guy on the Tollway," he continued, as they walked into the drugstore. "That's why I made such a quick exit. I just wanted to lose him."

Inside the store the pharmacist told Gacy he was late.

"What do you mean?" Gacy said in a loud voice. "You just saw me in the last twenty-four hours." The pharmacist looked at Gacy with a puzzled expression.

A clerk behind the counter spoke up. "John, there's a call here for you from Gail." Gacy picked up the phone and said, "Hello? Hello?" Then he hung up immediately. There was nobody on the line, he told Albrecht, but Gacy hadn't given the caller time to respond.

About a half hour later, Gacy walked out the back door of the drugstore. Seeing Hachmeister, he quickly stooped as if to pick something up, then went back into the store. A few minutes later he went out the front door, telling Albrecht he had to get a tool from a nearby rental shop.

"Hey, I wasn't trying to get away from you guys," he said to Hachmeister, who had moved to the front. "I was just getting something outside."

When he came out of the rental shop, he still refused to go near Albrecht's car. Then he confided to the officers that he wanted some consideration in the event he was arrested. He asked that they let him call his attorney. He said that he was prepared for arrest now that his bond money had arrived from out of state. Gacy went on to say that because his life had been threatened, the officers were now being followed. He looked at Albrecht. "Hey, you're not bugged, are you, Mike?" he asked. He went up to the officer and began frisking him.

Greg Bedoe was pressuring me to draw up another search warrant. What he'd heard from Gray and Walsh about wallets and IDs in Gacy's garage had convinced him that we had to have another look. He was sure we'd find things that would be plenty helpful in the investigation. I wanted to wait. Bedoe's argument was the standard one: "We have to get inside. You're the lawyer. You figure out how to do it." Now that we had Gacy pretty well hemmed in, I countered: "Let's not rush in like fools; let's do some more work."

I talked with Tovar, and was annoyed to hear that he had not made any progress checking the names in Gacy's address book. This morning, however, he had something else on his mind. His interest had been piqued by the similarity between Szyc's missing TV and the one in Gacy's bedroom. He had compared notes with Kautz, who had inventoried the items in Gacy's house during the search. The two men agreed that the sets could be the same. The papers Mrs. Szyc had given us didn't show a picture of her son's set, only the model number. Tovar planned to get an illustrated manufacturer's brochure, then check with the evidence technicians to see if Gacy's set appeared in any of the pictures taken on the search inside his house.

He called the sheriff's ET laboratory in Maybrook and asked if they could print a copy of the picture of Gacy's bedroom; they said they'd have it ready by the time he came to pick it up. He then called the offices of Motorola in suburban Schaumburg. The woman he talked with could not help him and said he would have to come out. When he got there, he was told that Motorola no longer had anything to do with TV sets; they had been bought out by Quasar, whose offices were in Franklin Park. Disgusted, Tovar returned to the station and called Quasar's customer service department. The man he spoke with was named George Dattilo. He gave him the model number; Dattilo said the set was manufactured in 1974 and that he would drop by the station with a descriptive pamphlet.

Robinson and Schultz came into the station several hours before they were to go on surveillance. They needed help. After several days and nights of high-speed chases, they were worried about their cars holding up—Robinson had already disabled one. Their driving philosophy was, get sideswiped, tail-ended, or anything, but keep the engine intact. Now, however, it was a question of just how much punishment the old vehicles of Delta Unit could take. Their cars were simply not competitive with Gacy's rented Volaré. The officers wanted something that, in Robinson's words, would "shit and git," cars that could take the punishment that Gacy dealt out. There were several autos in the department that met the specifications, but they were assigned to senior officers who were unwilling to risk their four-wheeled perks in a contest with Gacy. Lang had sought to borrow cars from both the county sheriff and the state, without success. Schultz and Robinson now turned to Kozenczak with their problem. To their delight, he told them to get on the phone and find whatever they needed.

The two officers were quickly dismayed by the response of car dealers and leasing firms. First, the high-performance cars they wanted were not available on a rental basis, and short-term leasing was out of the question. When the dealers learned that the cars would be used for high-speed surveillance work in and out of shabby sections of Chicago on a murder investigation, they politely said they were not interested. It was too bad, but Schultz and Robinson were stuck with the Batmobile and a few other junkers decorated with beer-can props. As they left with Lang to begin their shift, they asked Kozenczak if he could keep on looking for them.

Tovar came into the Detective Bureau with the color photo from Gacy's bedroom and the Quasar brochure. Bedoe and I and a group of detectives gathered around to look at the pictures. In each one, there was a beige twelve-inch Motorola television set. They were identical. The cover of the manufacturer's brochure, showing the set and a simulated television picture, was especially ironic. On the screen of the television was the face of a clown.

Schultz had just set a bag of four large cream-and-sugar coffees on the car seat when his portable radio crackled. "We're already moving," Robinson said. "We're heading for the Tollway." It was just after noon and Gacy was hurriedly departing from the drugstore in Waukegan. Schultz raced up a diagonal street through a residential area, hoping to intercept him. When he reached Grand Avenue, he looked left and right. No sign of Gacy or Robinson.

He turned west, then radioed his location.

"You're ahead of us," Robinson told him. Schultz braked, then spun into a U-turn. Luckily, traffic was light. As he accelerated, he felt first warmth, then a stinging sensation on his right thigh. The coffee had spilled. As he was groping for the bag, two cars whizzed by in the opposite direction.

"You just passed us," Robinson said on the radio. Schultz braked and made another U-turn. Now the coffee was sloshing all over the seat and seeping into the brittle cracks in the old vinyl. Cursing loudly, Schultz tried to squirm out of the hot puddle in which his crotch was immersed. It was no use.

"He's doing better than a buck," said Schultz. "Where the hell are we going in such a big hurry?"

"Believe it or not," Robinson radioed back, "Gacy told me we were going to be at his attorney's office by 1 o'clock." Neither had any doubt they would easily make the thirty-five-mile trip in a half hour.

Schultz was keeping his eyes fixed on the speeding Volaré

and the string of green traffic lights ahead of him on U.S. 41, but a movement in the rear-view mirror distracted him. He looked and saw that Robinson's car was engulfed in a swirling wreath of bluish gray smoke. His transmission diaphragm apparently had broken, and the engine was drawing in the fluid and burning it.

"What did you do to your car?" Schultz exclaimed.

"The hell with it," Robinson radioed. "I'm just going to keep going until it dies." The cars were now closing very quickly on a red light.

"Dump it here by the stoplight," Schultz said.

"Make room, I'm coming in," Robinson replied, pulling out on the snowy shoulder. He grabbed his radio and raced over to Schultz's car. Although the light by now had turned green, Gacy calmly got out of his car and walked back to see what was happening.

"What are you guys doing?" he asked.

"You son of a bitch," Robinson yelled. "They're going to give me five days off without pay for burning that car." Schultz, his trousers by now sodden with cream-and-sugar coffee, rolled down his window and snapped at Gacy like a Doberman. They both cursed Gacy's recklessness and hurled threats of arrest at him while the contractor stood on the highway like a chastened schoolboy as the backed-up traffic pulled around him. But when it was evident they weren't going to arrest him, he became inattentive. He'd heard it all before.

"Hey, I was just doing fifty-five," Gacy said. The officers roared in disagreement. "Look," he said, "if you don't believe me, why don't one of you ride with me?"

"That's a great idea," Robinson said, getting out with his radio, slamming the door, and stalking over to Gacy's car. "Now try to get away from me, asshole."

Robinson settled his six-foot, five-inch frame diagonally on the seat of Gacy's car to keep an eye on him. Up to now, the officers hadn't even frisked Gacy—they didn't know whether he was carrying a weapon or not. But Gacy was making no threats. He had lost his earlier belligerence and now was trying to make amends for discommoding his buddies the coppers. If only his private investigator could find the missing boy, he lamented, they could all cut out this fooling around.

A voice on Robinson's radio interrupted him. "Ron," Schultz said, "glance over at his speedometer and see what it says. If it's still reading fifty-five, then we've got to get that car in for work. Mine says eighty-five."

Robinson looked and radioed back: "You're right."

Gacy held his pace through Chicago's Northwest Side. He did most of the talking, rambling on while Robinson played the good listener. It was just like some of their previous conversations in bars and restaurants, except now there were just the two of them, and Gacy's hand was on Robinson's knee.

After the high-speed chase on the Kennedy Expressway and the arrest of Don Morrill on Friday night, it was clear to the Des Plaines officers that Gacy's friend Ron Rohde was no one to tangle with. Rohde, a short man with a full red beard and a weathered complexion, was a powerfully built cement finisher in his mid-forties. He was obviously a man of his own principles who didn't like being bothered by anyone and didn't bother anyone in return. It was rumored that he had chased with a hammer a Chicago inspector looking for a payoff, then doused the man with concrete. The officers were convinced he feared nothing. When Rohde came into the station on Tuesday for an interview, he was handled very gingerly.

Rohde had been loyal to Gacy up to now, but there were things about their relationship that angered him—and he was obviously fed up with the police surveillance. He disliked Gacy's calling him his "best friend," and he became livid when we said that Gacy had told Gray and Walsh that Rohde worked for him.

"I'd never work for that motherfucker," Rohde yelled in his rasping voice. "He's lucky I even give him jobs!" Rohde was an independent contractor who occasionally did cement jobs for Gacy, and that was it.

His rampaging in the Detective Bureau entertained us all for a while, but enough was enough. "Sir!" I said sharply. "This is a police station."

Rohde immediately became very meek; he even apologized. He was very polite and cordial after that, and Bedoe and Lang took him into an interview room.

Rohde confirmed everything Walsh had told us about Gacy's

activities the previous Tuesday night. Gacy was to have had some checks signed, then meet Walsh at the tree lot. He never showed up. Gacy, meanwhile, had proclaimed to Rohde his innocence of the boy's disappearance.

Bedoe asked him about his property in Wisconsin. Rohde said it was a seven-hour drive, one way, from Chicago. So that wasn't the gravesite—Gacy couldn't have driven there and back on Tuesday night.

When had Rohde last seen Gacy before the night of December 12? Gacy, Rohde said, had been at a party he and his wife had given in early December. John had gotten drunk and somebody had taken him home. Gacy was a bad drinker, Rohde said. After three or so, he'd get kind of "happy."

Had he ever seen Gacy fight? Bedoe asked him. *"Fight!"* Rohde cackled with amusement. "Haw! He's a pussy!" Rohde said that once when Gacy owed him money, Rohde called him and asked when he was going to repay the debt. Gacy gave him a lame excuse. Rohde told Gacy to pay up, or else. "Who do you think you're talking to?" Gacy told him, then hung up. Rohde stormed over to Gacy's house and pounded on the door. Walsh, whom Rohde thoroughly disliked, let him in.

"Give me my goddamned money," Rohde yelled at Gacy.

"Get the hell out of here," Gacy yelled back, "or I'm going to call the police."

"Well, as long as you're on the phone," Rohde said, "you might as well call an ambulance." And Rohde punched Gacy in the mouth. Then, for good measure, he turned and punched Walsh.

Rohde was apparently convinced that Gacy had had nothing to do with Rob Piest's disappearance, and though they didn't take his word for it, both officers accepted his good faith. When Bedoe asked Rohde if he was gay, he thought the witness was going to come over the table at him.

"Look," Bedoe said, "Gacy may be a friend of yours, but we wouldn't have two guys following him and bring you and others in here if we didn't think it was worth our time."

At the end of the interview, Rohde conceded that the police must know what they were doing. It was clear that he, too, wouldn't mind knowing just exactly what the hell was going on.

* * *

On the drive back from Waukegan, Schultz kept radioing the station to report the demise of Robinson's car. Each time he transmitted, he got the same reply: "Unit calling the station, you are unreadable." Schultz shouted ever louder into the radio. The only result was increasingly frayed tempers at both ends.

His first message had been picked up by Lang as he ferried Albrecht and Hachmeister back to the station, but the Delta Unit commander decided that something might be gained by having Robinson ride with Gacy, and so he continued on his way. His two passengers were furious that they were not going back to the action but decided it was best not to challenge Lang's decision.

Gacy led Schultz to LeRoy Stevens's office. After Gacy had gone inside, Schultz took the opportunity to call the station from a pay phone in a bank across the street. When he came out he was dismayed to see that Gacy's car was gone—and no sign of Robinson.

When Gacy decided to make a quick departure, Robinson had frantically tried to radio Schultz, but his batteries were too weak to send a good signal. Now Schultz looked at the spot where Gacy had parked and for once was grateful for his driving style. The contractor had left deep tracks of slush when he had pulled out and made a left turn onto busy Milwaukee Avenue. Turning northwest, Schultz drove about a block before he saw Gacy's car parked on the street in front of the Gale Street Inn.

He went inside and found Robinson, Gacy, Stevens, and the lawyer's secretary ordering drinks and lunch. "Want something to eat?" Stevens asked him.

"No!" Schultz said angrily. "I'll just have coffee." Only now, in the heat of the restaurant, did he have any hope of drying out his coffee-soaked jeans. He was hungry and would have ordered food, but he had only a few dollars in his pocket and was worried about the bill.

"What's the matter, buddy?" Robinson asked. "Don't you want any lunch?"

"I'm just too pissed off at these people to want to eat," Schultz said. He left the table and made another call to the station. He asked Kozenczak if he had lined up some better cars for them. The lieutenant said he hadn't had a chance. Schultz sulked for the remainder of the meal. His temper didn't improve when Stevens picked up the tab.

Back to Stevens's office. At 4 o'clock, after Gacy had spent an hour and a half there, lawyer and client emerged and announced that they were going downtown on the subway. Gacy and Schultz parked their cars in the lot at the nearby Jefferson Park Terminal. As the train clattered along the median strip of the Kennedy Expressway, Schultz nodded toward the rush-hour traffic on the roadway and commented how much easier it was keeping tabs on Gacy this way; Stevens chided Schultz about his earlier anger over Gacy's driving.

Gacy got off the train at the Daley Center complex of city, county, and state offices; Stevens stayed on, saying he had some Christmas shopping to do and would join them later.

In the lobby of the center, a man nodded a hello at the two officers and greeted Gacy warmly, wishing him a Merry Christmas. He was Illinois State Attorney General William Scott.

Gacy took an elevator up to the offices of the Building Department, where, he said, he had to get some papers that Stevens needed to incorporate some of his property. The offices were closed. Robinson rapped on the glass door until someone responded. Flashing his badge, he said: "Urgent police business," and Gacy got his papers.

The three men then wandered outside to the block-square plaza. Chicago's tall Christmas tree was now fully lighted, and between it and the brooding Picasso sculpture lay a crystalline field of ice sculptures depicting a sailing vessel, Santa Claus and reindeer, and Nativity scenes. Gacy explained to the officers how the sculptures were made: blocks of ice were fused together with water in a freezer, then chisels and shavers were used to shape the design. When he worked as a chef, he said, he had known many of the sculptors, who also did catering business.

It was cold, and they decided to get a cup of coffee while they waited for Stevens. They crossed the plaza, which was thronged with office workers hurrying to buses and trains or heading for State Street, a block away, for last-minute

Christmas shopping. At Randolph and Dearborn, the tinkle of Salvation Army bells pierced the din of traffic, and above the crowded sidewalks the marquees of once stately movie theaters blazed with their current fare: *Black Jack*, *Black Belt Jones*, *Big Bad Mama*, and *Toolbox Murders*.

Gacy and the officers decided to order sandwiches as well. As they moved through the line to the cash register, Gacy turned to Schultz, who was last, and said, "Your turn." Schultz had just enough to pay the bill. As they ate, Gacy told how he had remodeled this restaurant and had paid off building inspectors to overlook code violations.

As they walked back across the plaza, Gacy remarked, "Did you hear about the big mistake they made? They poured the concrete in the wrong spot. They had to redo the foundation." Robinson and Schultz looked at each other, puzzled. They didn't know what he was talking about.

Stevens was standing, shivering, outside the Daley Center. "Where have you guys been?" he asked as the three men approached. Schultz and Robinson noticed that despite Stevens's professed need to do Christmas shopping, he was carrying no packages.

They boarded a crowded subway. As well as the dank odor of the tunnel, the smell of burning brake shoes was in the air. The train waited at the next stop for several minutes, then the conductor announced that because of mechanical problems the train would make a nonstop run to Jefferson Park. Many of the passengers got off. The officers took a seat facing Gacy and Stevens across the aisle.

When the train got moving, Stevens said loudly that Gacy should consider taking a vacation. His client pulled out a big wad of bills, mostly in $100 denominations, and began counting them. They discussed destinations: Little Rock, where Gacy could visit his mother; Palm Springs; Belgium. The officers quickly joined in the spirit of the conversation.

"Are you really planning on leaving, John?" Schultz asked. "If you do, remember I told you to buy three tickets."

"It's no problem if you don't want to pay, John," Robinson added. "I've got my credit card, and we can go anywhere you can go." Gacy chuckled, then he and Stevens held up a newspaper and conversed behind it for the rest of the trip.

Back at Stevens's office, the lawyer asked the officers if they would help carry out several cases of liquor he was giving as Christmas presents. Not all of them fit in the trunk of the attorney's car, so he told them to put the rest in Gacy's trunk. Stevens drove away, and Gacy and the officers stopped for a beer at Coach's Corner. Then the contractor said he was going home.

Now the driving conditions were barely tolerable. The temperature was dropping, and an east wind off the lake was bringing fog and a sleety drizzle. The streets had turned to a glaze. Even Gacy reduced his speed, a rare concession.

Robinson was riding with Schultz now, and on the way to Summerdale they speculated about Gacy's travel plans. They concluded that Stevens's "Christmas shopping" had actually been a trip to a travel agency to buy Gacy's tickets. As to destination, Gacy himself had seemed to favor Little Rock.

Robinson began complaining about the mess in the car. Schultz just listened and grinned. Robinson had sat there in the restaurant like King Farouk, stuffing himself courtesy of LeRoy Stevens. Now, for all Schultz cared, Robinson could soak his tail feathers in the coffee for a while.

"You *know* it's the same goddamned TV," Bedoe said, pounding on my desk. Here we go again, I thought. The macho cop wants to kick down the door and go in and read the serial number. I was ready to admit that Szyc's set and Gacy's seemed identical, and that was a remarkable coincidence. But I still did not have what I needed to get another search warrant signed by a judge: proof that a crime had been committed. We still had found no trace of Rob Piest, and our best lead was Kozenczak's anonymous tip. Cliff Johnson had taken his helicopter up to search for the landmarks the woman caller had described, and I was waiting for his report.

I thought it likely that Szyc had been in Gacy's house, but we had no proof. Even proving that Gacy had Szyc's TV set wouldn't establish that, although it would sure help in getting a warrant, and I agreed it was important to have that serial number.

Our surveillance officers seemed to be the best candidates for the job now that Gacy was inviting them into his house.

Schultz and Robinson were told to try to cop the number if they had a chance, but I warned them not to get caught. They now had Gacy's confidence, which was useful in itself; I didn't want them to do anything that would alienate him and sabotage the investigation.

We also had to know more about Gregory Godzik, who, like Szyc, had apparently been seen after his reported disappearance. We had to keep trying to find relatives of Butkovich and Hattulo. And we had to talk to Kim Byers again now that we knew it was her photo receipt in Gacy's trash. We were moving toward a second search warrant, but from a legal standpoint we had a long way to go.

Tovar and Kautz spent much of the afternoon pursuing the Hattulo investigation and calling the people listed in Gacy's address book. Some of the names were marked with an "H"; the officers guessed this might stand for "homosexual." Those of Gacy's friends and acquaintances who were reached were reluctant to talk. The officers sensed that most of them were gay.

Tovar found out from the Texas Department of Public Safety that a Charles Antonio Hattula, born in the early 1950s, had once been issued a driver's license that listed a Houston address. Checking with the telephone company, Tovar was told that the residence had an unlisted number. He then talked to the Harris County sheriff's police in Houston, and they agreed to send an officer to the house to inquire about Hattula.

Now, presumably with the correct spelling, Tovar checked the microfiche listings and found that Hattula did have an Illinois license, with a Chicago address. It had expired in April, 1978, and he had never applied for a renewal. Checking the name with Chicago police, Tovar found that Hattula had been arrested for possession of marijuana there, as well as in Freeport, Illinois. The detective was now sure he had the right spelling: Hattula's identification record showed his employer as PDM. Tovar set out for 11th and State Street to pick up the records and Hattula's photo.

About half an hour later, Kautz received a call from the sheriff's police in Houston. They had spoken with Hattula's aunt, who said that her nephew had drowned on Mother's Day, 1977, in Freeport. Calling authorities there, Kautz was told that Hattula had fallen off a bridge over the Pecatonica River. His death had been ruled accidental.

As the officers stood in the drizzle, waiting for Gacy to unlock his kitchen door, they heard his dog barking in the back yard. They looked around and saw it tied to a stake.

"John, who left that dog out in this weather?" Schultz asked indignantly.

"I had to tie him out this morning," Gacy replied. "There was nobody here today to let him out."

Schultz scolded Gacy for his cruelty, but Gacy paid no attention. Once inside, he walked quickly over to the door to the front of the house and closed it. The officers smelled the same odor they had noticed the previous night, when they had watched Gacy clean up the dog mess. But tonight there was no mess in the kitchen—the dog had been out all day. And the odor was just as strong as before.

Schultz and Robinson had discussed how they would get the serial number of Gacy's television set: Schultz would reconnoiter while Robinson distracted Gacy. The contractor made it easier for them by ushering them into the recreation room. Robinson went to the bar and asked Gacy to make him a drink. If this didn't distract Gacy long enough, he planned to ask him to demonstrate a card trick. There was a knock at the door. It was Wally Lang, who had brought another car over for Robinson. Lang came in, and Schultz excused himself to use the toilet.

He walked back through the kitchen. So far so good: Gacy, who seemed to prefer keeping visitors in the newer part of his house, had not insisted that Schultz use the washroom next to the bar. Schultz took a deep breath as he edged into the hallway. He glanced into the darkened plant room with all Gacy's clown paintings, then walked to the bathroom midway down the hall. He switched on the light and exhaust fan, then flushed the toilet to cover up any sounds he made. From his earlier tour of the house, he knew that the bar, where Gacy was standing, was on the other side of the wall.

Quickly he walked into Gacy's bedroom, past the bed, over to the dresser on the far wall. The television set was right where the ETs' picture had shown it. He flicked on his cigarette lighter and peered around the rear of the set, but he couldn't find the serial number. With growing anxiety, he moved the set out a little farther and swept his lighter back and forth. He finally found a number but had difficulty reading it in the flickering light. He read it to himself several times to commit it to memory, then hastily retreated to the bathroom.

Schultz flushed the toilet again. As he was running some water in the washbasin, he felt a shaft of warm air coming up from the register by the toilet bowl. The furnace had just turned on, and a vile odor was wafting into the bathroom. From his own home-repair experience, Schultz knew that there probably was a leak in the ductwork and the blower was drawing in air from the space below.

I was checking on the progress of the helicopter and dog team searches when Bedoe came to me with renewed enthusiasm.

"We've got Ed Hefner in there," he said, "and he told us he dug under some concrete for Gacy in the last couple weeks. It's at a house, and he thinks it's somewhere in Norridge."

This sounded interesting: a fresh hole in the ground near some existing concrete footings could be just the sort of place Gacy might use to dispose of a body. Bedoe wanted to take Hefner out to find the house right away. Let's do it, I said. But first I wanted to know what else had come out of the interview.

Bedoe said they'd learned that Hefner had worked for Gacy for about a year and he'd met him when Gacy brought his wife to the Good Luck Lounge, where he tended bar. Gacy had told Hefner he planned to open a bar and wanted Hefner to run it. For various reasons, the deal had fallen through, though Hefner was not unhappy about it. Gacy had propositioned him sexually, but nothing ever happened after Hefner threatened to beat the contractor if he ever laid a hand on him. Hefner went on to say that in the last couple of days, he had overheard Gacy tell Walsh at a job site, "Don't talk to anybody about what we're talking about."

Just then, a commotion erupted in the Detective Bureau. Someone called, "Gacy's slipped the tail." The monitor in Kozenczak's office was alive with excited chatter as Schultz and Robinson reported that Gacy had eluded them, and they thought he might be heading for O'Hare. They said that he might be going to Little Rock, or even leaving the country for Belgium. I told the detectives to start checking the airlines for likely flights.

"What jurisdiction do we have at O'Hare?" Kozenczak asked.

I tried to decide quickly what to say. "They're law officers," I bluffed. "Stop the goddamned plane!"

After Lang had departed and Schultz returned to the recreation room, the officers at the house heard Gacy tell someone on the telephone: "I'll call you back in five minutes." Gacy then grabbed his coat and dashed out the door to his car without a word. Schultz and Robinson followed him south on Cumberland. Just before a busy intersection, Gacy made a quick turn into an alley behind a drugstore. Schultz and Robinson were close behind him. Gacy then slipped between the building and a dumpster that apparently had slid on the ice into the center of the alley. Schultz braked and aimed his sliding car for the same opening. His bumper and quarter-panels ground against the dumpster and the brick wall, but he made it through. Robinson, seeing that the big old Ford that Lang had delivered to him would not fit, stopped and went around the other way to the front of the drugstore. The two officers met. Gacy was gone.

Quickly they searched the parking lot, then one at a supermarket across the street. There was no sign of him anywhere. They rushed over to Rohde's tree lot, then back to Gacy's house, then to the Shell station Gacy patronized. He had to be running for a plane, they decided. Robinson parked his car and got into Schultz's for the race out the expressway to the airport. On the way, the station radioed: there was a Delta flight leaving for Little Rock in just a few minutes from Gate H-8-B.

The officers ran into the terminal, now surging with holiday travelers. At the security checkpoint they hurriedly explained their mission. The guards stared at them suspiciously, especially at Schultz in his coffee-stained jeans. One of the guards said he would have to check with his superior before he could let the two officers through.

Robinson looked at Schultz. "The hell with this bullshit," he said, and the two of them took off running down the concourse, dodging arriving passengers, with several shouting security guards in their wake.

At the gate, Schultz mollified the guards while Robinson checked with the airline agent. There was no Gacy on the flight, nor had anyone in a black leather jacket boarded the plane. The agent suggested they try the main counter in the terminal. There the clerks checked the reservation computers of Delta and the other airlines at O'Hare. No John Gacy was listed on any flight they could find.

Discouraged, Schultz and Robinson got back into their car just as Lang's voice was coming over the radio: "The car's at the tree lot. Come over here right away." Lang's tone spoke volumes, and the message was: "How the hell did you guys manage to screw up?"

Lang had not opposed the surveillance team's decision to go to O'Hare, but he was sure Gacy was elsewhere. A short time after Schultz and Robinson had cased the tree lot, Lang and Sommerschield drove by it, and, lo, there was Gacy's car parked conspicuously under a street lamp. Gacy, obviously pleased with himself, was visiting with Rohde. "I wasn't trying to lose them," he told Lang. "Honest. I parked and waited for them by the drugstore."

When Schultz and Robinson arrived, Lang was fairly caustic. "Do you think you can keep him this time," he said, "or do you want me to stay here?" Schultz mumbled that they could handle it themselves. Lang and Sommerschield followed Gacy to his house, while the two surveillance officers went to get the other car.

Not until evening were we able to question Kim Byers, who had been in a swimming meet at Maine North High School. Yes, the photo receipt was hers, and she remembered filling it in on the evening of December 11 at Nisson's. She explained that she had put on Rob's parka because she was cold. And with a little embarrassment she told us that she had put the receipt in the pocket of the jacket because she hoped that Rob would notice it and ask her about it.

This was the missing piece in the puzzle, and a second

search warrant was practically assured. We now had absolute confirmation that Rob Piest had been in John Gacy's house.

After the day's activities, Schultz and Robinson were glad enough to see their midnight relief. Gacy had just led them to Mr. K's Restaurant near his house when Lang arrived with Albrecht and Hachmeister. The new crew just slid into the booth with Gacy, who once again was eager to talk.

He now put a price tag on the suit that was naming Albrecht and all the others: $750,000. Des Plaines had violated his civil rights, and his attorneys were going to "indict," as he put it, all its detectives. Gacy mellowed, however, and began talking about his work as a clown. All of it, he said, was volunteer. He used the name Pogo. He had dressed up as Uncle Sam at one of his big summertime parties. Talking about parties, he said that he had been to some bisexual affairs and saw nothing wrong with what went on. He said he thought people should do whatever they wanted, as long as it didn't infringe on other people's rights and no force was used. Gacy said he had encountered many homosexual pharmacists in his work, but he always made sure they didn't bother his employees.

Gacy said he always maintained a formal employer-employee relationship with the people who worked for him, and as a result, no one really knew him. He was strict and would not allow his workers to smoke any grass on the job. He said he had told all of them to cooperate in the investigation and even had paid them for the time they were being interviewed. He threw in that Walsh and Gray were "real ladies' men."

After giving a detailed accounting of "all but a couple of minutes" of his time on the Monday night that Rob Piest disappeared, Gacy told the officers about his life as a prominent businessman in Waterloo, Iowa, back in the 1960s. He said he owned three Kentucky Fried Chicken outlets, as well as another restaurant, a motel, and a clothing design firm. He said he ran a prostitution ring at the motel, both gay and straight, showed pornographic movies, and, at private parties, had naked girl dancers who would engage in sex. At the time, Gacy said, he was running for alderman on the Democratic ticket. But he was set up by the Republicans and double-crossed by the sheriff and finally arrested for "inducing acts of prostitution." The town came down on him hard. He was convicted of a felony and served time. At that point, his first wife divorced him, taking him for $160,000, three cars, and his house. Gacy said he managed to get out with $40,000, but he had to pay all the legal fees.

After coming back to Chicago, Gacy said, he had been arrested late at night for assault and deviate sexual charges because he had picked up a hitchhiker who wanted to give him a blow job. Gacy said he stopped the car and threw the guy out on the expressway. The charge, he said, was eventually dropped because the man was a fence and no one believed his version of what happened.

With all the strain he was under now, Gacy said, he was contemplating a plane trip.

"Make sure it's after midnight, so we can go with you," Albrecht said.

"How about Hawaii?" Hachmeister asked.

Gacy went home at about 1 o'clock. Hachmeister parked on a side street, while Albrecht stayed on Summerdale in front of a neighbor's house. The freezing rain pelted their cars, obscuring vision through the windows. About an hour went by. Then Albrecht saw car lights in his rear-view mirror. The car stopped, then a little later he heard a door slam. He looked in the mirror again, but the car was gone. He got out and peered down the street. It was empty. Albrecht got back into his car. All he heard was the rain.

About twenty minutes later, he saw two cars come around the corner behind him. They both turned out their headlights and pulled up about seventy-five feet behind him. A large man got out of each car. Albrecht saw the man nearest him hitching his belt. They began walking toward Albrecht's car, one in the street, one along the curb. Through his rain-splattered rear window Albrecht could see little but their silhouettes. He picked up his radio.

"I think we've got company, Dave," he said. Albrecht reached for the gun he kept stuck in his belt.

Hachmeister heard the alarm in his partner's voice. He started his car and came around the corner, his lights out. He accelerated down Summerdale, then pulled up with the front of his car angled toward Albrecht's to give himself cover when he got out. But now the men were alongside Albrecht's car, and their faces reflected the glow of a distant street light. It was Bedoe and Hein, who'd been out having a few beers.

Albrecht cursed the two sheriff's policemen as he put his gun back into his belt. The two got into Albrecht's car, and Hachmeister joined them. Bedoe told them about the fruitless search that he, Hein, Kozenczak, and Kautz had made with Hefner. They had spent hours traversing glazed streets looking for the house with the freshly dug hole next to concrete footings. They didn't think Hefner was lying, but he couldn't remember where the house was. Discouraged, Hein and Bedoe had stopped at a bar, then decided to go out on their own to search. They set up checkpoints where they met every half hour. It had been another wild goose chase.

Bedoe told the surveillance officers to press Gacy whenever they could. He said they'd learned that Gacy hated to be called a "jagoff" and that he was upset about his father's death. The officers, he said, should make reference to these things when the situation was right, to unsettle Gacy until he reached the breaking point. Bedoe warned them, however, that Gacy could crack under pressure and that they didn't know what his reaction might be. He was not acting like a textbook homicide suspect and could be very dangerous. "Watch yourselves," Bedoe said.

At about 3:30, Hein began nodding off, so he roused himself and left on the long drive south to his home. Bedoe continued to fill the surveillance officers in on the progress of the internal investigation. Albrecht and Hachmeister were grateful. There was never enough time to share information with the others involved in the case. Soon the conversation tapered off, then ceased entirely. There were only the sounds of the icy rain pattering on the car and the snores of Greg Bedoe coming from the back seat.

Wednesday
December 20, 1978

This was the tenth day of the Piest investigation, and the signs of wear on all of us were most visible. We were by now uncommonly grateful if we could get two or three hours' sleep before rising in the winter darkness to start a new day. The few meals we managed to eat would have offended any nutritionist. Mostly, we did without them. As Greg Bedoe said, you'd look at your watch at 8:30 at night and remember that you hadn't had dinner *or* lunch. He himself lost fourteen pounds during the investigation.

The surveillance officers were lucky to have eight hours off duty. When they arrived home, they were ready for a couple of beers and, besides, their wives were eager to hear about their adventures. When they finally went to bed, they slept fitfully because they were so keyed up. The stress of high-speed driving in adverse weather, plus the specter of the unknown danger they faced, made relaxation only a fond memory.

Everybody had gripes. Delta Unit by now had exhausted its supply of serviceable cars. Robinson and Albrecht complained about the big Ford they were given to drive, but that was about the last train out, and there was little hope of getting any help from the car dealers. Communications by portable radio were becoming a great problem. The officers had asked Lang to borrow some of the sheriff's radios, but he had not followed through. Transmissions from these units are boosted by repeaters located all over Cook County, expanding the range of their reception. The officers were also miffed at Lang for not supplying them with fresh batteries, which they felt they didn't have time to purchase in the heat of the surveillance. The radio operators in the station were tired of being screamed at by surveillance officers trying to make themselves readable over the airways.

Perhaps the main complaint among the surveillance officers was the lack of information about their colleagues' activities. Rarely did they have a chance to talk to the officers they were relieving, and they felt that Lang told them very little about the internal investigation. One day, Albrecht and Hachmeister wandered into the Detective Bureau after their surveillance shift to see what they could learn, and they were confronted by Lang. "Go home and get some rest," the sergeant told them, "or I'll pull you off the case." They knew that he was acting in their own interests, but they were angered at being cut off. Finally, they solved their problem by visiting with Kozenczak when Lang was not around. The lieutenant, they found, was very willing to share information with them and curious to know about their activities. Oddly enough, Kozenczak was not getting the same good marks from some of his own detectives: his men felt similarly starved for information, and some of them felt their time was being wasted on a fruitless search for the anonymous caller's landmarks.

After some of the surveillance officers complained to Kozenczak, the lieutenant called Lang in and told him that he was spending too much time in the station away from his troops in the field. Moreover, the presence of two supervisors in the office led to some confusion. Lang frequently was asked questions that were properly Kozenczak's to answer. In responding, he might unwittingly be short-circuiting the orderly flow of communications and leaving Kozenczak out of the loop.

I think Kozenczak and Lang were each trying to find his own niche in the overall operation. Kozenczak carved out the anonymous tip as his territory and concentrated on that. Lang took a while longer to find his handle. After the first few days he rightly concluded that his presence with the surveillance team was not necessary; three cars following Gacy just led to massive traffic jams. At that point, after consulting with a psychiatrist, he decided to work on Gacy psychologically. Now whenever Gacy approached him at the twice-daily shift changes, Lang deliberately would not respond to Gacy's mood. If the contractor cheerfully initiated a conversation, Lang would be curt and unsympathetic. Then, maybe a shift or two later, he would apologize: "John, I'm sorry I said that. I was really tired." Once, when Gacy said that he was not into violence, Lang peeled back his shirt, revealing a bulletproof vest. "John," the sergeant said, "I don't really believe you're nonviolent."

The investigation was severely taxing the resources of the whole department. The Youth Bureau, Delta Unit, and the Detective Bureau had been given over wholesale to the Gacy case and had all but ceased activity on their other work. With detectives working sixteen- to twenty-hour days, overtime was mounting up and threatened to put a great strain on the department's year-end budget. But perhaps our biggest worry of all came to pass on this morning when I returned a call to Gacy's attorney Sam Amirante. "We've filed the suit," he told me. "It's due for hearing on Friday morning."

"Get out! We're moving!" Albrecht turned around to the rear seat and shook Bedoe. Awakening in a surveillance car in the foggy gloom of Wednesday morning, Greg was completely disoriented. "What's going on?" he mumbled.

"Gacy's moving," Albrecht said. "You've got to get out."

Gacy was indeed on the move. Hachmeister had driven around to the front of the house and pulled into the contractor's driveway. When Gacy came out of the house about 8:15, he said nothing to the officers. He got into his car and drove up as if he intended to ram Hachmeister's. The officer obliged him by backing into the street but made the mistake of turning his car the same way Albrecht's was facing, east, Gacy's normal direction of departure. Today, Gacy went west.

Hachmeister struggled to get his car turned around on the street, now glazed with last night's freezing rain. Gacy zipped down Summerdale, through the single track of icy ruts in the next block. By the time Hachmeister reached them, two eastbound cars were coming through, forcing him to wait. Albrecht, meanwhile, was trying to eject Bedoe from his car and get it turned around. A moment later, he was on his way, leaving a bleary-eyed and bewildered investigator standing in the middle of the street.

Gacy turned north and began racing up Cumberland. In a few blocks, he came up to two lanes of cars stopped at a red light. Gacy pulled out to the left around the traffic, into the southbound lanes, and weaved through the intersection. When Hachmeister got to the Kennedy Expressway, he stopped on the overpass and looked east and west. No sign of Gacy. He drove to the Shell station, a few blocks away. No one there had seen Gacy.

Albrecht, meanwhile, got on the expressway going west, since Gacy had said a few days earlier that he might soon be going to Raphael's place in Glenview. The officer put his portable red light on the dashboard and radioed his destination to Hachmeister.

Although Albrecht had Raphael's address, he did not know Glenview very well. Once he found the right street, he peered at mailboxes, looking for numbers. Finally, he saw a big house surrounded by trees. Gacy's car was parked in the driveway.

Albrecht pulled in. Gacy came out of the house, took a picture of Albrecht and his car, and went back inside. Then Raphael came out and walked over to the policeman's car. He was quite curious about the investigation. Albrecht said he couldn't comment on police activities but asked if Raphael minded if he parked in the driveway.

"I don't mind at all," Raphael said, "but John doesn't like it."

Gacy came out of the house again. On the walk to the driveway, he slipped on the ice and landed on his back. Raphael rushed over to him. "Better come here and look at him," Raphael said. "He's hurt." Albrecht walked over. Gacy's eyelids were twitching, as if he were struggling to keep them closed.

"Come on, John, get up," Albrecht said. "You're all right." With Raphael's assistance, Gacy grudgingly got up, his hand on his lower back, and walked slowly back to the house. Hachmeister had finally caught up and pulled in just in time to witness the fall. He was momentarily delighted: if Gacy had had a heart attack, that would mean the end of the surveillance.

Gacy and Raphael came out of the house, and the two drove to a restaurant. The officers sat at another table. After they all had breakfast, they drove to a hardware store, where the policemen watched the two men load about ten bags of salt into Gacy's trunk. Back at Raphael's, they unloaded the salt and started spreading it on the driveway.

"How's the back feel, John?" Albrecht asked. Gacy scowled.

Gacy left Raphael's. He was driving recklessly again, despite the dangerous road conditions. The officers had noticed that when Raphael was riding with him, Gacy drove cautiously. Now he was apparently venting his frustration and anger with a high-speed run into the suburb of Niles.

Gacy went into the lot at a Sportmart store he was remodeling. After remaining in front with Albrecht for a few minutes, Hachmeister decided he should cover the rear of the store. Just as he got to the alley, Albrecht radioed him that Gacy was leaving. Hachmeister accelerated, then slowed to turn at the corner of the building. To his horror, he saw the side of a diagonally parked semitrailer blocking his way. He hit his brakes but his tires couldn't grab the slick pavement. Seeing the bed of the trailer coming at his windshield, Hachmeister dove down onto the console. The hood of his car plowed into the undercarriage of the truck bed. Miraculously, the car stopped before the windshield hit the trailer. Hachmeister sat up and put the car in reverse. He couldn't move it; it was wedged under the truck. Hachmeister saw several men on the dock look at him curiously, then go back to work unloading the truck. The officer jumped out, flashed his badge, and got them to push him out. He finally caught up with Gacy and Albrecht at the Shell station.

On the way, Gacy had zoomed through school zones filled with children. Now he and Albrecht were having a heated exchange, which Hachmeister joined with relish.

"The only reason I drive fast," Gacy said angrily, "is because you guys do. It's your fault." Oblivious to the illogic of his remark, he stomped into the station. By the time he came out, his temper had cooled and he apologized. "I'm not mad at you guys personally," he said. "I know you're only doing your job, but I'm getting behind schedule." There was no doubt the surveillance was wearing him down.

After stopping at home, Gacy ran several errands, including a visit to the regular Democratic organization offices in Norridge. Shortly after 1 o'clock, he met Chris Gray and his girlfriend at the pants store where she worked. He took them around the corner to a restaurant. The officers sat at a separate table. Hachmeister ordered Gacy's party a round of drinks. After lunch, he went out to call Lang. When the bill was presented, Albrecht found himself stuck with five checks, food and all.

Gacy and Gray then drove to a secondhand shop on the Northwest Side of Chicago, where Lang made the relief rendezvous with Robinson and Schultz. As the officers were milling around their cars, Gacy came out of the shop and took more pictures of them. They assumed he was illustrating his lawsuit.

"Here, John. Let me see that," Robinson said, after Gacy pulled a print out of the camera. Gacy refused. "Come on, John, all I want to do is autograph it for you."

Gacy's face brightened. "Will you sign it for me?" he asked. Robinson nodded. Gacy still didn't seem to trust Robinson and held the print while the officer signed it: "To my good friend, John. Love, Ron."

Another of the pictures would bring Albrecht a lot of ribbing from his associates. By now it was evident that Gacy had taken a fancy to the officer, with his soft blond hair and Teutonic good looks. Gacy had photographed Albrecht as he was leaning over, talking to another officer in one of the cars. "Look at the picture that Gacy took," the other policemen would chortle, ". . . of Mike's ass!"

It had been no secret that Gacy's lawsuit was in the works, and now the timetable was established. We had less than two days to wrap up our case. Sam Amirante had brought me a copy of the complaint and, just as the surveillance officers had reported, they were seeking $750,000 in damages.

Amirante, whom I knew well from his work as a public defender, had tried hard to persuade us to drop the surveillance and avoid the suit. He had called me several times every day saying, "John's a good guy. I've worked with him in politics. He's been over to my house with my kids. These guys are just harassing him."

My response, of course, was to stall him. I tried to make it sound as if a lawsuit would be just a waste of his time, that we had just a few more things to tie up.

In his suit, Gacy named the City of Des Plaines and several police officers, including Chief Lee Alfano, Kozenczak, Vande Vusse, and Albrecht, as well as others whose identities Gacy didn't know. Gacy complained that the police had deprived him of his rights by holding him captive in the police station the previous Wednesday and not allowing him to talk to his attorney for five hours. He also complained about the search of his house, the seizure of his vehicles, and the presence of the surveillance units, which were harassing him, detaining his friends, and ruining his business dealings. As a result of all this, the complaint said, Gacy had suffered severe mental anguish, loss of use of his personal property, loss of reputation, expenditures of money, and deprivation of his liberty, his right to be free from unreasonable searches and seizures, and his right to privacy. The suit asked for a temporary restraining order, putting an end to the police harassment.

Gacy's attorneys could easily get a temporary restraining order without our even being in court. The theory behind the law is that nobody is going to be hurt by a little cooling-off period, at the end of which the court can review the merits of a permanent injunction. In this case, nobody would be hurt but us. If Gacy got a ten-day TRO, that would be the end of this investigation.

From the docket slip, I saw that the suit had been filed in Federal District Court late the previous afternoon. At least now I knew where LeRoy Stevens did his Christmas shopping.

Tovar's efforts to find Jeffrey Rignall, the young man who had filed a battery complaint against Gacy earlier in the year, finally paid off on this Wednesday afternoon. He told me he had the man's lawyer on the phone and asked if I would talk with him. The attorney told us that Rignall was in Florida and chided us for not finding and talking with him before. I said we'd like to interview his client, and the lawyer was agreeable as long as the state would pay to fly him up. He would not give me Rignall's phone number and said he would relay any messages.

I decided to let the matter rest for the moment. For one thing, I would have to get approval to spend the money to fly Rignall to Chicago, and nobody at the state's attorney's office downtown knew anything about the Gacy investigation. Besides, our most important goal now was getting another search warrant, and Rignall's story was not germane to those efforts. I was eager, however, to check out immediately one allegation in Rignall's complaint: that Gacy had used a rag soaked with a fluid that was possibly chloroform. Together with the brown bottle we had found during the search of his house, this gave us an interesting indication of his method of operation.

Another lead that had got pushed aside was Cathy Grawicz's remark that as a teenager Gacy had worked in a Las Vegas mortuary. We wondered if he was necrophiliac and if he might have been fired for that reason. Tovar called the police in Las Vegas, asking them to check with the city's mortuaries to see if any records of Gacy's employment were available. They said they had to have our request in writing before they could act on it. Tovar sent off teletype messages, but we heard nothing further from Las Vegas for the rest of the day.

Bedoe, Tovar, and Ryan began preparing subpoenas for Gacy's telephone and credit records. The telephone company keeps logs of metropolitan calls for about six months in case there are questions on billing. These logs, known as MUD sheets (for message unit detail), show all numbers, Chicago and suburban, dialed from a subscriber's phone. We thought that records of Gacy's calls and credit information might fill in some of the gaps in our investigation.

The interviewing continued. Robert L. Zimmerman, an employee at the Shell station, confirmed that he had been entertained at Gacy's house, once at a big summertime party and several times playing pool. Zimmerman told Tovar and Adams that Gacy wanted to make a bet with him and another employee before a pool game. If Gacy lost, he would give the winner either a blow job or the amount of money they agreed on. Zimmerman said he told Gacy that he didn't get turned on by that and left the gathering. He added that Gacy dealt in drugs.

I was hoping to hear from Schultz that he had successfully got the serial number from Gacy's television set and that it matched the one on Szyc's. When his report came through, it told us nothing we didn't already know: in his haste and nervousness, Schultz had memorized the model number.

On the way downtown, with Gray driving, Gacy stopped at a heating company just northwest of the Loop. The officers observed that Gray's way of driving was strongly influenced by that of his boss—or perhaps he was taking orders from Gacy.

When Gacy returned, he gave the officers a jar of peanuts. They continued on to City Hall. Gacy got out and went into the building. Gray and the two officers circled the block. Gray stopped to get a soft drink, and Schultz went with him. Robinson somehow got separated from them and circled the block four times before he caught sight of Gacy's car again. Gacy came out about twenty minutes later and got in the passenger side of his car. Before exiting the Loop, Gray made a fast right-hand turn from the left lane of a one-way street, and Robinson and Schultz followed. The three of them left the intersection in a turmoil.

Gacy next stopped at a drugstore on the Near North Side. Twenty minutes later, Gray came out and said that Gacy was in a partying mood and that because the two officers had been so decent, he wanted to rent a hooker for all of them that evening. He thought Gacy would foot the entire bill. Great idea, the officers exclaimed enthusiastically. They drove to a tavern to make the rendezvous.

On the way, Schultz and Robinson conferred by radio and agreed that this was surely a blackmail setup to give Gacy more picture-taking opportunities. "Don't worry," Robinson said. "Since John's paying the bill, John should go first. Nine days now that he hasn't been with a girl—for a real T and A man, that doesn't make sense."

They parked at a tavern and Gray went inside. A short time later, a frowzy redhead came down a gangway between some buildings. Gray returned and he and Gacy huddled on the sidewalk.

"She shouldn't be allowed on the street without a leash," Robinson told Schultz.

Gray came back to talk to the policemen. The lady wanted more money than John wanted to pay. The party was off.

Gacy dropped off Gray, then drove home. He did not invite the officers inside, so they got out the football game. Half an hour later, Gacy came storming out.

"Your boss has gone too far this time," he said angrily. "He's overstepped his boundaries. He's fucking up my business and everything. From now on, I'm not telling you where I'm going." He hurriedly got into his car and sped off. On the Kennedy, he accelerated to a hundred miles an hour. Schultz was preparing to force him off the highway when Gacy turned off at the Lawrence Avenue exit. He was going to Walsh's. A radio message from the station explained Gacy's rage: Dick Walsh was back in for questioning.

Tovar and Ryan were sent to pick Walsh up and interview him. They'd made this run before, and it was hoped Walsh would be more open with them. Whatever the outcome of the interview, Kozenczak was preparing to give him a polygraph test. On the way to the station, Walsh insisted that he knew nothing more and said that by now he was so annoyed that he was going to talk to a lawyer.

In the interview room, the detectives came down hard on Walsh. To try to shake something loose, they told him Gacy was saying things about him. They talked about the death penalty and how Walsh could turn state's evidence if he were involved. They asked him about Rob Piest. Walsh stood his ground for almost two hours. Towards the end of the interview the officers eased off. They didn't want to upset him too much before putting him on Kozenczak's lie box. At the lieutenant's suggestion, they took him out for dinner; he had prime rib.

When they returned to the station, Kozenczak took over the questioning and made a daring gamble. He laid all our cards on the table, telling Walsh all the things we had learned about Gacy that we had thought best to withhold: You are driving a car that belonged to a guy who is missing—and we believe he is dead. The same guy's class ring was found in Gacy's house, and we think his TV is in Gacy's bedroom. Kozenczak, moreover, told Walsh that he would ask him on the polygraph examination whether he had engaged in sexual relations with Gacy.

Walsh broke down crying. After he regained his composure, he said he knew nothing about John Szyc. He thought the car had been stolen; at least that's what Gacy had told him. Walsh consented to submit to the lie detector.

Kozenczak focused his test on Rob Piest's disappearance. He asked Walsh if he had caused or taken any part in it, and whether he had helped remove Piest's body from a vehicle or hide it. He asked if Walsh knew where Piest was now. Walsh answered no to all these questions.

When he talked to me afterwards, Kozenczak would not commit himself. He felt Walsh was being basically truthful, but the test results were hard to interpret. In his official report, Kozenczak said that because of "erratic and inconsistent responses" on Walsh's polygraph records, the lieutenant was "unable to render a definite opinion" as to the truthfulness of his answers.

When we heard from the surveillance officers about Gacy's angry trip to Walsh's house, Greg suggested to Lang that we tighten the screws. "Let's piss him off even more and bring Gray back in," he said.

Police commonly use a bluffing game when they interrogate a witness. They tell Jones that Smith has just spilled the beans and that the police now know the whole sordid story, and if Jones doesn't come forward and tell them what he knows, he'll be in a heap of trouble. Tonight we didn't have to bluff. Bedoe and Lang laid it all out for Gray, as Kozenczak had done with Walsh: the Szyc car, the ring, the television, Gacy's previous arrests.

"Here's the rap sheet, Gray," Greg said, leaning across the table. "See what it says there? It says sodomy. You know what sodomy is? Ten years in jail. What did Gacy tell you, that he showed stag films to a bunch of teenagers? That's a lot of bullshit."

I went in with the officers to make it more official. Okay, Chris, the party's over. We're not kidding. Even the state's attorney is here.

Gray related an experience he had had, during the two

months he stayed with Gacy. He and Gacy were up late drinking, celebrating Gray's birthday. Gacy wanted to show him the handcuff trick. Gacy put the cuffs on himself, turned around, and click; he had got them off. Now you try it, Chris. Gray didn't want to; he was drunk. Finally, he consented, and Gacy snapped the cuffs on him. So what's the trick? asked Gray, unable to free his hands.

"The trick, Chris," Gacy said with a leer, "is you gotta have the key." Gacy then grabbed the handcuffs by the chain and began swinging Gray around the room, growling. Gray finally broke loose and kicked Gacy in the head, knocking him down. He recovered the key and freed himself. By the time Gacy got up off the floor, he had calmed down and said nothing further about the handcuffs.

On another occasion, Gray said, he accidentally broke a statue that had been painted by Gacy's father. Gacy went into a rage and threatened to kill Gray. The youth locked himself in his bedroom until Gacy quieted down.

Gray said he finally moved out after Gacy almost depantsed him one night. Although the two had retired separately, Gacy kept calling in a high-pitched voice from his bedroom: "Chris, Chris. You know what I want." Then he came into Gray's bedroom. "Chris," he said, "you really don't know who I am. Maybe it would be good if you gave me what I want." Gacy jumped in bed with him, Gray said, "and damned near tore my pants off."

"Pants?" Greg asked. "You mean you slept with your pants on?"

"I had to," Gray said. Gacy frequently came into his bedroom in the middle of the night with an erection and tried to slip it to him. One night a fight ensued. Gray knocked Gacy to the floor, straddled him, and was about to strike him, when Gacy just gave up and feigned unconsciousness. Gacy finally got up and walked out of the room. "You're no fun," he said in a sort of giggle, then went back to bed. By that time, Gray had had enough of living with John Gacy.

The officers turned their questions to the search of Gacy's house a week ago. Gray related Gacy's fear of finding policemen hidden in his attic or crawl space. Gacy had asked him to go up and check the attic. Gray refused and said do it yourself. He told of Gacy's anger about the mud on his carpeting near the closet door and his trip into the crawl space.

"What the hell's in the crawl space?" Bedoe asked. "Were you ever down there?"

Yes, Gray said, he'd been down there, once spreading lime, and another time digging.

Digging? We all looked at him intently. Why were you digging?

Because Gacy said there was too much moisture down there, and he had to have pipes laid, Gray said. Gacy put up stakes to mark where they were to dig, then sent Gray and Walsh down.

"Show me where you were digging," Bedoe said, handing Gray a pad and pencil. Gray drew a diagram, locating the sump pump and the trenches he had dug.

At one point, Gacy had stuck his head down the trap door and started yelling at Gray. "Don't go over there," he shouted. "You go straight where I told you." Gray had started to take a shortcut and had veered from the line Gacy had indicated.

I looked at Gray's drawing. If Gacy had ground-water problems, the two or three trenches that Gray had dug made no sense because obviously they wouldn't drain into the sump. I asked Gray how wide he made the trenches for the tiles—six or eight inches?

"No," Gray said. "A foot and a half, two feet."

"How deep were they?"

"A foot and a half, two feet."

Did Gray ever lay any pipe? He hadn't. Did he know what Gacy did with the trenches? He didn't.

"What was there where you were digging, when you veered off?" Bedoe asked.

Just some dirt piled up, Gray said. It was a mound about six inches high, he guessed.

"How long?" Bedoe asked.

"About as long as this," Gray said, indicating the five- or six-foot desk we were sitting at. He pointed to his diagram and indicated where he had seen other similar mounds.

Greg looked at me, and his expression said it all: "Jesus, are they in the crawl space?" He would later say that the hair on the back of his neck stood up when Gray mentioned the desk top. I thought about Gacy's funeral home experience. Was he cutting up bodies and burying them beneath his house? The pieces were fitting together. Missing persons, kids digging, lime. If Gacy had a water problem, why were the trenches so large, why didn't they have any relationship to the sump pump, why was there no pipe? Gacy had something down there, and he was afraid to have it uncovered.

I knew Bedoe would be at my jugular for a search warrant the minute our interview was over. We had only one day left before the hearing on the harassment suit, and after that, we would have little chance of searching Gacy's house again. I planned to go out for a beer with Bedoe and Hein to sort it all out. Meanwhile, we had to be cool with Gray, just in case he went back to Gacy and reported the details of our interview, although there appeared to be little chance of that. We were convinced that he would cooperate fully from now on. Chris Gray had scared us just as surely as we had scared him. When he left that night, I don't think there was any doubt in his mind that we regarded John Gacy as a dangerous killer.

When Tovar and Ryan took Walsh home about 9 P.M., Gacy was still there waiting for him. By now Walsh was so fearful of the contractor that he asked the detectives to accompany him up to his apartment. They did. Gacy was very unhappy about the presence of the officers. He told Walsh that he was going to find a lawyer for him and that any further communications with the police must take place in the attorney's presence. When the tension subsided, Tovar and Ryan left.

About a half hour later, at 11:45, Gacy came out. Where to now? Schultz and Robinson asked.

"We're going for a *long* ride," Gacy snarled.

"How far?" Schultz asked. "I don't have much gas."

"Tough shit," Gacy said. He got into his car and roared off. The officers clocked him at a hundred miles an hour on the expressway. He turned off at Touhy Avenue and headed west toward Des Plaines.

Schultz spotted one of the few filling stations still open at that hour and radioed Robinson. He said he *had* to get gas and that he'd do his best to catch up. Screeching up to the pump, he got out and put $7 worth of fuel into his tank. Then he threw the gas hose and the money—all the cash he had—on the pavement and jumped back into his car. The attendant came out shouting, but Schultz was gone.

They ended up at Sam Amirante's offices in Park Ridge. LeRoy Stevens was just arriving and told the officers that Gacy would be there for only about fifteen minutes. Lang drove up with Albrecht and Hachmeister shortly after midnight.

On the way back to the station, the officers stopped for coffee, and Lang told Schultz and Robinson about the interview we'd had with Gray. He related Gray's story of digging trenches in Gacy's house and how Gacy had angrily warned the youth not to dig through one of several mounds of dirt in the crawl space. Lang said the police suspected that the mounds were graves.

At home, sitting in front of the Christmas tree his children had decorated, Schultz was sipping a beer and thinking about Gray's story. Suddenly he knew, without a doubt, what he had smelled last night in the waft of air from the register in Gacy's bathroom. He had smelled that odor many times before, in the Cook County morgue.

Thursday
December 21, 1978

Gacy's visit with his lawyers was turning out to be more than a fifteen-minute session. Amirante had his offices in the front of the building, and the policemen could see lights burning but no activity. At about 1 A.M., Albrecht decided to check some restaurants and bars in the area to see if Gacy and the lawyers had gone out for refreshments. Nothing much was open in Park Ridge, a dry community, so he drove into the adjoining Edison Park neighborhood of Chicago. After checking several places, he stopped at one, where he met an off-duty Des Plaines officer and one of the radio girls and had a beer with them. Hachmeister was irritated when Albrecht returned without a bottle for him.

At 2 o'clock, still no activity. Albrecht decided to go up and knock on one of the windows. Just as he was approaching the building, Amirante came to the door and invited the officers inside.

The lawyers were very solicitous. They offered coffee and a bottle of Canadian Club to the policemen and helped move out chairs into the hallway so they would be more comfortable. From there, the officers could see through the glass entrance into Amirante's outer office. After reassuring Albrecht and Hachmeister that Gacy was still on the premises, the lawyers went back into the offices, behind locked doors. Only once did the policemen get a glimpse of Gacy. The lawyers, however, were constantly moving about the suite, working in shirt-sleeves, their ties pulled loose.

At about 3 A.M., the officers rapped on the glass and motioned to the attorneys. They explained that it had been a while since they had seen Gacy, and after all it was their job to watch him. The lawyers were visibly nervous. They hedged. How do we know Gacy is back there? the officers asked. Don't worry, one of the lawyers said. He's sleeping in the back office.

Albrecht and Hachmeister looked at each other and broke into an unrehearsed skit. "Oh, man, you shouldn't let him go to sleep," Hachmeister said. Stevens and Amirante looked at him quizzically.

"He's a real bear when he wakes up," Albrecht said. "He goes bananas."

"We've seen him early in the morning," Hachmeister said. "If he's sleeping in there, you'd better stay away from him, because there's no telling what he's going to do."

Judging from the attorney's initial nervousness and the length of the meeting, the officers surmised that Gacy had told them something they hadn't known before. Now, seeing the lawyer's wide-eyed reaction to their improvisation, they knew they had struck a nerve.

Stevens and Amirante quickly agreed to bring Gacy out. They went inside, and a few minutes later emerged from the back offices, gingerly leading a half-asleep Gacy. The contractor dropped on the couch in the outer office and resumed his slumber. The attorneys came back out to the hallway.

Amirante told the officers they should park their cars so as to pin Gacy's in. Stevens, puffing on a cigarette, said that Gacy had been saying some very strange things. The police, he said, should shoot out his tires if he tried to leave. Hachmeister said they obviously couldn't do that: If Gacy wanted to leave, he was free to do so. Why were the lawyers so concerned? Stevens said they had nothing to say about it; it was just best they didn't let Gacy leave. The officers noticed that the cigarette Stevens was puffing on was unlit.

About an hour later, the attorneys announced that they would be leaving, one at a time, to shower, change clothes, and prepare for the coming day. Stevens left first and Amirante came and sat in the outer office across from where Gacy was sleeping. He kept paging through a law book, but he was not concentrating on it. He just stared at Gacy for a long time.

The officers, meanwhile, sat out in the hallway keeping their vigil. Now they were audience, waiting for the actors on the other side of the glass to begin their drama. Occasionally the policemen got up and paced the silent corridor, then stopped at the window and looked down at Gacy. He lay supine on the couch, his arms at his side, in rumpled white shirt and wash pants. A salt-and-pepper growth of beard stubble covered his jowls. He slept roughly, as if snoring, with his mouth slightly open. He had a meanness of expression even in sleep.

Albrecht decided to break the monotony at about 4:30. He was out of cigarettes and wanted some coffee. Let's tell Sam, he suggested to his partner, that I have to leave and you have to go out to your car for security reasons so we have radio contact.

Amirante was appalled when he heard their plans. Don't leave, he implored them. He would send out for breakfast, get them cigarettes and coffee, anything they wanted. Just don't leave. Why not? they asked. Just don't leave, he said. The officers went out anyway, if for no other reason than to test his reaction. Looking back through the entrance from the outside, they saw Amirante take up position where they had been sitting—in the hallway.

Albrecht returned about a half hour later. About 5:30, Stevens came back and Amirante left. As they walked through the outer office, the lawyers looked at Gacy warily and gave the couch a wide berth. Stevens joined the officers in the hallway.

None of the surveillance officers liked Stevens. They thought he fancied himself a smooth talker, and they disliked his lordly manner. Gacy had wanted to stay at a hotel that night, Stevens announced, but the lawyers advised him to stay in Sam's offices. They would, of course, be going to Federal District Court in the morning with the matter of the harassment suit. Stevens went on to say that Gacy was upset because the lawyers had told him that they might not be able to have the surveillance stopped. Once again, however, he made the usual request: Why don't you guys just save us all the aggravation and call it off? The conversation became a jousting match, building up and tearing down the image of the client sleeping on the other side of the glass. Mostly it was a game to see what the other side knew. We've talked to Gacy's second wife, Stevens said. She says John's a fantastic guy. John's quite a bullshitter, Albrecht said. And so on.

After Stevens went back to the offices, Albrecht lay down on the hallway floor and fell asleep. It was becoming daylight now and people coming into the building looked askance at the figure with a gun sticking out of his blue jeans that lay sprawled in the corridor. Hachmeister roused him.

Amirante returned at about 8 o'clock. Twenty minutes later, the lawyers gently awakened Gacy. The officers went outside and started their cars. Gacy came out in a hurry. Without acknowledging their presence, he got into his car and roared off. Reaching a stop sign at busy Devon Avenue, he made a left turn, and Albrecht just squeezed in behind him before an oncoming surge of rush-hour traffic reached the intersection. Once again, Hachmeister was left behind.

Gacy's destination was the Shell station, where by now owner John Lucas was referring to him and his police escort as the "circus train." Gacy had initially told Lucas that the policemen were his "bodyguards." Lucas knew better after Gacy had told an attendant, "Watch me lose these guys." Although Lucas had originally tabbed Gacy as a good, responsible businessman who promptly paid his monthly bills of $300 or $400, he was now becoming increasingly wary of him.

When Hachmeister pulled into the station, he hopped out of his car and immediately lit into Gacy for driving like such a jagoff and endangering the lives of little children in busy school zones. Gacy had lost his swagger and ebullience. He stood with his shoulders stooped and his head hanging down. Meekly, he walked over to Albrecht and pleaded, "Would you ask Dave to stop yelling at me?" Albrecht told him he certainly did drive like a jagoff, and he'd better slow down or they'd bust him.

Gacy walked over to the pumps, which were tended by a youth named Lance Jacobson. Gacy pulled a clear plastic bag containing some hand-rolled cigarettes from his pocket and nudged the attendant. The young man said no, he didn't want them. Gacy looked surprised. The two then went into the station; the officers followed. Gacy said he wanted to talk to Lucas alone. Albrecht and Hachmeister walked back out to the pumps. They watched as Gacy slipped the plastic bag into Jacobson's pocket. This time the young man offered no resistance. Gacy then initiated what appeared to be several emotional gestures of farewell to Lucas, double handshakes and pats on the shoulders. Albrecht suggested to Hachmeister that he stay behind—and let Gacy see him doing so. Gacy came out and drove off, Albrecht following, as Hachmeister sauntered into the station.

Lucas handed him the bag, which Jacobson had just given Lucas. It was marijuana.

"I didn't want to take it," Jacobson said. "I told Gacy he was crazy. He said, 'Take it. The end is coming. These guys are going to kill me.'"

Gacy had told Lucas not to put any more charges on his account "unless it's me."

"We've been friends," Gacy had said. "You're like a brother—I can't take much more." Then he had said his goodbye.

After crossing the intersection, Albrecht saw Gacy craning his neck to see what was keeping Hachmeister. In the process, the contractor veered off the road onto the muddy shoulder. He braked quickly, then tried to ease back on the road. Momentarily, he got stuck. His wheels spun furiously, throwing up mud, gravel, and ice. Finally he gained enough traction to get back on to the road, where he made a fast U-turn.

Hachmeister saw Gacy returning to the station, and he pocketed the marijuana. He began discussing transmissions with Lucas, who picked up his cue perfectly. Gacy came running in.

"What's the delay, Dave?" he asked. "Is there a problem?"

Hachmeister said no, he was just getting some advice regarding his car.

"Well, *I'm* ready any time *you* are," Gacy said impatiently.

The "circus train" moved on, stopping briefly at Summerdale. Gacy came out, looking no less disheveled and wearing the same clothes as he had before. He went to Rohde's house, stayed about a half hour, then bade another emotional farewell on the doorstep. Rohde beckoned Gacy to come back, but Gacy kept walking to his car. He was crying.

He returned to the Shell station, and from their cars, the officers watched another round of handshakes and back pats. Lucas looked over at the policemen with an embarrassed expression. Gacy seemed about ready to keel over.

On the expressway, Gacy's head began bobbing and his driving became erratic, as if he were drunk. Alarmed that he might try to commit suicide by ramming a bridge abutment, Albrecht pulled alongside. Gacy was holding something up to his chin, and Albrecht thought he was shaving. He honked. Gacy looked over from his hunched position and glared. Albrecht caught a glimpse of the object in Gacy's hand. It was a rosary.

Gacy got off the expressway at Lawrence and turned on to a side street to the south. Near a lumberyard, he slowed down, and Albrecht had a moment to scan the surroundings. He saw building materials, gravel, heavy equipment—the landmarks Kozenczak had sent him out to find! They all matched the description he'd been given. This *had* to be the site the anonymous caller had tried to direct them to! Just as he was radioing his discovery to Hachmeister, Gacy accelerated. A few minutes later, he drove up to Chris Gray's house. Dick Walsh was parked in front, taking tools out of the trunk of a car and dumping them on the parkway.

"Come on into the house," Gacy told him. "I have something I want to tell you."

"No!" Walsh said adamantly. "I got problems with my wife, my mother, my family. The police have been over to my house every day. We can't take any more. I don't want anything more to do with you!" He continued piling tools at the curb.

"Please," Gacy begged. "This may be the last time you'll ever see me."

Walsh ignored him for a moment, then finally relented. He was not in Gray's house long. When he came out, Albrecht asked what was wrong.

"He's really upset," Walsh said, turning to his car. "I don't want any more problems."

Gacy came out with Gray and walked up to the officers. They had to meet Stevens at Di Leo's, a restaurant on

Chicago's Northwest Side. Did the officers mind if Gray drove? They didn't, but they advised the youth to use caution.

It was noon when they arrived at the restaurant, and the parking lot was crowded. Gray stopped in front of a gas station across the street, and the officers parked in front of and behind his car. Lang was just arriving with Schultz and Robinson, and while Gacy went over to talk with his attorney under the restaurant canopy, the officers changed shift and Hachmeister and Albrecht got into Lang's car for the trip back to the station. While Gacy was talking with Stevens, Gray came over to Schultz's car, looking dazed.

Gacy is very depressed, Gray told the officer. He had been popping pills all morning. He was going around saying goodbyes to everybody; now it was Stevens's turn.

Why is he so depressed? Schultz asked.

"I guess he was up all night," Gray said, "and he told his lawyers he'd killed over thirty people."

Schultz's eyes bulged. "Where's he going from here?" he asked excitedly.

Gray said Gacy wanted to go to the cemetery to say goodbye to his father's grave. "I'm really afraid the guy might try to kill himself and kill me with him. When we leave here, don't lose us, *please!*"

Schultz grabbed his radio and called Lang: "Request you return immediately. I have important information." Seeing he was low on gas, he hurriedly backed the car to an empty island at the service station.

Gray walked over to Robinson's car and began repeating what he had just told Schultz, reiterating the fears he had for his own safety. The conversation was interrupted when Gacy returned from the restaurant. "Let's go," he told Gray.

Robinson jumped into his car, which was parked in front of Gacy's, and twisted around to see which way Gray would be going. Gray pulled out and went straight ahead, and Robinson fell in behind him.

"Stick with him!" It was Schultz's voice coming over the radio. Robinson looked back through his rear-view mirror. His partner was still pumping gas.

* * *

Early Thursday morning, when the surveillance officers were beginning their all-night vigil at Gacy's lawyers', I told Hein and Bedoe that we had enough on which to base a complaint for another search warrant. I wasn't prepared, however, to draft it at that late hour—I thought we should sleep on it. Instead, over a few glasses of beer, we talked about where we stood.

We were almost sure that Gacy had disposed of Rob's body on Tuesday, December 12—the night he was hours late for his appointment with Kozenczak, the night he finally showed up with mud on his shoes. Yet the next day the search team found no signs of digging in the crawl space. Nor did the crawl space fit the description of the gravesite Kozenczak's anonymous caller had supplied. From what Gray had told us, we knew there was something in that crawl space—we had probable cause for search, and it was likely we'd find some bodies. But his story did not tell us anything about Rob Piest. Then again, we had the photo receipt, which definitely established Rob's presence in Gacy's house immediately after his disappearance.

We went over and over it. Every time one of us thought he had put it all together, someone else would say, "Yes, but what about . . . ?" and counter with contradictory evidence. Still, the pressure was on, with Gacy's harassment suit hearing and probable restraining order just a day off. We had to act. I told Hein and Bedoe that we would resume our case for the search warrant at 8 A.M.

In the bright sunlight of morning, the photo receipt from Nisson's was still out highest face card. I was hoping that the envelope containing Kim Byers's photos would be returned by the laboratory today so I could have the state crime lab compare it and the stub to see if the two matched. That would give us the further legal leverage of having expert corroboration of what Kim had told us. The clincher that I was waiting for, however, proved to be waiting for me next door at the Des Plaines police station.

One of my assistants, Larry Finder, and Kozenczak said that Schultz just revealed something very interesting that I should hear. Schultz, unable to sleep all night, had come in at daybreak hoping to find Kozenczak there early. He wanted to tell the lieutenant what he had smelled from Gacy's register two nights before.

Schultz's story would certainly help us get the warrant, but I had to make sure we were on a solid legal footing. Was Schultz in Gacy's house legally? Yes, he had been invited in. Recent marijuana case law had toughened the standards on what an officer could say, as an expert, about what he had smelled: I asked him what he thought the odor smelled like, where he had encountered it before, how many times, and so on. A judge, for instance, might ask, How do you know the odor wasn't dead pigeons? Schultz's forty-odd visits to the Cook County morgue sounded convincing enough to me. Let's write the warrant, I said.

Bedoe started on the rough draft, but he was so exhausted he was making a typographical hash of it, and besides, I knew this one needed legal expertise. I sat down with Finder, a good attorney, and outlined what we needed. We would name Rob Piest as the victim and list the crime as murder. The photo receipt stub would be the main evidence demonstrating probable cause, and Schultz's story about the odor of death would be used in backup. Kozenczak would be the complainant. We would attach the first search warrant to the complaint as evidence that a judge had already given the police department credence in the investigation.

The Detective Bureau, meanwhile, learned that Kim Byers's photo envelope had been received by Nisson's. Kozenczak sent Adams and Pickell to retrieve it. When I compared the torn edges of the envelope and stub, I had no doubt that they had once been the same piece of paper. Giving us same-day service, a state crime lab forensic scientist, George Dabdoub, confirmed this, and also helpfully opined that the small brown bottle recovered on the first search emitted a chloroformlike odor.

In Kozenczak's office, excited voices came over the monitor. Gacy had almost slipped the tail again, and all three units of the surveillance force were now pursuing him.

When Lang heard Schultz's urgent message, he made a U-turn and raced back south toward the restaurant. Just before he reached the gas station, Gray and Robinson passed him in the

opposite direction. As Lang made another turn, Albrecht
jumped out and raced toward Schultz's car, which was just
pulling away from the gas pumps. He pounded on the trunk.
Schultz stopped and Albrecht got in. Schultz hurriedly explained what Gray had told him, then radioed the details to
Lang, who, with Hachmeister, was now third place in the
chase. While he was trying to operate his radio, Schultz's
driving was so erratic that Albrecht grabbed the unit and told
him to concentrate on the road. Schultz raced at sixty miles an
hour through the busy diagonal intersection of Elston and
Milwaukee.

Fearing that Gacy might attempt suicide, Lang radioed the
station for instructions: Should we take him down? After a
moment, Kozenczak replied, "If you have an arrest, take him.
Otherwise, use your discretion." Lang said that they had no
grounds.

"We've got marijuana!" Albrecht said to Schultz in a
sudden revelation. "Dave should have it." By now, Schultz
had closed the gap on the first three cars. He swung out
alongside Lang's car, and Albrecht yelled across to Hachmeister in the passenger seat.

"Dave, where's the marijuana?" Several pedestrians eyed
the procession—the new, longer circus train—suspiciously.

"In my pocket," Hachmeister said. He explained the gas
station incident to Lang, who then radioed Kozenczak.

We were monitoring the exchange in the station. Kozenczak
turned and looked at me as if to say, What now? Oh, my God, I
thought. All I needed were a couple hours more to complete
the search warrant, and I was sure that, from that, I would have
a valid arrest for murder later on. On the other hand, in his
present state it was possible that Gacy might kill someone, or
himself. If we took him on marijuana, I'd have Gacy's lawyers
to contend with—would we be able to hold him? The pressure
was tremendous. The five or ten seconds I stood there,
computing all the considerations in my mind, seemed like an
eternity. Finally I said to Kozenczak, "Yeah. Take him down."

At fifteen minutes past noon, on a bright and sunny
December 21, at the corner of Milwaukee and Oakton in the
suburb of Niles, the four surveillance officers and their
commander pounced on their quarry. For eight days and nights,

the policemen had tracked him, each convinced that their team had the edge on the other, that the final glory of slipping the handcuffs on Gacy would be theirs. All along, Gacy had played one team against the other, telling the morning shift that they were great guys, but their counterparts were schmucks. In the evening, he repeated the story in reverse. But whatever competition had developed dissolved as the four officers and Lang played the final act of the surveillance drama to an astonished audience of motorists and diners at the corner McDonald's.

Schultz pinned Gray in from the left front. Robinson and Lang pulled up behind Gacy's car, and all five officers surrounded the vehicle, Robinson and Hachmeister with guns drawn.

Robinson opened the door on the passenger side. "Get out of the car, John," he said, sticking the pistol at Gacy's right ear. "You're under arrest." The usually mild-mannered Hachmeister came over and unleashed a torrent of profanity. "We've got you now, you jagoff," he sputtered.

Gacy responded in a surprised and wounded tone. "What's the matter? What have I done?"

The officers spread Gacy over the trunk of his car and frisked him. Hachmeister recovered some pills in an unmarked container. Robinson handcuffed Gacy, who was then placed in the rear seat of Schultz's car. Gray was told to come with them all, driving Gacy's car. Then, like the triumphal procession from *Peter and the Wolf*, they drove to the station.

On the way back, Gacy spoke as if he was bewildered that his pals had turned on him. "What's this all about?" he asked repeatedly. "Hey, we're friends, we've come a long way. Can't you level with me?" Schultz, driving with Albrecht, simply told him that it was nothing personal, but they were ordered not to talk with him for the moment. It would all be explained at the station. Albrecht read him his Miranda rights.

Hachmeister and Robinson went to the Shell station to get Jacobson's version of the marijuana incident and bring him to Des Plaines for a statement. Jacobson said that he initially had rebuffed Gacy's offer of the joints, but when he was in the station making change for another customer, Gacy slipped the bag into his pocket. Rather than make a scene, he just left it there until Gacy left, when he immediately gave it to his boss.

The Des Plaines station was a scene of excitement and some confusion. The police hadn't been expecting John Gacy so soon, and now that they had him, they weren't quite sure *why* they had him. While Kozenczak held a debriefing in his office to get a clearer picture of the situation than the radio reports had provided, Robinson processed Gacy for arrest, shooting mug shots and fingerprinting him.

Although I would have preferred their delaying the arrest to keep Gacy's lawyers out of the picture as long as possible, I was not unhappy with the situation. Delivery of marijuana was a felony, and I was sure we could detain Gacy on that until we got the search warrant executed. We also had the unlabeled bottle of forty pills, apparently Valium, that Hachmeister had taken from him. If the lawyers' pressure for his release on the charge built up, we could hold him for maybe thirty-six hours on suspicion of murder.

Our technical equipment came to our aid—by not working. In any felony arrest in Illinois, the suspect is fingerprinted and the prints sent by facsimile to Springfield. There, the prints are compared with both the Illinois and Federal Bureau of Investigation files to make sure the police have the right person in custody. Furthermore, a suspect can't be released on bond until his prints are received and placed on file for future reference. Today, the Des Plaines department's facsimile machine was malfunctioning, which assured us of a fortuitous—and fortunate—delay in processing Gacy.

Now Lang had something he wanted to try in case we had to release Gacy and start surveillance again. A couple of days before, he had come to me with a proposal to install a tailing device called a bird-dog on Gacy's car. This is an electronic unit that emits a continuous signal that can be monitored by the police. This, he thought, would help cover those lapses when Gacy succeeded in shaking the surveillance as well as permit operation at less than breakneck speeds. Of course, it required a court order to permit installation on a suspect's car.

In the turmoil of the investigation, I had not pursued the order, but Lang had gone ahead and arranged with the Illinois

Department of Law Enforcement to have a unit sent up from Springfield. It had arrived this afternoon.

Lang and Schultz took a one-hour crash course in its operation, normally a forty-hour endeavor, then installed the device on Albrecht's car. Get lost, they told him and Hachmeister, and we'll find you. Hachmeister, fuming because he hadn't had the chance to complete the paperwork necessary on Gacy's arrest, thought the bird-dog was a total waste of his time.

Albrecht—and Hachmeister, under protest—drove to the nearby community college, parked, and waited. Lang and Schultz promptly found them. Next, Albrecht went to the municipal parking garage, which rises between the train tracks and the business section of downtown Des Plaines like a Chinese Wall, and drove up several levels. This proved more difficult for the spotters because of interference from the structural elements of the garage. Hachmeister said he'd had enough and got out in disgust. He walked across the tracks to the station and continued his paperwork. Lang finally found Albrecht and sent him out one more time. Again they located the officer, this time having coffee at his brother's house. Lang decided that the bird-dog was ready, should it be needed.

After Robinson finished processing Gacy, I told him and Schultz to sit with their friend, listening to what he had to say, making him as comfortable as possible. They told him that they knew he had something heavy on his mind and that they would be good listeners if he wanted to get rid of his burden. Gacy said he didn't want to talk now, but when he did he wanted Schultz to head the inquiry. "You go out there and arrange it," he said, "or I'm not saying anything to anybody— and I've got a lot to say." At Gacy's request, Schultz called LeRoy Stevens and suggested that Stevens call Amirante.

Later, it was Jim Ryan's turn to sit in a locked interview room with Gacy. Mostly they made small talk, and Gacy seemed fairly relaxed. Christmas was now just four days away. Gacy said he hated holidays. Ryan mentioned Rob Piest, how upset his family was and what a miserable Christmas they would be having. Gacy said he understood that, but there was nothing he could do to help them.

We were racing against time to get the search warrant

finished. Although the marijuana arrest was solid, I wasn't totally confident of our ability to detain Gacy on suspicion of murder because we had no body as evidence. At this stage, it all depended on what we found in his crawl space.

I kept revising the search warrant, trying to make it airtight. I called Judge Peters. He would be leaving for home at 4:30. I was sure we wouldn't have the complaint ready by then. We would have to take it out to his house to have it signed.

When Sam Amirante arrived at the station, the conversation went just as I had expected.

"What do you have this guy in here *now* for?" he demanded.

"Marijuana," I told him.

Sam shook his head. "You know," he said, "you guys are just asking for more trouble. We've filed the lawsuit. It will be up in Federal District Court tomorrow. These guys are going to be in trouble for holding him. This is just more harassment."

Sam kept asking me what we planned to do. Keep him in the station? Go out to the house? He was probing to see how much we knew. Now that the processing was over, he wanted to see his client.

Amirante spent about an hour with Gacy, while the atmosphere in the Detective Bureau became almost electric in anticipation of the search. The crawl space, of course, was our main target. Tovar, however, was obsessed by the television set, whose serial number we still had failed to get. I conducted another briefing session with the detectives who would be going on the search, then told Greg to notify the sheriff's evidence technicians and investigators to stand by.

Finally, we had the wording I wanted, and I read the draft over the phone to Peters, just to make sure. Now all it needed was retyping and a warrant number assigned. I was just telling Kozenczak how to get out to Judge Peters's house when I got word that Amirante wanted me. It was urgent.

"Gacy's having a seizure!" he told me excitedly. His client had pains in his chest and left arm and was having difficulty breathing. In unison, Tovar and I turned to the radio desk and said, "Call the paramedics." In minutes there were sirens outside and the crew came rushing in with a litter. They eased Gacy down and gave him oxygen, then hooked him up to their telemetry device so that the staff at Holy Family Hospital could monitor his heartbeats. Pickell rode in the ambulance for security. With a flourish of flashing lights and piercing sirens, they drove off into the night. What a godsend, I thought.

"You see what you guys are doing?" Amirante said to me. "You're going to *kill* the man!"

"Dave, I Want
to Clear the Air"

One of my assistant state's attorneys, Bill Ward, had been intrigued by Gacy's attempt to visit his father's grave at Maryhill Cemetery in nearby Niles. Ward had gone out there himself in midafternoon. At the grave, he saw footprints in the snow leading up to the marker and, behind it, several newly dug graves covered with boards. Ward realized with mounting excitement that the surroundings virtually matched the landmarks in the sketch in Kozenczak's office. When Bill returned and described what he had found, I agreed to go back to the cemetery with him later that Thursday afternoon when we had the opportunity.

We didn't have time until the search warrant was done, nor had I had a chance to take an hour or two to go Christmas shopping as I had planned with Brett, the eleven-year-old I sponsored in the Big Brothers program. Brett and his friend George had sat around the police station watching the activities with great interest. Now Bill and I herded the boys into my car in the early evening and drove to the cemetery. When we arrived, George bridled at going any further.

"I ain't going in no cemetery," he announced.

"Are you going to stay in the car?" I asked.

"No, man," he said. "Don't leave me here."

"What are you so scared about?"

"If you get lost," George said, "they can find you. But they can't see me in the dark." We compromised by holding one another's hands.

When we got to the site, I thought immediately: Now we've got it. The landmarks fit perfectly. I shined my flashlight at a spot alongside a small lake, and there I saw evidence of freshly poured concrete covered with straw. There were the graves, newly dug, just as Bill had described. Surely this was the place the mysterious caller had in mind—the very spot that Gacy was leading us to in his final hour of freedom. We had just decided to postpone further investigation until daylight so as not to obliterate the footprints, when we were interrupted. An urgent message for me to call the station had come over the radio of one of the Niles squad cars accompanying us. Kozenczak had returned from Judge Peters's house with the signed search warrant, and the way was clear for our return to 8213 Summerdale Avenue. I arranged for Brett and George to be taken home, and set out for Gacy's house.

At the station, the Detective Bureau was like a staging area before the assault on the Normandy beaches. Bedoe turned to Larry Finder and suggested he come along to see what they found. Larry demurred. His grandmother was cooking a sweet-and-sour meatball dinner just for him. He couldn't disappoint her. Besides, he didn't think we'd find anything, but he asked Greg to call him just in case. "Well, ye of little faith, you'll be sorry," Bedoe said as we hurried out to the cars.

Robinson got the news as he was driving Chris Gray home. Gray had been cooperative. Since driving Gacy's car to the station after the arrest, he had waited around patiently. He was totally dejected, and the least we could do was offer him a lift. Schultz radioed Robinson from his car, in which he was proceeding to the search. "The warrant's signed," he told Robinson. "We're on our way to Gacy's house."

Kozenczak, radioing from his car, angrily interrupted the transmission, telling Schultz they didn't want that on the air. It was now just a matter of time before the press would come swooping in.

The house on Summerdale was surrounded by a fleet of police vehicles, marked and unmarked, such as this quiet street had never seen. Three dozen law enforcement officials would visit the premises before the night was over. Now it was posted with Cook County sheriff's police officers, who had jurisdiction in unincorporated areas, and more cars were arriving by the minute. The unofficial assumption was that if Rob Piest's body was found, and no others, the case would remain with the Des Plaines Police Department. If other bodies were discovered, it would become the county's.

Inside, officers quickly removed the trap door leading to the crawl space. The ground below was under water; the electric cord to the sump pump had been disconnected. One of the officers plugged it in, and an anxious gathering waited in the front room with Gacy's clowns and plants while the water level receded. Schultz shined his flashlight around the opening, then zoomed it in on a bit of matted substance that attracted his attention. It was light brown hair, caught on some subflooring. Looking in the closet above the trap door, the officers saw that the hanger pole was scored with the sort of marks a hawser makes on a wooden bollard.

Other officers combed the premises for additional evidence. Tovar and Kautz went directly to the master bedroom to compare the serial numbers on the television and the clock radio. The officers rotated the TV set on Gacy's dresser and read the number on the identification plate. Gacy had John Szyc's television set. The officers checked the radio. It was the same story. Schultz, Adams, and about a half-dozen other men made a thorough search of Gacy's garage and workshed. They found wallets and IDs, as well as personal jewelry and pieces of plywood that appeared to be stained with blood. Kautz uncovered more IDs in the attic. In the recreation room, Tovar found an object no one wanted to examine too closely: a foot-long vibrator encrusted with fecal matter.

They also found pictures showing Gacy posing with Mayor Michael Bilandic and Rosalynn Carter. One politically disgruntled policeman muttered that he hoped they'd find her husband in the crawl space. The black humor had begun.

In the office off the clown room, the policemen found numerous ball-point pens of the sort Gacy obviously had distributed as mementos. They advertised PDM, Gacy's candidacy for the presidency of a local Jaycee chapter, and his summer parties.

After they had run the sump pump for about ten minutes, the

investigators decided to venture into the crawl space. ET
Daniel Genty had been curious about Gacy ever since he had
visited the house two years before while following up a report,
as a uniformed policeman, of a runaway teenage girl. In the
Piest investigation, he had helped process Gacy's vehicles and
had pleaded to be included on the search team if they ever got
another warrant. Now he was donning his coveralls and
fireman's boots, preparing to make the descent with Investigator Phil Bettiker, a bomb technician who had previously
done ET work.

Down in the crawl space, Genty moved eastward on his
hands and knees to a spot just below the kitchen. There he saw
hair sticking out of the ground. Shining his floodlight to the
southeast, he saw a long depression that looked like a dry lake
bed with cracks in the yellow gray covering of lime. At the
edges, it broke off, exposing a thin line of raw dirt around the
circumference of the depression. Something had caused it to
settle. He slithered on his stomach over a black drain pipe from
the bathroom and moved to a spot in the southwest corner,
where the ground was wet and spongy. He pulled up his boots
all the way, then shined the light on several puddles still
remaining. The two smaller ones were of clear water. A third
contained a reddish purple liquid in which hundreds, maybe
thousands of hairlike red worms a couple inches long were
fibrillating like creatures in a tidal pool. When he shined the
light on the puddle, the worms quickly withdrew into the mud.

Genty knelt down, propped the light at his side, and stuck
his entrenching tool into the ground. After two shovelfuls, he
saw whitish bits of a soaplike material floating up to the surface
of the murky water. He recognized this as adipocere flesh, body
tissue that has chemically changed to an almost lardlike
substance from being immersed in water. He called Bettiker
over as a witness.

The fresh excavation smelled like a sewer. Above the two
investigators, the floor creaked under the footsteps of officers
searching a bedroom, and bits of dust and spider webs,
dislodged by the movement, floated across the beam of the
floodlight. Genty dug further until, about six or seven inches
down, his shovel made a grating sound, as if it had hit a drain
tile. He worked his entrenching tool and finally brought the

object to the surface. It was a bone, seemingly from an upper arm, which his shovel had hooked at the elbow. Some hair strands had caught on the tool. When he first brought up the bone, its remaining body tissue was pinkish. A moment after it was exposed to the air, it turned gray.

Genty turned to the officers who were poking their heads through the trap door.

"Charge him!" he said.

"What?" Kozenczak asked.

"I've found one."

"What do you mean, you've found a body?"

"Yeah."

"Is it Piest?"

"I don't think so. This has been here too long."

Bettiker requested more illumination, and Karl Humbert, who had been photographing in the house, brought down another floodlight. The moment it was plugged in, the other lights in the crawl space blew, leaving the three investigators in total darkness.

While the officers above looked for the fuse box, the three men squatted on their haunches in the pitch black. The smell was becoming obnoxious and they fumbled to don charcoal-impregnated odor masks. Working in their coveralls near the heat-distribution box, Genty and Bettiker had begun to perspire. Now they sat waiting in the stinking darkness, listening to Tovar at the trap door imitating the call of an owl.

Five minutes later, the lights came back on.

Genty took a shovelful of his findings over to the trap door and stood up.

"What the hell is *that*?" several people asked.

"It's a body," Genty said.

"How the hell do you know that?"

"See the hair sticking out?" Genty said, pointing.

"Better call the medical examiner," one of the sheriff's policemen said.

"I think this crawl space is full of kids," Genty said. He stooped down and returned to the gravesite. The three men went to the northeast corner of the crawl space. After lifting several shovelfuls of muck, Humbert struck something solid and pulled it up. It was a kneecap. Next, they went to the southeast corner, where Humbert unearthed two long bones, probably from a lower leg. They were totally black. The investigators decided to wait for the arrival of the county medical examiner, Dr. Robert Stein, before disturbing any more remains. They came out of the hole.

Bettiker notified Lieutenant Frank Braun of the sheriff's police, who would personally take charge of the body recoveries now that the magnitude of the job was becoming known. Genty called his supervisor, Sergeant Donald Des Ré Maux, who was incredulous when his ET told him that they had found possibly three human bodies and that, according to a tipster's report, there might be three more buried in the crawl space. But Des Ré Maux, who had organized the sheriff's evidence technician unit in the early 1970s, was supremely confident in the ability of his men to function smoothly as a professional team, with or without his personal direction. He had been planning to leave early in the morning on a Christmas holiday vacation.

"Are you still going?" asked Genty, standing at the phone in mud-smeared boots and coveralls.

"Sure," Des Ré Maux said. "You handle it."

At about 11 P.M., Dr. Stein arrived with his investigator, Frank Flannigan. As medical examiner, Stein had the usual responsibilities of county coroner: it was his job to view the remains, first to determine if they were human, then officially to pronounce the person dead. Usually he worked in the Morris Fishbein Institute of Forensic Pathology, the Cook County morgue. Tonight, however, after hearing Braun's terse summation—"Doc, I think we've got a big one"—he had thought it best to come to the scene of the discovery.

Stein put on a disposable paper jumpsuit and went down into the crawl space with the investigators. They showed the doctor the kneecap found in the northeast corner.

"Yeah," Stein said in his high-pitched voice. "It sure looks like a human body." Humbert brought him the long bones. "Oh, definitely," Stein said.

"We have another one over there," Genty said. "Want to crawl over?"

"No," Stein said. "That's enough for me. I know what we're up against."

The men sat for several minutes on what appeared to be an unused footing, playing the floodlights on the crawl space floor and the underpinnings of the house itself. Only the front, original part of the house was built above the crawl space. The dining room and recreation area in the rear, built upon joists resting on the ground, appeared to be of more recent construction. The men came out of the trap door and went into the dining room, where we had a general conference around the table.

Stein announced that he wanted the recovery of the bodies to be made with the thoroughness of an archaeological dig. This meant the removal of the surrounding earth from the remains, then the meticulous retrieval of all skeletal matter and artifacts. Of course, the big problem was how to engineer the recovery. It was virtually impossible to expect the ETs to dig on their knees with less than three feet of headroom. Some of us wondered if the house could be raised off its foundations and moved. Someone suggested making an excavation through the side of the house from a lower level. We also discussed ripping up the floor. There were questions of legal rights and the problem of possibly having to restore the house to its original condition. We deferred any decision on how to recover the bodies until morning. The matter of security was raised, and it was decided to post round-the-clock guards of sheriff's policemen and seal the house from intrusion. We discussed how to keep the results of our investigation from the press until Gacy was properly charged.

The topic flew out the window when we heard a commotion at the patio door. Tovar and Ron Russell, of the sheriff's police, had intercepted a visitor. Most of us recognized him, though not as a member of the law enforcement community. It was Jay Levine of Channel 7.

While the search was going on at 8213 Summerdale Avenue, Gacy himself was undergoing a detailed examination at Holy Family Hospital in Des Plaines. The medical authorities, however, were unable to find any evidence of a heart attack, and their assistants were openly voicing their diagnosis that the closely guarded patient was just bullshitting. Shortly after 10

P.M., Gacy was released into the custody of Pickell and Hachmeister, who had been sent to assist.

Kozenczak had just told Hachmeister over the telephone that bodies had been found at the house and to guard Gacy carefully. Hachmeister tightened his handcuffs on Gacy with relish, then told the nurses that if they thought they had had a big time tonight, they should tune in the news tomorrow. He pushed Gacy, who he thought looked like a standing blob of jelly, into the back seat of Pickell's car and got in with him.

Back at the station, Pickell drove into the security garage, adjacent to the main building, where Albrecht met them. As the two surveillance officers led Gacy into the security area, Hachmeister unleased a volley of invective.

"Okay, you jagoff," he said, "the game is over. You're under arrest for murder. We've found bodies."

Not unmindful of its humiliating effect, they gave him a strip search to see if he had any drugs. Holding his rosary, Gacy stood passively, his shoulders sagging, his stomach protruding. They took his clothes and gave him prisoner's garb to wear. Gacy asked them to let him keep the rosary. They did. As Gacy sat on the slat bench in the security room, Albrecht read him his Miranda rights from a card. Gacy said he understood them. He read and signed, in a shaky hand, a written Miranda waiver. Then Hachmeister was called from the room.

Gacy sighed and told Albrecht that he had known it was all going to end ever since he talked with his lawyers the night before. "Have you been in the crawl space?" he asked softly. Albrecht nodded. "That's what the lime was for," he said.

"What do you mean?" Albrecht asked.

"The lime was for the sewage dampness—and what you found there." Gacy said that there were four different Johns, and he didn't know all their personalities.

"How many bodies are in the crawl space?" Albrecht asked.

Gacy shook his head. "I'm not sure," he said.

"Is the boy from Nisson's there?"

"No," Gacy said. "He's not there." He added that he would have a hard time pinpointing where he was, but that he could find him.

Through the window in the door, Hachmeister motioned to

Albrecht. Outside in the hallway, Hachmeister told him that Lang didn't want the officers talking to Gacy anymore.

"We've got a signed Miranda waiver," Albrecht said angrily. "There's no problem!"

I had just got back from Summerdale, and when Hachmeister told me about Lang's instruction, I immediately overruled him. "Get back in there and get what you can," I told him.

When the two officers went back in to Gacy, Hachmeister softened his manner. He didn't want to be left out of any further confession.

"John, I'm sorry I flew off the handle," he said. "There's been a lot of pressure, and I just lost my head a little bit."

"That's okay," Gacy said, nodding. "I understand." He looked up at Hachmeister. "Dave," he said, "I want to clear the air. I know that the game is over. The lime was used to cover the smell. The bodies have been down there a long time. And there are more bodies off the property."

The officers looked at Gacy for a moment, saying nothing. "But why did you kill them?" Hachmeister asked.

Gacy appeared occupied with his own thoughts. Finally he said, "I'm bisexual, not homosexual. I never used force. It was always by consent. I never forced anybody because I'm not strong enough to fight—especially with my heart condition."

Now he was becoming less introspective, and his inquisitorial manner returned. "Who else do you have in the station?" he asked. "There are others involved."

"Directly or indirectly?" Albrecht asked.

"Directly," Gacy said. "They participated."

The officers asked who they were.

"My associates," Gacy responded.

"You mean Walsh and Gray?" Hachmeister asked.

"Yeah," he said. "Walsh and Gray. Is Gray here now?" Before the officers could answer, Gacy had another question. "How did you know there were bodies in the crawl space?"

"John," Albrecht said, "we're on surveillance. We don't know what the others are doing. We haven't seen the search warrant."

Gacy straightened up and looked Albrecht in the eye. His

old swagger had returned. "Mike," he said, "you know I won't be in jail very long. I won't spend a day in jail for this."

"Do you want to elaborate on that?" Albrecht asked. Gacy shrugged.

Schultz walked into the room. "Well, John," he said, "I imagine you have a lot on your mind to unload. Do you still want to speak with us now?"

Gacy replied that he had a lot to say but asked if they could move to another room because he was chilly. The men collected a few chairs and moved into the nearby phone room.

"John," Schultz asked, "where is Rob Piest?" Gacy looked at him quizzically.

"The boy from Nisson's," Albrecht interjected.

"Oh," Gacy replied. "I didn't know his name. No, he's not in the crawl space."

"Where is he?" Hachmeister asked.

"I don't know," Gacy said. "I didn't transport him."

"Who did?"

"I can't say," Gacy replied. "But you'll find out when LeRoy gets here. He knows. I told my lawyers everything last night."

"You know, John," Hachmeister said, "you don't have to speak with us if you don't want to."

"I know that," Gacy replied.

"John, do you recall when your dad died?" Albrecht asked him. Gacy said he did. "You weren't able to go to the funeral, were you?" Gacy shook his head. "And the prison officials didn't tell you about it until after your dad was buried. Wasn't that around the Christmas holidays?" Gacy nodded and said that that had bothered him a lot. "Well, that's why we want to find Rob Piest's body—for the family."

"The body is in a location about an hour or hour and a half drive from here," Gacy said. "But you'll never find it."

"Well, if you'll just tell me where it's at," Albrecht said, "and if I can't find it, I will tell you, John, that I can't find it, and you were right." Albrecht immediately shuddered at his own garbled syntax and regretted breaking the continuity of the questioning. Hachmeister came to the rescue.

"Is the body above ground, or is it buried?" he said.

"Above ground," Gacy replied.

"How did he die?" Hachmeister said.

"They were all strangled," Gacy said. "None of them were tortured." He went on to explain how he got his victims to handcuff themselves, then later told them that the trick was to have the key.

As for Rob Piest, Gacy said, he put a cord around the youth's neck and had twisted it twice, when his phone had rung. Rob was still standing when Gacy left the room to answer it. When Gacy returned from his conversation, Rob was on the floor, convulsing. He had urinated all over himself. Gacy picked the body up and put it on the bed. "At that time," he said, "I felt he was dead."

At 11:30 Sergeant Lang came to the door and said they would have to move to another room outside the security area. Once relocated, Gacy announced that their conversation would end in fifteen minutes.

"We haven't pressued you, have we, John?" Hachmeister asked.

"No," he said. "Everything I've said has been voluntary." Gacy then mentioned "Jack," one of his other personalities, and said that Jack didn't like homosexuality. Schultz, sensing the groundwork for an insanity defense, immediately got him off the subject.

"But why death?" he asked.

"Because," Gacy said, "the boys sold their bodies for twenty dollars. They killed themselves."

"How could they strangle themselves?" Schultz asked.

"Because of what they did," Gacy answered. "They put the cords around their necks. They killed themselves."

"But why didn't you bury them all under the house?" Schultz asked. His tone was admiring: "You had a great plan. Nobody would ever find you out."

"Because of my heart condition," Gacy said. "I couldn't dig a grave anymore. Besides, the crawl space is full."

Lang came in at 11:45 and asked to speak with the three officers. The interview was over.

The three surveillance officers relayed what they had learned to those of us in the Detective Bureau, all the while complaining about Lang's cutting them off short. Meanwhile, Greg Bedoe and Earl Lundquist, another sheriff's policeman, showed Gacy pictures of some of the youths we thought were probable victims. He identified three by name: Butkovich, Godzik, and Szyc ("the guy with the funny name. You'll get a kick out of that story"). After a few minutes, however, Gacy said he wanted his lawyers present before he talked anymore. The officers told him that he'd probably decide to clam up once his lawyers talked with him, and tried to persuade him to continue his statements. Gacy was adamant. "My lawyers work for me," he said. "They'll do what I tell them to do. We can clear a lot up, get to the bottom of this, but I want my lawyers present."

Although it was well past midnight, the police station was throbbing with activity. Assistant state's attorneys, sheriff's policemen, and the evening shift of Des Plaines patrolmen, who had been relieved at 11:45, were all milling around the Detective Bureau. Some officers were discussing how to recover the bodies at Summerdale, some were processing evidence and writing reports on the day's events. As I tried to sort out the kaleidoscopic happenings of the last twenty-four hours, I began to consider getting another search warrant in the morning to assure the legality of the recovery operation.

I also engaged in a cat-and-mouse game with Sam Amirante. Gacy's lawyer had been to the house during the search, and he had been not-so-politely told by Bedoe to leave. Consequently, he wasn't sure what we had found or learned. Back at the station, we spoke to each other a couple of times, each of us trying to ferret out what the other knew. Now I decided to open up the discussion: I told him we had found human remains. Sam sat in his chair speechless, averting his eyes, shaking his head in disbelief. I knew that Gacy had confessed to him the night before; Sam obviously had hoped I could tell him that Gacy had been lying.

LeRoy Stevens arrived and the two lawyers were ushered into the room where Gacy sat. As they met, I tried to map our strategy. We knew Gacy wanted to talk, but we didn't know whether his lawyers would allow him to.

I had a court reporter standing by in the event Gacy chose to give a formal statement, but I was reluctant to use him. Gacy could put anything he wanted into the record—including his whole "John/Jack" split-personality scenario—and his attorneys could demand the presence of a court reporter. In that case, I would be forced to decide whether to accept the risk to the prosecution, or simply to do without any further statements from Gacy. That had its drawbacks, too: although we weren't looking for a confession at this stage, we did want information that would help us find Rob Piest, as well as any other victims.

As we waited for word from the lawyers, we tried to decide who would take any statement Gacy might make. Everyone was clamoring to be included, but the selection had to be limited, preferably to those officers whom Gacy liked and trusted. After about an hour, the suspense was broken when Amirante came out and announced, reluctantly, John wants to talk.

Fortunately, he did not ask for a court reporter. We decided to send in the four surveillance officers—Bob Schultz, Ron Robinson, Dave Hachmeister, and Mike Albrecht, who would take the official notes—as well as Greg Bedoe and Earl Lundquist to represent the sheriff's office. And so, in a small conference room, seated at a table, with his two lawyers at his side, John Gacy began his statement to the six police officers. The time was 3:30 A.M.

It all started, Gacy said, in 1974. Since then he had murdered twenty-five or thirty young men, all homosexuals or bisexuals, all of them hustlers. All the victims willingly came to his house, and all were killed there. By now, he said, he had lost count of the number buried in the crawl space. The last five victims, all killed in 1978, he dropped into the Des Plaines River, southwest of Chicago, off the bridge on Interstate Highway 55. One, he thought, might have landed on a barge. All but one he killed by looping a rope around their necks, knotting it twice, then tightening it, like a tourniquet, with a stick. A couple of times, he said, he had to tighten the knot more than once when the victims showed signs of reviving. On two or three occasions, he said, he had "doubles"—nights when he killed two people. Some of the victims, he said, convulsed for an hour or two after his "rope trick." In the crawl space, he either soaked the bodies with acid or put lime on them and buried them under a foot of earth. Sometimes he buried one on top of the other. He disposed of their personal effects in the garbage. Gacy said that the investigators wouldn't be able to find all the bodies—he would have to show them.

There was hardly a sound from any of the listeners except the scratching of Albrecht's pencil on a notepad. Some of the officers sat at the table, some stood, others sat on the floor of the tiny room, against the wall. Gacy spoke as if he were holding court, frequently leaning back in his chair and talking with his eyes closed. He had overcome his fatigue and was speaking with a renewed air of confidence. Just as he wanted, the room belonged to John Gacy.

The Piest boy, he said, didn't know what awaited him at Gacy's house, but he had wanted to make easy money. He had run up to Gacy's vehicle, asking about a summer job. The boy said he would do almost anything for money—but he lied, Gacy said ominously. Later at the house, the boy had his hand on the doorknob when he said, "Gee, I thought you were going to kill me." Gacy told the officers that he knew right then that the boy was not going to leave the house. Rob asked why Gacy was putting the rope around his neck. Why did he ask? the contractor said rhetorically. He was stupid, that's why. Gacy related how he was interrupted by the phone while strangling the youth, then recounted the events of the evening he had spoken of in his statement the week before—his visit to Northwest Hospital and to his aunt's house.

After sleeping in bed next to the corpse all night, Gacy got up at 6 A.M. and moved it to the attic. There it lay, even during the visit on Tuesday of the two police officers, "Asshole"—as he referred to Kozenczak—and Pickell. After they left, he had just brought the body downstairs when he heard the bell ring at the rear door. He left the body in the hallway while he went to the door. It was Walsh, ready to go Christmas-tree shopping. Gacy said he couldn't go, and Walsh left. Gacy moved his car to the back door, wrapped the body in an orange blanket, and put it in the trunk. Gacy said he recalled being "higher than a kite."

He drove south on the Tri-State Tollway to Interstate 55. Reaching the bridge over the Des Plaines River, he saw a barge passing underneath and continued on. He turned around and came back in the northbound lanes. He began hearing reports on his CB radio of an unmarked "smoky"—a patrol car—on the bridge, so he doubled back again. He made several passes before concluding that the CB reports were probably referring to him. He stopped and dumped the body over the rail.

On his way back toward the city, Gacy said, he threw away the blanket, although he wasn't sure why he did because there was no blood on it. He lost control of his car on the Tri-State and slid into a ditch. A truck stopped, but the driver was unable to help him. Gacy jacked up the car and put his spare tire under a wheel, but he couldn't get out. He got back into his car and soon fell asleep. At about 2 A.M., a tow truck stopped and pulled him out. He drove to the Des Plaines police station to see "Asshole" but found that he had left.

Gacy described his encounters with several other victims. The one before Piest, Joe from Elmwood Park, was into sadism and bondage and wanted $20 more for everything he did. Gacy just wanted to get blown. Joe, too, went to the river in Gacy's trunk. Another victim, Gacy said, pulled a knife on him, took money from his wallet, then said he wasn't done with Gacy sexually. This enraged the contractor, who first showed the youth some magic tricks, then got the rope around his neck. He was buried in the crawl space.

Gacy said he killed his first victim by stabbing him. Gacy was married then; his wife was away. The two men had sex, then went to sleep. Awakening, Gacy saw the man coming at him with a knife; the man stabbed him in the right forearm. They fought, and Gacy got the knife away from him. Gacy finally stabbed the man to death and buried him in the crawl space.

Several years ago, Gacy said, he had a drag queen, who danced for him. "He was real weird," he said. "God didn't put people on earth to do that." Gacy read him a verse from the Bible: "Yea, though I walk through the valley of the shadow of death, I will fear no evil." He twisted the rope twice, then finished reading his victim the Twenty-third Psalm before twisting the rope the final time.

Gacy told of bringing two youths home one night. He told one of them he would tighten the rope around the boy's neck three times, so he would get an erection, then Gacy would blow him. Gacy twisted the rope until the youth died. He went into the other room and told the other boy his friend was dead.

The boy didn't believe him. Gacy led him, handcuffed, to the other room and strangled him in front of the body of his friend.

Occasionally an officer asked a question, but mostly it was Gacy who spoke, continuously, clinically, without any discernible signs of remorse. At first he made pointed and repeated reference to Jack Hanley, his "other" personality. "You would have to ask Jack that," he would say in response to a question, or, "That was Jack talking," as an afterthought to his own remarks. As he went on, however, he mentioned "Jack" less frequently; then, for a long while, not at all. At one point, Stevens asked a question, adding, "Isn't that right, Jack?" Gacy made no acknowledgment of the question until Stevens called him John.

Gacy said he frequently used the name Jack Hanley in his early morning prowling. He cruised the streets around Bughouse Square, a park on the Near North Side that was a gathering place once shared by radicals and off-beat humanity, now a homosexual hustling-ground. With his black car and spotlights, dressed in his black leather jacket, Gacy commonly convinced his prey that he was a policeman, and they did as he told them. Sometimes he threatened them as cop Jack Hanley; other times he gave them his "Hanley" name as someone they could call at City Hall if they ever needed help.

At Bughouse Square, Gacy didn't have to look far for potential partners. After stalking one, he would offer the youth a cigarette, then ask if he were interested in having a party. The discussion would turn to price, which ranged from $5 to $50. Gacy said he had encounters with 150 such people, and he paid all of them. He added that he didn't always have sex with the young men he picked up. Sometimes they went to his house, undressed, and just sat talking. Some had hard-luck stories. These he let go. He even gave a few of them money. The sex he did have was always oral, unless his partner consented to something else. He never bothered straight people.

The books taken from his house, Gacy said, were not his. He would not spend money on that type of reading matter. He used the books only to stimulate some of his victims.

Over the years, Gacy developed a fixed schedule for his cruising. After working long days in construction, sometimes until 10 P.M., he would go whoring late at night. After making his liaisons, he had sex between 1 and 3 A.M. Except for two victims, one of them Rob Piest, all died between 3 and 6 A.M.

Gacy was adamant on one point: he was *not,* he said, a homosexual. In fact, he had a very strong fear of being one. He disliked gay men and queens and the bars they frequented. "A man is a man," he said, "and if he didn't like girls, there was something wrong with him." He didn't like sadism and masochism and thought that those who practiced such things were very weird. Nor did he like to be propositioned. He once threw a man out of his car for offering him $10 for sex. Gacy found that insulting. *He,* John Gacy, would make any and all propositions. He was always the dominant one. As for those who sold their bodies, he had utmost contempt. If they lied to him, or were greedy and tried to rip him off, they would have something done to them.

Gacy mentioned Jeffrey Rignall and acknowledged that he had been charged with attacking the man, although he was vague about the details. He spoke of his sexual relationship with both Gray and Walsh, how they complied when they wanted something of him. He told his version of the fight with Walsh at the tavern in Cicero, after which he was hospitalized. He described the last moments of a victim, probably Szyc, who had his car title with him. Gacy said he later gave the vehicle to Walsh.

Gacy told of other victims, identifying them by where he met them or where they were from, but he said he was unable to recall any names the investigators didn't already have. In that sense, Gacy was still in control, giving nothing away. He did, however, say that the crawl space was not the limit of his activity at 8213 Summerdale: John Butkovich was buried under the garage.

When he finished his statement an hour or so before dawn, he left the assemblage of police officers awestruck, some disbelieving. Thirty bodies. Could it be possible? Or was Gacy lying again?

Bedoe openly and profanely voiced his skepticism. He went back to Gacy and asked him to go over his account of Rob Piest's disappearance. Gacy stuck by his story. The boy had not been coerced to come with him from Nisson's, and his body was indeed in the Des Plaines River. One of the sheriff's investigators called the state police to see if they had a log entry corroborating Gacy's story of being stuck on the Tri-State Tollway early on the morning of December 13. They did. Now we knew how the mud got on his car and in his trunk and were inclined to believe his story about dumping Piest's body in the river.

Gacy now was in the company of his older sister in a small interrogation room. At his request, she had been awakened by a sheriff's policeman and brought from her home to the station. She was sobbing hysterically at Gacy's side, begging her brother to tell the police everything he knew. While she cried, a dazed Amirante walked aimlessly in the corridor, and the combined forces of sheriff's and Des Plaines police planned their next move: the trip to the bridge on Interstate 55.

"A Pack of Dogs Chasing a Bone"

Larry Schreiner, a Chicago vice detective for many years, is a free-lance journalist. His competitors say he's the kind of guy who sleeps with police radios stuck in his ears. Chicago crime reporters have never been starved for lack of material, and the events of Thursday, December 21, would make yet another of the city's legendary police stories. Late that evening, Schreiner found himself mapping the path of the next day's stampede.

When he received word from a tipster who had monitored some of the afternoon radio traffic, Schreiner was not entirely unfamiliar with the Gacy case. Living just a few blocks from the contractor's house, he himself had listened to the surveillance transmissions with growing interest. He also recalled an incident of a month before when, on a busy thoroughfare, his vehicle had been cut off by a black car sporting red and white spotlights. Thinking he knew all the local politicians, he made a license check and learned that the car was registered to PDM Contractors at 8213 Summerdale. With the house at that address now under surveillance, he saw an interesting story taking shape.

Arriving at Gacy's place shortly before midnight, Schreiner spotted an old police buddy who told him, "I can't say anything, but don't leave this house." After the main group of investigators had left, Schreiner cooked up a ruse with the one other journalist then at the scene, a free-lance photographer. While the photographer knocked on the front door, Schreiner slipped back to the rear of the house, switched on his floodlights, and made some shots through the windows on 16 mm. film. Next, he began canvassing the neighborhood. By dawn, Schreiner's footage was appearing with Jay Levine's reports on Chicago's Channel 7 and the ABC network, and he was calling in as a "man on the street" from the telephone in his car to Wally Phillips's popular morning radio show on WGN.

Late Thursday evening, the city desk at the Chicago *Sun-Times* was having trouble getting solid information on the story, so they called their ace crime reporter, Art Petacque, at home for help. Petacque, who had been told earlier of Piest's disappearance by a colleague who was a neighbor of the boy's parents, made a few calls. The reporter, who is well known for his pipeline to the sheriff's police, talked to a source, who, in turn, called the Des Plaines police and got Gacy's telephone number for him. Petacque called the house, talked with a sheriff's policeman he knew well, and was told that they had two bodies and that Gacy had said he had killed more than thirty. By sunrise, the final Friday edition of the *Sun-Times* was alerting its readers to yet another crime story that would dominate news coverage in the weeks ahead.

When on Friday morning Eugenia Godzik walked into the kitchen of the modest white house where she lived with her parents on Chicago's Northwest Side, she found her mother, Mrs. Eugenia Godzik, in tears. The radio on the counter was tuned to Wally Phillips. The talk was of Gacy . . . bodies . . . Gacy.

"That's the man Gregory worked for," Mrs. Godzik cried in anguish. Gregory, a slender, handsome seventeen-year-old with long blond hair and gray eyes, had vanished a little more than two years earlier, in fact, two years to the day before Rob Piest's disappearance. It was a Saturday night. His sister, Eugenia, six years older than Gregory, and her parents teased the boy for not going to mass with them: they knew that Greg had just made up with his girlfriend, Judy Patterson, and had a special date planned. The last verified reports of anyone seeing Gregory Godzik came from Judy and her mother, who said goodnight to him at their house shortly after midnight.

Like Rob Piest, Greg had no reason whatever to run away. He was a warm and loving boy who always stayed close to home. He had been working since he was in the seventh grade, delivering newspapers and cutting grass; now a senior at Taft High School, he was enrolled in an afternoon work program. He was planning to go to college in the fall.

He loved animals and had many pets, and was forever nursing injured crows and stray cats back to health. To his sister he was a sentimental pussycat. The playing of "Auld Lang Syne" on a New Year's Eve television show reduced him to tears. He was devoted to his mother, a woman of joyful disposition who happily mended his friends' jackets during their frequent visits to the Godziks. Greg never left the house without kissing his mother goodbye.

Although he and Judy had temporarily fallen out, he was obviously smitten by her and had told his mother fervently, "She's the girl I love, and I'm going to marry her." Mrs. Godzik had cautioned him to go easy and said that he was still young, but if it was meant to be, it *would* be. Greg was overjoyed when Judy agreed to a reconciliation, and he grabbed his mother and danced round and round with her while telling her of his forthcoming big date on Saturday night. Greg was becoming very conscious of his appearance, and, for Christmas, he had asked for clothing and a special hairbrush. His family had complied with his wishes. Now, more than two years later, as Schreiner's reports were coming over the kitchen radio, Greg's gifts lay in another room, still unwrapped.

On Sunday morning, December 12, 1976, Eugenia Godzik had peered into her son's room and saw that his bed was still made. Alarmed, she hurried down to the living room and den. She saw no sign of Greg anywhere. She called his friends. Several of them had seen Greg and Judy the night before, but not since. She called the Chicago police and was told that it was department policy to do nothing for twenty-four hours. Kids, after all, run away by the thousands, they said, and within the one-day grace period many of them return home.

Later that day, a friend of Greg's came by and told Mrs. Godzik that another youth had seen Greg's car parked near a pet store in Niles. Sure enough, his burgundy-colored 1965 Pontiac Catalina, which he had bought for $80 two months earlier, was there, its doors unlocked. That was an unmistakable sign something was amiss: the car was Greg's greatest pride, and he always locked it.

The two years since he had vanished had been a time of great hope and heartbreak for the family, especially for Mrs. Godzik, who, after her work as a Chicago school lunchroom supervisor, pursued every avenue she could think of to find her son. After learning little from his friends and schoolmates, she called his employer. Only a few weeks before his disappearance, Greg had come home with the news that he was quitting the lumber company where he was working for $2.20 an hour. A contractor named John Gacy had offered him $5.50, plus the promise of summer employment and the opportunity to travel out of town, where, Greg was told, the money was really big. Mrs. Godzik was not pleased about Greg's working in construction and told him that leaving town was out of the question. Still, Greg brought home reports of what a nice guy his employer was, how he performed as a clown for children, how he'd always treat his workers to a Coke at quitting time. Only once was she truly upset by his job: Greg came home late and the family was already sitting at the dining table. "Where have you been?" she asked.

"I was working at Gacy's house," Greg replied. "We had to dig trenches for some kind of tiles."

Four days after his disappearance, Mrs. Godzik called Gacy, who said that Greg had left a message saying he would be at work the day before, but he had never shown up.

"How do you know it was Gregory?" Mrs. Godzik asked.

"Because I have a tape recording of it," Gacy answered.

"Do you still have it?"

"No, I erased it."

The next time Mrs. Godzik called, Gacy said he still owed Greg some money and would come by sometime and give it to her. (He never did.)

Gacy tried to reassure Mrs. Godzik. "You know how these kids are," he said. "I told Greg I ran away when I was eighteen. I told my mother I was going for gas, and I didn't come back for I don't know how long. You know, that could have happened to Greg."

"But he's not the type," Mrs. Godzik said anxiously.

Don't worry, Gacy said. He'll come back.

The last time she called Gacy's house, a youth answered the phone. He had not seen Greg for some time.

"What are you doing there?" Mrs. Godzik asked.

"I live here," the youth replied.

"Don't you have a home?"

"No, I don't want to live at home."

"But doesn't your mother want you home? I can't stand it without my son. I think you belong at home, not with strangers."

"Oh, this guy's real good to me," the youth replied.

The Chicago police made routine follow-up checks after Greg's disappearance, but they went to no great lengths after the boy was reported seen by several witnesses at Taft High School. The police did not check with Gacy until nearly three months had passed. Once a young officer enthusiastically told Mrs. Godzik he had learned that a youth fitting Greg's description was working at a lumber company. Excited, Mrs. Godzik went to see for herself. The boy was not her son.

She called halfway houses and any institutions that she thought might deal with runaway youths. Only the Salvation Army offered her any help. The other organizations brushed her off, saying that she was intruding into their confidential sphere. In desperation, she turned to a professional investigator.

Anthony J. Pellicano, Jr., is a wiry, long-nosed private detective who once told the Chicago *Tribune* that he was "the greatest investigator in the city." Pellicano rode the crest of publicity. He had gained fame in his specialty of uncovering illegal wiretaps and had been credited with finding Yoko Ono's missing son. On the day he contracted with the Godzik family to search for Greg, he scored another publicity coup by finding the reamins of showman Michael Todd, which had been stolen some days before from a cemetery in Forest Park. He made the discovery in the presence of police and a television news anchorman.

Mr. Godzik was a retired shipping clerk, Mrs. Godzik's wages were modest. Paying Pellicano's fee would severely strain their finances. Nonetheless, they settled on a price of $15,000 of which $5,000 would be paid as a retainer and the remaining $10,000 when Pellicano found Greg, either dead or alive, within the two-year life of the contract. "I don't know how I can pay you ten thousand dollars," Mrs. Godzik told the investigator, "but I would work my fingers to the bone if you would find Greg." The family scraped together what they could and borrowed the remainder of the $5,000 from Mrs. Godzik's mother.

Despite Pellicano's reputation for a high success rate, the Godziks were unhappy with him from the start. Although Pellicano warned them that he could not give them a step-by-step accounting of his efforts and promised a written report only when he had fulfilled his mission, the Godziks felt that he did not press the investigation with the vigor they expected. They thought he should pursue such leads as Greg's friends might offer; Pellicano later said he chose to act on the information he got from law enforcement sources. The Godziks later insisted that they had given him Gacy's name; Pellicano said they never did, that they told him Greg worked at a gas station. But despite whatever failures of communication may have existed at the time, Mrs. Godzik continued to pin fervent hopes on Pellicano to find her son alive.

In mid-December, 1978, Eugenia Godzik was especially saddened when she heard the news of Rob Piest's disappearance. "Oh, I feel so sorry for that family," she told friends. "I know what they are going through."

Mrs. Godzik's last sign of hope came on her birthday, the night before the news of John Gacy filled the airwaves. Arriving home from an errand, she saw her daughter sitting in their living room in the company of police officers. Mrs. Godzik's mouth widened into a bright smile and she asked eagerly, "Oh! Did you find Gregory?"

"I have some bad news for you," one of the officers said. "Your house was burglarized."

With just a hint of approaching daylight in the southeast, a three-car procession departed from the police station for the bridge over the Des Plaines River on Interstate 55. Schultz had come to me earlier, saying that Gacy was willing to make the trip, but he had asked one favor in return: he wanted the police to take him to Maryhill Cemetery for one last visit to his father's grave. "He's got it," I told Schultz. We would do our best, security requirements permitting, to honor his request.

In the company were Schultz and Robinson, Gacy's two attorneys, his older sister, and Pickell, Bettiker, and Sommerschield. Gacy rode with Schultz and Robinson. He kept nodding off to sleep. During his waking moments, his conversation with the officers was light. As they drove the fifty-odd miles, the sky gradually turned brilliant orange in the east, giving promise that the shortest day of the year would be sunny and crisp. Soon the flow of semitrailers rolling in from the West Coast became mixed with a greater surge of commuter traffic as the morning rush hour began.

They crossed the bridge going south, then took the Arsenal Road turnoff to get back into the northbound lanes. A state police marker car was waiting for them at the river. As the officer diverted traffic into a single lane, Gacy and his police escort walked out onto the windy span. When they came to the fifth upright structural beam, Gacy stopped, looked over the low railing, and pointed to the water, about forty feet below. Robinson and Schultz each clutched one of his arms, for fear he might jump. This, Gacy said, was where he had dropped Rob Piest and the other four bodies.

The river at the bridge is about a hundred yards wide. The banks were lined with shelves of ice and snow, but the mainstream was open, and the surface of the deep bluish brown water was ruffled by a brisk wind out of the southwest. As the officers peered over the railing, the long shadows of the traffic passing against the sunrise flickered over them. Suddenly they were motioned back to the cars.

A television truck had parked a couple of hundred yards south, and a minicam crew was running toward them. The officers hustled Gacy to the cars and hurriedly departed. As they drove off, they looked back and saw a newsman running alongside the state policeman's car, trying to question him. It was Jay Levine.

A large crowd of curiosity seekers had gathered at 8213 Summerdale, and the press was there in force. Police had roped off the front of Gacy's property and erected barriers, closing the street to all but local residential traffic and law enforcement vehicles. Since the search, a parade of police brass had been visiting the site. Some officers were not always recognized in the confusion of a multijurisdictional crime scene. Deputy Chief Richard Quagliano of the sheriff's police was denied entrance by one of his own men until the young officer was set straight, and Chief Alfano of Des Plaines encountered a similar challenge. The house was already creaking under the footsteps of Des Plaines and sheriff's policemen and medical examiner's and state's attorney's personnel; now Chicago policemen were dropping by, wanting to view the horrible scene that lay just beyond their jurisdiction.

When Robinson and Schultz arrived with Gacy their car was escorted through the surging mob into the driveway and back to the garage. Reporters and crews immediately went crashing through the side yards of the neighbors to get a view of the confessed mass-murderer. Police responded by roping off the entire property.

Shielded by several officers, Gacy was led into the garage, where he immediately began complaining about the disorder left by investigators. Bettiker reminded him that he was there to point out the location of the body buried in the floor. They moved to the narrow workshed area in the southeast corner. There Gacy again complained about the mess and began tidying up the shelves and cabinets. Officers noticed numerous jars of Vaseline amidst the construction material. Gacy began moving some tools and iron bars, and Bettiker again told him to get down to business.

"What do you think I'm doing?" Gacy snapped. "Give me something to mark with."

One of the officers handed him a can of black spray paint. It didn't work. He was given another. Gacy then sprayed a large square on the floor with an X inside. "Dig there," he said. Asked if he knew who the victim was, Gacy replied, "John Butkovich." Like the others, Gacy said, the youth had been strangled. His head was to the south. Gacy picked up a sledgehammer and tapped it inside the mark as if taking aim. Bettiker told him that the police would do the digging.

Now, as a conciliatory gesture, I had Gacy brought inside the house because he had expressed concern about his dog and his plants. He erupted in anger when he saw his house in disarray and mud tracked over his floors, and said he was all through cooperating with us. We had expected that, and that was why we had taken him to the garage first. He was bustling about, taking off his coat as if he planned to stay, when I got tired of his antics. "Why is this man wandering around loose?" I shouted to a couple of officers milling around. "Cuff him!" Gacy, sulking, offered no further information. I ordered him taken back to the station.

By now, Gacy's unlisted phone number, which was on his various business cards, had gotten into the hands of many reporters, as well as cranks who were calling for the sport of it. The officers who answered call after call would listen for a moment, then slam down the receiver, cursing. Braun told Bedoe to arrange for new phone service.

After Gacy's overnight confessions, we were exhausted to the point of virtual numbness. The previous week had been sleepless enough, and now some of us had been on the job for almost thirty hours straight. Our physical depletion was almost total. Still, we had to keep going. I went back to Des Plaines.

We could not hold Gacy on the marijuana arrest any longer. His processing complete, he would be able to post bail. We would have to charge him with murder or release him. But could we hold him without bond for the murder of Rob Piest when we had no body, despite Gacy's confessions of other killings? If the defense objected, as they surely would, we could agrue that Dr. Stein had not yet made any identifications and hope that the judge would deny bail.

It took several hours and numerous telephone calls with my superiors, Larry O'Gara and Bill Kunkle, before I had the criminal complaint for the murder of Rob Piest prepared and ready to take to the judge. Lang and Ryan rushed Gacy from the police station into the Civic Center and up to Judge Peters's tiny third-floor courtroom, fighting off newsmen all the way. The room had but two pews, and it was jammed. My assistants Mike Corkell and Larry Finder appeared with me, and Sam Amirante stood beside a very haggard looking Gacy. I was so tired I could hardly think.

Kozenczak was the state's witness. First, he was sworn to the complaint, which he had signed, charging Gacy with murder. The subsequent hearing went raggedly, probably because both sides were exhausted. I argued against releasing

Gacy because of the murder charge and his prior criminal record. In the end, Judge Peters denied bail, and I was greatly relieved. He set a preliminary hearing for December 29, the Friday before the New Year, and ordered Gacy transferred to the Cook County Department of Corrections. At Amirante's request—the lawyer said he thought Gacy was a "very sick individual"—Peters ordered the prisoner sent to Cermak Hospital, the medical wing of the jail. I offered no objection.

A search warrant is valid only while the police officers remain on the premises, and so we would have 8213 Summerdale guarded by police twenty-four hours a day until the last body and pertinent piece of evidence was recovered. While we had valid legal position—that police were now simply processing a known crime scene—there was no sense in taking any chances. To assure our legal situation, I had Finder prepare two more search warrants, one that would inform the court of Gacy's admission that he had buried a body in his garage, and the other attesting to the presence of human remains in the crawl space. Both were signed on Friday afternoon.

Because of the overriding necessity to find Rob Piest's body, I turned next to organizing a search of the Des Plaines River downstream from the I-55 bridge. Special Agent Wayne Fieroh of the Illinois Department of Law Enforcement told me they could supply a helicopter from Springfield. Next I called the sheriffs of Will and Grundy counties, through which the Des Plaines flows before becoming part of the Illinois River. Personnel there, working in conjunction with local fire department divers, are accustomed to dealing with bodies that float downstream from Chicago. I sent two of my assistants, Frank Nolan and Bill Ward, to monitor the river operation.

Late in the afternoon, in the rear of the police station, Finder saw Gacy sitting in an interview room. Gacy beckoned to him. He wanted someone to talk to. Finder warned him that he was an assistant state's attorney and any statements Gacy made might be used against him.

"You've never done anything wrong to me, and I've never done anything wrong to you," Gacy said, "so there's no reason we can't talk." When Finder asked if Gacy's lawyers would approve, Gacy said that they worked for *him* and if *he* wanted to talk, he would. Corkell came in, and Finder said that if the conversation were to continue, he would have to read Gacy the Miranda rights. Gacy replied that he had been given his rights so many times, he knew them by heart. He took Finder's plastic card and read them himself.

Finder was just asking about Rob Piest when LeRoy Stevens joined them. He had no objection to Gacy's talking. The contractor repeated his plea to visit his father's grave, and Finder agreed to relay his request. After Stevens left, Finder asked Gacy if he was relieved to have confessed. Gacy said he was, but that he was was also unhappy. He offered nothing more. Finder gave a policeman some money to get Gacy a cup of soup, and he and Corkell left.

About forty-five minutes later, in the Detective Bureau, Albrecht told Finder that Gacy still wanted to talk, this time with Albrecht and Finder. Albrecht had just moved Gacy to the lockup. The contractor was sitting on the cot in his cell when they arrived.

"Hello, Larry," he said, looking very alert. "Where's my soup?" Finder said it should be coming shortly and once again went through the Miranda briefing. Gacy impatiently recited the rights from memory, then started to talk about Rob Piest.

Gacy said that he had returned to Nisson Pharmacy to pick up his appointment book because he relied on it heavily. When he left the drugstore, he saw Rob Piest come out the door and motioned to him to get into his car. Piest told him he wanted to discuss a job. Because the boy said he had only a half hour or so, Gacy said they would drive and talk.

Gacy continued his own version of that evening. He said he set out for his house, and on the way he said that he was a very liberal person; Rob said he was, too. Gacy asked if he would have sexual relations with a man. Rob didn't think he would. Asked if he would do it for a lot of money, the boy said, according to Gacy, that he'd do almost anything for a lot of money. Gacy said again that he was bisexual and that he never forced sex on an unwilling partner.

At the house, Gacy said, he showed the boy some of his clown tricks, including the one with the handcuffs. Once he was manacled, Rob became distressed but did not try to stop Gacy from removing his pants. Gacy then tried to give him a blow job, and the boy broke into tears. The contractor said he had only one thing more to show Rob, the rope trick.

Finder asked Gacy to explain it. The contractor asked if he could have a piece of rope.

"There's no way I'm going to get you any rope, John," Albrecht said.

"Shit, I'm not going to kill you," Gacy said. "I'll tell you what. Larry, stick your hand through the bars and make a fist." Reluctantly, Finder complied. "Now pretend your fist is a head and your wrist is a neck." Gacy took his rosary out of his right pants pocket, looped it around Finder's wrist, and tied a series of three knots. Then he stuck a pen between the second and third knots, saying that it was just like the stick he used for the real thing. Three or four quick turns, and the victim was strangled. Finder, who is Jewish, later said that Gacy's explicit demonstration, added to his own sense of mystery about the powers of the rosary, made his knees turn to jelly.

Gacy said he then took the boy's body to bed and slept next to it. He showed the two men how, the following morning, he had slung it over his shoulder and carried it up the attic ladder.

Albrecht asked if he had had anal intercourse with the body.

"I didn't," Gacy said, "but Jack might have."

"Did Jack usually have anal sex with his victims?" Albrecht asked.

Gacy nodded and said he couldn't get an erection any other way.

Albrecht asked how he managed to get the rope around the victims' necks. Gacy replied that sometimes he didn't have to—the boys themselves would put it on, anticipating an interesting trick. After repeating his earlier account of the disposal of Piest's body, Gacy reflected for a moment. The appointment book at Nisson's—that was the rub. Had he not forgotten it, he said, he would not have killed Rob Piest and none of this would have happened.

Gacy now described his encounter with his first victim, the one he said he stabbed to death in 1974. He said he met the young man in the Greyhound bus station in downtown Chicago. The man wanted to cruise the city, looking for girls. After they searched in vain, Gacy tried to find out if his companion was bisexual. He asked if there was more than one way to have sex. When the young man said that two males could do it, Gacy feigned ignorance. His companion said that either a guy or girl could give a blow job, it was all the same. They drove to Gacy's house and had sex. After killing the young man the next morning, Gacy buried the body in the crawl space and poured concrete over it.

Gacy said that he had sexual relationships with males in his house while he was married. His wife was often away, either for the night with friends, or out of town.

Albrecht asked Gacy if he could precisely locate the bodies in the crawl space. Gacy asked permission to draw a diagram, and Albrecht gave him a pen and a blank receipt form for prisoners' belongings. As he drew his sketch on the back, Gacy asked if Gray and Walsh had been arrested yet. He said they were guilty of being his accomplices, then backed off and said that they had only dug trenches. He said that the officers were mistaken if they believed that he had used lime to dissolve the bodies. The crawl space, he said, had always been musty from the dampness, and he had used the lime only to get rid of the odor.

Gacy drew the first portion of the diagram very neatly, using a line to designate each grave. He indicated the concrete under which his first victim was interred. He said that some of the trenches had more than one body in them and he could no longer remember the number. As he was finishing his sketch, he clenched his fists tightly, closed his eyes, and remained motionless for almost a minute. He then relaxed, opened his eyes, and looked at the diagram. "What's going on?" he asked. "Oh, I see Jack drew a picture of the crawl space." This seemed very contrived to Finder and Albrecht, and they said they would see him again after he got some rest. "What did I say?" Gacy asked, in a wounded tone as the two men departed. "What did I do wrong?"

About an hour later, Albrecht and Finder returned to the lockup with pictures of two victims whose bodies had been found in the Des Plaines River. Ward had brought the photos back from the search operation. Rounding a blind corner, Finder jumped in a jolt of fright, almost knocking down Albrecht: He had seen the figure of a man in front of the cell and at first glance thought it was Gacy. It was Officer James

Kinsella guarding the prisoner, who now was placidly sleeping on his cot.

Albrecht awakened Gacy and showed him the photographs, one of which was of a Frank Landingin, whose bond slip had been found in Gacy's house. Gacy said he had known Landingin from a bar in Franklin Park but he didn't think the man was one of his victims. He said he was not familiar with the other one at all.

When Eugenia Godzik heard the horrifying news on the radio in her mother's kitchen, she picked up the phone and dialed 911, the Chicago police emergency number. She explained why she feared that her brother might be among the victims buried in Gacy's crawl space, and she begged for help. The dispatcher knew nothing about the reports from Summerdale and kept telling her to calm down. Finally, he said he would take her number and call back. Eugenia telephoned one of her girlfriends and asked to speak with her father, a Chicago homicide detective. He knew nothing about the case either but said he would check. Five minutes later, the Godzik's phone rang.

"Eugenia," the detective said, "it's very, very serious. There are many bodies. Tell your dentist to be prepared to send in Greg's records."

She called the family dentist, John Davis, who was not yet in his office. He returned her call at 8 o'clock and said he would begin gathering the necessary material. Gregory had had root-canal treatment for an infected tooth just before his disappearance; Davis had X-rays of that work and of the gold crown he had put in. The dentist also had made a point of keeping the models he'd made of Greg's teeth, knowing that the boy was missing and that they might be needed for identification.

Davis called the Chicago police and was told they were not involved in the case. He called the sheriff's police, but they didn't know where he should send the records. He talked to someone on the *Tribune*'s city desk, who didn't answer his question and instead began pumping the doctor for information. Davis hung up. He began making duplicates of the models, just in case.

That evening Davis got a phone call at home from a man asking if the dentist would meet him after dinner and give him the records. It was Pellicano. Davis knew that the Godziks had hired a private investigator, but he told Pellicano that he couldn't release anything until first he checked with Mrs. Godzik.

By the time Davis talked to her, she was worn down from the ordeal of facing the horde of reporters camped on her doorstep, and she readily gave her permission to release the records to Pellicano. Davis, however, recognized the stress she had been under, and first called two lawyer friends. Neither was home. Davis decided to try the sheriff's police again. This time he insisted on talking with someone involved in the case. He was put on hold for a long time. Finally, a sergeant came on the line. The officer told him that under no circumstances could he give any evidence to anyone except the sheriff's police.

Minutes later, Pellicano called back, asking Davis to meet him right away at the dentist's office. Davis declined and turned the materials over to a sheriff's investigator the next morning.

By Saturday morning, I was alarmed by some of the information pouring out of the press. Obviously there were leaks galore, from the sheriff's policemen, from Des Plaines, maybe from my office as well. Jay Levine had developed the story on his own the first night but, as he would later admit, a policeman's leak was what had sent him scurrying to the river. A day later, parts of Gacy's statements were appearing in the press, plus a lot of other information that was dreadfully erroneous. This torrent of leaks could jeopardize the prosecution.

Gacy was still in custody of the Des Plaines police, and Kozenczak was getting anxious to send him to the Cook County jail. Suburban police departments are not equipped to lodge prisoners for very long, especially those who attract press attention and present security problems. Kozenczak, therefore, eagerly accepted the suggestion that his own people drive Gacy to Cermak Hospital rather than wait for the county van to pick him up. Tovar, Ryan, and Adams would make the trip.

They brought a stake-out car with Indiana plates into the security garage while guards got Gacy ready. Tovar, meanwhile, announced the plan to several members of the press in what his partners regarded as a bid to get on television. By the time the garage doors were opened and Gacy was hustled into the car with his jacket pulled up over his head, the cameras were ready and rolling.

"Look at them!" Gacy said as they drove through the throng. "They're like a pack of dogs chasing a bone." After reflecting a moment on his notoriety, Gacy asked if local TV anchorman Walter Jacobson and columnist Mike Royko had called asking for him. He was told they hadn't. "They're good friends of mine," he said. "I figured they'd be calling." A press caravan fell in behind the Des Plaines car, one vehicle with a camera poking out of its sun roof.

Gacy reminded the officers that he still wanted to see his father's grave. Tovar, driving, cleared his throat. He had hoped the subject wouldn't arise.

"Look behind us, John," he said. "Do you want them to take pictures of you and go stomping all around your dad's grave?" Gacy thought about it a moment. Screw it, he said finally. He wouldn't give them the satisfaction.

Gacy said he remembered Tovar from the day he'd come into the station and asked Adams and Ryan how they fit into the investigation. Tovar said that if they talked about the case, they would have to read him his rights again.

"Shit," Gacy said. "They've been given to me so many times, I know them by heart." Tovar recited them anyway, then asked Gacy about his last five victims. As far as Gacy recalled, he had dumped them all in the river, and the Piest boy was the last one.

"How many did you kill?" Tovar asked.

"I told my lawyers thirty or thirty-five," Gacy said. "But I don't know, there could be thirty-five, forty-five—who knows?" In his rear-view mirror, Tovar saw Gacy smirking.

"Are you religious?" Adams asked. "Do you go to church?" Gacy said he used to. Tovar asked him about the victim before Rob Piest.

Gacy said his name was "something-Joe" and he thought he was from Elmwood Park. "People into that kind of sex," he said, "you only know by nicknames." The youth was a weird little guy, Gacy said, into masochism. "But I took care of him," he said jauntily. "I tended to his particular sexual inclination." Gacy explained that he had put the youth into the two-by-four, doubling him over and chaining his wrists and ankles together. "Since he liked pain," Gacy said, "I did the ultimate number on him." Tovar asked how he got the idea for the board. "From Elmer Wayne Henley," Gacy answered. "The guy in Texas."

As Gacy rambled on, he glanced over his shoulder. "Hell, if I was driving," he said, "I would have lost those assholes a long time ago." He asked again: "Were the officers sure Jacobson and Royko hadn't called? Are you being careful in my house?" he continued. "Making sure it isn't damaged."

In his mirror, Tovar could see that Adams was seething over Gacy's flippancy.

"Did the Piest boy suffer when you killed him?" Adams asked. Gacy said he didn't remember and changed the subject.

Adams turned and stared at him, hard. "I asked you, and I'm going to ask you again: Did the Piest boy suffer when you killed him?"

Gacy got the message. "No," he said seriously. "I don't think he did."

The officers drove in the entrance of the Cook County jail at 26th and California Streets, where they were informed they would have to escort Gacy themselves to the Cermak Hospital facility. At four minutes before noon on Saturday, December 23, 1978, they surrendered custody of their prisoner to county authorities. It was the thirteenth day of the John Wayne Gacy case, and the Des Plaines Police Department would never be the same again.

By the time Christmas was over, most of us would agree that it was the worst holiday in memory. Physically we were all burned out, but it was probably the realization of the evil we had uncovered that dispirited us most of all. Not even the triumph of the arrest seemed to mitigate this assault on our sensibilities.

On Friday night, I gathered my staff to talk things over. We went out for a few beers, more to escape than anything else.

Already the specter of power politics was looming in the state's attorney's office. My bosses downtown had dispatched one of their top trial lawyers, Bob Egan, to help us, and several of my assistants warned me that our staff was on the verge of getting shunted aside. I thought they might be right.

The Des Plaines police were facing a similar problem, even though they had broken the case. Since the sheriff's police had taken command of the scene at Summerdale, their vehicles were prominently displayed in the glare of television flood-lights, and their activities were getting the major share of the coverage. The Des Plaines police simply didn't know how to react—they were novices alongside the more worldly sheriff's department, which had a well-oiled machine specifically tuned up for publicity outreach.

Soon internal dissension and jealousies would erupt within the Des Plaines force itself, as several officers began taking credit for cracking the case singlehandedly. The department formed into factions, with the surveillance officers pitted against the detectives and the patrol division resentful of both.

For the moment, however, most of us were simply content to take a well-earned two-day respite and put the case out of our minds as best we could. It had been a remarkable piece of investigative work and, despite a few flaws, I was proud of our accomplishment. Without the perseverance of the Des Plaines detectives, without the dogged pursuit by the surveillance force and the psychological effect it had on Gacy, and without the sharpness and persistence of investigators Greg Bedoe and Sergeant Joe Hein, it could not have been done.

When the hunt was over, Bob Schultz went home and got into a hot tub his wife had drawn for him. As he lay in the soothing water he broke into tears. He sobbed unabashedly for ten minutes. He was not the only police officer who cried.

Before Greg could put this phase of the case behind him, he had to resolve something in his mind. On the first day of the recovery at Summerdale he had watched the evidence techni-cians at work in the crawl space, and he could not comprehend the reality of the bones they brought up. Unrecognizable, they were only what other people said they were; they meant nothing to him. On Saturday afternoon, he went back to the house to try to understand. It was not until he saw a human skull that he knew in himself that this place was the graveyard of formerly living men.

Even John Gacy was moved. "Dear Mom and family," he wrote in a letter on Christmas Eve, 1978. "Please forgive me for what I am about to tell you. I have been very sick for a long time (both mentally and physically). . . . I wish I had had help sooner. May God forgive me. . . ."

The Crawl Space

In the news on the morning the Gacy case broke, officials in Washington announced that it would cost $4 million to airlift the 911 bodies of victims from the Jonestown, Guyana, mass slaying of the previous month. Our task was no less disturbing: recovery of the—God knew how many—bodies of victims from John Gacy's crawl space. Already people were making allusions to two other cases of mass-killings: Juan Corona, who was found guilty in California, in 1973, of murdering twenty-five migrant fieldhands; and Elmer Wayne Henley, Jr., who was convicted the following year in Texas for his participation in a homosexual torture ring that killed twenty-seven boys.

These were ominous comparisons, and not just because of the magnitude of the crimes. Both convictions had been reversed by higher courts earlier in the year, Corona's in May, and Henley's the day before Gacy's arrest. We wanted to avoid any errors in the recovery and identification of the bodies that might later help overturn a conviction. The Cook County sheriff's police was ordered to conduct an operation that would be exemplary in its professionalism.

It soon became obvious that this would be no leisurely excavation in the Yucatán, with camel's hair brushes and renewable grants. The pressure from the press and the families of the missing youths was tremendous. Nonetheless, we proceeded with great care. The evidence technicians would be governed by strict rules of accountability. The crawl space would be divided into quadrants, and all remains described in precise measurements. The technicians were expected to recover every bit of evidence, human or otherwise, even if that required sifting through every cubic centimeter of earth.

After a professional house mover inspected the crawl space, we discarded the idea of raising the dwelling. That would require jacking pads, which obviously would disrupt the buried evidence, and there wasn't sufficient clearance at the side of the house to bring in the necessary long I-beams. Furthermore, the rear addition would have to be disengaged from the rest of the house, causing substantial damage. We were still assuming that after we did what was necessary to recover the bodies, we would have to restore the house to the condition in which we found it. In any event, raising the house would expose the excavation to both the weather and the public. Finally, in the interests of expediency and legality—and because it was the most feasible plan—we decided to remove the flooring to gain access to the crawl space.

Sergeant Ernest Marinelli, a large and gregarious man in the criminal intelligence unit who had worked as a rough carpenter in college, was assigned to deal with structural matters. Almost immediately he and his men saw that Gacy's 1950s-vintage house was much sturdier than contemporary models; their saws soon burned out cutting the oak flooring. They sought the help of the neighboring Rosemont and Chicago fire departments, who obliged by bringing in huge gasoline-powered K-12 saws and exhaust fans. Now Gacy's house resounded with the deafening chatter and shrieking of radial blades passing through hardwood, pipes, and electrical cables as the firemen cut the floor in checkerboard fashion.

Out in the garage, a contingent started on the recovery of the body whose grave Gacy had marked with spray paint. Using an air hammer and compressor, men proceeded to remove the concrete floor. The space in the narrow shed was so confined that chips kept ricocheting off the walls, hitting the officers. To open up the work area, Earl Lundquist and Ron Russell ripped down a wall.

The contents of the freezer in Gacy's garage had caused some speculation when investigators found frozen meat and a container full of what they thought might be blood. Dr. Stein quickly ordered serological tests performed. The meat proved to be not of human origin, and the "blood" was nothing more than stewed tomatoes.

Inside the house, officers moved Gacy's furniture and possessions to the rear addition. The amateur electricians on the force went through the crawl space rewiring the cables that the fire department saws had chewed through, so that power could be restored. Lundquist was told to arrange for new utility service, on the assumption that Gacy shouldn't have to pay for the lighting and heating of the destruction of his house. Officers ripped out a non-load-bearing wall between the "clown room" and Gacy's office and removed a patch of flooring in the northeast corner. After they removed every third floor joist, they were ready to begin the recovery.

Evidence Technicians Daniel Genty and Karl Humbert went down into the crawl space and began excavating the area where the kneecap had been found. From the start, they encountered the problem that would plague them throughout the entire recovery: the water table. As soon as they removed some dirt, the hole filled with water, and from then on, the soil was mostly liquid mud. They tried several kinds of submersible pumps, to no avail. The inlets kept getting clogged with bits of floating adipocere flesh. Ultimately, they bailed by hand.

They soon learned that larger tools were useless under such conditions and they would have to dig by hand. The surgical gloves they customarily wore were torn by the bones and gravel, and they had to use ones of thicker rubber, taping them at their wrists to keep out the slime. They filled plastic buckets with muck, then lifted these to the floor above, where a crew plumbed their contents for overlooked bits of bone or other evidence. Those working without gloves quickly felt the sting of the lime Gacy had used. The men emptied the buckets in back of the house, in a corresponding quadrant pattern, and planned to pour the dirt through fine sieves when it dried out. This idea was abandoned in a couple of days; instead of drying, the dirt froze into solid moguls.

Connective tissue having decomposed, the skeletal remains of the first body, like most of the others, were disjointed, and it was impossible to bring up the bodies intact. The diggers simply handed up what they thought to be bones to the technicians, who put them in Gacy's deep-fry basket and rinsed them in a bucket of water before passing them on to Stein. Even in the early stages, it was apparent that it would be impossible to recover most of the small toe and finger bones from the watery mud. Only when they found shoes or socks still on the victims could they recover all the footbones intact. When Genty and Humbert were recovering the last remnants of Body No. 1, they encountered sobering proof of Gacy's intensive burial system, a recurring problem that would complicate identification: At the feet of the first body was the skull of another.

By the end of the first day, the officers had recovered one body and part of another. Just as Gacy had said, human remains were found under the concrete in the workshed. The accumulation of the marsh gas produced by decomposition was so strong, however, that Stein ordered that recovery be suspended to give the grave a chance to air out.

As darkness fell and Christmas decorations flickered on up and down Summerdale, the crowd of onlookers and newsmen stood fast. Inside, officers were washing off in Gacy's bathtub and beginning what would become a daily ritual of decompression before they set off for home and normality. They had observed that Gacy had stocks of various supplies in case lots: breakfast cereal, perfume, soaps, all the sort of merchandise one finds in full-service pharmacies—and beer was no exception. By the end of the recovery operation, the officers would have worked their way through Gacy's entire stash of nearly two dozen cases of Old Milwaukee.

During the week of the surveillance the interest of the police in John Gacy had not gone unnoticed by his neighbors, but they were hardly prepared for what happened now. Yet, despite their complaints of reporters trampling all over their yards and shrubbery, many were delighted to be thrust into the floodlights as instant news sources. A few even opened their homes to reporters, only to be rewarded later with sizable phone bills. For the moment, everybody was dredging up all sorts of "we should have known" recollections. One neighbor stopped Lang and mentioned that every time he had walked his dog in front of Gacy's house, the animal had gone over and sniffed the foundation. "If only dogs could talk," he said.

Most of the people on Summerdale who would comment regarded John as a good neighbor, although some had misgivings about his sexual inclinations. One of Gacy's neighbors, Edward Grexa, was particularly annoyed by Gacy's habit of touching. "Keep your damned hands off me," he snapped on several occasions. Gacy always apologized. Even when Gacy was married, neighbors noticed that at his parties he surrounded himself with "pretty boys," and his ever-present circle of teenage youths sealed the verdict in many minds.

Still, no one suspected Gacy's dark side. Grexa, among others, had remarked to Gacy about the constant turnover of his young associates, but the contractor always had a ready answer: the kid went back to Texas, or the boy got too mouthy and he had to can him. Unknowingly, perhaps the closest anyone came to the truth was on a hot day the summer before. Anthony DeLaurentis, a neighbor across the street, was mowing his lawn and having an increasingly difficult time tolerating the odor of some water that Gacy was draining into the street. Gacy, who had a big black hose coming out of his crawl space, explained with some embarrassment that his sump had overflowed. He apologized for the smell and said he would have the mess cleaned up by sundown.

Perhaps there had been other signs, but who could say then what they meant? One morning, about 3 o'clock, Grexa looked out his window and saw Gacy struggling to lift a heavy object from his car. Grexa could not see what it was and went back to bed. On another occasion, he saw Gacy digging late one night in the back yard, where he was building himself a brick barbecue.

"Hey, John," he called. "What are you doing—digging your own grave?"

"That's not very funny," Gacy replied.

One summer Gacy told DeLaurentis that he was going to New York to build an ice cream parlor and asked if DeLaurentis would watch his house. Sitting in their kitchen late one night, the DeLaurentises were startled by what sounded like a scream for help. They ran outside to investigate. The street was deserted. DeLaurentis looked across at Gacy's house. The light was on in his master bedroom and a heavyset figure was silhouetted against the window. A couple of days later, DeLaurentis told Gacy what he had seen and asked if he had, indeed, gone to New York. Gacy said he had and that DeLaurentis had probably seen his bookkeeper.

Despite his professed heart trouble, Gacy never seemed to stint on his own work, even on the hottest days, when neighbors would see him hefting boulders in his yard or emerging covered with mud from a job in his crawl space. He was always offering neighbors the use of his tools, even his assistance. Rosemary Gosinski recalled the time her husband had borrowed a saw to cut down a tree, but didn't know how to use it. Gacy came over to show him, then climbed up the tree and proceeded to cut it down himself. Mrs. Gosinski shuddered, fearing the contractor would have a heart attack. Her gratitude vanished, however, when he sent them a bill for his services.

The neighbors felt warmly toward the John Gacy they saw at Christmastime, when he gave them hams or baskets of fruit, or showed genuine kindness to their children. Yet there was always a facet of his personality, partly boastful, partly ingratiating, that turned them away. John Gacy always seemed to be striving for a state of social grace that he never quite attained. The neighbors were regularly invited to Gacy's huge theme parties (which several regarded as big tax-writeoffs), yet many chose to avoid them because they were such improbable, almost awkward gatherings of people ranging from minor political figures to construction trade go-fers.

But Gacy's ebullience never completely covered unsettling evidences of a basic insecurity. When a bowling partner called him an SOB, Gacy upbraided him at length for the insult to his mother. When DeLaurentis expressed dissatisfaction with Gacy's remodeling of his recreation room, Gacy was at first servile, then began cursing his teenage crew. Alden Jones remembered that Gacy would get furious at parties when other men danced with his wife. The Joneses got to know Gacy when he came to one of their parties uninvited, tagging along with the Grexas. Although Gacy was congenial and tried to be helpful—he offered to assist Jones remodel his restaurant— Jones never encouraged his friendship. After a while, Gacy got the message and dropped Jones from his party invitation list, an acknowledgment of his failure to forge a desired social bond. "He wanted to be accepted in the group of friends I associated with," Jones said, "and he never was."

Greg Bedoe was not told until the second day of the recovery that Gacy had drawn a map of the crawl space. It was still sitting around the statiton in Des Plaines. He politely suggested that it might be useful to the people digging and took it to the house. The map proved reasonably accurate, although Gacy's body count was wrong in several places where the remains were intermingled.

The day before, when Genty and Humbert had uncovered Body No. 1, they had found the skull of a third body (the remains in the garage were assigned No. 2). Now, when they unearthed the feet of No. 3, they found the skull of a fourth body buried under it. Learning from this experience, they later returned to the first gravesite, and, sure enough, found remains of yet another body at a deeper level.

In an attempt to avoid mixing the remains of one skeleton with another, ET Pat Jones devised a system of marking a body's depth with lines of tape on his gloves or sleeves. He would extend his arms down no deeper than the marks indicated to avoid the possibility of exhuming the wrong remains. Later in the recovery, ET Alan Kulovitz encountered such an intermixture of two skeletons that, by the time he uncovered the spines and rib cages, he could only guess how the remains should be apportioned. Putting one body bag on the left, another on the right, he simply gave each one alternate handfuls. He later learned from the people identifying the remains that he had given one bag two left arms, and the other two rights.

Several days after their recovery, bodies 3 and 4 were identified by dental examination. Body No. 3 was John Szyc, Body No. 4 was Gregory Godzik. Since very soon after their disappearances about two years before, they had been sharing a common grave—made, in all likelihood, by Godzik himself when Gacy had him dig "trenches" for "some kind of drain tiles."

After four bodies were exhumed, the recovery was suspended over Christmas Eve and Christmas Day. Returning on December 26, we continued our work. Marinelli's crew removed more flooring and joists and restored some bracing. The ETs seasoned in the pit separated and formed new teams. Everyone, including ET night boss Dan Zekas, ET commander Lieutenant Al Taylor, all the way up to Chief Edmund Dobbs of the sheriff's police, got his turn digging. The exploration of the 28-by-38-foot crawl space expanded.

Where investigators found that the gravel and tarpaper originally laid down in the crawl space was still intact, they were reasonably certain there were no graves below. But in the settled areas, where the ground was soft, they poked rods into the earth. When they were withdrawn, they were invariably redolent with the odor of death.

As the recovery continued, disturbing new evidence was uncovered. Some of the bodies were found with ropelike ligatures around their necks. Others had cloth, often bikini shorts, impacted in the throat area. Could some of the victims have suffocated from the obstructions in their throats? More alarming, could some of them have been buried alive? In the pelvic region of a few bodies, the ETs found foreign matter— wadded-up cloth in one case, a prescription bottle in another— that Gacy apparently had pushed into the victims' anuses.

As the policemen tore up more of the floor and walls, more of the forced-air heating system became disrupted, and, with the steady flow of traffic in and out of the house, the furnace worked almost constantly. The diggers in the crawl space were at one moment overheated by the hot air from disconnected ductwork, then chilled by drafts from the outside when the doors were opened. Within a few days nearly everyone had upper-respiratory infections.

The evidence technicians also feared contracting disease from pathogens in the graves. Anyone with the slightest laceration was sent to a hospital for a tetanus booster shot. The men shaved only at night so as not to risk exposing a fresh nick to the crawl space environment.

When uncovered, the decomposing bodies emitted marsh gas, or methane, and hydrogen sulfide, which mercifully dulled the men's sense of smell. Sometimes those in the pit became so inured to the odor they had to rely on the more sensitive noses above to signal them when they were getting close to a new discovery. When one body was unearthed, it began to bloat with gas so rapidly that Dr. Stein had to cut open its abdomen to release the pressure.

When all discernible remains were removed from an excavation, Dr. Stein viewed them, pronounced the victim dead, and assigned a morgue identification number. The ETs tagged both the remains and the body bags—usually the skull was placed in an inner bag to prevent loss of teeth—then stacked the bags near the front door, awaiting the late afternoon run to the morgue. In the crawl space, all that remained were the simple stake markers, appropriately numbered, placed at the spot from which each victim's skull had been recovered. Very soon, the hole from which the body had been taken was full of dark water.

To the amazement of observers, every day the policemen ate a hearty lunch. As Genty said, there is nothing worse than dealing with something yucky on an empty stomach. For most of the officers, the excavation was harder physical labor than they were accustomed to, and they worked up substantial appetites. Moreover, lunch was a welcome chance to relax and blow off some of the pressure they had accumulated in the pit.

The kitchen was a kind of neutral zone between the trenches in the front and the command post in the dining-recreation area at the rear. Lundquist used Gacy's microwave oven to warn up the food delivered by caterers. At first, the men got their meals from the flight kitchens at nearby O'Hare, but they soon tired of Chicken Kiev and Beef Granada and switched to more mundane fast foods and delicatessen fare. The officers were highly amused when a local hotel sent over several trays of "finger" sandwiches. In the pecking order of dining room seating, the diggers were first, the dirt carriers next, the others last.

If mealtime at noon and happy hour at the end of the day were necessary relief valves, so was morbid humor. A visitor might have been even more shocked by the jokes coming from the sheriff's policemen than by what he saw in the crawl space. It was not that the men lacked human feelings. On the contrary, their work was so devastating that those feelings had to find an

outlet that would allow them to do their jobs. Sergeant Des Ré
Maux, back from vacation, watched his men closely for signs
of depression. "If they're not grab-assing and busting each
other's balls," he said, "then I'm worried about them."

The result was a steady stream of jokes, most of them utterly
tasteless. Once all the bodies were removed, some of the
policemen planned to put plastic skeletons in the crawl space,
install a glass floor, and turn the house into a gay disco. They
cautioned each other at lunch: Don't throw your chicken bones
in the pit, or Dr. Stein will go berserk. They had good and bad
news concerning a strident tyke who was then selling cars on
local television. The bad news was John Gacy's escape from
jail. The good news: Timmy from Long Chevrolet was
missing. And everybody, of course, knew that Gacy wouldn't
be going out this New Year's Eve because he couldn't dig up a
date. As Pat Jones said, it was like whistling when you're
afraid.

The officers had a ghoul pool, in which they bet on how
many bodies eventually would be recovered. The estimates
ranged from five to twenty-four. Everyone was low. Taking a
cue from a movie just opening in Chicago theaters, they got
themselves T-shirts emblazoned with "The Body Snatchers,
No. 803640," the six digits referring to the case number, with
large numerals "27," signifying the body count, on the other
side. (That number also proved low.)

A brisk souvenir trade flourished as policemen grabbed the
ball-point pens advertising Gacy's theme parties or construction firm and the calling cards announcing himself as Democratic precinct captain, and filled requests from, among others,
prosecutors and members of the judiciary. The demand for
bricks from the house was strong, too.

As a final commemoration of their presence at 8213
Summerdale, the officers rigged up on one wall an ornate
backdrop consisting of a blowup of Gacy, Polish flags, dildoes
shaped in the caricatures of Santa Claus and a preacher, and
other miscellaneous Gacyana. A number of officers posed for
formal pictures in front of it, riot helmets neatly tucked under
their arms, and the day's body-count chalked on a mug-shot
clapper board. The men were sparing no effort in busting each
other's balls.

After the levity, however, the reality of the job remained. From the beginning to the end of the excavation, the ETs photographed the graves and remains to guard against later errors in evidence identification. In the early stages, the operation was videotaped. To ensure uniformity and accuracy, one of the unit's top record men, Charles Pearson, was given the job of site historian. He logged all activities, made necessary measurements, assigned body numbers, drew up the plat map, and prepared the written reports.

In the back of the house, Lundquist and others combed through all Gacy's personal property and set aside anything of evidentiary value; the remainder of his effects was packed up and sent to a warehouse for storage. As Marinelli and his crew continued to pull up flooring and rip out walls and insulation, they kept finding more evidence: a bloodstained pad under a bedroom carpet, more IDs, more sex books. All this was sent to the sheriff's crime lab at Maywood. '

By now the floor in the front of the house was little more than an open grillwork of joists traversed by a plank catwalk. The policemen watched apprehensively the day Sheriff Richard Elrod inspected the site. Despite his crippling injury at the hands of Weathermen rioters in 1969, Elrod insisted on walking on his crutches across the narrow gangway so he could view the crawl space. When he made it to the kitchen, the investigators breathed easier and went back to work. Among other visitors that week were Dick Walsh and Chris Gray, who were asked to show the officers where they had dug trenches. Neither was very happy about being there, and both were very wide-eyed at what they saw. County inspectors also came to the house to check on health and safety matters; they insisted that everyone wear hard hats.

Having found a body buried under a concrete slab, the investigators worried that there might be others entombed in a mysterious pad that ran all the way across the crawl space. After studying the plat map and survey records of the house, however, they determined that it was a footing for the original foundation that had been poured in the wrong location. This was apparently what Gacy meant by his offhanded remark to Schultz and Robinson at the Civic Center the week before.

At the end of each day's work, Dr. Stein and either Chief

Dobbs or Lieutenant Frank Braun, the officer in charge of the recovery, would go to the front steps and make the obligatory remarks to the press about the body count, which, between Christmas and New Year's Eve, went from four to ten to fifteen to twenty-one and finally twenty-seven. Then the bodies were placed singly in a wire litter and carried by a group of officers to the waiting van for the trip to the morgue. For the legions of reporters and camera crews camped outside, it was the media event of the day. For those policemen who relished publicity, it was their chance to get ten seconds of exposure as pallbearers on the 10 o'clock news.

Des Plaines policemen following the story on television resented the sheriff's department's expert choreographing of the daily event. They had been totally pushed from the limelight—or almost totally. Tovar remained at Summerdale as Des Plaines's liaison officer and often appeared as a pallbearer. His colleagues accused him of choosing his wardrobe—red and blue, and green and blue, rugby shirts—with the capabilities of color television in mind.

The evening press conference was not well suited to all deadlines. Art Petacque immediately acquired the new phone numbers at Gacy's house and frequently called for updates. He would identify himself as "Lieutenant O'Malley" and ask to speak with one of his sources. "Just a minute, Art," the policemen who answered customarily replied. Faced with a midday deadline for the *Tribune*'s afternoon edition, Ronald Koziol would call a source at the house and get a cryptic report of "two at the door" for a preliminary body count. A Detroit newspaper reporter casually walked into the house and was promptly arrested.

Another *Tribune* reporter had a different problem. On a follow-up assignment to Jonestown, Michael Sneed called the city desk with the massacre story from Guyana and found that nobody at the *Trib* was interested in talking to her. Finally, her editor explained what had just broken.

"Oh, my God!" she wailed over the telephone, recalling a conversation we had had the week before. I had known her from previous stories she had covered, and I had mentioned to her that I thought what I was presently working on might eventually be right up her alley. She was interested, but terribly rushed: Her plane was leaving for Guyana within minutes. At that stage, I couldn't give her any details, so she opted instead to fly south to follow "the greatest story of my career."

By late afternoon, the press corps was sensitive to every official movement. Whenever an investigator opened the door, even to get a breath of fresh air, virtually every floodlight would flash on in anticipation of newsworthy activity. Noticing this, Bettiker, who views the world through thinly slit eyelids set into an unimpeachable poker face, decided to have some fun. He and a colleague stuffed a mound of food and beverage debris into a body bag and nonchalantly carried it out the door. The front of the house lit up like a stadium. As the cameras rolled, the men walked out toward the van, then suddenly veered off. With a one-and-a-two-and-a-three they tossed the body bag into the dumpster and sauntered back into the house. When they watched the 10 o'clock news that night, the officers who had been bona fide pallbearers were convinced that the television people had tried to get even with them by zooming in tight and cropping out their faces.

By the Friday after Christmas, the count stood at twenty-seven bodies, twenty-six from the crawl space and one from the garage. On Saturday, investigators began tearing apart Gacy's back-yard barbecue pit, where Edward Grexa had observed him digging late one night, but suspended work until they could get equipment to break up the concrete base. In the attic, after removing floorboards, they found more pornographic books, some bong pipes for hash or marijuana, and a bag of police-type stars and badges. The crawl space, however, yielded no further human remains. The diggers cautiously wondered if perhaps their job was done.

Work was suspended for the two-day New Year holiday, and on the last day of 1978, the snows came. Thirty inches already had fallen during the season, and the New Year's storm added nearly ten inches more. On their return in early January, the investigators were prevented from doing any further excavation outside because of the snow and the frozen ground. On the heels of the storm, an Arctic air mass moved in and kept Chicago in below-zero lows throughout the first half of the month. The plans to dig until everyone was sure there were no more bodies would simply have to wait for a break in the weather.

County highway workers were brought in to excavate the crawl space down to the substratum of clay. Before the dirt was removed on a conveyer belt through the side of the house, ETs sifted through it once again for further evidence. Acting on a statement Gacy had made at Cermak Hospital, investigators probed under the floor in the utility room and found a blue down-filled nylon parka. It was Rob Piest's.

The break in the weather we were hoping for in January never came. On Friday the 12th, it began snowing again and didn't stop until early Sunday. By then, twenty more inches had fallen, bringing the city to a standstill. O'Hare was closed over the weekend, rapid-transit trains were stalled with frozen switches and traction motors, roadways were barricaded with seven-foot drifts, and Chicago schools shut down for a full week. This January—which would still see another thirteen inches of snowfall—would set a record with the worst combination of snow and cold in Chicago's history. The entire winter would prove to be a record-breaker, with nearly ninety inches total snowfall. Roofs sagged and leaked, and some collapsed. Authorities were alarmed that the murder rate was soaring; they attributed the increase to an epidemic of cabin fever.

After the big snow, the activity at Summerdale came to almost a complete halt. Mostly now it was a custodial operation to keep the search warrant alive. It was apparent that the remainder of the work would have to wait until the approach of spring.

Among the people who gathered on the street in front of Gacy's house during the week after Christmas, there was no group more pitiable than the relatives of missing boys. There was little they could learn at the scene, but they didn't know that. Jostled by the horde of onlookers at the police lines, they kept their vigil, straining their ears for bits of information from reporters or law enforcement people.

When the digging was resumed on the day after Christmas, an officer on guard duty was approached by a young woman named Kari Johnston Betleg, who told the officer that her brother Rick had been missing for two years.

Rick Johnston, a slender and slightly built youth of five foot six, would have started his senior year of high school in the fall of 1976. He had been a wrestler in junior high school, and early each morning would run around the golf course near his home in west suburban Bensenville. He was an avid reader and a Tolkien fan. A budding environmentalist, he deplored the needless use of cars he saw all around him and chose to ride his bicycle everywhere.

On August 6, 1976, Rick had a ticket for a rock concert at the Aragon Ballroom on Chicago's North Side. He loved music and, especially after having two wisdom teeth pulled, he was looking forward to the diversion of the concert. There is no direct public transportation from Bensenville to the neighborhood of the Aragon, and Rick announced to his mother, Esther, that he would ride his bike. That was impossible, she replied. The distance was too great, and the trip would be too dangerous. Rick had been to Chicago only a few times and was anything but streetwise. Finally his mother said she would drive him. Rick said he would probably meet some friends at the concert and ride home with them.

Esther Johnston set out with her son in rush-hour traffic, driving eastward across the city on busy Lawrence Avenue. Rick's mother hadn't been to the Aragon since the days of the big bands, and she was shocked by the deterioration and the altered demography of the surrounding community. When they got to the ballroom, she considered waiting until the concert was over, but discarded the idea; Rick would be safer at the concert than she would be driving around the neighborhood. Rick leaned over and kissed her. If he didn't get a ride, she said, be sure to call either her or Kari. One of them would pick him up. She locked her doors and braced herself for the long trip back out Lawrence Avenue. When she arrived home, she passed through the kitchen and noticed an open book on the table. It was the family Bible. Rick apparently had been reading it just before he left for the concert.

Later that evening, Esther Johnston lay down on the living room couch to wait for her son. This was her usual practice, especially since her divorce from Rick's father. Rick had not arrived by midnight, but it was likely that he and his friends were getting something to eat. By 2 A.M. she was worried. By 4, she was truly frightened, but hoped that Rick was spending the night with one of his friends.

By daylight, Esther Johnston was frantic. She began calling Rick's friends; none of them had gone to the concert. At 11 A.M., she called the Bensenville police. They talked about the twenty-four-hour grace period, but they came by her home at 2 P.M. "Lady," the policemen told her, "if something happened to your son, you'd know about it." Esther Johnston called her other son, Greg, who came in from Galena, Illinois, to help in the search. They called hospitals. One listed a boy who fit Rick's description. Greg checked. It was not Rick.

That evening Kari and Greg took pictures of Rick to the Aragon, where they showed them to policemen and guards. They had not seen him, and they warned Kari and Greg that they should be very careful on the streets. This was a high-crime area.

After talking with Chicago and Bensenville police and a couple of newspaper reporters, the family became convinced that Rick had been picked off the street by representatives of the Unification Church of Korean evangelist Sun Myung Moon, whose cult was active in the neighborhood around the Aragon and in the suburb of Itasca, near Bensenville.

The Johnstons embarked on an odyssey that would last more than two years. As Kari said, "It was as if God put the Unification Church there so we wouldn't go crazy in all that time, wondering what happened to Rick." They spent thousands of dollars on telephone calls, checking leads and talking with other parents whose children were missing, or with workers who specialized in cracking the Moonie citadel. They hired a private detective. Greg traveled to Tennessee, Pennsylvania, and New York for information. Every time they approached a Unification Church establishment, they were rebuffed, stonewalled. Calling the offices in New York, Esther Johnston started crying, pleading for information on her son. The man on the other end simply laughed at her. They sent legal documents to the headquarters; the reply came back that the church didn't have Rick.

If Rick had indeed been absorbed into the Moonies, it would

be that much harder to bring him home after he turned eighteen. The Unification Church had scheduled a massive rally in Washington, D.C., for September 18, 1976, just a week before the boy's birthday. Joined by Rick's father and several friends, the Johnstons went to Washington.

They combed through the crowd on the Mall surrounding the Washington Monument. They spoke to park policemen, one of whom promised to have a photograph of Rick copied and distributed. Mrs. Johnston talked to a reporter, who said he had infiltrated the Unification Church but had left after they announced plans to ship him to Japan; that convinced her that they probably had sent Rick overseas. The Johnstons studied the faces of the clean-cut true believers with the glassy stares until it was so dark they could no longer see them. Hobbled by an earlier tail-bone injury, Esther Johnston slowly made her way across the Mall as the last embers of the Moonies' fireworks display fell from the sky. Her throat was burning from the acrid pall of smoke. She was depressed, knowing they would not find Rick there.

The Johnstons never gave up hope that Rick might one day emerge from the Moonies, and they waited, holiday after holiday, for a phone call. His friends continued to drop by the house to offer help and consolation. One of them reported what a girl at school, an amateur psychic, had said: Rick was underneath a house, where it was very dark. He had no shoes, and his feet were very cold.

After the news of John Gacy broke, it was not his name that told Mrs. Johnston that her search might be over. It was his address. Summerdale is less than a mile north of Lawrence Avenue. Esther Johnston shared her fears with her daughter: What if Rick had taken a Lawrence Avenue bus to the end of the line and tried to walk, or hitchhike, home from there? What if he had met John Gacy?

So on December 26, 1978, Kari went to 8213 Summerdale and told her story. The officer reported the details and suggested that Kari turn her brother's medical records over to the sheriff's police.

At 2:05 P.M. on Friday, December 29, Rick Johnston was found. His was the twenty-third body removed from Gacy's crawl space. The remains were under the laundry room, commingled with those of another body. The identification was made at 10 A.M. on New Year's Day, from the dental X-rays the family had supplied.

After Rick's funeral, a simple and devastating administrative error, now two years old, gained currency. In their original missing-person report, the Bensenville police had logged the date of Rick's disappearance, August 6, 1976, as 06 08 76. In subsequent records, and now in news reports and other published material, the date was misread as June 8, 1976. This was the cruel slander that Esther Johnston had to endure in the midst of her grief: that she had bided her time and waited two months before reporting her son missing.

Identification

After Gacy's confession that he had thrown the bodies of his last five or so victims into the Des Plaines River, we turned our attention to the Will and Grundy county "floaters" reported to us before his arrest. One of them had been identified as Frank Landingin, a homosexual who had a previous arrest record for theft and battery. Landingin's body had been found by duck hunters on November 12. His bond slip had been found in Gacy's house, and Gacy had recognized his picture.

The other body, which had a "Tim Lee" tattoo on its upper left arm, had not been identified since its discovery on June 30, 1978, by a barge crewman at Dresden Island Lock and Dam. Although the body was badly decomposed, Grundy County authorities had been able to lift fingerprints from it. Searches of Illinois and FBI files, however, had proved negative. Periodically, Grundy officers had checked Chicago, and the DLE had searched its computer files, but no indication of a missing "Tim Lee" had ever materialized.

After Gacy's arrest, Bill Ward developed an interesting, albeit off-the-wall, theory that he was convinced would help us identify "Tim Lee." Since Grundy authorities had suggested that Lee might be Oriental, and because Ward had seen a menu from a Chinese restaurant among Gacy's personal effects, he was sure that if we searched hard enough, we would find a stir-fry chef somewhere who would know him. After he and several investigators called dozens of Chinese restaurants without success, Ward finally had to admit he was grasping at straws.

A story in the Chicago *Sun-Times* in early January gave a better lead: a young man with a "Tim Lee" tattoo was known in the North Side gay bars he frequented as Timothy O'Rourke.

Grundy County asked the Illinois Bureau of Criminal Identification to compare the Tim Lee fingerprints with any they had on a Timothy O'Rourke. This time the match was made. A *Sun-Times* reporter told Grundy investigators he had located O'Rourke's father, who said his son had a "Tim Lee" tattoo on his arm. The younger O'Rourke, he said, was interested in karate and a great fan of Bruce Lee. Dental records and X-rays confirmed that the body with the tattoo was, indeed, Timothy O'Rourke.

In the wake of the *Sun-Times* story, Chicago Investigator Jerry Lawrence received a telephone call from a Donita Ganzon, a transsexual who said she remembered O'Rourke's "Tim Lee" tattoo very well and who offered further information: O'Rourke had mentioned that a man named Gacy had promised him a job, but he later said he thought Gacy was giving him the runaround. Ganzon said she had asked if Gacy was gay, and O'Rourke just smiled. Shortly after midnight one morning, O'Rourke said he was going out for cigarettes. Ganzon never saw him again.

Frank Landingin, the other floater, had last been seen by friends early on November 4. His body was found eight days later. The cause of death was asphyxiation. His mouth gagged with a pair of his own bikini underpants, Landingin apparently had inhaled his own regurgitation. The autopsy also determined that within an hour and a half before his death, Landingin had eaten a large meal—the presence of bean sprouts suggested Chinese food—and that he had had sexual relations; his seminal vesicles were empty.

From interviews with his family and friends, investigators had learned that Landingin, nineteen, was a somewhat violent youth who dealt in drugs, hustled, pimped, and operated on the fringes of North Side gang activities. Though often jobless, he always had money. Landingin had a record of about a half-dozen arrests in the year before he disappeared, mostly for battery and auto theft. Although investigators initially had not established any clear-cut tie with John Gacy, the manner of Landingin's death—especially the underpants in his mouth—and the homosexual/drug activity in Gacy's "cruising area," certainly pointed to a likely connection.

In response to our request for assistance in finding the body of Rob Piest, Will and Grundy county authorities enlisted the aid of several local fire departments, which sent out their boats to search on the Saturday before Christmas. They cruised from a point several miles upstream of the I-55 bridge all the way down to Ottawa, Illinois, about forty miles away. A helicopter borrowed from the Illinois Department of Transportation scouted the same portion of the river. In the week after Christmas, the search continued with the added help of divers from a local scuba club.

They had no success. Greg Bedoe, Frank Nolan, and Bill Ward witnessed the search in the first days and talked to lockmasters, boat people, and old river hands. There were so many variables, they learned; it might be spring before Rob Piest's body could be recovered, and it was possible it might never be found.

Bodies dumped in the river initially sink. Only when decomposition sets in is sufficient buoyant gas produced to bring them to the surface. The cold water, therefore, might preserve Rob's body so well that it would be months before it came up.

The condition of the body at the time it was dumped was another consideration. Will County police told of cases in which corpses in a state of rigor mortis had plunged straight to the bottom and got stuck in the mud like statues. There they would remain unless disturbed by the prop wash of passing boat traffic.

Barges were another problem. Bodies could get stuck in the cables and struts of towing rigs. It was theoretically possible for a floater from Illinois to end up in New Orleans, or to get stuck under one of the large flotillas of barges temporarily moored at various havens on the river, or to be completely dismembered by the screw of a tug.

The river banks were lined with inlets where ice had formed, and outside the channels the bottom was littered with all manner of junk and natural snags. The places where a body could remain hidden were too numerous to count.

The odds were discouraging, but on Thursday, December 28, we learned that a body had been spotted from a tug just downstream from the I-55 bridge. If this body was Rob Piest, it would help convict John Gacy of murder.

Bedoe, Hein, I, and Wayne Fieroh of the DLE were in the Des Plaines police station when the call came in from Will County. The four of us jumped into Fieroh's unmarked squad car and headed southwest at speeds reminiscent of the surveillance.

The body had been spotted just before dark about a half mile downstream from the I-55 bridge by one of the tug's crew. The boat stood by until a unit of the Channahon Fire Department arrived and retrieved the body, which was then taken to a funeral home in New Lenox.

It would not be easy for me or Greg Bedoe to view the corpse because of our involvement with the Piest family—by now Rob was very real to us. Even though he was dead, I kept thinking, how awful being in that cold water. When we got to the funeral home, county authorities had the body in the basement. Although it was not recognizable because of bloating and skin slippage, it appeared to be a teenage male of about 150 pounds. We were puzzled, however, because it seemed so short, about five foot two. I went upstairs and asked Deputy Coroner Karl Kurtz if a body could shrink. Yes, he said, possibly an inch or two. That didn't explain the discrepancy: Rob Piest was five foot eight.

While Bedoe and I were conferring in a corner, one of the Will County officers asked if we knew whether Piest had been circumcised. We called Kozenczak, who checked. Rob had been circumcised; the youth on the examination table had not. This was not Rob Piest.

Two days later, the victim was identified by fingerprints as James Mazzara, twenty, of Elmwood Park. He had a record of arrest in Chicago for possession of marijuana and criminal damage to property, both the previous year. I sent Bedoe and Joe Hein out to talk to the youth's family.

It was a nasty evening, with freezing drizzle glazing the streets. A young woman answered the door. This was James's sister, Annette. Her father was not home, and the officers asked Annette to get her mother. It was obvious that the family was anticipating bad news. The officers told Annette about the events in Will County, then waited while she spoke to her mother in Italian. The older woman wailed and screamed, and her daughter cried. The television in the living room was on for the evening news. A picture of John Gacy flashed on the screen. The mother spoke urgently to Annette, who relayed her message: "He did it, didn't he?" The officers said they didn't know.

Calmer now, Annette talked to the officers in the kitchen. The family had last seen James on Thanksgiving. When he didn't show up for Christmas, they suspected something was wrong, but they hadn't reported him missing. He lived in Chicago, but Annette wasn't sure where. They had no telephone number for him, and only "Clark Street" as an address. As far as she knew, he worked in construction. He'd told her at Thanksgiving not to worry, he was doing all right. He mentioned the name of a bar which she and some friends later checked, looking for him. It was a tough gay establishment. The officers asked if James had any nicknames. She said his friends called him "Mo-Jo." John Gacy had said on his way to jail that his penultimate victim was "something-Joe" from Elmwood Park. "Mo-Jo" sounded pretty close to the mark.

At the request of the state's attorney's office—and from what he called a desire to set the record straight—Gacy consented to an interview with a member of my staff and several sheriff's policemen in the second week of his confinement at Cermak Hospital. At 4 o'clock on January 3, Larry Finder, Greg Bedoe, and Phil Bettiker filed into a library/conference room at the hospital, where Gacy and Sam Amirante were waiting. Frank Braun and Joe Hein joined them later.

"Hi, Larry," Gacy greeted Finder, and the men exchanged handshakes all around. Gacy was clean-shaven and seemed to be in a cheerful mood. He sat at the head of the conference table, with Amirante on his right, and the others seated themselves along the sides.

"Do you believe the bullshit the press is creating?" Gacy

asked no one in particular. "They want to dig up the Winston Ice Cream Shop at State and Division just because I worked there and someone smelled an odor. That's the reason I wanted to talk to you—so every time they find a body, they don't blame me for it."

Gacy said it would be foolish to rip out all the concrete at the store—there were no bodies there. Finder nodded, then told Gacy he was under no compulsion to speak to the officers and began reciting the Miranda rights. As he had in previous interviews, Gacy pre-empted the reading and summarized his rights himself. He then went over some of the subjects he had covered in earlier statements and elaborated on others at the request of the interviewers.

Gacy said that he never had sex with most of the hustlers he picked up at Bughouse Square because they would raise the price. All of them were white, he said. He would never have sex with Puerto Ricans or blacks. Over the last five years, he estimated, he had had about 1,500 relationships—which made it rather hard for him to remember the identities of the twenty-seven victims buried at his house. Toward the end, the killings became less frequent because he worked so hard during the day that he was too tired to cruise at night. Gacy explained that the "H" he had marked in his address book alongside some of the names signified that they were "tricks"—or homosexuals. He said he had had his first sexual relationship with a male when he was twenty-two.

Asked why some of the bodies had plastic bags over their heads or upper torsos, Gacy said he had put them on if the victims started bleeding from the nose or mouth. Sometimes, he said, he stuffed a victim's sock in the mouth, but he never used underpants. The blood in the green-carpeted bedroom, he said, had come from a body he had stashed feet-up in the closet shortly before his remarriage. He sometimes stored corpses under his bed, though never for more than twenty-four hours. After he'd filled up the crawl space, he had considered putting bodies in the attic but rejected the idea because of the possibility of excess "leaking."

When asked to explain his remark that the victims had killed themselves, Gacy said that when he twisted the cord around their necks, the victims began to convulse, which made the rope tighter, and thus "they killed themselves." Asked about the rope trick, Gacy explained his procedure, then offered to demonstrate it on Braun. The lieutenant said he would pass, and everybody, including Gacy, laughed heartily.

Between puffs on an A & C cigar Braun had given him, Gacy went through several rolls of Certs and a Hershey bar and rejected the hospital dinner as looking like something he had once stepped in. Earlier he had chided Bedoe for bringing cigars he thought were not very good and advised Finder that he didn't like nuts in his Hersheys.

Gacy said that he had killed for either of two reasons: the victim raised the originally agreed upon price for sex, or he posed some sort of threat—such as telling the neighbors about Gacy's sexual activities. Those who showed remorse after engaging in a homosexual act he put in the second category. He had his employees dig trenches in the crawl space so he would have graves available. Several times he referred to the space as his "burial grounds."

Gacy said his relationship with "Joe" from Elmwood Park began shortly after Thanksgiving. Joe liked to beat Gacy during sex; Gacy said he did not like S&M. Joe tried to raise the price after one long bout and threatened to tell the neighbors he'd been raped if Gacy didn't pay. Gacy performed the rope trick without even having to bind Joe's hands and dumped the body in the river the next night. When shown a picture of James Mazzara, Gacy said the boy in the picture could be Joe if the hair were shorter.

Gacy said he had buried John Butkovich in the garage because he already had a trench there for drain tile he no longer intended to install. The two had had an argument over a paycheck when Butkovich wanted to quit and go to Puerto Rico. Butkovich, Gacy said, had charged some carpeting for his apartment to Gacy's account and had never paid for it. If he wanted to collect his salary, Gacy told him, he'd have to work until the next payday and reimburse the contractor for the carpeting. Butkovich came to the house that night with friends and demanded the money, but left after Gacy refused to pay. Later the same night, Gacy encountered Butkovich while cruising in Chicago. Butkovich had been beaten in a fight, and Gacy took him home and cleansed his wounds. The same argument resumed, and Butkovich began hitting Gacy. The contractor finally calmed him down and showed him the handcuff trick. Butkovich became enraged and threatened to kill him. Then, Gacy said, he performed the rope trick.

Gacy said he did not remember Jeffrey Rignall. At first, he denied the chloroform allegation, but later said they may have "chloroformed together" by their own choosing. He said he never used chloroform on any of his victims; he kept it only because some of his partners liked to use it to get high.

Gacy said he met John Szyc, whom he described as a "he/she," at Bughouse Square. After Szyc demanded more than $20 for the sex they had engaged in, Gacy showed him the rope trick. He said the costume jewelry and wigs in his dresser belonged to Szyc.

Gacy said that he was not sure why he had killed Rob Piest. He recounted his activities of December 11 at Nisson Pharmacy and how he had invited Rob to join him in his vehicle. Contrary to reports in the press, he said, he did not offer Rob a job. He did, however, offer Rob $20 if the boy would let him perform oral sex. Rob was not handcuffed at this time, Gacy said, but the sex act never took place because of Rob's inability to get an erection. When Rob became frightened and said he thought Gacy was going to kill him, Gacy said he reassured him, saying there was no reason to be scared. The contractor, however, became worried that the boy might tell other people and decided to kill him. Despite his earlier statement that the crawl space was filled, he said now that only "Jack" knew why he had disposed of Rob's body in the river.

Late one Saturday night, Gacy said, Greg Godzik needed a ride, and Gacy picked him up. They drove to the contractor's house, where they smoked some marijuana. Gacy said he talked Godzik into performing oral sex on him, after which Godzik became sullen and expressed shame. Gacy said that "Jack" thereupon decided to perform the rope trick.

Shown the picture of Rick Johnston, Gacy recalled that the boy was from Bensenville and that he had picked up Rick in his "cruising area." The body, he said, was buried under his house.

When Gacy was shown a picture of Frank Landingin, he said he could not identify it, although he had recognized the youth when shown the picture by Finder in the Des Plaines jail. Gacy did, however, recognize Landingin's bond slip, which, he said, he'd found in the victim's wallet after he was killed.

Gacy said that his first killing took place in January, 1972, and the second in January, 1974, about a year and a half after his marriage. He did not kill anyone, he said, during the time his mother-in-law lived with him and his wife. Gacy said he could not stand his wife's mother and eventually had to get a court order to get her out of the house. He said the report in the press that he had been seen burying a handgun was correct. The gun, he said, belonged to his mother-in-law, and he had buried it under his stoop because guns scared him.

After saying again that there were no bodies buried under his driveway, Gacy suggested that the officers check with Ron Rohde, who had poured the concrete in front, and the asphalt company that put in the rest of the driveway. He had been planning, within the next few months, finally to solve the problem of the odor in the crawl space by filling it in with twelve inches of poured concrete. The only thing holding up the work, he said, was getting the building permit.

Finder asked Gacy about the book he was carrying with him, *Modern Currents in Political Thought*.

"I read all heavy stuff," he answered. "Politics is power. Power depends on consent."

At the end of the four-hour meeting, one of the officers asked Gacy if he would submit to further interviews to assist in identification of the victims.

Only, he said, if the jail personnel treated him like a human being. "Some of the guards asked me how I was able to sleep in a house with bodies in it," he said indignantly. "I half expected them to throw peanuts at me—like I was an animal in a zoo."

As soon as the recovery operation got under way at 8213 Summerdale on December 22, police and the county medical examiner's office began preparing for the task of identifying the victims. From Gacy's first confession, we expected to find John Szyc, Greg Godzik, and John Butkovich, in his "burial grounds." But who were the two dozen others and what had brought them here? Were they runaways who had innocently accepted his hospitality, or hustlers engaged in the ultimate transaction, or simply kids whom Gacy had kidnapped from the streets?

Through the news media, both local and national, we requested information from families and friends of missing boys and young men. A toll-free hotline number was established by a Houston group for runaways who wished to have word relayed to their families that they were not among Gacy's victims. As the sheriff's office in Niles set up the administrative machinery to deal with the public outreach, the work began in the Cook County morgue to identify the remains.

Dr. Stein called in Charles P. Warren, associate professor of anthropology at the University of Illinois at Chicago, to do the initial processing of the bodies. From an examination of the bones and their patterns of growth (and, to some degree, the teeth), a physical anthropologist is able to establish a body's sex, race, approximate age, and stature. In two separate examinations, Warren prepared forms listing this information as well as a complete skeletal chart for each set of remains, noting any unusual osteological features, such as a healing of fractures.

From Gacy's statements and the findings of Warren and his staff, we determined that the typical victim was a Caucasian male in his teens or twenties. Families of missing persons who would be excluded by reason of race or age were discouraged from sending in material. If, after talking with the parents on the phone, the investigators believed the son fit the victim profile at all, they requested medical records and X-rays, preferably dental.

Some correspondence came in from out of state, pathetic notes written by parents who had lived in anguish for years. Others, unaware that most remains were nothing more than skeletal, called in, asking if any of the victims had, say, blue eyes or freckles. Some families, particularly those who were Appalachians living in the North Side neighborhoods around Gacy's cruising area, were poor people whose sons had had little or no medical care, or else they were ignorant of the existence of any records. Some parents were cooperative; others were not. Among those who were not, many obviously were repelled by the homosexual implications of the case or just simply did not want to face the possibility that their sons were in the crawl space.

A large room at the sheriff's headquarters in Niles was given over to Gacy evidence. Phil Bettiker, along with Irv Kraut of the sheriff's police and Jerry Lawrence of the Chicago department, emptied the containers of property seized at Summerdale and meticulously sorted it, piece by piece. All jewelry, trinkets, keys, pins, and other miscellanea that could have belonged to victims were photographed in color. If relatives saw something familiar in the photo book, the investigators showed them the actual item. Several body identifications were corroborated by personal property identification. One young woman spotted her boyfriend's belt buckle and a religious medal she had given him shortly before his disappearance early in 1978.

Investigator Paul Sabin set up a massive filing system for the incoming reports and X-rays, and Bettiker and Lawrence tracked down medical records that the families of missing youths were slow to, or unable to, locate.

Dr. Edward J. Pavlik, who would head the team of forensic odontologists that was to make the dental identifications, read Stein's announcement of his appointment in the newspaper before he got the official call. He had been a consultant to both the sheriff's police and the medical examiner's office and, before that, to the Cook County coroner. Recognizing the scope of the Gacy case, Dr. Pavlik immediately called for the assistance of Drs. James Hanson, Ralph Remus, and Jerry Kadlick. On the Saturday before New Year's Day, they began the work of identifying the remains.

Working with the cleansed skulls, the dentists first replaced any teeth that had fallen out into the body bag of the victim. Certain teeth—mostly those in the front—fall out after death because their roots are conical and there is no connective tissue to hold them in. Any dentist, of course, knows where a given tooth belongs, and there is only one way it can fit into its socket. Fifty-three teeth, in total, were missing from all the victims.

Next, Pavlik and his staff charted the teeth of each victim, noting the condition of each of the five surfaces of each tooth. There are five possibilities for each surface: it can be healthy, diseased, missing, or repaired either with a filling or a crown. Those teeth that had fallen out after death and had not been recovered were charted as "LPM," lost post mortem. Dentists can easily tell from a jawbone if a tooth was lost after death. If that is the case it leaves sharp edges on the bone socket. When a living tooth is removed, these edges round off as the bone heals and eventually fills itself in.

When the dentists finished charting the teeth and taking X-rays, they made comparisons with the records sent in. Pavlik designed a master chart, listing each victim and the status of each tooth, from number one to thirty-two. If a chart came in showing a specific bit of dentistry, such as a crown on the lower-right first molar, the dentists could run down the column on the master chart for that particular tooth to see which, if any, of the victims had had such work. If they noted a similarity, then they checked another specific piece of dentistry, and so on, until the victim was either identified or the submitted record ruled out.

Pavlik and his staff were dealing with three possibilities: consistencies, inconsistencies, and incompatibilities. When everything they saw in the comparison was similar, those were consistencies. It is possible, however, for a dentist to find five things consistent and still not be comparing the same person's teeth. Perhaps half the people in the country have four wisdom teeth missing, and even more may have a silver filling in a given molar. From X-rays, however, a dentist can see the specific shape of a filling—the little points, ragged edges, knobs, and so on—that make it unique. A forensic dentist can make a positive identification from an X-ray of just one filling.

Inconsistencies are dissimilarities that are explainable. A tooth may have had, at its last ante-mortem charting, a two-surface silver filling, yet a post-mortem record may show it as having a gold crown—dissimilar dental work, yet a conceivable progression of treatment. The reverse, however, would be an incompatibility: a tooth that had a crown in 1963 could not have a two-surface filling in 1970. One incompatibility is sufficient to rule out any further comparison.

When the dentists had the necessary records to work with, the identifications went smoothly. Bettiker even gained sufficient experience to make unofficial identifications himself.

Getting proper records to work with, however, proved to be difficult. Pavlik was surprised that fewer than 300 X-rays were sent in, considering the tens of thousands of missing-person reports filed every year. Some of the records were too old to be of use, such as X-rays taken when the boy still had mostly baby teeth. Some of the dentists had sold their practices—and their records—to someone else; others were simply careless in their record-keeping and sent in charts with obviously erroneous entries. Pavlik had the most difficulty getting usable material from dental clinics. One dentist simply wrote entries such as, "pink envelope," "yellow envelope," etc., in his record of treatment. Pavlik and his staff surmised that the man was keeping a duplicate set of books for reasons known only to him.

On occasions when Pavlik lacked sufficient medical records from which to identify the victims, he sought help from the investigators, who resorted to old-fashioned detective work to get them. The mother of one missing youth recalled that her son had been hospitalized for a stab wound in the chest; the hospital still had the X-ray, at the top of which a small segment of the boy's jaw appeared. Another mother remembered that her son had been taken to a hospital after he had sniffed glue, and they still had a skull X-ray on file. From those films the dentists were able to identify both boys as Gacy victims.

For skeletal identifications, Stein employed Dr. John Fitzpatrick, radiologist on the staff of Cook County Hospital, as a consultant. Dr. Fitzpatrick compared post-mortem X-rays of the victims with ante-mortem film sent in, which he also read for any unique skeletal features.

Although radiological identifications have been made for more than sixty years, they are not all that common. Consequently, they have tended to be eclipsed by dental authentications, which are favored by the law enforcement community because of their widespread use and virtually unimpeachable track record. A person's bones, however, may have anomalies that one either is born with or acquires through disease or trauma. Fitzpatrick searched for these sort of features. The skull, especially the sinuses, the transverse processes, the spine, the trabecula, or inner lacing, of the bones—all these present signatures of individuality that Fitzpatrick was able to note in his comparisons.

In the aftermath of Gacy's arrest, the Chicago police became increasingly embarrassed by the disclosures of his earlier encounters with them. They responded the best way they could, by assigning Jerry Lawrence, one of their top homicide detectives, to the case to facilitate cooperation with the investigators. Chicago had massive files on missing persons from the metropolitan area, and Lawrence was able to cut through the red tape whenever necessary, even if it took a visit to his boss, Joe DiLeonardi, then chief of the homicide division and later superintendent of police.

When the voluntary flow of information on missing persons from relatives and other sources began to slow down, investigators ordered all the Chicago police reports on such cases filed from 1972 until Gacy's arrest. After conducting a computer search, the records division turned over 45,000 case reports that fit the description of possible victims of Gacy. With the assistance of Chicago investigator Ed Curtiss, officers began a laborious manual search of these records to find the disposition of each case and learn if the person was ever found. Many of the complainants had moved several times, and others hadn't had telephones when the report was filed. Some of the cases, like John Szyc's, had been cleared because the person had been reported seen by witnesses of varying degrees of reliability.

After making an analysis of Gacy's financial records, especially travel documents and employee time cards, investigators constructed a pin map showing every job Gacy was known to have worked on anywhere in the country. Officers called police departments in those locales, requesting any information they had on missing persons. This study also helped us to establish Gacy's presence in Chicago at the times each of the known victims was probably killed.

Investigators talked with friends of some of the missing youths and visited gay bars. It soon became apparent to them that Gacy had cut a wide swath through the homosexual community. To some, he was known as a "chicken-hawk," an older man who looks for young men and boys. Many thought he was a policeman. The friends of one youth at the bar where he was last seen referred to Gacy as "the cop" and said that their friend, a hustler, had gone off with the man in the black car, expecting to rip him off.

Once a youth was identified, the investigators checked his background. Some of the victims had indeed been street hustlers—but far from all. Nonetheless, many families of missing boys feared the taint of association with hustlers and homosexuality and were reluctant to come forward. Some, undoubtedly, still have not. By June, 1981, twenty-four of John Gacy's victims had been identified, most of them through dental comparisons. The nine unknown young men were buried on June 12 in separate cemeteries. Burial expenses were paid by the Funeral Directors Association of Greater Chicago, and each stone bore the simple inscription, "We Are Remembered."

In the end, the investigators had the painful task of informing parents that their sons had been identified. Some of the families were uncomprehending. A few reacted violently, as if they wanted to annihilate the bearer of bad tidings. Most, however, were prepared for the news and took it stoically, some with a sense of relief that the uncertainty was over.

After telling the Szyc family that John had been identified as one of Gacy's victims, Officer Kraut had to ask their help in pushing his squad car through the snow piling up in their street. When he called on Esther Johnston, she cried softly and asked if Rick had felt any pain. Kraut did his best to reassure her that he hadn't.

Perhaps it is some comfort to the Piest family that their son is not one of the nine boys still unidentified. When the river search at Christmastime failed, Rob's family once again mobilized to find him. Harold Piest took time off from work and went to the Des Plaines River and made repeated searches on his own. The family turned to Dorothy Allison, the psychic, in hope that she could provide some clue as to where the body was. They brought her to court one day so that she could see Gacy and possibly divine something from her observation.

When Mrs. Piest talked to me about engaging a psychic, I told her that she should go ahead if it would give the family any relief. I don't have much faith in psychics, and I was particularly soured on the subject when I learned that Kozenczak's "anonymous woman caller," whose leads we actively—and unsuccessfully—pursued in the week before the arrest was actually a psychic whose help he had requested. I thought Kozenczak's failure to tell us this at the time was an unforgivable breach of conduct.

When the spring thaw came, there was new urgency in pursuing a river search. The tremendous runoff from melting snow could cause the river to overflow great distances into adjoining woods and fields, vastly increasing the area we would need to search. Too, river veterans recalled seeing huge tree trunks being swept through the floodgates by the voluminous flow and emerging completely shredded. Our hopes of finding the body at all were rapidly fading as the weather changed.

Shortly before noon on April 9, about five or six miles downstream from the I-55 bridge, a man on the towpath saw a body floating face down in the river, about five feet from shore. He reported what he had seen to the lockmaster at Dresden, who called the Grundy County sheriff's police, who in turn summoned the Morris Fire Department and a crime technician to the scene.

We knew about this from one of the Grundy dispatchers we had befriended in the course of the investigation, who made an unofficial call and told me that Braun had already left for the scene.

I arranged to meet Bedoe and Hein at a rendezvous point on the Tri-State Tollway, and we rushed to the Des Plaines River in Greg's undercharged economy car, his flashing portable light on my knees. When we arrived, Braun was a little sheepish: He knew the case was in the hands of the prosecution and that he should have notified us. He said he first wanted to make sure the report was not a false alarm.

The body, badly decomposed, had been taken to a funeral home in New Lenox. It was apparent that we would need dental records to make an identification, and I called Kozenczak, who brought down Rob's dental file. I could not reach Dr. Stein, but I did get Dr. Pavlik, and asked him to work on the identification. The body was X-rayed at a Joliet hospital, and

Pavlik and three other dentists made the record comparison. At about 9 o'clock that night they agreed unanimously that the body was Rob Piest's.

Three days after Easter on a warm and sunny April 18, Robert Jerome Piest was buried in a mausoleum vault in the gently rolling greenery of All Saints Cemetery. His funeral mass in Our Lady of Hope Roman Catholic Church had drawn a large gathering of his classmates and friends; most of the Des Plaines officers involved in the case were there, too. At the wake, where his coffin was covered with a blanket of red roses, his family took Greg, me, and several of the others aside and thanked us for all we had done. I, for once in my life, had no words.

Portrait of
an Evil Man

When Gacy arrived at Cermak Hospital in the Cook County jail, the executive director posted a series of strict rules governing his confinement. For his own safety, Gacy was isolated from all other inmates. All jail personnel, except those directly assigned, were instructed to have neither contact with nor discussions about him. Gacy quickly developed the notion that he was a Very Important Prisoner and boasted in a letter to a friend of his "nine bodyguards."

Although he was normally in good spirits, Gacy reacted angrily to press coverage of his case, which he believed was distorted and full of falsehood. He was also feeling the walls of loneliness closing in on him, a thought he expressed in a letter to Ron Rohde thanking him for taking the time to write. In the same letter, Gacy said, "My life is like [being] in a dark tunnel, not knowing how long it is or even if I am going in the right direction." In another letter, he pondered the ultimate forces of good and evil: "Since the dark shadow of Satan has come over me, it seems that my fair weather friends have run away. . . . When things were good and I was giving, everyone was on my bandwagon, but as soon as I am accused and suspected, they run and hide. May God have mercy on them. . . . If it wasn't for God's will, I would have never given or helped so many people. Oh, I am no saint or anything like that, just one of God's children. I do not take the right to sit in judgment on others or myself."

Nonetheless, Gacy seemed very demanding to those observing him. He complained periodically to jail officials about his treatment. On one occasion, he addressed a guard by surname alone and snapped an order at him. He still behaved importantly: He asked Fr. Joseph R. Bennett, the Catholic chaplain at the jail, to ask Cardinal Cody, the Chicago archbishop, to visit him, and commented to Rohde that Sheriff Richard Elrod had already paid him a "social" call, though of course he hadn't.

For reading matter, Gacy asked Charles Fasano, who acted as liaison between prisoner and administration, to bring him copies of *Playboy* and *Hustler* and daily newspapers, as well as a book on criminal justice. He asked Fr. Bennett to bring him a Bible.

Throughout, Gacy expressed his confidence that he would be acquitted and talked of once again being free, when he would need round-the-clock bodyguards. "I got the case beat," he told Rohde in a phone conversation. "You can take that to the bank." Asked how the bodies got into his crawl space, Gacy replied that he was out of town a lot and that five or six people had keys to his house. He went on to say that both his attorney and the psychiatrist for the defense saw no problem at all in getting an acquittal. He vowed that, once free, he would take action against everyone who had violated his civil rights, including, I assumed, me.

Gacy caused a flurry of excitement when guards found him under his cot with a towel around his neck, and a few officials expressed fears that he was contemplating suicide. Gacy denied he'd made such an attempt—he was just cooling off, he said—but he did tell Fasano that if what the press was saying was true, then his life was not worth living. To Fr. Bennett, however, he disavowed any such thoughts.

Despite the gloom of life in jail, however, Gacy on occasion made light of his situation. "I have canceled the party this year," he told Rohde in a letter. "I know how you were looking forward to it. Even with the expanded yard space provided by the county, there just is no place to cook."

In his statements, Gacy had told us a lot about his mode of operation, his sexual activities, and some of the victims he had disposed of. According to him, they were bad kids, they had sold themselves, they threatened him—they killed themselves.

Despite the horror of the confessions, I thought his stories were somewhat clinical, somewhat pat, and no doubt sparing of substantial detail. Not until we interviewed some of his still-living victims did we get the other side of the story. In many cases, they contradicted what Gacy had told us, and their narratives made me wonder at times if there was any limit to the man's brutality. Almost as disturbing to us was the evidence we saw that his pattern of sadism and violence had continued unchecked in the face of complaints about him to the police by at least five known victims—three of them in Chicago. Gacy always landed on his feet, and in his final year of freedom he was an arrogant bully convinced of his immunity to prosecution.

In the course of checking into James Mazzara's background, Greg Bedoe had learned that a man called Arthur Winzel (not his real name), now living in California, had suffered at Gacy's hands. After some months, Bedoe had located him in Los Angeles and spoke to him on the phone. Bedoe and I flew to Los Angeles to interview him. On arrival, we drove to Hollywood, only to learn that Winzel had quit the gay bar he was working at. We found him in his apartment the next day. We took him to a restaurant, where, over coffee and lunch, he told us his story.

Winzel told us he'd had a rough childhood, living in foster homes, and he admitted to having a juvenile record. A homosexual street hustler, he was also an alcoholic who consumed about a fifth of liquor a day. After he had left Chicago for the balmy climate of Southern California, Winzel had been shocked to hear in January from a homosexual friend that John Szyc's name had been listed as a possible victim of Gacy's. Winzel had dated Szyc and lived with him for several months before his disappearance. Although, by January, Winzel had forgotten John Gacy's name, he recognized his photograph in the newspapers his friend had sent.

Early one morning in the autumn of 1977, as he had been leaving a gay bar on Chicago's North Side, Winzel saw a black car with two spotlights pull up. The driver—John Gacy—rolled down the window and asked, "Do you want to get high?" They drove, saying little, to Gacy's house, where the contractor took Winzel in to the bar. Greg and I asked Winzel to describe the recreation room and interior layout of the house, which he did faultlessly. Gacy took some marijuana out of the refrigerator and rolled a few joints. Winzel took a couple of puffs, whereupon Gacy offered him some Valium and yellow downers he kept in a cabinet near the bar. Gacy, Winzel noticed, did not take any pills.

Sitting on the couch, Gacy told Winzel that he liked S&M and asked if he knew what it was. Winzel did, but decided to play dumb. Gacy went into another room, came back with a gold badge that said "Detective," and told Winzel he worked downtown in the narcotics division. Had Winzel ever been handcuffed during sex? Gacy asked. No, said Winzel, and he didn't like the idea of it. Gacy suggested they move into a bedroom. Turning on the bathroom light, he told Winzel to get undressed. "Remember," Gacy said several times, "I'm not going to hurt you." Winzel, believing that Gacy was a cop, albeit a kinky one, did what he was told. There was no mention of money.

Explaining that this was the only way he could get it off, Gacy cuffed Winzel's hands behind his back and put shackles on his ankles. With Winzel lying on his back on the bed, Gacy, naked, straddled him and rubbed his penis on Winzel's abdomen. Gacy got up and told Winzel, "If you don't obey your master, there's only one recourse." Winzel asked what that was. "Death!" Gacy said, fishing a piece of rope and an eight-inch stick out of the closet. Winzel was becoming frightened, and he asked to use the bathroom.

Winzel was able to slip his hands beneath his buttocks and bring the handcuffs to his front. When Gacy walked into the bathroom, Winzel told him he'd had enough; please remove the handcuffs. Gacy sat on the sink and calmly reassured Winzel that he was not going to hurt him. Gacy was so persuasive that Winzel was voluntarily handcuffed again behind his back within a few minutes.

Back on the bed, Gacy tried to act very considerate and said that this was the only way he could have an orgasm. He took the rope and looped it around Winzel's neck and tied two knots. See? he told Winzel. It's loose.

We asked Winzel to show us how Gacy tied the rope. Winzel pulled out one of his shoelaces, put two loops in it, and inserted a short piece of wood in the second loop. Bedoe nodded. This was exactly the "rope trick" Gacy had described after his arrest.

It soon became apparent to Winzel that Gacy was truly working at turning the stick. Winzel tried to tell him to get this fucking thing off, but he could only gasp. Now he knew he was fighting for his life. In desperation, he twisted his body, sliding his hands to his left side, and succeeded in grabbing one of Gacy's testicles and inner thigh. He squeezed as hard as he could. In agony, Gacy released the stick. Winzel had Gacy remove the rope before he loosened his grasp.

As they both dressed, Gacy moaned about the pain Winzel had caused him. He then went and got a small-caliber pistol. "I wasn't going to hurt you," he said. "If I was going to kill you, I would have used this." Winzel told him to take it easy.

Gacy dropped off Winzel at a transient hotel on Chicago's North Side. There Winzel showed a friend the red welt on his neck and the marks on his wrists and ankles and later showed them to a bartender at a nearby homosexual club. After we returned from Los Angeles, the two men confirmed this to Bedoe. Although Gacy had told Winzel his name, Winzel chose not to report the incident because, through the homosexual grapevine, he was told that Gacy was indeed a cop.

In contrast to Winzel, an admitted street hustler, Robert Donnelly was a straight youth of nineteen who had taken a job before continuing in college. In the aftermath of the deaths of his father and grandfather, he had been hospitalized for stress, but now, in the summer of 1979, Donnelly was beginning to get his life in order. He would eventually receive a state scholarship and a federal grant for his college education.

After reviewing police reports of a complaint Donnelly had filed against Gacy, I interviewed the youth, who painted the most chilling picture of Gacy we had yet seen.

On December 30, 1977, after a few beers at a friend's house on the Northwest Side of Chicago, Donnelly left shortly past midnight and walked to a bus stop. A dark-colored car pulled up with one of its spotlights trained on Donnelly. The driver, later identified by police as John Gacy, asked the youth for identification. As Donnelly was leaning in the passenger door to show his ID, Gacy pointed a gun at him and said, "Get in, or I'll blow you away." Gacy was dressed in dark blue pants, black shoes, and a black leather patrol-type jacket. Donnelly, having noticed the PDM plate, assumed he was a policeman and he complied. "Lean forward," Gacy said. "I want to put cuffs on."

"What's going on?" Donnelly asked.

"Shut up," Gacy said. "If you're smart, you'll keep quiet." Whenever Donnelly began to speak, Gacy told him to shut up. When they got to the Kennedy Expressway, Gacy stopped. "Get down on the floor!" he yelled. At Gacy's house, the contractor led him in by the handcuffs and pushed him down on the couch in the recreation room. Still carrying the gun, Gacy left the room and came back wearing jeans and an unbuttoned shirt.

"I'm thirty-five years old," he said as he went to the bar and poured himself a drink, "but people don't respect me." Gacy had two or three drinks out of the bottle, then offered Donnelly one. The youth refused. "Have it anyway," Gacy said, splashing the drink in his face. "Girls are ungrateful to me, even though I have money," Gacy continued. "Women are hung up on looks, and that's all." He again offered Donnelly a drink; the youth again refused. "Drink it anyway, you ungrateful little bastard," he said, grabbing Donnelly by the throat and pouring it down. "When somebody offers you something, you should take it." Gacy picked up the gun and walked over and uncuffed Donnelly. "I don't want to shoot," he said, "but I will if I have to. This house is soundproof."

Gacy told Donnelly to toss over his identification cards and sit in a chair. Donnelly gave him his wallet and Gacy rummaged through it while holding a gun on him. He asked him questions about himself, his employer, and other information on his ID cards. Gacy told Donnelly to sit at the bar, where he poured him a drink. He slid the handcuffs down the bar. "Put these on yourself," he said.

"What if somebody comes?" Donnelly asked. Gacy slapped him with the back of one hand.

"I told you, people don't respect me," Gacy said in a tough voice. "You don't either. I ought to kill you now." Gacy pushed Donnelly onto the couch, sat on his back, and pulled his head up by the hair. Donnelly screamed. "Shut up!" Gacy said, slamming the youth's head down. Gacy pulled Donnelly's pants down, forced his knees apart, and raped him. Donnelly struggled, then momentarily passed out.

When Gacy was finished, he held Donnelly down by his shoulders. "If you fight me now," he said, "I'll kill you." He got up and told the youth to pull his pants up, then grabbed him by the handcuffs and led him into the bathroom. The tub was already full of water. Gacy shoved Donnelly's face into the wall, slipped a rope around his neck, and twisted it. "This is a lot of fun, huh?" Gacy said. He alternately twisted the rope and banged Donnelly's head against the wall. "How does this feel?" Gacy asked. He then tripped Donnelly, knocking him to the floor, then pulled him up on his knees. Gacy shoved the boy's head into the water, holding on to the rope. Donnelly tried to hold his breath, then passed out.

When he awakened on the floor, he was naked and handcuffed in back. Gacy was standing in the doorway. "We're having fun tonight, huh?" Gacy said. Gacy ducked the youth's head under water again. Donnelly passed out once more. When he woke up, Gacy was sitting on the toilet. "Looking for me?" Gacy said, laughing. He then stood up and urinated over Donnelly. Gacy picked up a copy of *Penthouse* and showed the youth some pictures. "Like this?" Gacy asked. Donnelly was too weak and dazed to respond. Gacy kicked him in the side and pushed his head underwater. Again, Donnelly fainted.

After the boy woke up, Gacy hauled him into a bedroom and tripped him. "You're just in time for the late movie," Gacy said, sitting on Donnelly's back and pulling his head up. "Look at this." A homosexual movie was being projected on the wall.

When the film was over, Gacy wondered out loud what kind of game they could play next. He told Donnelly to sit up against the wall. Gacy got a chair and gun and sat facing Donnelly with one foot on the youth's stomach. "We'll play Russian roulette," Gacy said, spinning the chamber of the gun. He pointed the barrel at Donnelly's head and pulled the trigger. *Click*. He spun the chamber again. *Click*. As he repeated the process, each time aiming at Donnelly's head, Gacy mentioned that he had killed some girls in Schiller Park. *Click*. "Girls are no fun to kill," Gacy said. *Click.* "Guys are more interesting to kill," he said. *BAM!* "Ha! Ha! You're *dead."* Gacy chortled. It was a blank. Gacy grabbed Donnelly by the throat and choked him until, for the fifth time, the youth passed out.

When he awakened, Donnelly was still handcuffed in back and naked, and had a gag in his mouth that was tied behind his head. Gacy was naked, too. He fondled Donnelly, then told him to roll over. The youth refused. "Do what I say," Gacy said, punching him and forcibly turning him over. Gacy then raped him with a dildo until the youth once again fainted.

"Isn't it fun screaming when nobody can hear you?" Gacy asked when Donnelly woke up, still gagged. Gacy began playing again with the dildo in Donnelly's rectum. When Donnelly showed signs of great pain, Gacy took the gag off, but warned him not to scream.

"Why don't you just kill me and get it over with?" the youth gasped.

"I'm getting around to it," Gacy replied. Donnelly screamed, then Gacy put the gag back until the youth promised to do it no more. Gacy then said Donnelly looked bad and pushed him into the bathroom. He stood there while Donnelly showered. After the youth dressed, Gacy said they were going for a ride. "I'm going to kill you," he said, striking him again.

Gacy led him, handcuffed, out to his car. It was daylight. "Don't wake up the neighbors," Gacy said. Inside the car, Gacy told Donnelly to get down on the floor. "How does it feel, knowing you're going to die?" he asked.

After driving to the Marshall Field's downtown store, where Donnelly worked, Gacy removed the handcuffs. "I'm going to let you go," Gacy announced. "But if you go to the cops, I'll hunt you down." Donnelly got out in a daze. Despite his warning, Gacy didn't seem to care what the boy did. "The cops won't believe you anyway," he said, then he drove off.

In spite of the battering he had received, Donnelly had the presence of mind to note Gacy's license number. He still thought the PDM had something to do with the police department. When Gacy's car was out of sight, the youth turned and fled. He ran north on State Street until a policeman, suspicious of his flight, stopped him and told him to quit running. Donnelly continued on for several blocks, then caught the subway at Grand Avenue. He went to the house of his cousin, who wasn't home. He then went to the house of his uncle, who listened to his story, then took him to Chicago's 20th District Police Station. He was told to go to Area 6 and talk to the homicide/sex investigation unit. There Donnelly filed a complaint, and the police took him to a hospital for treatment.

On the evening of January 6, 1978, John Gacy was arrested at his house on suspicion of deviate sexual conduct. He showed little concern, even inviting the investigator in for a drink while they waited for a backup squad car to arrive. His invitation was declined. Gacy had little dispute with Donnelly's story, except he said he had not used a gun and there was no force. The slave-sex routine, he said, was by mutual consent.

In reviewing the case and after interviewing both Donnelly and Gacy, an assistant state's attorney rejected felony charges. It was just as Gacy had said: "They won't believe you."

We began preparing the state's case against John Gacy in the first week of the New Year. It was a hectic time. The holiday blizzard, although just a taste of what was yet to come, had brought just enough snow to make travel very tedious, especially for those of us making all kinds of interagency trips to coordinate the prosecution. And, as if the snow were not enough, a storm of controversy was being generated over material currently appearing in the press.

A gag order had been issued by Circuit Judge John White the week before, barring the law enforcement community from releasing information that would prejudice Gacy's right to a fair trial. Nevertheless, leaks were spouting freely. Within hours of Gacy's January 3 statement at Cermak Hospital, reports of his confession were appearing in the news. This situation, I felt, could seriously hinder our efforts to prosecute, and it surely would be the end of any furhter cooperation from Gacy himself in identifying his victims.

Unfortunately, Dr. Stein also made some inadvertent comments which would prove troublesome. When he was asked by the *Tribune* what kind of man could bury bodies in his own crawl space, Stein responded, "A schizophrenic, of course." Then, the next week, in a taping for a radio show on WMAQ,

Stein said that the person burying the bodies could be sane and could get the death penalty.

Amirante responded angrily to the leaks and statements and drew up motions seeking contempt citations against both Sheriff Elrod and Dr. Stein. The next day he added to the list Lieutenant Braun, Investigator Bettiker, Deputy Chief Richard Quagliano of the sheriff's police, and *Sun-Times* newsman Art Petacque. We wholeheartedly, though certainly not openly, endorsed Sam's actions.

I had a friendly chat with Stein over coffee. He, too, was concerned about putting the prosecution in jeopardy and agreed to measure carefully any future statements he made to the press. The sheriff's police were another matter. I kept hoping for an upper-echelon knuckle-rapping that would stop the leaks and get us all pulling together as a team, but, to my knowledge, it never happened. Meanwhile, I let it be known that I would seek to put all the interviewers involved in the Cermak statement on the lie box to see who did the talking. There was much high-level hand-wringing and, of course, denials all around. No admissions were ever made, but at least the threats seemed to stanch the further flow of unauthorized information.

Judge White had issued his protective order in Circuit Court proceedings in Des Plaines on Friday, December 29. Despite heavy security, including SWAT officers on the Civic Center roof, Gacy did not appear at the hearing because of the judiciary's fears for his safety. Amirante sought dismissal of the sole murder charge against Gacy because the body of Robert Piest had not been found and asked for Gacy's release on bail. Both matters were continued.

The prosecution team was taking shape. Bernard Carey, the state's attorney, had named his number-two advisor and deputy, William Kunkle, as chief prosecutor. I was amused, and flattered, when Kunkle asked me if I minded if he prosecuted the case with me. Of course I didn't mind and thought it classy of him to ask. I found Kunkle hard to get to know, but I got along with him well. On one hand, he's a quiet-talking, sensitive man with a very sharp mind. On the other, he's a chunky, strong guy who loves gourmet dining and motorcycles. Among the top honchos, he had the most experience in trial work. Since I had been on the case from the beginning, it was assumed I would continue on the team. Bob Egan, a versatile and well-regarded trial lawyer from the state's attorney's headquarters at 26th and California, would be the third member.

At this stage, there was no grand strategy for Gacy's prosecution because we were still enmeshed in an active investigation. We still hadn't found Rob Piest's body, we didn't know how many victims Gacy had killed, or who most of them were, and our main concern was simply to establish control over the various elements of the investigation. One thing we did decide in the initial stages: We would go for the death penalty.

In the second week of January, a Cook County grand jury indicted Gacy on seven counts of murder. The six victims so far identified were Butkovich, Godzik, Szyc, Johnston, Landingin, and Mazzara. Gacy was also charged with killing Rob Piest after committing the other felonies of deviate sexual assault, aggravated kidnapping, and taking indecent liberties with a child. Under Illinois law, a murder committed during the commission of another felony is punishable by death. Furthermore, anyone convicted of two or more murders since the death penalty went into effect the previous February could be similarly sentenced. The disappearances of Rob Piest, Landingin, and Mazzara all took place after that date.

On January 10, in the packed courtroom of Judge Richard Fitzgerald in the Criminal Courts Building, Gacy listened as Amirante entered a plea of not guilty to each of the charges. We were separated from the spectators by a partition of bulletproof glass, and the security was tight all over the building. I watched Gacy, dressed in brown sport coat, white shirt, and polka-dot tie, for the entire proceedings. He showed little emotion, and when the death penalty was mentioned, he just kind of looked up in the air.

After the pleas were entered, Fitzgerald assigned the case to Judge Louis B. Garippo, who continued the proceedings in the same courtroom rather than risk moving Gacy to his own. Garippo ordered a behavioral-clinical examination to be conducted by Dr. Robert Reifman, assistant director of the Psychiatric Institute of the Circuit Court of Cook County, to determine Gacy's fitness to stand trail and his sanity at the time the crimes were committed. Reifman would determine whether Gacy was able to cooperate with his attorneys and if he had sufficient understanding of what he was charged with.

Gacy's attorneys, Sam Amirante and Robert Motta (LeRoy Stevens was apparently handling Gacy's legal affairs in civil matters only), filed a motion seeking an end to any further excavation of Gacy's property because of the damage it was causing. Kunkle responded that the search would end when investigators were sure there were no more bodies on the premises. Garippo continued the motion and denied bail.

The Piest family was present. Without my knowledge, they were kept behind the glass partition. I tried to bring them into the open courtroom, but a deputy told me that for security reasons they had to remain where they were. This was their first of many courtroom appearances as they listened to the developing case against the man charged with killing their son.

Before Gacy's next court appearance, both the Secret Service and Chicago's large Polish community were embarrassed by the publication of a photo found at the house showing Gacy shaking hands with President Carter's wife. Gacy had been director of the Polish Constitution Day parade for the previous three years. That position was his entree into the photo opportunity during Mrs. Carter's visit to Chicago in 1978. In the photograph—inscribed, "To John Gacy. Best Wishes. Rosalynn Carter"—Gacy was wearing the Secret Service's "S" lapel pin, indicating that he had security clearance to be on the reviewing stand with her and later attend a reception for her. The Secret Service promised an investigation of how Gacy happened to be cleared.

On January 30, we sought a court order for the continuing excavation of the lot at 8213 Summerdale to ensure its legality. Previously we had been relying on the validity of the search warrants, but now that the physical destruction of the house was so extensive we wanted stronger protection and we now had the time we didn't have in December to seek a court hearing. Judge Garippo, however, gave the defense a week to file a motion challenging the search warrants and this brought the excavation to a halt for the time being.

At our next court date, February 16, the defense filed

motions challenging Gacy's arrest on the drug charge and the validity of the search warrants. Garippo, however, refused to quash the arrest; he also denied a motion to quash the search warrant issued the day of Gacy's arrest.

Probably the most interesting news from the proceedings was announced shortly after Gacy was led in. In a letter to the judge read into the court record, Dr. Reifman announced that Gacy was, in his opinion, mentally fit to stand trial.

I was greatly relieved when, on February 21, Judge Garippo upheld the validity of all the search warrants. The same day, Garippo signed the order allowing us to resume the excavation at Summerdale. Chicago, however, was still in the throes of its most severe winter in history. The previous seasonal record for total snowfall had been broken by five inches, and there were almost two feet of snow still standing on the ground. Spring, by calendar reckoning—which, in Chicago, is foolishly optimistic—was still a month away. Even if we had been allowed to excavate the property while the order was pending, we wouldn't have got very far.

Nevertheless, we wanted to finish the task soon; the cost of keeping a dozen men on security and away from other work was mounting. In a few days, with just a hint of moderation in the weather, the sheriff's police began exploration of the grounds. In early March they broke up the concrete stoop near the rear sliding doors, where they recovered the revolver Gacy had said he'd buried there. A week later they began ripping up the patio around his back-yard barbecue pit.

Dan Lynch, a heavy-equipment operator for the county highway department, peeled off a layer of asphalt, then one of concrete with his hydraulic shovel. Either Genty or Marinelli watched every excavation he made, looking for signs of pertinent evidence. As Lynch dug below the concrete, he found the ground still locked in frost, and the shovel clawed at the semisolid chunky layers. Suddenly he stopped. "Do you smell something?" he asked Genty. The ET went into the hole and probed with his hands. What Lynch had smelled was definitely the odor of decomposing remains. County laborers continued digging by hand. In a mushy substratum, they came upon a human body wrapped in several plastic bags. There was a wedding band on the ring finger of the body, the first indication that any of Gacy's victims might have been married. Investigator Irv Kraut, who witnessed the recovery, recalls that he felt a chill when, at the moment the covering of plastic bags was removed, bells from a neighboring church started chiming.

This discovery substantiated our case for continued digging, despite Gacy's statements and his attorneys' assertions that we were just on a fishing expedition. Gacy had said that the crawl space and the gravesite in the workshed were the extent of his "burial grounds" on Summerdale. Either he no longer remembered, or he was lying. The sheriff's police continued with their plans to excavate every square foot of the property down to the layer of hard clay.

On March 15, while further dismantling the interior of the house, officers found Jeffrey Rignall's driver's license under a cupboard in the recreation room. The next day, a week after the body by the barbecue pit was discovered, Marinelli was walking on the joists of the dining room floor, which was being removed, when he chanced to poke a crowbar into the ground beneath. He was probing a pile of old ceramic tiles, which tumbled into the hole the bar had made. After a little digging, the officers came upon a hip bone, then some arm bones. Beneath the very floor on which they had set up their command center and eaten their noonday meal, they had found the twenty-ninth body buried at 8213 Summerdale. This would be the last, although the excavation would continue until that much was established with certainty.

Because the house was now a gutted shell, unsafe to occupy, the sheriff's police set up a trailer on the parkway and street out front, from which they conducted their remaining business. After removing the access portal to the crawl space, which would be used as evidence, it became largely a matter of waiting for court approval to demolish the remainder of Gacy's house.

Although we originally had planned to "rip and restore" the house, that idea was soon discarded because of the unusual problems we faced in the recovery of evidence. When investigators found objects squirreled away in increasingly improbable places, they had to be sure they recovered them all. And when Gacy's layered system of burials was revealed, they had to dig so deep—for the sake of thoroughness—that they weakened the footings the house rested upon. They reached a point where it would be more economical to raze the house and build a new one.

The structure was now clearly unsafe, and because we wanted to remove it to permit total excavation of the premises, we filed suit seeking the court's permission to demolish it. Housing Court Judge Richard Jorzak ordered the house razed on March 27, but he withdrew the order the next day after Amirante and Motta complained that LeRoy Stevens had not informed them of the proceedings. After about a week's delay, the court finally approved the demolition, and on April 10 the wrecking began.

The policemen had left the driveway intact to give heavy equipment a firm foundation from which to operate. When word was received, Lynch energized his machine, which had been poised for the job, and began tearing off portions of the front roof. In the following two weeks, the house was torn down, the debris removed, and the rest of the grounds completely excavated. Marinelli got friends in the earth-moving business to haul in loads of fill to bring the lot up to proper grade.

Although it was by then spring, little seemed to grow on the vacant lot on which a comfortable, well-maintained house had stood. For the next two years, only weeds and sparse clumps of field grasses poked through the gravelly subsoil that had been the burial grounds of twenty-nine bodies. As the sheriff's police prepared to leave after four months at the scene on Summerdale, they routinely photographed the barren premises. That done, the last detail of officers collected their gear and departed. Genty wrote the final log entry: "No further action taken at this time."

In little more than a month, the same team of sheriff's and medical examiner's personnel that had worked together at the site of the nation's greatest mass-murder would be ordered to another nearby scene to recover and identify more bodies. On a bright afternoon in late May, American Airlines flight 191, bound for Los Angeles, would lift off a runway at O'Hare, drop an engine, and bank into a fatal arc, taking 275 lives with it. This, the country's worst air disaster, would happen just six miles away. I remember seeing the giant DC-10 fall from the sky as I had lunch at the Tollway Oasis, a mile away. I hitched a ride to the scene with a state trooper, and I spent the rest of that day helping police and fire officials in a futile effort of rescue.

From Dr. Reifman's report, and those of other doctors, we could gain some insight into the working of the mind of the man so far accused of seven murders. From interviews with family members and associates conducted by both the state and the defense, we were beginning to fill in the pieces of the mosaic that was John Gacy's background.

A. Arthur Hartman, Chief Psychologist of the Psychiatric Institute, the Cook County Court's forensic clinic, found Gacy to be, at deeper levels, "very egocentric and narcissistic with a basically antisocial, exploitative orientation. One reflection of this is his development of a technique of 'conning' (his own use of the term) or misleading others in his business or personal dealings." Hartman found Gacy's "severe underlying psychosexual conflict and confusion of sexual identity" most significant.

Gacy's denial of guilt through the use of "Jack Hanley" appeared to Hartman to be "a conscious evasive device. . . . No scientifically valid division in consciousness, memory or identity could be observed as between John Gacy and 'Jack Hanley.'" Hartman's diagnostic impression of Gacy was a "psychopathic (antisocial) personality, with sexual deviation"; he noted also "hysterical personality and minor compulsive and paranoid personality elements."

In midsummer we got the reports of the psychiatric examination conducted at the request of the defense and by order of Judge Garippo. As we expected, the psychiatrist whom Sam Amirante had chosen, Dr. Richard G. Rappaport, concluded that Gacy was "insane at the time of the alleged crime." Rappaport's findings were based upon sixty-five hours of his own psychiatric interviews, plus the reports of other consultations and interviews he had ordered.

From a neurological examination, an electroencephalogram impression, a computerized tomographic brain examination, and a chromosome analysis, Rappaport concluded that Gacy showed no evidence of any organic brain disease. Rappaport also disposed of the multiple-personality theory; in the five months he examined Gacy, he had seen no sign "that more than one personality actually existed." He said that Gacy had used the name "Jack Hanley" merely as an alias to prevent his own identification.

Reviewing the myriad medical records from Gacy's past, for all his heart attacks, fainting spells, and seizures, Rappaport found that it was questionable that he had had "any real physical illness of any magnitude." As to heart attacks and brain damage, the doctor's diagnosis was negative, and he felt that Gacy's fainting spells were brought on by anxiety.

Rappaport said that Gacy had a "borderline personality organization with the subtype of psychopathic personality and with episodes of and an underlying paranoid schizophrenia." Although he regarded the latter as the severest part of the illness, he did not see it as dominant. The paranoid schizophrenic psychosis, Rappaport said, occurred when Gacy was under "particularly stressful conditions," especially when he was indulging in alcohol or drugs: "At these times he loses control over his defenses as inhibitions are removed and the underlying psychological conflicts are expressed in the concrete form of acting out."

The doctor said that Gacy fit, to a high degree, the following characteristics of borderline personality: "Intense affect (such as angry eruptions in an impulsive manner), usually hostile or depressed . . . the depression characterized by loneliness rather than guilt or shame . . . a history of impulsive behavior . . . a lack of integrated identity or self-concept, difficulty with self-image and gender identity . . . superficial interpersonal and chaotic sexual relations . . . use [of] primitive ego-defense mechanisms, such as splitting, projective identification and gross denial."

Rappaport supported his diagnosis of psychopathic personality by attributing these characteristics to Gacy: "Unusual degree of self-reference . . . great need to be loved and admired . . . exploitative . . . charming on the surface, cold and ruthless underneath . . . noticable absence of feeling of remorse and guilt . . . history of continuous and chronic antisocial behavior."

Although Rappaport declared Gacy competent to stand trial,

he concluded that if Gacy did commit the murders he was responding to "an irresistible impulse which was allowed expression by the loss of ego controls under the influence of alcohol, drugs, extreme fatigue, and the stress of psychological conflicts within him. His victims were representations of these conflicts. It was at these particular instances that he was unable to conform his conduct to the requirements of the law." Even though Gacy knew that squeezing a neck could cause death, Rappaport believed, he could "justify his behavior to himself as a warranted act. It thus conformed to his private code of morality."

After getting Rappaport's reports, we immediately moved to get rebuttal evidence. For this purpose, we turned to the prestigious Isaac Ray Center, part of the department of psychiatry at Chicago's Rush–Presbyterian–St. Luke's Medical Center. Gacy was examined by several members of the Isaac Ray staff, including its medical director, Dr. James L. Cavanaugh, Jr., a psychiatrist.

Pointing to Gacy's apparent inability to recall all the pertinent details of five of the murders, and little, if any, of the other twenty-eight, Dr. Cavanaugh found the results of Gacy's alcohol-electroencephalogram significant. Within a period of seventy-five minutes, the examiners gave Gacy six ounces of 100-proof Scotch whiskey while taking a continuous EEG recording. An hour after the test, Gacy vomited and showed significant signs of inebriation. Although the test was conducted in the Psychiatric Institute, Gacy got the notion that he and Cavanaugh were sitting in a hotel room and that the two should have a few more drinks, then do a little cruising. He showed no cognizance of Cavanaugh's identity and professed to believe that it was December, 1978. Under questioning, Gacy had no recollection of any of the crimes he was charged with or of having been incarcerated for almost eleven months. After half an hour, he tried to leave and had to be returned to his room in full leather restraints.

Cavanaugh and his superior at the medical center, Dr. Jan Fawcett, concluded that in Gacy's repetitive murder pattern, "a psychological mechanism or repression, in which he attempts to spare whatever conscience he had from awareness of and responsibility for his actions, could explain the 'patchy recollection.'" They also saw the possibility that "the defendant's degree of intoxication could be so extreme that recollection of some or all of the details of what transpired could in fact be missing—e.g., 'a blackout,'" such as he had in the Institute.

In their report, the doctors concluded that, at the time of the murders, Gacy did not demonstrate any mental illness or defect that prevented him from understanding the criminality of his behavior, or from conforming his conduct to the requirements of the law. For at least the last fifteen years, they said, Gacy had demonstrated a "mixed personality disorder," which included obessive-compulsive, antisocial, narcissistic, and hypomanic features. He abused both alcohol and drugs. The crimes he committed resulted from "an increasingly more apparent personality disorder dysfunction, coupled with sexual sadistic preoccupations within an increasingly primary homosexual orientation.

"Narcissistically wounded in childhood, by a domineering and at times burtal father figure and inability to physically participate in athletics, [Gacy] continued to fail to master psychosocial milestones, in part because of a series of apparent psychosomatic disorders. Increasingly obsessed with his sense of failure (constantly emphasized by his father), he dedicated himself to a career of productive work," which brought him positive social feedback. "Simultaneously, however, his rage at his presumed powerlessness, due to a pervasive, defective self-image, began to merge with sadistic elements in a slowly unfolding homosexual orientation. [This] began to center upon young men with whom he re-enacted the projected helplessness and sense of failure that he himself continued to experience. His sadistic, homosexual conquests were much more gratifications through the exercise of power than erotic experiences motivated by unmet sexual needs. Murderous behavior became the ultimate expression of power and control over victims rendered helpless. . . .

"With each murder victim he was presented with undeniable evidence of his crime (a dead body), yet [he] continued with the same patterns of behavior. Ultimately, he came to justify murder as socially acceptable because of the degraded nature of his victims (human trash) and his increasingly egocentric conviction that he would never be apprehended because of his own cleverness in concealment and a disordered belief that his murderous behavior was of assistance to society."

Gacy, the doctors concluded, "demonstrates a personal career of too much success [and] ability to sustain interpersonal relationships, manipulate his environment, and control his surroundings to be seen as suffering with any . . . major psychiatric illness. . . . Finally, like a good sociopath, he has come to see his current predicament as the complex by-product of others' incompetency [or] cunning, or the price he has to pay for the moral depravity of a group of young men with whom he had the misfortune to come in contact. If these rationalizations are ever punctured, or if he later begins to understand more of the psychodynamics surrounding his behavior or comes to conclude that society's retribution is inevitable, completed suicide will be likely to emerge to him as a final solution."

In the opinion of his younger sister, Gacy "was a walking replica of Dad" in his temper, mood, and work habits. John Wayne Gacy, Sr., a machinist born in Chicago at the turn of the century to Polish parents, was a generous, hard-working perfectionist, a stern parent, and a good provider. He was also a drunkard, with what his children called Jekyll and Hyde personalities, and a wife-beater. He was undemonstrative, he could not reciprocate feelings. His only show of emotion came when he cried as his son was sentenced to prison in Iowa on a sodomy conviction.

When his son was two and his wife, Marion, was only recently back from the hospital with their three-week-old daughter, Gacy, Sr. came home one night and knocked out several of his wife's teeth. She fled to the street while John, Jr., and his older sister screamed in terror. Their father came out of the house and pummeled his wife more, knocking her to the sidewalk. The police finally interceded. As John, Jr., grew older, he tried to come to his mother's aid in family scenes. For his efforts, his father called him a mama's boy or a sissy. The children loved their father, but each night at the dinner table they fearfully waited for his rantings in the basement to stop.

Then the elder Gacy, always drunk, would emerge, and the meal could be served.

As a young child, John, Jr., was loving and eager to please. A neighbor recalled that he enjoyed helping her mother garden. Even as a boy, she said, he was a hard worker. Rarely, however, did he please his father, whose meticulous standards of craftsmanship the boy was unable to meet. When he failed, his father called him stupid.

Once, Marion Gacy found a bag full of her underpants under the porch where John played. John liked the feeling of silk or nylon. In a psychiatric interview, Gacy later recalled that his mother had made him wear a pair of her underpants to embarrass him. His younger sister recalled their father whipping him with a leather strap after he was told about it.

Gacy himself told the court's psychiatrists that his psychosexual history began between the ages of six and ten, when a teenage daughter of one of his mother's friends undressed him and played with him. He also recalled wrestling at age eight or nine with a contractor who liked to pin Gacy's head between or under his legs. Between ages ten and twelve, he got a whipping from his father after a girl complained that Gacy and her brother had taken off her underpants. Gacy said he began dating at sixteen and had his first intercourse at eighteen.

In his early twenties, he preferred "normal" sex with his girlfriends. He said he did not want oral sex because he couldn't kiss the girls afterward. He was upset when, at twenty-one, his first proposal of marriage was rejected; he married for the first time a year later. He had his first homosexual experience after his wife's pregnancy. He said he got drunk with a friend, who performed fellatio on him. Gacy never had any talks about sex with his father, but had the father known his son was homosexual, Marion Gacy later said, he would have killed him. Gacy said his instruction came from his mother, who told him that sex was beautiful, and it should never be forced on anyone.

Gacy was an intelligent child, but by the end of his grade school years he was given to daydreaming in class and was developing a resistance to his teachers. He began to suffer from a series of seizures and fainting spells and was peridoically hospitalized. These episodes continued into his adult life.

Sometimes he complained of shortness of breath and pains in his chest. His problem was diagnosed in childhood as recurrent syncope, leading to probable psychomotor epilepsy later on. As a teenager, after a seizure at a friend's house, Gacy was given the last rites by a hurriedly summoned priest. Neither the cause nor the cure was ever determined with certainty, and after he was an adult, his associates tended to regard his affliction simply as heart trouble.

Gacy finished eighth grade at a vocational grade school, then continued in a similar course until midway through his sophomore year. He got superior marks in English, excellent in general science, and fair and good in mathematics. His conduct received generally favorable ratings.

In high school Gacy developed signs of what one of his brothers-in-law later described as a "hang-up" with uniforms. Both his sisters spoke of his activity in a Civil Defense organization that allowed him to go to accidents and fires with a flashing blue light on his car. Gacy's father, who had loaned him money to buy the car, finally got tired of all the running around and removed the distributor cap. Gacy, who by then had left high school, became angered with his situation at home and departed, without notice, for Las Vegas.

George Wieckowski, manager of the Palm Mortuary in Las Vegas, recalled that Gacy was employed by both the funeral home and an ambulance service they used. Wieckowski remembered the youth as polite and always cooperative. He thought that it was unlikely that Gacy ever had much contact with the bodies, other than unloading the ambulances, and he said he never heard any complaints against him.

Back in Chicago, as a young man in his early twenties, Gacy found the sort of work in sales that would bring his manipulative talents to the fore. He took a job with the Nunn Bush shoe company, which sent him to Springfield, Illinois, and there he got his first taste for political involvement.

At the store in Springfield to which Gacy was sent to work as a salesman, he met his first wife, whom he married after a nine-month courtship. After his apprenticeship, Gacy was promoted to manager of his department. When his wife gave birth to their son, he was a typically proud father. A neighbor noted that he was both loving and attentive to the boy and seemed to be a devoted parent. With his new family, his reputation for hard work, and his wholehearted involvement with the Jaycees, John Gacy appeared headed for a bright future.

From Springfield the road to advancement led to Waterloo, Iowa. Waterloo was the place where it all began to unravel, where the warning lights would be noticed but their messages ignored.

Waterloo
and After

Waterloo, Iowa, is the seat of Black Hawk County. It is a mundane manufacturing and meat-packing town of about 75,000 set in the midst of prime Iowa corn country. Like many another midwestern county seat, its 1920s-vintage downtown surrounds a turn-of-the-century limestone and granite court-house, this one of French Renaissance styling, housing the governmental offices. John Gacy, his wife, and young son moved to this mostly working-class community in early 1966. Greg Bedoe, Joe Hein, and I followed thirteen years later, to learn what we could.

In announcing his arrival to take over management of three Kentucky Fried Chicken outlets in the city, the Waterloo *Courier* probably took Gacy's résumé at face value. It reported the somewhat exaggerated biographical data that Gacy had managed several stores in Springfield and held a degree in accounting and business management. Gacy was brought to Waterloo by his father-in-law, Fred Myers, Jr. Myers had acquired the Kentucky Fried Chicken franchises a few years before and now needed help running them. Although he never liked Gacy and had tried, right up to the wedding, to persuade his daughter not to marry him, Myers made the offer as an accommodation and to be near his daughter and grandson. As far as Myers was concerned, Gacy was a braggart and liar. Nonetheless, Myers paid him well—nearly $15,000 a year, plus 20 percent of net income.

Armed with his diploma from Kentucky Fried Chicken University, Gacy arrived in Waterloo ready to make his mark, rumbling to all the employees how he was going to change things. The employees, however, didn't take Gacy that seriously, and most of them quickly developed a dislike for him. "He was no threat" at all, one of them told us. Despite Gacy's bombastic utterances, Fred Myers was still the boss.

Early on, Myers was angered when Gacy kept passing himself off as the owner of the stores. Gacy's practice of giving free chicken to friends in the Jaycees also upset him. Although Gacy frequently talked about how much he was doing for the business, Myers said that he actually made little dent in the work load. Moreover, Myers said, he would have "come down hard on Gacy" and probably fired him had he not been his son-in-law.

Gacy immediately turned to the Jaycees in Waterloo for social diversion and to advance his status. He quickly cemented a friendship with Clarence Lane (not his real name), who would soon become president of the local chapter. Gacy openly discussed with Lane his ambition to make a name for himself in the Jaycees and someday wield the gavel himself. Lane was impressed by Gacy's willingness to work and, once he was president, harnessed what he called Gacy's natural talents as a hustler and con-man to help him on the membership drive. In one day, Gacy recruited twenty new members.

During Lane's presidency, Gacy held the office of chaplain and added ecumenical prayer breakfasts to Waterloo's civic calendar. His proudest achievement in this office was bringing the honorary national president and author of the Jaycee creed to Waterloo. Gacy got his picture in the newspaper (the caption identified him as "Colonel," an appellation his cronies used in recognition of his association with Kentucky Fried Chicken), and the acclaim he got from this programing coup assured his shot at the presidency the following year.

Of the fifty or so official Jaycee activities during the year, Lane estimated that Gacy attended 90 percent. The unofficial side of Jaycee social life, however, proved to be an even more enticing diversion for Gacy and some of his colleagues. In the mid-1960s, Waterloo was a wide-open and permissive town, and some of the Jaycees flourished in this atmosphere. The group was involved in prostitution, pornography, and various other vice activities. In the opinion of David Dutton, a county attorney at the time, the motel Gacy said he owned, which was managed by Lane, was the hub of those activities.

Gacy did a lot of socializing at the bar in the motel, and he and Lane frequented a night spot that featured strippers. Gacy, says Lane, was sleeping around a lot at that point, and his friends frequently heard Gacy bragging about having sex with one of his employees and other women, especially at the motel. "If you listened to Gacy," another close friend, Steve Pottinger, said, "he laid a hundred women." One of his partners recalled that Gacy was good in bed, but rather weird. He choked her, the woman said, when she refused to give him oral sex after intercourse.

Gacy by now was "kind of casual" about his wife, Lane said. Gacy "controlled" her, Pottinger said, and other friends would notice that in public there was never any show of affection between them at all. On several occasions, in his wife's presence, he offered her sexual favors to other men. When he made the offer behind her back a few other times, the price he named was a blow job.

Myers could never understand what Gacy was doing with the money he was earning, especially after he learned that his own wife was helping their daughter pay phone and utility bills. He assumed that Gacy was gambling. He did know, however, that one of the activities keeping his son-in-law out late at night was his membership in the Merchants Patrol, a sort of cooperative security force of "door-shakers" who guarded their own establishments against break-ins.

Gacy was what his wife called a "police freak," and he found a comfortable association in the group. She recalled his intense curiosity about emergency vehicles, which he followed at high speed with his portable red light flashing. Gacy liked to be known as having influence with the police and, according to Lane, he solidified the ties several times a month by taking fried chicken to them and to the firemen, gratis.

Gacy took his male employees with him on night patrols and thus established himself as a power figure to the youths. One former employee, Russell Schroeder, said Gacy always wanted to be in charge and that he always carried a handgun.

Schroeder and other former employees recalled that Gacy would take them out to steal auto parts while he monitored police calls on his radio. Gacy would honk his horn whenever a squad car was getting close.

Gacy was not in Waterloo long before those he encountered had formed definite opinions about him. To Donald Voorhees, Sr., a former Iowa state representative and Jaycee, Gacy "could have been successful in just about any enterprise." As a Jaycee, Gacy was regarded as a bright and dynamic member with the sort of drive that any organization values for getting its worthy projects done. To Lane, he was also a charitable man: he gave money and chicken to underprivileged children at Christmastime.

But there was another side to him. Dutton saw Gacy as "a kid trying to make it in an adult world." His certificate commissioning him as an honorary "Kentucky Colonel" was very important to him, and he loved being addressed as "Colonel" by his friends. He told Lane that he was also a colonel in the "Illinois Governor's Brigade." To Voorhees, Gacy was a boastful, arrogant know-it-all. To many others, he was a braggart striving to achieve big-man status with all his talk of money and connections.

Dutton attributed Gacy's prominence in an organization such as the Jaycees to his "unique ability to manipulate people and ingratiate himself." Always he catered to the influential by doing them favors. Myers well knew Gacy's ability to promote himself; in his son-in-law, however, he saw a person who was not particularly charming, but rather one who told people what they wanted to hear.

Gacy, to Dutton, was a very goal-oriented man who planned his moves impeccably. If Gacy thought he could intimidate someone, he would. "He wanted to dominate everyone," Pottinger later said. "I once told him he had a problem because his ego was more important than living."

Robert Beener, the chief of police, thought of Gacy as a wimp and a coward. Gacy disliked being told what to do, and something either had to go his way or not at all. The sheriff, Robert Aldrich, pointed out that Gacy would never confront an adult; a juvenile, maybe, but never an adult. Nor, when something went wrong, would Gacy ever admit fault. He always transferred blame, said Dutton, to someone "who was out to get him." His quick temper sometimes made him a terrible loser. His wife recalled a card game they played with friends. In a fit of anger after losing, Gacy threw all the cards and money on the floor. She said that even after she and Gacy went home, his anger persisted and culminated in a sort of seizure. He had to be rushed to a hospital.

Gacy chose his tactics carefully to fit his purpose, using aggressive hard-sell where it worked, manipulation where it didn't. "He could adapt his nature to any situation he was in," says Dutton. "He was a complete chameleon."

Although Gacy hired young people of both sexes for the stores, he associated closely only with the boys. Gacy set up a social club in his basement recreation area, where, for the payment of monthly dues, the boys were free to drink beer and other alcoholic beverages. Because many of them were under age, they found the club a convenient arrangement. Gacy had a pool table, and it was here that he apparently devised the strategy of challenging the boys to a game "for a blow job." If he failed at that, he tried a pseudo-scientific approach: The governor of Illinois, he told the boys, had commissioned him to conduct sexual experiments, some heterosexual, but mostly homosexual, in the interst of scientific inquiry. He even had a certificate attesting to his membership on a sexual commission. He lectured the boys on sexual morality, saying that homosexual relationships were not wrong if the participant believed they were not. To those who seemed incorrigibly heterosexual, he promised the services of his wife—as long as Gacy got oral sex from the youths as part of the deal. For the truly intransigent, he spoke ominously of connections he had in Chicago that would get rid of anyone he wanted. In such a manner, Gacy began to manipulate and intimidate the second group of what Dutton called his two main social outlets in Waterloo, the Jaycees and the young boys who worked for him.

Edward Lynch was sixteen in the summer of 1967, when he was working for Gacy as a cook and dishwasher in one of the stores. Although he was not a member of the "club," Gacy invited him one night to his house to watch some films, shoot pool, and have a few drinks. His wife was in the hospital, having delivered their second child. After several games of pool, Gacy made his blow-job proposal, then became angry when Lynch won and refused the prize. Gacy suggested they go upstairs. In the kitchen, he grabbed a carving knife and told Lynch to "get in the bedroom." He backed the youth into the room, and they struggled on the bed. When he saw that he had cut Lynch on the left arm, Gacy stopped and apologized and got a bandage.

They returned to the basement. Lynch wanted to leave, but Gacy insisted on showing some of his pornographic films. When they were over, he brought out a chain and padlock and said, "Let me try something." Used to taking orders from Gacy, Lynch allowed him to chain his hands behind his back. "Can you get them loose?" Gacy asked. Lynch couldn't. When he sat the boy down in a straightback chair, Gacy straddled him and got on his lap. He began rubbing Lynch's thighs. The youth drew in his legs, dumping Gacy on the floor. Gacy then rolled a cot into the room and pushed Lynch down on it. He put another chain on the youth's feet, then began choking him. Lynch struggled, then lost control of his bladder. He decided to pretend he had blacked out and lay perfectly still. Gacy eased up, then became concerned when Lynch didn't move. "Are you all right?" he asked the boy, who was dazed. Gacy agreed to take him home.

In later discussing the attack with a friend, Lynch was surprised to hear that he, too, had had strange encounters with Gacy. This boy was Donald Voorhees, Jr., who, though not a full-time employee, did various odd jobs for Gacy. Voorhees was interested when Gacy told him he could earn $50 or so by assisting him in research for his sex education committee. Voorhees was fifteen at the time.

Over a period of several months, in various locations, including Gacy's house and the motel, Gacy forced Voorhees to submit to oral sex. Often he got the boy drunk on whiskey or vodka before the encounters took place; Gacy himself did not drink. After the "experiments," Gacy would debrief Voorhees, asking his feelings and reactions. Usually, he gave him several dollars as a "gift."

The arrangement had Voorhees very confused, and he began to feel guilty about it. Gacy, however, told him not to discuss the "experiments" with anyone and threatened him with his organized crime contacts in Chicago. Finally, both Voorhees and Lynch became so upset that they decided to tell their parents.

Voorhees made his disclosure one evening after Gacy's name came up at the family dinner table. Donald Voorhees, Sr., had known Gacy through the Jaycees and had socialized with him on various occasions. Now, with Gacy's star ascending in the Jaycee organization, he was making a run for the presidency, and he had asked the senior Voorhees to be his campaign manager. Voorhees, then running for the state presidency of the Jaycees, suspected that Gacy was merely trying to ride his coattails. In any case, he was considering the matter and told his family of Gacy's invitation. Donald, Jr., implored his father not to get involved—and the whole story of his relationship with Gacy came out.

Both Lynch and Voorhees, Jr., gave statements to the police on March 11, 1968. The elder Voorhees urged County Attorney Roger Peterson to prosecute Gacy, and the grand jury heard testimony of the two youths on April 8.

On May 2, Gacy was given two polygraph examinations by the police. He asserted that he had not engaged in homosexual acts with anybody and that he was telling the truth. The examiner, Lieutenant Kenneth Vanous, found reactions "indicative of deception" and concluded that Gacy "did not tell the complete truth." The joke in the county attorney's office was that the only thing Gacy got right was his name, and the following week the grand jury indicted him on a charge of sodomy.

Gacy continued to deny any guilt and tried to disparage the reputations of his accusers. Many people in the community were persuaded and believed he was innocent.

In July, Gacy requested another polygraph examination, this time administered by the prestigious Chicago firm of John E. Reid and Associates. Gacy answered no to four questions about sex with Voorhees. Noting "significant emotional disturbances indicative of deception," the examiner concluded that Gacy was not telling the truth. Gacy finally amended his story, admitting that he had had homosexual relationships with Voorhees, but that he had paid the boy for them.

Despite the evidence of the two polygraph tests, nothing much happened in the weeks after Gacy's arraignment. The community was split into Voorhees and Gacy factions, and the accused had a substantial following, both inside and outside the Jaycees, that was convinced he was being framed. Too, Gacy claimed that he had a lot of incriminating information about several police employees involved in the goings-on at the motel, and for this reason—not to mention all the free fried chicken—there was talk that authorities were reluctant to push the matter any further. Toward the end of summer, there were growing indications that, but for a foolish move by Gacy himself, the whole case was fading away.

On the night of August 30/31, Gacy was making the rounds on his Merchant Patrol with his eighteen-year-old employee Russell Schroeder. Gacy had never made sexual overtures to Schroeder, a big youth who played both football and basketball, but he had been curious to hear about anything that had got Schroeder into trouble. On this night, however, the talk mostly concerned the businesses they were checking—and breaking into.

At Brown's Lumber Company, Gacy took a metal bar he kept by his car seat and pried the office door open. He told Schroeder to get the money out of the soft-drink machine, and he picked up a can of varnish and an extension cord. Gacy told Schroeder how easy it was to break into places with his metal bar.

About 6 A.M., while dropping off Schroeder at his car, Gacy remarked that there was a youth named Donald Voorhees, a witness against him in a criminal matter, who was spreading lies about him. Gacy said he wanted someone to beat up Voorhees for him. Schroeder didn't give it much thought at the time, but, several days later, after getting jilted by a girl, he talked to Gacy, who suggested he vent his anger and frustration on Voorhees. Gacy pointed out a picture of Voorhees in a high school yearbook and offered to pay off the debt on Schroeder's car, about $300. Schroeder agreed to do the job. Gacy gave him a can of Mace.

Schroeder found out the boy's class schedule at West High School and met him shortly after three o'clock. Schroeder introduced himself as a "big brother," representing one of the school's social programs, and asked Voorhees to drive out into the country with him, where he had a big cache of liquor. Voorhees accepted the invitation, and they drove out to a wooded park along Black Hawk Creek. Schroeder got out and started leading Voorhees into the park. Suddenly he whirled around and sprayed the Mace in Voorhees's face. Voorhees recoiled in pain and ran blindly, trying to wipe the chemical out of his eyes. Finally he fell into the creek. Dousing his face with water, he asked Schroeder what was going on. Schroeder said that somebody had accused Voorhees of stealing "some wheels." Voorhees denied this, and Schroeder said okay, he would take him home.

When Voorhees walked up the creek bank, Schroeder sprayed him again with Mace and hit him with a heavy stick. The two began grappling, and Schroeder tried to hold Voorhees's head under water. Voorhees broke loose and ran into a nearby cornfield. Unable to find him, Schroeder got into his car and cruised along some of the back roads. Finally he drove back to town. After taking a shower, he drove to Gacy's house about 6:30 P.M. Gacy was not at all pleased to see him— or to be seen with him. He took the can of Mace and told Schroeder he didn't want to know anything about what had happened. Schroeder left.

Voorhees, meanwhile, called the police in nearby Hudson from a farmhouse. They didn't believe his story at first, but after seeing the signs of struggle at the park, they changed their minds. The police reported the incident to the county sheriff.

After Voorhees identified Schroeder's picture, the sheriff's police picked up the older boy for questioning. Schroeder said that a guy he knew only as "Jim" had paid him $10 to scare Voorhees, whom Jim suspected of stealing his tires. Schroeder denied the attack and said he had never even seen any Mace. Gacy later told him the police couldn't prove anything—it was just the Voorhees boy's word against Schroeder's. Gacy continued checking with Schroeder to see if he was sticking to his story, and on Monday of the following week he told him that either Gacy or his father-in-law would help the boy with his attorney's fees.

Schroeder, however, folded under the pressure, and later that afternoon, in the presence of his father and an attorney, admitted that his earlier statement was false and told the police he wanted to set the record straight. Gacy's involvement was now out in the open and his motive for having the Voorhees boy beaten was clear for all to see. County Attorney Peterson filed three charges against Gacy in connection with the beating and, on Thursday, after Schroeder implicated him in the lumberyard break-in, Gacy was jailed in lieu of $10,000 bond.

At his court appearance on September 12, Gacy was ordered to submit to a psychiatric evaluation at the Psychopathic Hospital of the State University of Iowa. Later that afternoon, some of the remarks that Gacy made to a deputy sheriff about the milieu in which he operated so interested the policeman that he called in six law enforcement officials, including Peterson, to hear Gacy's statement. For several hours into the evening, Gacy told them what he knew—both from observation and hearsay—about the seamy side of Waterloo. He talked of gambling, prostitution, pornographic movies, wife-swapping, the shenanigans of some of his Jaycee associates, both at the motel and on the road at conventions, police corruption—and he supplied numerous names of friends and associates. He tried to make it clear that John Gacy was not the only sinner in Waterloo.

After the sheriff's police deposited Gacy at the Psychopathic Hospital, ward attendants there noticed that he immediately began feeling out his environment. He was friendly and cooperative and made it known that he was a private patient there to be helped. By the second day, he was denying that he had done the things he was accused of. He also appeared to be "overly defensive when supporting a point of view." In the first few days, his moods and activities varied. He boasted of how much money he made, he cried for an hour, refused to eat, and seemed depressed for the rest of the day. Talking with his wife on the telephone, he said that the Voorhees boy was lying. He became angry and told her he would not agree to a divorce, saying that her parents were telling her lies.

After several days, Gacy focused his attention on another patient, whom he saw was a rule-breaker. Gacy began tattling on him as well as ordering him to perform such tasks as making his bed. Toward the end, he became somewhat fatherly. The attendants noticed Gacy becoming meddlesome in ward affairs as well. He threatened to report one shift for not mopping the floors.

Gacy freely expressed his opinion on everything. He expounded on civil rights and emphasized his dislike for "queers." He boasted frequently about the new cars he drove and about the money he made; he offered to pay an attendant twice his present wages to leave the hospital and work for him. When playing pool, he had ready excuses for losing, which he usually did: the table wasn't level, his back gave him problems, and so forth.

By the second week, he was openly referring to himself as the "barn boss." He was the self-proclaimed Bible teacher and had assumed the responsibility of directing newly arrived patients about the ward. He constantly tried to manipulate the attendants to obtain privileges.

During his seventeen-day stay at the hospital, the staff administered psychiatric interviews and physical and psychological testing, in addition to observing his behavior in the ward. Dr. Eugene F. Gauron wrote that Gacy would "twist the truth in such a way that he would not be made to look bad and would admit to socially unacceptable actions only when directly confronted." Gauron regarded him as "a smooth talker and an obscurer who was trying to whitewash himself of all wrongdoing."

Gacy scored a Full Scale I.Q. of 118, putting him in the "bright normal range." His highest verbal subtest score was in comprehension, indicating, Dr. Gauron said, "a high degree of social intelligence or awareness of the proper way to behave in order to influence people.

"The most striking aspect of the test results," Dr. Gauron continued, "is the patient's total denial of responsibility for anything that has happened to him. He can produce an 'alibi' for everything. He alternately blames the environment, while presenting himself as a victim of circumstances and blames other people while presenting himself as the victim of others who are out to get him. Although this could be construed as paranoid, I do not regard it that way. Rather, the patient attempts to assure a sympathetic response by depicting himself as being at the mercy of a hostile environment. To his way of thinking, a major objective is to outwit the other fellow and take advantage of him before being taken advantage of himself." Dr. Gauron also noted Gacy's propensity to behave impulsively: "He does things without thinking through the consequences and exercises poor judgment."

Gacy is loquacious and circumstantial, but also coherent and goal-oriented, Dr. L. D. Amick wrote in his discharge summary; and, "he does not seem to have remorse over the admitted deeds, which are a part of his present difficulty."

The doctors determined that Gacy was competent to stand trial. In their letter to District Judge Peter Van Metre, Dr. Leonard Heston and Dr. Amick said they had diagnosed Gacy as an "antisocial personality." Such persons, the doctors wrote, "are basically unsocialized, and [their] behavior patterns brings them repeatedly into conflict with society. Persons with this personality structure do not learn from experience and are unlikely to benefit from known medical treatment."

Gacy now contended that Voorhees had offered his services to others and that the acts committed with Gacy were commercial transactions. He put himself at the mercy of the court and pleaded guilty, perhaps in the belief that his standing in the community would bring leniency and no greater punishment than a reprimand and probation. Indeed, probation was the recommendation of Parole and Probation Officer Jack D. Harker in a presentencing investigation he made at the request of the court. Harker presented Gacy's explanation that his offense was of an experimental nature, and the officer thought that Gacy was sufficiently imbued with the work ethic to make good under supervision back in Illinois.

Despite Harker's recommendations, and much to Gacy's shock, Judge Van Metre decided against probation. "The particular pattern you seem to have chosen," the judge said, "is to seek out teenage boys and get them involved, either in sexual misbehavior or in other misbehavior, and, unsatisfactory in many respects as imprisonment is, at least that will ensure for some period of time that you cannot seek out teenage boys to solicit them for immoral behavior of any kind."

On December 3, 1968, Judge Van Metre sentenced the convicted sodomist to ten years' imprisonment.

* * *

When John Gacy arrived at the Iowa State Men's Reformatory at Anamosa, he seemed determined to be a model of good behavior to qualify for early parole. Conscious of the homosexuality that pervades every prison, he went to some effort to isolate himself from inmates so inclined. Obviously fearing attack, Gacy quickly befriended three inmates, Raymond Cornell, Larry Polsley, and Duane Fulton, all former partners in crime. The other prisoners knew that these three would defend one another, and Gacy curried their favor for the security their group offered. Gacy always disguised his sodomy conviction, saying he had been charged with showing pornographic films to teenagers. In the protective circle of his three new friends, he loudly voiced his disdain for "fucking queers."

Assigned to work in food service, Gacy soon manipulated himself into the unofficial position of straw boss of the kitchen. Under his stewardship, the quality of the food improved, and the kitchen was spotlessly maintained. Gacy, however, didn't limit his supervision to the inmates; he openly bossed the guards as well. When a known homosexual was assigned to his staff, Gacy protested and got the man transferred because he didn't think such a person should be involved in food service. Polsley recalled Gacy taking good care of his friends, inviting them to select in advance the best cuts of meat and giving them extra mushrooms and other special treats.

Cornell noticed that Gacy closely identified with the guards because he, himself, enjoyed being boss. From his hosts, Gacy wangled civilian shirts and his favorite cigars. Though he never knew where it came from, Cornell noticed that Gacy always had money, and Cornell suspected he was loan-sharking on the side. As a commissary worker, Gacy had a "late-out" card that meant he didn't have to return to his cell until midnight.

Gacy and his friends, says Fulton, were known as "power inmates," prisoners who participated in such activities as the Jaycees to improve their chances for parole. Gacy took up with the Jaycees where he had left off—except for the illicit doings. He was a director of the prison chapter and served as chaplain. At Christmas he was Santa Claus. For his dedicated service, he won a "Sound Citizen Award."

Once, while working on a miniature golf course the Jaycees were building, he and Polsley argued over a construction matter, and Polsley threatened to fight him. Gacy suddenly developed one of his seizures, clutched his chest, and turned pale. The other inmates knew that he was physically weak and did not exercise at all. When Gacy talked of being on a mob hit list, Fulton concluded that he was paranoid.

Although the other inmates thought Gacy was being overbearing and determined to get his own way, they generally expected him to become a wealthy man once he was free. He followed *The Wall Street Journal* and taught several prisoners how to read stock tables. Frequently he discussed his business plans for the future. While Gacy was momentarily content to bide his time, it was clear that he wanted out of the prison system.

Gacy's great sadness of his first year at Anamosa was the divorce action his wife brought against him. He expressed bitterness about his father-in-law's prompting in the matter and later complained of how Myers had taken him for all he had. He was returned to Waterloo in September, 1969, for the hearing, where he saw his wife for the first time in a year. Although visitation of his two young children was left pending, he would never see them again. Back at Anamosa, he told his associates that as far as he was concerned his children were dead.

Within six months of his imprisonment, Gacy was applying for early release under supervision. The State of Iowa Board of Parole informed him that such a request was premature but said they hoped he continued making progress. A month later he sought approval to engage in community service outside the reformatory. Peter Van Metre, the judge who sentenced Gacy, had no objection, so long as the prisoner acted correctly, but he cautioned: "I am rather pessimistic about any long range change in [Gacy's] character. I believe, from what I know, that he is likely to behave properly so long as under supervision and the threat of possible harmful consequences for misbehavior." Black Hawk County Attorney David Dutton was not so sanguine: "I do not feel that John Gacy should receive any consideration or leniency at this time," he wrote. "Mr. Gacy has always had the capacity to manipulate his environment and most people in it for his own ends. I would be highly suspect of his 'changed attitude.'"

Gacy's family in Illinois maintained their loyalty and sent letters to the institution, pledging that they would help him find work and provide a loving and stable environment during his parole. Because the health of Gacy's father was deteriorating fast, the family pleaded for John's release on compassionate grounds as well.

In a report written on September 4, 1969, nine months after Gacy's sentencing, Correctional Counselor Lyle Eugene Murray reviewed the inmate's progress. Gacy got good marks for his work in the kitchen, and Murray listed the various courses he had enrolled in and mentioned Gacy's plans to take the General Education Development test. Murray noted the need for further counseling, but he viewed Gacy's regular attendance at mass and involvement in the Jaycees as positive factors. Although he conceded that Gacy should look at himself in greater depth, Murray questioned whether there was much more Gacy would gain by remaining at Anamosa. Murray said that Gacy, if he returned to his parents, "would very likely not be involved in the same type of offense as he is presently incarcerated for." The following day, a preparole committee recommended Gacy for favorable consideration.

Although the board turned down his request, Gacy took the news with equanimity and set about improving his chances for release on the next docket, in May, 1970. After completing sixteen high school courses, he received his diploma in November, and started taking college-level classes. He plunged into the Jaycees with new fervor, serving on twenty-three committees and winning the vote as top member in the chapter.

On Christmas Day, 1969, Gacy's father died. When he learned of the death, John went through an emotional period of readjustment during which he cried often and required considerable support from the staff.

The preparole committee, on March 13, 1970, again recommended Gacy for consideration, and a psychiatric evaluation was ordered. During the interview, Gacy told the consultant, Dr. Richard Lee, that he no longer entertained the unconventional attitudes he had once espoused. Diagnosing Gacy as a "passive aggressive personality," Dr. Lee also recommended paroling him. "The likelihood of his again being charged with and being convicted of antisocial conduct," Lee wrote, "appears to be small."

This time, the parole board responded favorably and set Gacy's release for June 18, 1970. As planned, he would go back to Chicago to live with his widowed mother and make a new start. Shortly after noon on the appointed day, Gacy's best friend from Waterloo, Clarence Lane, picked him up at the release center in Newton. Gacy had been incarcerated for twenty-one months of his ten-year sentence. All along, Lane had been convinced of Gacy's innocence and had remained loyal to him. Lane told Gacy, almost jocularly, "Now that it's over with, keep your nose clean."

"Clarence," Gacy earnestly told his friend, "I'll never go back to jail."

Living in Chicago with his mother, Gacy had to observe a 10 P.M. curfew under the terms of his probation. Through the kindness of a family friend, Eugene Boschelli, Gacy got a job at Bruno's Restaurant, which Boschelli managed, in downtown Chicago. Although Boschelli later said he never truly liked or fully trusted Gacy, he thought he was a good chef. Bruno's was a favorite gathering spot for some members of the Chicago Black Hawks hockey team, as well as for city policemen and politicians. In this kind of Runyonesque atmosphere Gacy came into bloom, first as a rapt listener, then as an ingratiating host. Among those he met at the restaurant was James Hanley, the Chicago policeman whose name Gacy modified for his street alias. Although Gacy dated a waitress who worked at Bruno's, Boschelli noticed that he was soon associating with men who were obviously homosexuals.

Gacy tried to arrange for regular visits with his children. In a letter to his former wife, he said he loved her as much as he had before and that he missed her and his children. Not receiving an answer, he wrote another letter shortly before Christmas. Although his tone became somemwhat more defensive, he pleaded for cooperation for the children's sake. He said he was sending a check to pay for some current pictures of the children and for their Christmas presents.

Gacy's letters apparently went unanswered, and the despair

he had known in prison returned. He made his mother get rid of all the pictures of his former wife and their children and told her that it was better he just consider them dead.

Gacy was eligible for discharge on June 18, 1971, a year after he got out of Anamosa. He received his certificate of release the following October. But even after twenty-one months in jail, Gacy had not reformed at all. Police records show that on two occasions before June, 1971, he had engaged in homosexual activity, thus violating the parole.

Mickel Ried told sheriff's investigators that shortly after arriving in Chicago in November, 1970, as a twenty-year-old discharged from the army, he had met Gacy, who was cruising on Clark Street. Ried said that Gacy took him to Gacy's mother's apartment and performed fellatio on him while masturbating himself.

In February, 1971, Gacy was arrested on a complaint of disorderly conduct filed by nineteen-year-old Alan Lemke, who said that he and Gacy had engaged in sex at Gacy's apartment. Gacy filed a similar complaint against Lemke, and the case was dismissed.

Gacy, meanwhile, went into business with Ried, painting and doing maintenance work for people Gacy had met in Bruno's Restaurant. His mother's apartment, however, lacked the necessary storage space for materials, and Gacy persuaded her to buy a house. She settled on the one at 8213 Summerdale, and they moved there in the autumn of 1971. Ried was one of several nonfamily members who lived with them and, by his account, he slept in Gacy's bedroom.

Even then, Ried said, Gacy was talking about playing policeman and handcuffing and beating the young men he picked up. Ried, however, never believed him. One day, Gacy took Ried to a nursery, where Gacy said he wanted to steal some shrubs for his house. Ried saw Gacy following him with a tire iron in his hand and asked what that was for. Gacy said "there might be trouble" but, when pressed, told Ried to forget the whole thing and returned to his vehicle. Ried thought Gacy had planned to kill him.

Several weeks later Ried was riding with Gacy. They drove into the garage, and Gacy closed the door. He asked Ried to look under the workbench and get a spare fuse. As Ried was stooping down, he felt a blow on the back of his head, then blood was running down his neck. He turned and saw Gacy holding a hammer. Ried grabbed him and asked why he had hit him. Gacy said he didn't know but said he'd had a sudden urge to kill Ried. The next day Ried moved out.

Soon after that, Gacy married Cathy Hull. The two had become reacquainted in May, 1971, when she was getting divorced from her first husband. She had known the Gacy family since attending school with John's younger sister, and she had dated John at age sixteen. After Gacy and his mother moved to Summerdale, he started going out with Cathy, and by Christmas he was talking marriage. After celebrating New Year's Eve at Bruno's, they had their first sexual relations, and Cathy became pregnant. Gacy was happy when she told him the news. He told Cathy he wanted a family of his own because he couldn't visit his children, and he said he loved her. Cathy miscarried in February. She moved into the house in March with her two daughters from her previous marriage. Gacy slept in the living room, where the two generally had their sexual relations, especially on Friday nights, when both their mothers went off together to play bingo. In July, they had a big wedding, then a reception at the house. Gacy did most of the planning.

By then, Gacy's mother had got her own apartment to avoid the congestion, and because her relationship with her son was becoming more strained. Gacy's contracting business was growing, and he was angered whenever the senior Mrs. Gacy, answering a telephone inquiry from one of his potential clients, referred to herself as "John's mother." It was just too unbusinesslike to suit the future chief executive officer of PDM. After her departure, however, Gacy invited Cathy's mother to live with them, probably on the assumption that they needed a babysitter for his wife's two young daughters. He would soon regret it and later complain that, after a year of her residence, he needed a court order to evict her.

Almost from the start, John and Cathy's marital relationship went into a decline when he took up with his circle of boys. Toward the end, the couple went weeks without even talking, and they coexisted separately, he in the recreation room, she and her children in the front of the house. The marriage was a lost cause, and they were divorced early in 1976.

Cathy recalled that the odor from the crawl space got worse during the period of their marriage. After she initially complained, Gacy spread lime. Once, when she was away, Gacy poured some concrete—he said, to stop the smell. It was especially bad in the bathroom and hallway. She wanted to call an exterminator, but Gacy said the dampness caused the odor. In the last months she was living at Summerdale, they were getting gnats and black bugs in the house, even during winter. Finally, she told Gacy that there must be dead mice in the crawl space and asked him to check. He said he would set traps. She was astounded by the non sequitur.

In the windup of our investigation, we talked to several more of Gacy's "living victims."

David Edgecombe worked for Gacy for several months before quitting to go on a trip. Late one night, he heard a knock on his bedroom window at his mother's house in Park Ridge. It was Gacy, who suggested they "go party." Edgecombe took along Ivan, his Siberian husky, just in case Gacy was angry about his quitting.

Gacy drove Edgecombe to the Democratic precinct headquarters, where he offered the youth $25 to drink a half pint of rum. Gacy didn't drink any. The next thing Edgecombe remembered was being in Gacy's workshed, handcuffed. Gacy was sitting on his stomach choking him, saying, "You son of a bitch, you'll never quit on me again." Edgecombe cried out, and Ivan began furiously barking and clawing at the door. Gacy got off the youth and offered to drive him home.

Sixteen-year-old Anthony Antonucci had his parents' approval when he accepted a job offer from Gacy, who had done some work on their apartment. The Antonuccis had met Gacy at the church of which they were members. Soon after Anthony started work, Gacy took him to the Democratic headquarters, offered him some whiskey, and suggested giving him a blow job. Antonucci thought Gacy was joking and refused. Gacy began tussling with the boy, who finally picked up a chair and swung it at Gacy. The contractor stopped his advances and took Antonucci to Summerdale. Cathy and the children were off visiting, and Gacy said he wanted Antonucci to be ready for an early job. The boy spent the night on the couch with nothing further said.

About a month later, Antonucci's parents left town on vacation. They had asked Gacy to keep an eye on their son. Gacy came by the apartment about midnight and told the boy he had been to a party in the neighborhood and just wanted to check on him. He happened to have a bottle of wine, a projector, and some stag films with him.

The two began wrestling, and Gacy managed to handcuff Antonucci behind his back. He didn't notice that one manacle was loose. He rolled the boy over on his back, pulled his pants down, then got up and walked into the kitchen. Antonucci, meanwhile, worked his right wrist out of the loose handcuff and remained on the floor waiting. When Gacy returned, Antonucci—who happened to be on his high school wrestling team—tackled him and held him down by pressing his knee into Gacy's neck. He slipped the loose handcuff on one of Gacy's wrists, found the key, and, after freeing himself, cuffed the contractor's other wrist.

As Gacy lay prone on the floor, he expressed wonderment over the boy's dexterity. "You're the only one," he said, "that ever got out of these and got them on me." Antonucci let him stew about it for ten minutes, then released him, whereupon Gacy left.

Several other youths told us of the homosexual experiences they had had with him. In one instance Gacy threatened to kill the boy if he didn't submit to anal intercourse, and in another case he persuaded the victim to inhale a chloroform-like substance before attacking him. Who knows how many more horror stories remain to be told? By his own reckoning, Gacy had hundreds of sexual experiences, and most of those the police learned of were anything but consensual. The August before his arrest, after eight years of indiscriminate promiscuity, Gacy finally encountered a modicum of—at least pathogenic—revenge: He was diagnosed as being syphilitic.

By late 1978, Gacy was showing signs that he could see the end was coming. Several times earlier he had remarked to his family that he would probably die violently before he was forty, but now he was voicing other premonitions. After visiting his mother in November, he told his older sister that Mrs. Gacy probably would not be coming up from Arkansas and spending any more summers with him in Norwood Park. He told her that if anything happened to him, he wanted her husband to take over his business.

The same month, returning from a funeral in Springfield, Gacy remarked to his sister as they approached the Des Plaines River, "If you fell off that bridge you could come up anywhere downriver." A few weeks later, on December 13, 1978, John Gacy threw the body of his thirty-third and final victim into the river from the same span. And, as perhaps he foresaw, it all came apart.

TRIAL

Preparation

From the start we knew it was likely we would be facing an insanity defense. Under Illinois law, a finding of insanity is tantamount to not guilty. Because the defendant presumably does not appreciate the criminality of his behavior nor can he conform his conduct to the requirements of the law, he is considered not responsible for his actions and therefore cannot be punished for them. Instead, he becomes a ward of the state mental health system, and those who take custody of him determine how long he will be sequestered from society. Nothing is certain about long-term incarceration, and possibly after a brief term he may be set free. This is what we sought to prevent in the case of John Gacy.

In Bill Kunkle, the state had a man of substantial trial experience with insanity defenses. A chemistry and biology major with a premedical background, Kunkle was highly conversant with the terminology and literature of psychiatry. He was our senior expert in insanity-defense cases.

Kunkle always tries, as I do, to get to the defendant's family and friends before the defense lawyers have a chance to make them part of their "team." "Relatives will not want to suggest that the defendant was 'crazy,'" he says, "until a defense lawyer points out the advantages of such a posture to them." He prefers to let the defense make the first move toward a psychiatric examination. If, on the other hand, the state calls for the exam, he says, "that shows a jury that there is some doubt in our mind about the guy's sanity." Gacy's first examination, of course, had been at the defense's request and by court order.

As Kunkle says, there are three basic philosophies of forensic psychiatrics. The first is, "It's all hokum; ignore it"; second, "It may be of some help, but the facts are more important"; and third, "It's very important." With Gacy, he chose a course midway between the second and third. When psychiatric witnesses contradict one another or the testimony is beyond the comprehension of the jury, he looks for a washout, trying to get the jury simply to disregard all of it.

"Most insanity defenses break down," Kunkle says. "They can show there's a mental defect, but they stumble when they ask, 'Did that defect make it impossible for the defendant to conform his conduct to the law or understand the criminality of his action?' " We knew that Gacy was anything but normal, but after Kunkle had Dr. Reifman critique the reports of Dr. Rappaport and the other defense analysts, we believed that their case for insanity could be dismantled.

We had demanded a thorough background check of Gacy and had amassed considerable evidence to support our contention that he was sane. In the end, the facts of the case themselves would be our most effective weapon: We would show that Gacy had dug graves in advance, made telephone calls during the killing of Piest, drawn an accurate diagram of the crawl space, and so forth. These were certainly the acts of a man capable of premeditation, acting in his own best interest under duress, and recollecting the details of his criminal activities. While Bill focused on the psychiatric questions, Bob Egan concentrated on the physical evidence and I on the police investigation. All our work had to constantly intermesh because the factual case must be built in such a way as to achieve the goal of defeating the isanity defense. The law allows us to anticipate that defense, so I instructed our investigators to gather facts about Gacy's drug and alcohol consumption. If we could show that Gacy usually reacted to those things by getting sick or passing out, that would defuse the defense's attempt to portray him as a violent captive of drug-related psychosis.

In felony cases, we often collect blood, hair, and handwriting samples from the defendant for identification purposes. In a rape case, police generally take pubic hair samples. In all cases, they collect certain materials for use as "negative evidence" in the event the defense tries to show that samples don't match and the police were careless in their investigation. In this case, we wanted to resolve the mystery of the forged title to Szyc's car. (Our handwriting experts, however, were never able to ascertain whether Gacy had done it or not.) Although Gacy's lawyers objected to our taking the physical samples, we got a court order allowing the investigators to do so.

On March 16, 1979, Sergeant Des Ré Maux, in company with Charles Pearson, Joe Hein, and Greg Bedoe, presented themselves in Gacy's room at Cermak to take the samples. After noting Gacy's and Motta's objections on the warrant, Des Ré Maux plucked hairs from Gacy's head, and a medical technician drew several vials of his blood. Des Ré Maux, however, decided to honor Gacy's request to pull out his own pubic hairs in private, and he detailed Pearson to accompany him to the lavatory.

"Hey, Des Ré Maux," Pearson said, moments later. "You'd better come here." The sergeant went to the door. He looked and saw that Gacy's pubic region was clean-shaven.

"Sorry, fellows," Gacy said sheepishly. "I got the crabs. I apologize, but you'll have to come back when it grows out."

Later, Genty would take delight in plucking Gacy's pubic hairs himself. Today, however, the officers would take what they could get, then rush back to Summerdale on more pressing business. Sergeant Marinelli had called Des Ré Maux moments before. Body No. 29 had just been found.

On April 23, a Cook County grand jury indicted Gacy on twenty-six other murders, bringing the total to thirty-three. Two days later, under heavy guard, the defendant stood in the courtroom beside his lawyers and pleaded not guilty to the charges. Gacy was now sporting a full beard, and he had lost considerable weight after going on a self-imposed Lenten fast. He had been rushed to Cook County Hospital a couple of weeks earlier, after twenty days of fasting on liquids only, complaining of stomach and chest pains. The diagnosis indicated hypoglycemia, or low blood sugar.

We announced that we were ready for trial on the Piest indictments, but our statement was mostly for the sake of good press action and to show that we were moving right along. It also had the practical effect, however, of making the defense think twice before demanding immediate trial and automatically putting into effect Illinois's "speedy-trial" provisions, which, by now, would have given us less than 120 days to start trial. Of course we were nowhere near ready, but we knew Gacy's lawyers weren't either, and the court had yet to rule on Gacy's fitness to stand trial.

In July, the defense filed a motion to consolidate all the indictments, which would force us to try all the cases at one time. (Earlier, both sides had agreed to transfer the Rignall case from another criminal court in Chicago to 26th and California.) Neither side, of course, wanted any testimony coming out of other legal actions that would hurt the main criminal proceedings. Now, however, we were being forced into an unfavorable position, even though we didn't necessarily want to try all the murder cases separately.

The defense, of course, was relying on the insanity issue: Here they had one of the greatest accused mass-murderers of all time, and everybody was saying, "He's gotta be nuts." The sheer number of his victims tended to corroborate that notion in the popular mind, and separate trials surely would have diluted his defense. Conversely, if we tried the cases separately and lost the first, we would have had thirty-two more chances. Consolidating them made it a most frightening all-or-nothing venture.

Under Illinois law, if the prosecution knows of other criminal charges that stem from activities happening at or about the same time—if they are all part of the same "course of conduct"—they must all be tried together. The Gacy murders, however, did not fit that description; all but his notorious "double" happened at different times. So, while we didn't truly want to try the cases separately—an endeavor that would have taken years—we also didn't want to play into the hands of the defense. Consequently, we opposed their motion. In August, Judge Garippo ruled against us, saying, "Let's get ready for trial." To avoid interference with the holiday season, he was hoping to have it over by Thanksgiving.

* * *

It was only at this stage of the trial preparation that I was finally transferred to 26th and California, the "Establishment" of the state's attorney's office. Although I hadn't worked full time for several years at the main Criminal Courts Building—traditionally the in spot of Chicago's felony trial activity—I thought it was essential for me to be at the headquarters during preparation of our case. Initially, my bosses just put me off, saying they didn't know when the case would go to trial. So for the first few months, I remained at my post in the Northwest suburbs as district supervisor.

Meanwhile, we heard continuing rumors of State's Attorney Bernard Carey's interest in the case. Carey, a Republican, was an elected official, and there was no doubt he was preparing for the November, 1980, elections, in which he expected to win re-election to his third term. It was widely assumed that trying and winning a case of this magnitude would virtually assure his victory. On the other hand, if he lost the voters would surely run him out of office. Carey's main drawback as a potential prosecution chief was that he had had no trial experience since taking office.

But in September Carey announced to the press that he was taking personal charge of the prosecution. He said he felt that a case as important as Gacy's demanded his personal attention and that as the county's top prosecutor it was his duty to step in. Some of us thought that he had never intended to make such an announcement, that an off-the-cuff remark he had made to a reporter after a speech got snowballed by the press and now made it difficult for him to back off.

Although he had promised to keep the prosecution team intact, his anticipated arrival certainly didn't ease our burden. We had no choice, however, but to go ahead, preparing witnesses so we would have the case ready, with or without Carey, on schedule. By Thanksgiving, he still hadn't taken part in the preparation, and the trial, having again been continued, was just weeks away.

Although he never made a direct statement that he would quit, in the second week of December Carey announced that it now was very unlikely that he would personally prosecute the case. Garippo, meanwhile, had postponed the trial until after the holidays, and it looked as if it might even still be under way at the time of the Illinois primary on March 18. The postponement, caused by the defense's motion for a change of venue, was another reason Carey gave for possibly removing himself: He would be too long away from his duties in Cook County. As it turned out, Carey never did step in, although he made symbolic appearances at both the opening and closing of the trial. In November, 1980, he lost the election to Richard M. Daley, the son of the late mayor.

Both sides, as well as the court, were greatly concerned about whether Gacy could get a fair trial in Chicago, but the problems of moving the proceedings elsewhere were many. Judge Garippo wanted to keep it in his home jurisdiction, and we did not relish the tremendous logistics burden—transporting records, evidence, police personnel, and witnesses—that a move would entail. On the other hand, the composition of the jury in a downstate city would be quite different from one chosen in Chicago, and likely more favorable to us; we knew we would be far better off in a smaller city, where we could find a good All-American, God-fearing, working-class jury. The central issue, of course, was pretrial publicity. Garippo had continued the original gag order, and the threat of contempt citations had mostly buttoned the lips of those who could have sunk ships by further leaking information to the press. Nonetheless, there was substantial coverage of the Gacy story in Chicago, and the identification of each body brought forth a flurry of the sort of feature coverage that Garippo thought would be particularly prejudicial. But the case was so notorious that, as with the Manson trial in California, it was doubtful a jury could be chosen anywhere that hadn't been exposed to considerable Gacy news coverage.

In late October, the defense finally made a motion to have a market research study made of possible sites in Illinois, analyzing the news coverage in those communities. The judge denied the motion and offered instead the proposal that he give the defense the privilege of unlimited juror challenges. This scared the hell out of us; the other side could then chop away at the jury candidates until they came up with an offbeat selection not unsympathetic to Gacy.

One of Garippo's main concerns was the great cost to the taxpayers that would result from conducting the trial elsewhere. Despite the importance of the case, he was determined to keep the spending at a reasonable level. But with unlimited challenges, the defense could prolong jury selection for months, and the costs would mount even if the trial were kept in Chicago. Thus Garippo had a knotty issue to resolve. There were several sound reasons for staying in Chicago, but he still had to give the defense every possible guarantee of a fair trial.

Several more weeks went by, and Garippo, seeing that even his revised timetable was falling apart, on November 20 gave the defense a ten-day deadline for filing a motion for change of venue. They responded on November 30, asking for a publicity analysis as well as a change of venue. Now it was virtually certain that the trial could not begin on January 7, 1980, as rescheduled.

In early December, the judge, Amirante, and I visited a market research firm in Chicago. Shortly thereafter Judge Garippo unenthusiastically consented to the defense request to make a study of press coverage in several downstate cities by compiling newspaper clippings. The court itself would survey the situation in Chicago. Garippo set January 7 as the hearing date for change of venue.

The judge had hoped that we would oppose the defense's motion for another trial site but, despite the hardships such a move would cause, we decided we would do better going elsewhere. A compromise, independently suggested by me and one of the judge's colleagues, was reached: going downstate to choose a jury, then sequestering them and bringing them back to Chicago for the trial itself. This effectively honored the defense's request for a change of venue, while greatly simplifying our logistical burden. It gave the defense a jury presumably untainted by the substantial Chicago-area pretrial publicity. And it effectively removed the built-in grounds for appeal the defense would have had if they had been able to argue that the defendant—denied the venue change—had not got a fair trial.

The media survey revealed considerable news coverage in downstate cities, although far less than that in Chicago. The defense would have preferred choosing a jury in a place like

Champaign-Urbana, home of the University of Illinois, where they could tap the population of college liberals. (Prosecutors try to avoid jurors who hold permissive attitudes, as well as people who work in or who are students of health care, education, and so forth, lest they be looked on by their fellow jurors as "experts.") We still wanted a predominantly working-class community. Not all the downstate candidates, however, welcomed the opportunity to participate in this momentous proceeding. Editorial writers in Peoria said that we could deal them out: their citizens already had done their duty in the trial of Richard Speck, a Chicago drifter convicted of the murder of eight student nurses in 1966.

The choice was Rockford, which, despite its proximity, ninety miles northwest of Chicago, had in Garippo's judgment the least amount of pretrial news coverage. We were quite satisfied. Rockford, Illinois's second largest city, is a manufacturing and commercial center with a sizable population of Swedish descent, and its values are the sort we were looking for.

In the final weeks before trial, we intensified our preparatory efforts. Our list of possible witnesses had run well into three figures, but now we were targeting on fewer than one hundred. We ran them through considerable preparation to ensure that they would be as comfortable as possible on the stand. Bill Kunkle, Bob Egan, and I each had our own witnesses, and after we prepared them for direct examination—testimony in response to our own questions—one of us put them through an imaginary cross-examination, anticipating questions we knew the defense would ask.

To prove murder, the state must first establish that the victim once lived. To this end, we planned to present the testimony of relatives and friends of those victims who had been identified. These witnesses were the most difficult to prepare, and we regretted having to put some of them on. They were still grieving enormously and when asked to recall the last moments of their son's life, they often broke down and wept uncontrollably. A few were reluctant to testify but were later persuaded to do so in the interest of seeing justice served. Many of the witnesses feared facing John Gacy. Some witnesses had things they wanted to say, as a final testamentary to the slain youth. This, they felt, was the only way to refute Gacy's slander that he was disposing of human garbage, and we would phrase our questions in such a manner as to allow them to make their statement. We took the witnesses into an empty courtroom to give them an impression of what it was like, and we showed them evidence we would be introducing, such as pictures of the victims. As best we could we prepared them to the point where, we thought, they could finally cope with the task of telling their story.

When Chicago news crews swept into Rockford to cover the jury selection, they were looked upon by some local observers as prime evidence of the world of difference between the Windy City and downstate. After it was all over, a Rockford columnist would invite us to take our crime, our lousy schools, and our Gacys with us—and good riddance.

Jury selection began, under strict security precautions, on Monday, January 28, 1980, in the Winnebago County Courthouse in downtown Rockford. Gacy was now in public view for the first time in months, and many of those who had seen him only in his mug shot were surprised that he could be taken for a typical businessman, dressed in his light gray tweed three-piece suit, with white shirt and black loafers. The suit was one of four his attorneys had bought for his courtroom appearances.

During the proceedings, Gacy smiled and sometimes laughed during moments of lightness in the questioning. (One juror promptly got himself excused when, asked his name by the judge, he fired back: "He's guilty.") Frequently Gacy took notes, studied legal documents, and huddled with his attorneys. At other times he turned in his chair and stared at various spectators and news representatives, watching them writing on their notepads and sketching him. By the end of the session in Rockford, Gacy was waving to members of the press.

Despite pessimistic predictions that we would be a month or more in juror selection, Judge Garippo was confidently saying he would have a jury within a week. He was right; it took four days. In Rockford, he did not need to question potential jurors to the extent he would have had to in Chicago, where news coverage had been much heavier and the likelihood of connection, however remote, between a juror and one of Gacy's victims far greater.

Garippo asked candidates about their family, job, religion, and so forth, then asked pointed questions about their views on homosexuality, insanity, the death penalty, and what they considered their obligations under the law. Those who said they could not serve impartially nor cope with the hardships of being sequestered for eight or ten weeks were excused. Each side had twenty challenges they could use to dismiss any candidates they regarded unfavorably. The defense used fifteen, we thirteen. The proceedings were quite monotonous— Gacy was visibly bored by Thursday—but they were conducted with Garippo's customary efficiency. By the fourth day, the twelve jurors and four alternates had been chosen and sworn. Seven were men, five women, all white and all from working-class backgrounds. Their ages ranged from twenty-one to seventy-one.

The opening statements in *The People of the State of Illinois* v. *John Wayne Gacy* were heard on Wednesday, February 6. The scene was now Chicago, in the seven-story gray limestone Criminal Court Building that rises like a butte out of the Cook County penal complex at 26th and California. The marble corridors were crowded with camera crews and onlookers queuing up to get passes admitting them to the trial. Extra pews had been brought into the huge, high-ceilinged courtroom and fifty seats reserved for the press, as well as several rows for the families and friends of victims.

Workmen had enlarged the jury box to accommodate the twelve regulars and four alternates. From the spectators' point of view, the jurors sat to the left of the judge's bench, facing the table where Gacy sat with his lawyers, Sam Amirante and Robert Motta. Our table was in the center facing the bench. Behind the defense stood our two largest exhibits, the four-by-eight-foot board on which we would display pictures of the victims—which became known among the prosecutors as the "Gallery of Grief"—and a four-by-twelve-foot plat map showing where the bodies had been recovered on Gacy's property.

When Garippo welcomed and reswore the jurors, all of us felt a great sense of excitement that, after months of arduous work and careful preparation, at last we had arrived at our destination.

The First Week

Bob Egan delivered the prosecution's opening statement. "I want you to picture, if you will, a young boy," he began. "He is fifteen years old, he is a sophomore in high school, he is a gymnast at the high school, and in the evening he works at a pharmacy." He recounted the fateful Monday night meeting of Rob Piest and John Gacy. He told of the overheard conversation, the forgotten appointment book, the invitation to go for a ride and discuss the job, the attempted sex, Rob's tearful fright, the rope trick. "Do you know how a tourniquet works?" Egan asked the jury as he described Rob's death. Then he talked of the activities of Tuesday, when Gacy took the body to the Des Plaines River "and threw him over the bridge like a bag of garbage. That in itself is not the horrible part of the story," Egan said. "The horrible part is that this was the last of thirty-three young men, people with their lives ahead of them, that John Gacy strangled—killed and buried."

For the benefit of the Rockford jurors, Egan gave them a quick tour of the Chicago area, mentioning the names they would be hearing in the days ahead: Norwood Park Township, Uptown, Bughouse Square, Des Plaines, Park Ridge, Niles, Bensenville. Then he listed each of the victims, starting with the boy from the Greyhound bus station—"I say 'this kid' because he is not identified"—and ending with the ten other youths that to us were still nameless at this point.

Egan traced the highlights of the Des Plaines investigation:

Gacy's appearance at the station muddy and four hours late, the photo slip Kim Byers had put in Rob's jacket, the stake-out that closed around Gacy ("a rat trapped in a corner"), Schultz's recognition of the odor at Gacy's house, and the discovery of the contractor's "burial site" on the second search of his premises. Egan described the circumstances of Gacy's statements and named the ten victims that Gacy "remembered" killing. The state, he said, was able to prove that Gacy murdered thirty-three boys because his actions were thoughtful, rational, and premeditated.

Egan reminded the jury that the psychiatrists who would be called to testify were just witnesses. "You can choose to believe them or not, and you can evaluate their testimony in light of the testimony of all the other witnesses. That means you can use your common sense." Egan urged the jurors to use their common sense throughout the proceedings, "and I think you will come to the conclusion that [Gacy] is nothing more than an evil, evil man."

Egan's statement left a stunning impression on the jurors and the courtroom spectators, who were learning some of the details of Gacy's killings for the first time. Gacy himself was no longer grandstanding as he had in Rockford; he turned his chair toward the judge's bench and solemnly listened to Egan outline our case against him. The silence in the courtroom was punctuated only by the sobs of Mrs. Lola Woods, mother of victim William Kindred. Judge Garippo admonished the jurors not to discuss the case and adjourned until afternoon.

Robert Motta made the opening argument for the defense. "Every man's death diminishes us in some way; we feel a loss," he said. "But no amount of vengeance or anger or sympathy can ever bring those boys back to life. They are gone; it is final." Motta asked the jurors to decide the issues "without any sympathy whatsoever, without any feeling or desire for revenge."

"Try to conceive of living there with twenty-nine bodies," Motta said. "Is this premeditation, or is it obsession; compulsion . . . the device of a deeply sick individual?" Motta portrayed his client as irrational, a man acting on impulse without intent, a victim of a chronic and severe mental disease.

"The evidence," he said, "will show that John Gacy is insane under any standards . . . that he could not control his conduct." He promised that psychiatrists for the defense would show Gacy to be "crazy all the time" except for his ability to control his deviant behavior by filling up his schedule and obsessively working long hours.

Then Motta turned to our list of medical witnesses and the biases he expected them to show. One he characterized as a professional witness, another was a "mechanic for the state." The choice facing the jury, Motta said, was simply this: Either John Gacy is evil, or he is crazy.

"The insanity defense," he said, "has been looked upon as an escape, a defense of last resort. The defense of insanity is valid and it is the only defense that we could use here, because that is where the truth lies. . . . If [John Gacy] is normal, then our concept of normality is totally distorted."

Opening statements are not evidence; they are strictly arguments by the lawyers in which each side lays out what it expects to prove. You have to be careful what you say: If you don't eventually prove what you say you will, either because you can't or because you're forced to change strategy in the course of the trial, the opposition will club you in their closing arguments and make you look bad to the jury.

After the opening statements, each side has the opportunity to present its case in chief. The state goes first because it has the burden of proving beyond a reasonable doubt that the defendant committed the crimes as charged. The defense is allowed to cross-examine each witness and try to poke holes in his testimony or, if possible, discredit him.

At the conclusion of the state's presentation of its evidence, the defense may make a plea for a directed verdict, in which the judge finds the defendant not guilty because the prosecution has failed to present sufficient evidence to sustain a finding of guilty.

Even if the judge does not issue a directed verdict of not guilty, the defense is under no obligation to press on. Because the defendant has no burden of proof whatever, they can choose to offer no evidence or they may offer whatever defense they have for the sake of their client's best interest. The issue of insanity can be raised only by the defense, and if that's the strategy they choose, that becomes a basis of their case in chief. In a long trial, jurors tend to remember the last words most vividly, so the state avoids playing all of its cards at the start—taking, of course, the heavy risk that it might never have the chance to play them if no defense is put on. Such strategy can be treacherous.

If the other side puts on an insanity defense, the prosecution should be prepared to match their medical experts one for one, knowing from discovery—the required pretrial disclosures— how many they have left on their roster. The prosecution's rebuttal is the opportunity for this, but testimony must be confined to rebutting what was presented in the case in chief— no new areas may be explored. And the defense, of course, then may introduce witnesses to rebut the testimony given during the prosecution's rebuttal. Since this can go on and on into endless surrebuttals, the state generally tries to exhaust the supply of defense witnesses and keep an ace or two in the hole to play at the very end.

Finally, the closing statements give the attorneys from both sides the chance to interpret what the opposition has presented and argue the deficiencies in its case. The jurors are the judges of whether the lawyers' arguments are corroborated by the facts of testimony. In the closing statements, the prosecution gets the last word because of its burden of proof beyond a reasonable doubt.

After Motta's opening statement, which lasted about an hour, Garippo adjourned court for the day, by far the shortest in the entire trial. Now the preliminaries were out of the way.

John Butkovich, who had disappeared in July, 1975, was the first of Gacy's known victims. We wanted to present our life witnesses in the order of the victims' disappearances, so John's father, Marko, was the first to testify when court resumed on February 7.

"When you last saw your son," Kunkle asked, "was he alive and well?"

"Yes," Butkovich replied.

"After he walked out of the door of your house, did you ever see him again?"

"No."

"Nothing further, Your Honor," Kunkle said, closing the direct examination.

After the cross-examination was conducted and the photograph of John Butkovich had been shown to the jury, we placed the picture in a slot on our huge display board with the name tag of the boy underneath. Amirante immediately requested a side bar, a conference with the opposing counsel and the judge outside the hearing of the jury. He objected that the cumulative placement of photographs of all twenty-two identified victims in full view of the jury would be highly inflammatory.

"We had a motion to consolidate," Kunkle told Judge Garippo, referring to the fact that there was now but one trial for all thirty-three counts of murder. "We have twenty-two identified victims [who] we don't intend to become nothing but numbers," he said. But Garippo sustained the objection, ruling that each picture should be on display only during the testimony relating to it.

Our next witness was Delores Vance, whose eighteen-year-old son, Darryl Samson, had disappeared in April, 1976. I asked Mrs. Vance what she had done after Darryl disappeared, and she replied in words that would become almost a litany in the procession of witnesses: She called the police, who made a missing-person report and told her that Darryl "had just run away."

Bessie Stapleton testified to the disappearance of her fourteen-year-old son, Samuel Todd, in 1976. The boy was last seen by his mother leaving for his sister's house. Mrs. Stapleton was overcome by grief when Egan asked her to examine a chain bracelet. She identified it as her son's, then, shaking, cried, "God, why?" and fainted. Attendants rushed to her side and escorted her from the courtroom.

Fifteen-year-old Randall Reffett had disappeared the same day Todd did, and we were sure that these two youths were the ones Gacy had spoken of as his "double" killing. Myrtle Reffett told the jury of seeing her son for the last time on the afternoon of May 14.

James Varga, the assistant state's attorney who had done legal research and helped us to prepare evidence for trial, questioned Shirley Stein, the mother of Michael Bonnin, seventeen. Mrs. Stein last saw her son on June 3, 1976, when he left home with a friend to do a painting job. She heard nothing further from or about him until the sheriff's police called on December 30, 1978, to inform her that Michael's fishing license had been found at Gacy's house. On cross-examination, Amirante continued a previous line of questioning by asking the color of Bonnin's hair (strawberry-blond). We assumed the defense was attempting to show that Gacy compulsively sought out young boys of specific physical characteristics.

Under my questioning, Esther Johnston recounted the events of the afternoon she had driven Rick to the Aragon Ballroom. After Mrs. Johnston testified, we brought back Bessie Stapleton, who by then had regained her composure. On cross, Amirante questioned Mrs. Stapleton about reports that her son had been seen several times in the months after his disappearance. His questioning seemed to accomplish little and may have even offended the jury.

When court resumed in the afternoon we put on both Eugenia Godziks—mother and daughter—as well as Greg Godzik's girlfriend, Judy Patterson. Judy testified that she and two other girls had gone to Gacy's house to see if he knew anything about Greg. Gacy was still saying that Greg had run away, but he did give the impression that he was trying to be helpful.

"He said to give [him] my address and phone number," Judy testified, "and that he was in the syndicate and that they were going to look into this in their own way. And he said, 'If you have any questions, call me.' He gave me his contractor's card, and I left."

After Judy Patterson's testimony, I sought to introduce into evidence several of John Szyc's belongings we had recovered from Gacy's house. Judge Garippo ruled that the high school ring was admissible. He did not allow the television set and radio, however, because they were recovered during the second search, when the sole object specified in the warrant was the body or remains of Rob Piest. Although the television and radio were not in themselves evidence that a crime had been committed, I did not agree with the ruling. Still, it didn't greatly harm our case.

The parade of life witnesses continued. Violet Carroll last

saw her sixteen-year-old son, William, just before midnight on June 13, 1976. William had said he would be back in an hour but never returned. He was Gacy's fifth victim in less than a month.

Rosemary Szyc told the jurors of finding her son John's apartment deserted and certain belongings missing. She identified the ring as her son's.

Bob Egan put on Roger Sahs to testify to the disappearance of his friend, Jon Prestidge, twenty, who had come to Chicago from Kalamazoo. Prestidge, who was thinking about going to school in Chicago, stayed with Sahs, whom he had met in a bar several months earlier. Sahs testified that he had last seen Prestidge on the night of March 15, 1977, after leaving a restaurant two blocks from Bughouse Square. Sahs said he had warned Prestidge not to go there.

Amirante tried to discredit the witness on cross, trying to get him to say that he had driven Prestidge to Bughouse Square to hustle gays and make some money. Sahs said he had put Prestidge's picture in a gay magazine, listing him as missing, but he denied Amirante's allegation about hustling. The defense was obviously trying to show that one of Gacy's victims got what he asked for, but Sahs came across as a gentleman, and I think that Amirante's attempt to impeach his testimony backfired.

The day was full of pain. As soon as they had testified, the witnesses were allowed to sit in the courtroom and watch the remaining proceedings. United in sorrow, they helped to console one another whenever one broke down. By the end of the trial, some of them would become close friends. Most of the witnesses had brought other family members with them for support; one brought her priest. After Bessie Stapleton collapsed, Harold Piest demanded that a paramedic and ambulance stand by in case his wife was overcome when she testified. We arranged for a fire department rescue crew to be on hand the next day.

During the day's testimony, Gacy had sat motionless, staring impassively. After each witness identified the photograph of a victim, one of us took it and showed it to the jurors. Although we were barred at this point from posting more than one photograph at a time, an interesting visual effect was taking shape on the board. Ten nameplates were now mounted on the display, each beneath the empty frame for the photograph. The defense had succeeded in keeping the pictures off the board, but they hadn't as yet noticed the unintended effect that made the empty rectangles above the names look like ten little coffins.

The jury heard testimony on the twelve remaining identified victims on Friday, February 8. Marie Todorich last saw her son Matthew Bowman, nineteen, after dropping him at a suburban train station on July 5, 1977. According to testimony by an uncle, Thomas Gilroy, twenty-one-year-old Robert Gilroy left his home, just four blocks away from Gacy's house, on September 15, 1977, to go for a riding lesson in the suburbs. Robert, the son of a Chicago police sergeant who had pursued the search both officially and on his own, was never seen again by his family.

Delores Neider was now revisited by tragedy. In November, 1972, her twenty-one-year-old daughter Judith had been stabbed to death in her apartment in Chicago; the killer had never been found. Now she was testifying to the disappearance of her nineteen-year-old son, John Mowery, a former Marine, whom she had last seen on September 25, 1977. John had been visiting his mother, borrowed an umbrella from her, then walked out into the rainy night. She never saw him again.

Norma Nelson, of Cloquet, Minnesota, last talked with her son Russell, twenty, on October 17, 1977, when he had telephoned to wish her a happy birthday. Russell, who had come to Chicago to study architecture, was planning to marry.

Joyce Winch, of Kalamazoo, Michigan, never saw her son Robert again after November 10, 1977, when the sixteen-year-old boy went off with a friend.

After an early break for lunch, testimony resumed with Albenia Boling, who had last seen her twenty-year-old married son, Tommy, on November 18, 1977. Later that evening, the young man called her from a bar, where he was watching *Bonnie and Clyde* on television; neither his mother nor his wife ever heard from him again.

Pearl Talsma told the jurors that her son David, nineteen,

another Marine, left for a rock concert on December 9, 1977; that was the last time she saw him.

Our third witness of the afternoon was brought into the courtroom in a wheelchair. She had been in an auto accident only days before and had left her hospital bed in order to appear. Amirante immediately offered to stipulate to her testimony to spare her the ordeal, but the young woman, Mary Jo Paulus, was willing to continue. I wanted the jury to hear her full story so I ignored Amirante's offer.

Miss Paulus, who had been engaged to victim William Kindred, identified a medallion found among Gacy's belongings as one she had given Kindred. I worried momentarily when she had some difficulty identifying Gacy, but she finally pointed him out. When I showed her the picture of Billy Kindred, she broke down. I had no more questions, and I left her sitting there for the defense. Perhaps I should have shown more sensitivity, but I wanted her grief to register on the jury. The judge decided to call a recess.

On cross, Motta came down on her needlessly hard, I thought, probing into the nature of her accident and whether she was on medication. At one point she interrupted and exclaimed: "I would like Mr. Gacy to please stop staring at me."

Francisco Landingin testified that he last had seen his nineteen-year-old son, Frank, on November 4, 1978, and Alberto Mazzara told of his family's last Thanksgiving with his son, James, twenty. Donita Ganzon was the witness for the third river victim, Timothy O'Rourke. The defense subjected Ganzon to what all of us felt was excessively harsh cross-examination on her sex-change.

Elizabeth Piest told of the events of the night of December 11, 1978, that would eventually lead to Gacy's downfall. Her grief was evident in every utterance, and she spoke slowly and painfully. Several times her voice broke with emotion, and she sobbed when I showed Rob's parka for her to identify. Wisely, the defense made no attempt to cross-examine her.

These first two days of testimony had been an ordeal for all concerned. We had assembled and put on the stand witnesses to the lives of twenty-two of Gacy's victims, and on Friday afternoon we returned to our offices and slumped into chairs, emotionally drained.

In a long morning session on Saturday, we laid the basis of the police investigation that stemmed from Rob Piest's disappearance from Nisson Pharmacy. Kim Byers, Linda Mertes, and Phil Torf testified to the events of that Monday night, and we focused on Kim's account of putting the photo receipt in Rob's jacket. We called Torf because we felt that his presence at the pharmacy long after closing might be used by the defense to show some sort of conspiracy theory, that Gacy might not have acted alone. By calling Torf ourselves, we showed we had nothing to hide. The defense put Torf through a fairly long cross, using him mostly as a character witness of Gacy's work habits.

Three Des Plaines police officers testified. George Konieczny recounted his late-night meeting with the Piest family and his filing of the missing-person report. Ronald Adams started with his call to Gacy on Tuesday and went through the first search, the identification of the school ring, recovery of the Nisson photo log, and the trip with Gacy to Cermak Hospital. Jim Pickell testified to the first visit of the police to Gacy's house and the contractor's statement at the station the following day. For dramatic effect, I saved one of Pickell's best quotes for my redirect examination.

What statement, I asked, did Gacy make after he said he was too busy with his uncle's funeral arrangements to come into the police station?

"He asked the question," Pickell testified, " 'Don't you have any respect for the dead?' "*

---

*Several months after the trial, on May 28, 1980, Jim Pickell died of a heart attack at age forty-one. His widow and some of his associates thought that the stress of the Gacy case had brought about a physical deterioration in Pickell and a change in his personality. Reporters referred to him as "John Gacy's last victim."

The Second Week

We resumed on Monday morning, February 11, with witnesses who testified to Gacy's activities after his trip on December 12 to the bridge from which he dumped Rob Piest's body. Dennis Johnson, a highway worker, told how he and his partner had found Gacy stuck in the ditch along the Tri-State Tollway early on the morning of December 13. Robert Kirkpatrick, the driver of the tow truck that was called, told the jury that when he arrived Gacy was asleep, slumped over the car's steering wheel. Officer Gerald Loconsole, the watch officer on duty the night of December 12/13, described Gacy's visit to the Des Plaines police station at 3:20 A.M. with the mud on his clothes.

Joseph Kozenczak, by now a captain, commented that Gacy looked different from when he'd last seen him: he'd lost a lot of weight in addition to his mustache. Kozenczak testified that he had come to my office seeking help and how that meeting led to the first search of Gacy's house. He related the details of his recovery of the photo slip from the kitchen trash.

Richard Raphael told the jury of his business relationship with the defendant and the meeting that Gacy had missed on the night Rob Piest disappeared. He spoke of how Gacy had summoned him the night of the first search and how his associate had thereafter become irrational and frightened. "It seemed," Raphael testified, "that his whole objective in life was to ditch the police."

We ended the day's testimony with two young men who both

had been sexually propositioned by Gacy. Robert Zimmerman, the Shell station employee, said Gacy had once offered him $300 a week to work for his firm and had entertained him at the house, where he made his pool-table proposal of money or a blow job for the winner. Gacy, Zimmerman said, freely offered both drugs and alcohol to the youths at the gas station. Zimmerman threw Amirante a little curve when the lawyer asked him how Gacy had acted at the theme parties, where only about 10 percent of the guests were in Zimmerman's age group.

"He was with us a lot," Zimmerman said, "and it struck me kind of odd that he was smoking pot with us. I asked him [if] he didn't care about his older friends knowing it. He said, 'No, if they don't like it, they can lump it.'"

Anthony Antonucci described Gacy's attempted attack on him while his parents were away on vacation and how he had got the handcuffs on Gacy. At the end of the day, Zimmerman remarked to reporters that he still wondered why he wasn't among the victims in Gacy's crawl space.

Two of the witnesses potentially most damaging to Gacy were Chris Gray and Dick Walsh, both of whom had lived with him. Because of their involvement in the crawl space digging, their testimony would be of great importance in helping us prove that Gacy's murders were premeditated. We knew the defense would probably try to portray the two as Gacy's accomplices and jump on the sex angle in an attempt to discredit them. When we explained this to Gray, he seemed truly fearful of being criminally linked with his former boss and pledged his full cooperation. As a result, we used him to paint the big picture based on his experiences with Gacy.

Walsh was another matter. As he had threatened, even before Gacy's arrest, Walsh had hired legal counsel, and we had not been able to interview him during the trial preparation. Walsh's lawyer was Edward V. Hanrahan, the Cook County state's attorney whom Carey had defeated in 1972. Hanrahan immediately sought immunity for his client. Because I knew Hanrahan—I had worked for him—I got the job of dealing with him. In office, he had a reputation of being very stern and tough, and I've always held him in the highest respect. The prosecution strongly opposed granting immunity because in the jurors' eyes it taints a witness and harms your case against the defendant. Hanrahan, however, was adamant. We went back and forth for months. In the end, Hanrahan relented, mostly, I think, because he was willing to trust me when I personally promised him that we'd stick to the questions he and I already had discussed and that we'd protect Walsh as best we could on cross-examination. Although his client was his main consideration, I knew Hanrahan was a solid law-and-order man who didn't want Gacy running free any more than we did. And so in a hectic session on Sunday, February 10, Kunkle prepared Walsh as a witness in Hanrahan's presence. Not being sure how Walsh would come across, however, we planned to give Gray the larger role and use Walsh mostly to fill in details. The defense objected to our putting Gray on—they said they hadn't been able to interview him because their investigators could never find him. Judge Garippo overruled them, however, but delayed the proceedings long enough for them to question him briefly. On Tuesday morning, February 12, Gray took the stand.

Gray gave the jurors a good insight into Gacy's drug and alcohol usage. "Did you ever notice any drugs in his house?" I asked.

A.   Yes.

Q.   Where did he keep these drugs?

A.   He had them in the refrigerator, behind the bar, in a couple of places, behind the pictures.

Q.   Did he ever offer these drugs to you?

A.   Yes.

Q.   How many times?

A.   Oh, just about any time that I really wanted them.

Q.   In your presence, did he ever offer these drugs to any other teenagers?

A.   Yes, but employees were free to . . . he used to, if we were all dragged out in the morning, he used to give us a pep pill and speed to get us going.

Gacy's supply of drugs was all but assured. "As we were remodeling the drugstores," Gray testified, "we'd have complete access to everything."

As to Gacy's consumption habits, Gray quickly exploded

what the defense would have liked the jury to believe, that Gacy became the criminal he was during abusive forays into drugs and alcohol. Gacy was affected by drugs, Gray said, "just once in a great while." Rather than becoming a raging fiend under the influence of drugs and alcohol, Gacy showed quite the opposite effects. "For the most part," Gray said, "he did a tranquilizer and had two drinks, and it just turned him in."

Q. Did he pass out?

A. Yes. He just dozed off right in the middle of a conversation.

Next, I focused my questions on the crawl space, where Gray's testimony suggested that Gacy paid more than just occasional visits.

Q. Mr. Gacy went down there with you, is that correct?

A. Yes.

Q. Did he have any shoes in the crawl space?

A. Yes, he had a pair of navy boondockers, ankle-high black boots.

Q. Where?

A. Right at the bottom.

Q. Inside the crawl space?

A. Yes.

Gray stepped in front of the judge's bench and, crouching in the well of the courtroom, demonstrated to the jurors how he had dug trenches with just thirty-inch-headroom. The jurors straightened up in their chairs and peered over the railing of the jury box.

On the morning of Gacy's arrest, Gray testified, Gacy broke down and cried, saying that he had confessed to thirty killings. "He said they were syndicate-related killings, but he swore up and down, 'I never had anything to do with this boy being missing.'"

When I asked Gray if Gacy had mentioned anything about Iowa, in order to establish that Gacy had said he would never go back to prison, he started to talk about the sodomy arrest. The defense immediately objected and asked for a mistrial on the basis that their presentation now was tainted. The judge sustained the objection but didn't declare a mistrial because, he said, the prison question would doubtless come up later when the psychiatrists were called.

On cross-examination, Motta hammered hard on the crawl space theme, questioning Gray about his digging, his access to Gacy's house, and so forth. Gray held up well. When asked if he had participated in sex with Gacy, Gray pleaded the fifth Amendment.

During the lunch break, Kunkle and I brought into the courtroom the hatchway to the crawl space that had been cut out of Gacy's floor. We placed it on a table that had been constructed to our specifications so that the hatch would be the same distance off the courtroom floor as the crawl space was deep. When the jurors returned, they stared at the hatch, transfixed. Walsh took the stand, and I kept my fingers crossed.

Kunkle directed his questions immediately to Walsh's knowledge of the crawl space. The witness had no trouble identifying the hatchway. Kunkle asked Walsh specifically about Gacy's behavior during the times of the killings. For instance, at the time of John Szyc's disappearance, Walsh said, Gacy was acting normal. We went into the car purchase to show that Walsh had nothing to do with Szyc's disappearance.

An hour before Gacy's arrest, while Walsh was dumping his boss's tools on the parkway at Gray's house, Gacy seemed emotionally disturbed, Walsh said. Gacy was "very nervous, breaking into tears."

Q. What did he say to you at that time?

A. He proceeded to tell myself and Chris about confessing to his lawyers the night before to over thirty killings.

Q. Did he say anything else?

A. That was the high point of the conversation.

Walsh told the jurors of digging a trench in which Gacy was supposedly going to have drain tile installed. This was where the unidentified thirteenth body was recovered. Walsh indicated the location on the plat chart.

Q. How deep a trench did you dig?

A. It was between my knees and my hips.

Q. And about how wide?

A. Approximately a foot.

Q. While you were digging, did you see any new drain tile?

A.   No.

Walsh refused to dig trenches the second time he was asked, but he did supervise other employees after Gacy had marked the location with sticks.

Q.   If someone deviated from the plan the defendant laid out, what would he do?

A.   He would get very upset.

Walsh also had noticed the boots Gacy kept at the crawl space entry.

On cross-examination, it was evident the defense really wanted Walsh's hide. Amirante chided Walsh about the "high-priced" lawyer he had retained.

Q.   For what reason did you have to hire an attorney, Mr. Walsh?

KUNKLE: Objection.

THE COURT: Overruled.

THE WITNESS: Cause it's my right.

AMIRANTE: Good answer.

Walsh denied ever having engaged in sexual activities with Gacy. When asked if he had forged the name of John Szyc on the car-title application, he denied that, too.

Amirante asked if Walsh had signed Szyc's name on the registration form.

A.   Yes, sir.

Q.   Okay. Were you ever charged with forgery for that?

A.   No, sir.

Q.   Did the state's attorney ask you about that?

A.   Yes, sir. They asked me if I signed the title itself.

Q.   What did you tell them?

A.   No, sir.

On redirect, Kunkle pursued the matter of the auto transfer. Showing Walsh the title itself, he asked if John Szyc's name appeared on it.

A.   Yes.

Q.   Did you sign that title?

A.   No, sir.

Q.   When Mr. Gacy gave you this title, was it already signed "John Szyc"?

A.   Yes, sir.

Kunkle then showed Walsh the title application form, listing him and Gacy as co-owners.

Q. At the bottom, where it says, "new vehicle information, from whom did you buy?" did you write in a name?

A. Yes, sir.

Q. What was that name?

A. John A. Szyc.

Q. Now, who told you to write in the name of the former owner on the application for plates?

A. The woman at the Elston Avenue—what you call it?—driving vehicle inspection building.

Q. And nobody charged you with forgery, did they, Mr. Walsh?

A. No, sir.

Q. Except Mr. Amirante.

On Wednesday, officers Dave Hachmeister and Bob Schultz testified about the surveillance. Here we sought to show Gacy the tough guy/nice guy, trying to con the police and calculating all the while. Schultz's testimony on the smell helped establish the validity of our reason for getting the second search warrant. The jury, of course, hadn't heard any of the motions challenging the warrants, and the defense, if it so chose, could reopen the whole issue. They didn't, however, and after the officers had told of the sometimes bizarre activities of those eight days of surveillance, the defense opted for only minor cross-examination.

On Thursday morning, February 14, I put Greg Bedoe on the stand to testify about the internal investigation. Because I had worked so closely with Greg and we had been over it all so many times, I tended to lead him and he tended to anticipate my questions. I wanted to get detailed testimony of the police work in the record to forestall any attempt by the defense to discredit it. Garippo, however, frequently sustained the defense's objections whenever he thought I was going into too great detail. We asked the court's permission to recall Bedoe for further testimony, and the defense withheld its cross until that time.

One of the most colorful witnesses of the trial proved to be

Ronald Rohde. The jury was sometimes amused by his remarks and appreciated his total candor. Rohde, a contractor for twenty-three years, had met Gacy in 1973, when Gacy stopped at a job site and asked if Rohde would be interested in bidding on some work he had. After a while, they became friends, and Gacy invited Rohde and his wife to a party. In telling the jurors about it, Rohde somewhat deflated his former host. "There were quite a few people there," he testified. "Contractors and, oh, I don't know. Nobody real important—not that I know of." Gacy grimaced.

Rohde said that Gacy had told him he had emphysema and heart problems. "I couldn't see how anybody in construction [could have] a heart problem, and I have been around John when he was wrecking."

"What kind of job would John do when he was involved in wrecking?" Kunkle asked.

"He was very active," Rohde said. "He was very good at destroying things." He added that he found it hard to understand how any contractor could do business at 3 A.M.

Kunkle asked Rohde what happened when Gacy got drunk.

A. He was like any other normal person. If he had too much, he'd just throw up and pass out, and that was the end of it. We would put John to bed.

Q. On these occasions, did you ever see any personality changes in him?

A. No, sir.

Rohde told of being upset over the surveillance, but Gacy had reassured him that "he was going to sue the city of Des Plaines, and he was going to get them off my back. . . . They were pulling in my neighbor's driveway, and I was not accustomed to living this way. I mean, I'm no saint, but I never had that problem."

Rohde recalled Gacy's visit shortly before his arrest: "He was kind of ragged, like he was up all evening. The first thing he asked me for is a drink, Scotch and water on the rocks." Rohde complied and invited Gacy to sit down in the kitchen. After a few minutes, Gacy said he had to go to the cemetery. "He says, 'I really came to say goodbye to my best friends for the last time.' I says, 'What the hell are you talking about?' He told me, 'Well, them son-of-a-bitches out there are going to get me.' He meant the police officers.

"He walked up and put his hands on my shoulder, and he starts crying and he says, 'Ron, I have been a bad boy.' I looked at him. 'Oh, come on, John,' I says, 'you haven't been *that* bad.' He says, 'I killed thirty people, give or take a few.' I didn't know what the hell to say. I looked at him, and I says, 'John, the only bad people that I know is Jesse James and Billy the Kid, and they are all dead.' He was crying." Rohde asked about the victims, and Gacy said they were bad people—black men—and they were scattered all over.

" 'Okay, John,' I said. 'You're full of shit.' I thought I knew this gentlemen very well. It would be like somebody's best friend giving you a shot right between your eyes. You know he's telling you the truth and you really don't know where to go with it."

Gacy picked up his coat to leave, Rohde said, and a rosary fell to the floor. He stooped to pick it up. "I says, 'Hey, you son-of-a-bitch, when did you turn so religious?'" Kunkle asked Rohde if he had known Gacy to be a regular churchgoer. "No way," Rohde replied.

As Gacy went to the door, Rohde grabbed and shook him. " 'John,' I says, 'for once in your life tell me the truth. Do you know the Piest boy?' He says, 'Ron, I swear, if he walked through the door, I wouldn't know him.'" At the door, while Rohde was pleading with him to come back in and talk, Gacy turned and asked for a gun.

" 'John,' I says, 'no way am I going to give you a gun. What do you want a gun for?' He says, 'If I'm going to go down, I'm going to take a few of those son-of-a-bitches with me.' I says, 'My friend, if you're going to go down, you're not using one of my guns.'"

Rohde told the jurors of Gacy's unexpected phone call from jail about six months after his arrest. "He kind of caught me off balance," Rohde said. "I says, 'How did you get phone privileges, John?' He says, 'Oh, I'm a celebrity here.'" After they joked around for a bit, Rohde got right to the point.

" 'John,' I says, 'explain one question to me—how the bodies got under the house.' There was a little silence. He says, 'There's going to be a lot of surprises—there's a lot of keys out to my home.' I said, 'Well, hey, you son-of-a-bitch, I ain't got one!' " The jurors laughed heartily.

Kunkle asked whether Gacy, in the phone conversation, had said anything about the case. Rohde replied that Gacy had told him that he had some doctors who were on his side and that Rohde could "take it to the bank and walk it in a year."

On cross, Amirante asked about Rohde's feelings. "You are extremely hurt and aggravated about this man, aren't you?"

A.   I don't have the hurt that some of these people in this jury room have. My hurt is completely different.

Q.   But it is a hurt?

A.   It's not a hurt.

Q.   An anger?

A.   John manipulates people to fit his way.

Q.   Is it . . .

A.   And he only told me what he wanted me to know.

Amirante asked Rohde if he wasn't surprised and shocked. "I believed John," Rohde said, "until the first body came up under his house."

It is essential for the prosecution to show in its presentation that the chain of evidence has been kept intact. We chose ET Daniel Genty to be our major evidence witness because of his long-term involvement in the recovery of bodies at Summerdale, from the night of their discovery to the very end.

Egan questioned Genty about his first descent into the crawl space, the night of the second search warrant. The ET knelt down in the well of the courtroom and demonstrated to the jurors how he had dug in the confined space and crawled on his stomach under the center support beam. Genty told the jury of the discovery of the remains beneath the murky puddles and the red worms. It was the jurors' first "trip" into the crawl space, and they listened raptly.

We recalled Hachmeister to testify that he had notified Gacy of his arrest on a murder charge after the police brought him back from the hospital. Next, we put on Mike Albrecht and questioned him about the statements Gacy had made to the police late that night. We aimed to show that Gacy, all the while, had known what he was doing and was even planning his defense. After Albrecht mentioned the defendant's statement that there were four Johns of different personalities, Kunkle asked if Gacy had been to his lawyers' office the night before. He had, Albrecht said.

Amirante asked for a side bar. Furious, the defense attorney charged Kunkle with directly attacking his integrity by suggesting that the lawyers might have put the split-personality ploy in Gacy's head, and he called for a mistrial. Judge Garippo said he hadn't interpreted things that way, but he warned Kunkle that we had better not make that suggestion in our closing arguments. It was a fair warning because the defendant, after all, is the one on trial, not the attorneys. Still, we were entitled to show Gacy's calculating mind in the days before his arrest.

Albrecht testified to numerous statements that Gacy had made to the officers: "Dave, I want to clear the air, the game is over"—to show that Gacy had known that he was a cornered criminal; "I won't spend a day in jail for this"—to show that Gacy already had his defense plotted; his detailed description of the death of Rob Piest—to show that he knew precisely what he was doing; his use of the name Jack Hanley—to show that he had planned ahead.

When Albrecht had finished testifying and the jury had been dismissed for the day, Amirante was still smoldering over what he regarded as prosecutorial misconduct. Again he asked the judge to declare a mistrial. "My client," Amirante said excitedly. "I have stifled him for thirteen and a half months. He's wanted to jump up in the courtroom; he's wanted to say things about the prosecutors. I don't let him say it because I figure what he says is a lie, to me, and I'm not going to let him impugn the integrity of another lawyer in the courtroom."

Garippo tried to calm Amirante, promising he would straighten it out in the morning. "I will take a shower on it," the judge said.

On Friday, we recalled Greg Bedoe to testify on the statements Gacy had made to police in the early morning hours after his return from the hospital. Here we were revealing to the jury Gacy's admissions to numerous killings, as well as showing that his rights had not been violated when he was giving the statements. Phil Bettiker's testimony took up with the trip to the bridge and continued with the return to

Summerdale, where Gacy had marked the grave of John Butkovich in his garage.

Kunkle wanted to get into testimony the demonstration of the rope trick that Gacy had performed with the rosary on Larry Finder in the Des Plaines jail. Larry was still skittish about the sacred symbolism of the rosary, and during trial preparation I had heightened his anxiety by telling him that he wouldn't be allowed to buy one in a store because he wasn't Catholic.

After Larry had described Gacy's demonstration of the rope trick, Kunkle asked Finder to join him in front of the jury box. As the jurors watched attentively, Finder took a rosary from his pocket at Kunkle's request. Judge Garippo came down from the bench for a better view.

"Assume that my wrist and hand are your wrist and hand through the bars of the Des Plaines [jail] when John Gacy told you he was going to demonstrate the rope trick on you," Kunkle said.

Finder looped the rosary around Kunkle's wrist and began tying it, just as Gacy had done. "First knot," he said. "Second knot . . . space between the second and third knot." Finder put a pen between the two outer knots. "And twist it."

Kunkle raised his fist to show the jurors.

Then Kunkle had Finder describe the diagram that Gacy had drawn showing where he had buried bodies in the crawl space. The defendant interrupted the proceedings.

"Your Honor," Gacy said, "I didn't draw that drawing."

Kunkle continued his questioning. When he had finished, the judge dismissed the jury and called Gacy to the bench.

"Mr. Gacy," Garippo said, "during the course of this trial, it is not proper for anyone to just get up and begin to speak. If you wish an opportunity to testify, you may testify or present any other evidence you may wish to, but we cannot have you getting up, especially in front of the jury, and making statements like that. You understand?"

Gacy said he did. Then Rafael Tovar completed the day's testimony by recounting the discovery and identification of John Szyc's ring and the trip with Gacy to the Cook County jail.

* * *

ET Dan Genty returned to the stand on Saturday morning and responded in meticulous detail to Bob Egan's questions on the body recoveries. Working entirely from memory, Genty reconstructed the exhumation of each body, from No. 1 in the crawl space and No. 2 in the garage, all the way to No. 29, found between the dining room joists just before the house was razed. Even the measurements he recalled with astounding accuracy.

A. Body No. 9 was face down with the head to the south. It was seven feet, six inches from the east wall, twelve feet, ten inches from the north wall. The only clothing found on this body was the elastic waistband from the underpants and a pair of socks, dark-colored.

Q. Now, how far under the surface of the earth was it?

A. It was very difficult to determine. We measured from the top of the pad, and it was twelve inches down from this cement pad (indicating).

Q. Approximately how thick was that pad?

A. Four inches.

On cross, Motta tried to get Genty's estimate of how long the remains had been in Gacy's crawl space.

A. I would say somewhere from six months to a number of years.

Q. How many number of years?

A. Five to ten.

Q. So it is from six months to ten years—that is as good as you can place the guess?

A. It's conceivable.

If the defense can't reasonably dispute the facts as stated, they usually try to poke holes in the police investigation and try to leave the jury uncertain. Sensing this sort of attempt, on redirect examination Egan asked Genty about the various factors that figure into the decomposition of a body.

"A cold temperature tends to slow decomposition," Genty testified. "The fact that the body may be under water would slow it down. The fact that it would be covered by earth would slow it down by preventing oxygen from reaching the body. The body that is, say, found outdoors in the summertime, with the warm temperature and the insects, could be completely denuded in two weeks. On the other hand, a body could lie in a protected environment and be virtually intact six months later, or appear to be. So there are many variables. The big thing is the environment in which the body lies."

"Would it also be correct to say," Egan asked, "that it is virtually impossible, down to the day, minute, or hour, to determine when a body died?"

"Absolutely," Genty responded. "That's one of the fictions we see on TV all the time—where they determine that the person died between 3 and 3:15. It just can't be done. There is no clock in a person. At best it would be a matter of hours that you can estimate time of death. And in this case, who knows?"

Bill Kunkle questioned Sergeant Ernest Marinelli on other aspects of the operation at Summerdale, and then Judge Garippo dismissed the jury for their second brief weekend.

The Third Week

On Monday, February 18, we were just a few days away from concluding our case in chief, and we had reached the point where we and the defense would stipulate that the remains of Gacy's victims had been correctly identified. Had the defense decided not to stipulate to anything, as Amirante had threatened late in the trial preparation, we would have had no choice but to bring the actual skeletal remains into the courtroom to establish the integrity of the chain of evidence. That possibility may have influenced his decision.

Jim Varga read the stipulations: that bodies 1 through 29 had been removed from 8213 Summerdale and taken to the county medical examiner, that the jaws, teeth, and X-rays of the remains were correctly numbered, that the ante-mortem X-rays were in fact those of the persons identified on them, and so forth. We then called Dr. Robert Stein.

We were worried about what the defense might do with some of the statements Stein had made to the press during the early phase of the recovery. Stein was worried, too. They could have tried to discredit him, but we needed his testimony and had to take the chance, hoping they wouldn't. Thus Kunkle kept his direct examination rather limited. Stein is an experienced forensic witness who keeps his answers short and to the point. He started by explaining to the jury the difference between the cause and manner of death.

"The cause of death," Stein testified, "is the initiating agent or agents which cause the demise of that individual. It could be a chemical. It could be physical. It could be biologic.'' For the manner of death, he said, there are five possibilities: homicide, suicide, accident, natural causes, or undetermined.

Stein testified that upon entering Gacy's house, he immediately smelled the same sort of odor he encountered in his work at the morgue. He described his trip into the crawl space with Genty, the start of the discovery, and the identification work.

When Kunkle asked Stein about Samuel Todd's chain bracelet, the youth's mother, Bessie Stapleton, broke down and sobbed. Motta requested a side bar, and the judge excused the jury. Garippo warned the spectators that there would be many moments of grim testimony and that anyone not able to handle it should leave the courtroom so as not to influence the jury. Amirante said that he had counted at least four of the jurors looking in the direction of Mrs. Stapleton as she cried.

A brief recess was called, after which Amirante objected to having family members in the courtroom at all during Stein's testimony and asked that they all be excluded. Garippo said he would take whatever steps were necessary as they went along.

Continuing his testimony, Stein said that in his opinion the cause of death of the six bodies found with ropes around their necks was asphyxia due to ligature-strangulation. As to the thirteen bodies found with clothlike material in the throat area, Stein gave the cause of death as asphyxia due to suffocation. Of the other ten bodies his office examined, Stein said, the cause of death could not be determined. As to the manner of death of the eighteen identified bodies from the crawl space and Rob Piest, Stein said they were, in his opinion, homicides. Naming each victim separately, Kunkle asked Stein if he had issued a death certificate in each case. "I did," Stein replied crisply.

On cross-examination, Amirante explored the doctor's testimony on the cause of death, obviously for the purpose of raising doubts in the jurors' minds whether the cause could be determined with any real certainty. Finally, Amirante brought up the question of auto-erotic asphyxia.

Q. Have you run across ligatures in incidents of accidental suicide, you might call it, whereby a person puts a rope around his neck in a sexual act and twists the knot in a fashion you have shown, in the form of a tourniquet, and accidentally commits suicide in the course of an orgasm?

Stein said his office attributes about fifteen or twenty deaths a year [his office handles thousands] to cases of that nature. Sometimes the person does not release the pressure in time, and he blacks out and dies. When this happens, Stein said, it is during masturbation.

Furious that the defense had suggested that some of Gacy's victims might have died in this way, Kunkle asked Stein on redirect examination if he had ever seen knots such as Gacy had used in any of the doctor's investigations of auto-erotic asphyxia.

A. No.

Q. If somebody used a ligature, a piece of rope like that, on an individual and strangled them to unconsciousness and not to death, and then killed them by stuffing a wad of cloth or paper in their mouth, would that make it any less a homicide than if they had accomplished it on the first try?

A. It is a homicide.

Q. If somebody used an appliance like this (indicating a rope) on a fifteen-year-old boy and then stuffed paper in his throat and he was not even dead yet and then dumped him in the river, and he drowned in the river, would that make it any less of a homicide?

A. No, it would not.

Q. If a person used an appliance like this on a teenage boy or young adult and strangled him to unconsciousness and then buried him in his basement and he died of asphyxia from his own grave, would that be any less a homicide?

A. It is a homicide.

KUNKLE: Nothing further.

The jurors' eyes were locked on Stein as he left the witness stand.

In the afternoon, Dr. Edward Pavlik, who by now had been named chief forensic odontologist for Cook County, took the stand and described to the jury the methods he used in making identifications. For Pavlik's testimony, we had two carousel projectors, one loaded with slides of ante-mortem X-rays we had got from the victims' dentists, and the other with the post-mortem films. While Egan projected the presentations simulta-neously on the screen, Dr. Pavlik showed the jurors the comparisons his team had made and explained the differences in the camera angles from which the X-rays were taken. He pointed to some of the specific identifying features, then compared images on the slides, showing how individual victims were identified.

Dr. John Fitzpatrick testified as to the identification he had made from the skeletal X-rays. On cross, Motta tried to get Fitzpatrick to say that radiological identification was not 100 percent airtight. "Actually," the lawyer asserted, "your science is one of probability as opposed to exactness."

"No," Fitzpatrick replied. "There are certain landmarks on these individuals that make it absolute. I'll bet my house on it."

Our last witness of the day, Daniel Callahan, the lockmaster at Dresden Island lock and dam on the Illinois Waterway, testified to the recovery of the first and last bodies from the river, Timothy O'Rourke and Robert Piest.

On Tuesday we put six witnesses on the stand who testified to the recovery and identification of the four river victims. Larry Finder returned on Wednesday and told the jurors of Gacy's plans to finally rid his house of the foul odor: "He said he was going to fill up the crawl space with poured concrete."

On that Wednesday, as I often did, I saw Gacy in the corridor leading to the lockup. I had been given a cigar the day before, and because I don't smoke and I knew Gacy did, I had passed it on to him.

"That was a good cigar, Terry," Gacy said.

"I'm glad you enjoyed it," I replied.

But, said Gacy, he was puzzled by one thing. What's that? I asked.

"I was surprised that the wrapper didn't say, 'It's a boy!'"

Larry's Wednesday testimony was the last we presented in this phase of the trial. Thus, in the middle of the third week of *The People of the State of Illinois* v. *John Wayne Gacy*, after the testimony of five dozen witnesses and much sooner than we had anticipated, we rested our case in chief.

We had learned through discovery that Gacy's lawyers were going to plead "in the alternative" allowed under Illinois law. By that they were saying that the prosecution can't prove our client guilty, but if they can, then he is not guilty by reason of insanity.

Garippo announced that the courtroom would be cleared so that the evidence could be laid out for the jurors' viewing. Afterwards, the jurors would be excused until the following day, when the judge would hear the defense's motion for a direct verdict of not guilty.

Before dismissing the attorneys, Garippo told us that he foresaw problems of insufficient evidence on the counts of deviant sexual assault and indecent liberties naming Rob Piest as the victim. Sufficient evidence, independent of Gacy's contradictory statements, would be necessary, he said.

This announcement left us somewhat perplexed. We didn't know what the judge wanted, nor what he would do. Although the law says a defendant's statements in a confession standing alone are not sufficient evidence for conviction, it does not say what else is necessary. Conviction on the Piest indictment would be our best hope of getting the death penalty. But we had exhausted our evidence on those charges, and there was little we could do but wait for Garippo's ruling, which for the moment he was reserving. Meanwhile, we put Jim Varga to work getting together more law on the subject.

Tomorrow it would be the defense's move, and we—especially Greg Bedoe and Joe Hein—would have a breather in the arduous and often hectic routine of lining up witnesses and getting them set for appearance. Now we had to be more flexible so we could react advantageously to the defense's strategy. We did not know whom they were going to call, and so we had to have voluminous material at our fingertips ready for cross-examination. From the defense's case in chief would come the showdown on the issue of insanity versus evil.

The defense began the proceedings on Thursday, February 21, with a motion for a directed verdict of not guilty, which Garippo denied. Then, to open their case in chief, they called to the stand Jeffrey Rignall, the young man who had charged Gacy with attacking him in March of 1978. We had considered using Rignall as a witness for the state but rejected the idea after publication of a book in which he related his account of Gacy's attack. Whichever side chose him as a witness would face having him cross-examined on anything that was in the book. We felt he would have been a difficult witness because the details in the book went far beyond what Rignall had told the police in their investigation. We thought we could get more from him on cross-examination than if he were our own witness. Sure enough, the defense put him on.

Over Kunkle's objection, Amirante asked Rignall if he thought Gacy could conform his conduct to the requirements of law.

A. No.

Q. How did you reach that opinion?

A. By the beastly and animalistic ways he attacked me.

When asked if he thought Gacy could appreciate the criminality of his act at the time, Rignall gave the same opinion, for the same reason.

On cross, Kunkle focused on any discrepancies he noted between what Rignall had reported to the police and what he had testified to. Although Kunkle directed some of his questions at what we thought was publicity-seeking on Rignall's part, the witness showed outward signs of stress while recounting his experience. At one point he wept on the stand; at another time he became ill and vomited, and Garippo had to call a recess. We were careful to show no reaction.

The defense next called Gacy's neighbor, Lillian Grexa. She testified that on December 16, 1978, Gacy had told her and her husband that he had given their names to his lawyer as character references and asked the Grexas if that was all right with them. He appeared very calm, Mrs. Grexa said. Although Mrs. Grexa was a witness for the other side, she was helping us prove our contention that Gacy was already methodically planning his defense.

Mrs. Grexa characterized Gacy as a stern boss, a good father, and a generous, warm, and good man who was always smiling. The only complaint she had about him, she said, was his reluctance to trim the six- or eight-foot hedge between their houses. I questioned her about that on cross.

Q. So once Mr. Gacy drove in the long driveway, once he got past the front, you couldn't see him, is that right?

A. We can't see his back door from our house at all.

This was another point for us because it showed that Gacy had gone to some trouble to conceal his activities.

In the course of building our picture of John Gacy, we had talked to many people who were potential defense witnesses, and we always tried to get to them before the other side did. In some cases witnesses will forget having talked to our investigators, or forget just what they said. Then, when the defense talks to them, they may neglect to repeat everything they told our people. This of course gives us the chance to embarrass the defense in court, as well as to bring out information favorable to our case. Such an opportunity arose when I questioned Mrs. Grexa about Gacy and drugs.

A. John, I says, are you dealing in drugs? I says, you know my feelings about drugs. I says, if I find my neighbors, my son, or you, or anybody I know that is dealing, I will turn them in.

Q. What did John say to you?

A. He said, no, I have nothing to do with drugs.

Q. Did you find out that he had any involvement with drugs?

A. I believe he was giving my son drugs.

That answer, I thought, transformed Mrs. Grexa from a solid defense witness into one favorable to us. Our long and careful preparation was paying off.

Then over defense objections, Mrs. Grexa repeated what she had told our investigators: "There is no way I am going to say that John is crazy. I think he is a very brilliant man." Enough, I thought. I sat down.

The defense's last witness of the day was Mickel Ried, who had lived with Gacy at Summerdale. Ried described the incident when Gacy had hit him on the head with a hammer in his garage and then apologized. When Amirante asked him whether he thought Gacy could conform his conduct and appreciate the criminality of his act, Ried said he didn't think Gacy knew what he was doing.

On cross by Egan, Ried told of Gacy's earlier attack on him

with the tire iron at the nursery. In this instance, it seemed that Gacy did know what he was doing.

Q. Now, when you turned around and you saw him coming, he stopped, didn't he?

A. Yes.

The defense called a correctional officer and a business associate of Gacy's as witnesses on Friday morning.

Oscar Pernell, a security guard at Cermak, told the jury about the towel incident. The defense was probably trying to show evidence of a suicide attempt, although Gacy had originally given the explanation that he was just cooling off. The incident was certainly weird, and the witness's testimony didn't help us.

James Vanvorous, a heating contractor and friend of Gacy who had co-hosted several theme parties, testified to Gacy's character. He regarded the defendant as hard working, demanding, and trustworthy. I asked Vanvorous on cross if Gacy had once told him that there was no job Gacy couldn't do once he put his mind to it. Correct, said Vanvorous.

The formal insanity defense began later that morning when Thomas Eliseo, a clinical psychologist from Rockford, was called to the stand.

We would have to do as much damage as possible to the defense's medical witnesses in order to keep an insanity defense from being established. If we could do that, we felt our doctors would be capable of rebutting their theories.

Eliseo had examined Gacy a few weeks before trial began, after it was known that the jury would be selected in Rockford. The defense probably figured that by this five-and-a-half-hour examination, Eliseo could provide a fresh diagnosis, untainted by pretrial reporting. Moreover, the jury might be favorably disposed to a Rockford expert.

Under Motta's questioning, Eliseo said he had found Gacy to be "of superior intelligence, about the top ten percent of the population—very bright." He said that Gacy did not have any major brain damage at the time he tested him.

Kunkle objected to what he foresaw as the defense's attempt to draw an inference between Gacy's mental condition at the time Eliseo examined him and his sanity at the times the crimes were committed. Motta responded that Eliseo would be testifying to "a continuing and uninterrupted mental disease that began some time early in Mr. Gacy's life." Garippo did not rule on the objection, electing to wait and see.

Asked for his diagnosis of Gacy as of the date he examined him, Eliseo responded, "Borderline schizophrenia or borderline personality, a person who on the surface looks normal but has all kinds of neurotic, antisocial, psychotic illnesses."

When Motta asked Eliseo to estimate the date of the onset of Gacy's condition, once again Kunkle objected. "There is no basis for any opinion at this time other than January 13, 1980," the date of the examination, Kunkle said. Garippo let Eliseo reply.

A. Paranoid people are usually paranoid most of their lives, and I would say somewhere since he was in his twenties—I would hypothesize after the death of his father in 1969—that is when it began.

On cross, Kunkle got right to the point.

Q. Doctor, you just said something about relying on the fact that his father died in 1969, is that right?

A. Well, he said 1969 to me.

Q. Did you have any source of that information besides what the defendant told you?

A. No.

According to his testimony, Eliseo had not read the police reports or the confessions, nor had he talked to anyone involved in the case, including the doctors, or read any of their reports. (He would later state that the defense lawyers had instructed him to ignore them.) On further examination outside the presence of the jury, Eliseo said that he could make the same diagnosis of paranoid schizophrenia based solely on the psychological test alone, apart from anything Gacy had told him.

Kunkle asked Eliseo how many cases he had seen of psychotics going seventeen or twenty years without being diagnosed or treated.

A. Few.

Q. Would you name those?

A. Particularly with paranoid schizophrenia . . . I don't want to name . . . Richard M. Nixon.

Q. You have treated President Nixon?

A. No, from what I have read and seen. King George III of England.

THE COURT: I have heard enough. You may step down.

When court resumed in the afternoon with the jury present, Motta posed a hypothetical question to Eliseo. He gave details of Gacy's activities during the period of the killings, then asked Eliseo to assume that the defendant was examined by a qualified psychologist who came to the same conclusion as Eliseo had. In Eliseo's opinion, Motta asked, did Gacy suffer from a mental disease?

He did, Eliseo testified. Paranoid schizophrenia, that it existed continuously during the period of his killings, and that Gacy could not conform his conduct to the requirements of the law and lacked substantial capacity to appreciate the criminality of his conduct during that time. "That does not mean he was psychotic overtly all of the time," Eliseo added, "but the condition was there, and probably he looked good, like most people do."

Kunkle objected. We went into side bar, each side snapping at the other.

"My motion is to strike all of his testimony," Kunkle said. "He had just said that he [Gacy] was not suffering from paranoid schizophrenia throughout—he said [Gacy] was only psychotic during certain times. You cannot be a paranoid schizophrenic and not be psychotic—that is a psychosis."

"Where did you get your license?" Amirante asked.

"The judge knows that," Kunkle said.

"Be quiet," Garippo said. He sustained the objection but refused to strike the testimony.

In response to questioning, Eliseo went on to testify that, while Gacy showed some traits of an antisocial personality, others were inconsistent with that diagnosis: his inappropriate affect, his grandiose thinking, his drive to build a business and be responsible and reliable. The defense was obviously anticipating the testimony of some of our doctors and trying to discount the diagnosis of Gacy's mental state made as far back as the time of his imprisonment in Iowa.

Kunkle kept hammering at the psychologist's diagnosis that Gacy was psychotic only at certain times. Eliseo had asserted that Gacy, during the act of killing, did not know it was wrong and only later understood.

Q. So, after the first one, he has now got a body, and he has put it in his basement, and he sure didn't understand during that first one, you say, but now he has buried the body to hide it from the police and the public, and now he is going to kill again. Do you think that is an indication that he didn't understand the criminality of his conduct when he is killing the second time?

A. At the moment that he did it, he was not aware of the criminality.

Q. Or the third?

A. Yes, I think all of them, he did not.

Q. Right through to thirty-three?

A. Yes, sir, that he was in a state where he was psychotic for that period and all he thought was to kill this person.

Q. He was psychotic for the whole period and all he could do was kill people?

A. No, not for the whole period, but during the time he actually went around and committed the act, not for the whole eight years or whatever it was, six years.

Q. Was he psychotic for eight years solid or wasn't he, yes or no?

A. Yes, but . . .

Q. Yes, but?

A. Yes.

KUNKLE: But for thirty-three bodies. I have nothing further.

The framework of our subsequent cross-examination and closing argument had been forged with this first expert witness. If we could force the others to testify that Gacy was insane *only* at the exact times of the murders, I thought that in closing argument I could portray their doctors as seers with crystal balls. I doubted that a jury would buy Eliseo's theory, especially since we could show that Gacy acted "sane" as a businessman and social being over the six years the killings occurred. The defense had now shown their cards: Their other experts had either to live with Eliseo's theory or flat out contradict him. Either way was fine with us.

* * *

Max Gussis, a sixty-six-year-old plumber who had done work for Gacy, was the defense's first witness on Saturday, February 23. Describing some of his jobs, Gussis related his impression of the crawl space, which he had seen the month before Gacy's arrest: "I noticed there was all kinds of lumps over there, and I just didn't understand why a contractor that had men working would keep a basement like that, never giving thought to anything else."

On cross, I tried to find out if Gussis had ever encountered the smell from the crawl space, and I got an answer of a man pretty well inured to his work environment.

Q.   You have been a plumber for forty years, is that right?
A.   That's right.
Q.   When you go on a job, do you smell much of anything?
A.   I hardly smell anything. Everything smells the same to me.

As far as Gussis was concerned, Gacy was sane.

Cathy Hull Grawicz testified, and didn't contribute much to the defense's notion that Gacy was a raging psychotic when drunk or under the influence of drugs: "If he had too much [to drink] and just couldn't handle it anymore," she said, "he would just be very quiet and sit down and pass out, or just fall right on the floor."

Amirante asked Mrs. Grawicz if the John Gacy she had seen in the news was the same man she had known.

"No, not at all," she replied.

"Sitting here in this court today," the lawyer continued, "how do you feel about John?"

"I feel sorry for him,' she said, leaning forward and looking directly at him. "My heart goes out to him."

Mrs. Grawicz was now sobbing, and Gacy put his hand to his eyes and wept. Garippo called a brief recess.

There was no need for a hard-hitting cross-examination, and we all agreed that I should be as gentle as possible with Mrs. Grawicz. When we resumed, she spoke about John Butkovich, how she had called him Little John and her husband Big John. She told of the argument he and Gacy had had over the boy's pay. I asked her to describe Gacy's physical strength and got an answer I hoped the jury would interpret as indicative that Gacy knew what he was doing.

Gacy, she said, was "very strong."

Q. Did he ever tell you why he didn't fight with people?

A. Yes, he said that he would think that he could probably kill somebody.

Q. With what?

A. His hands.

Mrs. Grawicz said that Gacy "had a memory like an elephant." She thought that he was sane all the time she had known him.

Paul James Hardy, a deputy sheriff detailed to Cermak Hospital, characterized Gacy as an ideal prisoner who presented no problems. On cross, Hardy said that Gacy sometimes associated with Richard Lindwall, a former high school teacher in suburban Northbrook who was accused and later convicted of sexually assaulting and murdering a seventeen-year-old boy. Like Gacy, Lindwall had gone cruising for young men.

After fifteen days of testimony, in which they had heard about seventy witnesses, the jury was dismissed for their third weekend.

The Fourth Week

Five lay witnesses testified for the defense on Monday, February 25, at the start of the fourth week of trial.

John Lucas told the jury of Gacy's activities at the Shell station, including the marijuana incident on the day of his arrest.

Gacy's seventy-two-year-old mother, Marion, came into the courtroom supported by a metal walker. With the appearance of his former wife and his mother, Gacy was now showing the first emotion he had since the trial began. "That's John over there smiling at me," his mother said when asked to identify him; at the end of her testimony she tearfully embraced her son.

When questioned by Motta, Mrs. Gacy characterized John as "a good and loving son." Motta asked how she felt when she heard the news of his arrest:

A.   I can't believe he would do anything like that, not my son.

Q.   As you knew him?

A.   I still . . . I would just like to erase everything.

Two of Gacy's childhood friends, Richard Dalke and Edward Kenneth Doncal, a doctor of chiropractic, testified. Dalke told of the card party at which Gacy had passed out and a priest was summoned to give him the last rites. Doncal recalled another card party at which Gacy began flailing his arms and had broken Doncal's glasses.

Gacy's younger sister, who lived in Arkansas with her husband and three children, described her brother as sweet, loving, understanding, and generous; like her mother, she spoke of her father's brutality.

She told how Gacy had bought her a freezer when her old one broke down. "It was with love," she said. "He had his biggest dream in life to help pay off me and my sister's mortgage so we wouldn't have to work."

Motta responded to the sister's emotional testimony with prodding, leading questions:

Q. Isn't he a fake? Couldn't he fake that?

A. No, he couldn't fake it. John always came through from the heart.

Q. Wasn't he a big phony? Everything was a sham, a front, isn't that right?

A. No, it's not right. He liked to show off when he did something, but that's not being a phony. He was proud of what he did. No one ever praised him. No one ever said, "Hey, John, you did a good job."

Over the next three days, the defense put on three more medical witnesses, whose testimony would wrap up their case in chief. Dr. Lawrence Freedman, a psychiatrist from the University of Chicago, diagnosed Gacy as a pseudo-neurotic paranoid-schizophrenic, whose mental illness stemmed largely from circumstances of his childhood, primarily his brutal father. Calling Gacy one of the most complex personalities he had ever encountered, Freedman said that the defendant showed "an extraordinary absence" of normal human feelings toward his victim.

But the weakness in Freedman's testimony that Kunkle zeroed in on was the psychiatrist's reluctance to give an opinion as to whether Gacy was insane at the time of the killings.

Robert Traisman, a clinical psychologist, testified to the tests he had given Gacy at the request of the defense's chief psychiatrist. Based on the Rorschach Ink Blot Test he had administered, Traisman said he found Gacy to be "a paranoid schizophrenic who had homosexual conflicts, marked feelings of masculine inadequacy, a man who had a lack of empathy, a lack of feeling for other people, an individual with an alarming lack of emotional control or ego control when under stress, who had strong potentials for emotional or ego disintegration and expressions of very hostile, dangerous impulses, either to others or to himself."

More important, Kunkle had noticed that Traisman's cover letter to his report was, as he put it, "much less a finding of insanity than the report itself," and this proved helpful to us in Egan's cross-examination:

Q. Would it be correct to say in your opinion, and consistent with your diagnosis, that John Gacy certainly knows the nature of any antisocial acts he might perform, and he would be quite cognizant of whether or not they are right or wrong on a moral level?

Over the defense lawyer's objections, Traisman answered yes.

Dr. Richard G. Rappaport, the defense's chief psychiatrist, was called on Wednesday afternoon, February 27. From the start there were indications that his would be very lengthy testimony. Under Motta's direct examination, Rappaport gave long answers defining basic terms of psychiatry. Sustaining an objection at one point, Garippo admonished him, "This is not a lecture. You are supposed to be answering questions."

As we expected, Rappaport gave his diagnosis of Gacy as borderline personality organization with a subtype of psychopathic personality, with instances of psychotic or paranoid schizophrenic behavior, the latter, however, not being the primary illness. Using a chart of an onion as an analogy, Rappaport told the jury that "in the psychiatric evaluation of an individual, as you peel back layers, you find out more and more and more about the individual and his understanding."

Rappaport testified that Gacy's affect was never inappropriate, that there was some evidence that he was an antisocial personality, and that he was probably not psychotic at the time the psychiatrist was examining him.

Knowing that we were reaching the culmination of the defense's case in chief, Kunkle went into cross-examination very aggressively, and at several points prosecution and defense engaged in heated exchanges. Prompted by a conversation he had had earlier with a news reporter, Kunkle asked the doctor if he had indicated his availability for news interviews after his first day of testimony. The defense lawyers objected. Rappaport said no. Asked how much money he expected to be paid by the county, Rappaport said that his time was probably worth twenty to twenty-five thousand dollars, a statement that probably hurt the defense.

For most of his cross-examination, Kunkle attacked Rappaport's basic diagnosis, part of which was that Gacy was a borderline personality who slipped over the edge into states of schizophrenia, a psychosis. Kunkle was convinced that both prevailing schools of thought ruled that possibility out: "One says that that can't happen," he said later, and "the other holds that once a borderline becomes psychotic, then he's not borderline anymore—and one doesn't go back and forth." Kunkle asked Rappaport if he thought an article by Roy R. Grinker, M.D., whom the psychiatrist had cited in his direct testimony, would be authoritative. Rappaport said he thought so. Kunkle asked if he agreed with Grinker's statement, "The borderline does not have the thought disorders characteristic of even latent schizophrenia. They do not have the capacity to develop schizophrenia." Rappaport said he did not.

Kunkle asked Rappaport if Gacy was floridly psychotic when he strangled Rob Piest.

A. Thinking he is the father and Piest the son, it was a psychotic delusion.

Q. How about when he laid him down on the floor and went on and answered the phone call from Max the plumber, was he floridly psychotic then?

A. I think he was under the same delusion, and was able to handle the phone calls.

Q. And what about when he handled the phone call from the hospital about his uncle, still floridly psychotic?

A. Yes.

Q. What are the symptoms of psychosis?

A. A person is out of touch with reality, a person who has thinking, mood, behavior disorder . . . you want me to go into more detail?

Q. No, that is all right. And the defendant was in florid

psychoses when he was handling his business on the phone with this Piest body in the other room?

A. Yes.

On redirect, Motta asked Rappaport, "Is it delusional to think that Cook County will pay you twenty to twenty-five thousand dollars?"

"Sure," the doctor answered.

The defense rested. The next phase of the trial would be ours, to rebut the evidence as to Gacy's alleged insanity that the defense had presented.

In the rebuttal, the prosecution is normally confined to refuting the defense's case in chief. But because Gacy's lawyers had used an insanity defense showing a long-standing mental condition, drawing on witnesses going back to his childhood, we were allowed to be equally wide-ranging in our rebuttal. We would counterattack with people who had known Gacy in Iowa, witnesses who would testify to his mental state at the time of his conviction for sodomy and convince the jury that he was not crazy at the time.

Our first witness on Friday, February 29, was Gacy's teenage victim in the sodomy case, Donald Voorhees, now twenty-seven years old. The judge had agreed to a defense motion and ordered a voir dire examination outside the presence of the jury to determine whether Voorhees was competent to testify. Staring vacantly through his granny glasses, Voorhees had difficulty answering the questions put to him. He responded slowly to Egan's questions, sometimes not at all, and he admitted that he had made a statement to the defense to the effect that he felt incompetent to testify. Seeing the state that Voorhees was in, Egan cut short his examination. Motta began, asking if the young man was seeing a psychiatrist.

A. Yes, sir, I am.

Q. How long have you been seeing him?

A. (No response.)

Q. For a while?

A. (No response.)

Q. All right, we will . . .

A. Ever since I heard that Gacy was out of prison. Yes, I have had problems.

Motta asked if Voorhees had had any medication today. No, the witness responded. "I drank one beer for breakfast."

In side bar, I told of interviewing Voorhees. "He is slow. He had been affected by this, but he knows what is going on. He can testify." I had a sickening feeling that all our work with Voorhees was crumbling. He had told us of his great fear of Gacy, and how his subsequent life, including a failed marriage, had been wrecked by what the defendant had done to him. Now, with Gacy sitting fifteen feet away and staring directly at him, Voorhees was falling apart. I desperately tried to persuade the judge that the witness had an important story to tell. Amirante requested that a psychiatric evaluation be made of Voorhees to determine his competence to testify. Garippo denied the motion and told us to try again, this time in the jury's presence.

Egan questioned Voorhees about knowing Gacy and doing work for him. When he got to Gacy's proposal for sexual experiments, Voorhees said only that Gacy "came on to me sexually" and could remember nothing further. The defense renewed their objections, and Egan again questioned Voorhees in voir dire. Voorhees's responses were painfully slow. Finally Garippo asked the witness to step down. In side bar, we discussed the possibility of deferring Voorhees's testimony until later, although we said it was unlikely he would get any better.

In the jury's presence, Egan withdrew the witness, and later in the morning Garippo ordered Voorhees's testimony stricken. It was regrettable that we couldn't use Voorhees, but I think that in his brief appearance he gave the jury a profound idea of the sort of havoc that John Gacy wreaked on the lives of so many of those he encountered.

Throughout the day, seven other witnesses from the Waterloo years took the stand. Russell Schroeder, now thirty, married and the father of one, told how Gacy had hired him to beat up Voorhees to persuade him not to testify in the sodomy hearing. The act done, Schroeder said, he returned to Gacy's house and found that his sponsor didn't want to know anything about the beating. Did he tell you why? I asked. "He didn't want to get involved," Schroeder replied.

"You like to make up stories, don't you?" Amirante asked Schroeder in a very forceful cross-examination.

"No," the witness replied. "John Gacy persuaded me to tell a lie so that he would not get involved, and after getting better advice, I decided to tell the truth."

Two other men who had been teenagers when they associated with Gacy in Waterloo took the stand. Richard Westphal told of Gacy's pool and blow-job strategy. Edward Lynch recounted Gacy's knife attack on him, and the chaining, padlocking, and choking incidents that followed. He drew a picture of the future mass-murderer from the point of view of a perplexed teenager. "I had watched two films previous to the stabbing incident. And then he had apologized and reassured me. I was sixteen and gullible. I believed him."

We put Gacy's friends from Iowa in the witness chair, too. Raymond Cornell, the ex-convict who had served time with Gacy and who now was the prison ombudsman at Anamosa, told how Gacy as a lead cook had given steak sandwiches and other food to inmates and staff alike in return for movie tokens, cigars, and other goods from the outside. He spoke of the privileges gained from being a prison Jaycee and how Gacy had availed himself of these emoluments as the chapter's "most decorated member." Cornell also expressed gratitude for the supportive friendship that Gacy had offered him, coaxing Cornell out of the throes of prison-induced depression.

Steve Pottinger and Clarence Lane, Gacy's cronies in the Waterloo Jaycee chapter, also appeared. Pottinger told the jurors he saw no difference in Gacy's personality and behavior before he went into Anamosa and after he got out. Lane acknowledged that Gacy had manipulated him. "I believed in his innocence on the first charge right up until this last incident," he said.

Lyle Murray, the former correctional counselor at Anamosa, described Gacy's educational progress during his stay as excellent, his record in the Jaycees as outstanding, and his work performance as good with the exception of a minor disciplinary incident. As a prisoner, he said, Gacy was "almost no problem" and had excellent institutional adjustment. He could be regarded, Murray said, as a model prisoner. I hoped the jury could see from this that Gacy did have the ability to conform his conduct to the requirement of the law.

Judge Garippo dismissed the jury for its first two-day weekend, advising the members who, like many of us, were "fighting all kinds of bugs," to get some rest and Vitamin C.

The Fifth Week

Our first medical witness testified on Monday, March 3. This was Dr. Leonard L. Heston, a professor of psychiatry who had been directly involved in the examination of Gacy before the sodomy conviction in Iowa. Over defense objections, Heston testified that he had diagnosed Gacy as an antisocial personality, one who comes into repeated conflict with society and social norms. The impairment, he said, was a defect in personality, and he regarded Gacy as sane at the time of the sodomy offense.

The person suffering from psychosis, Heston said, "is unable to meet the demands of an ordinary environment because of a disturbance of thinking or mood. If one takes that definition literally, simple drunkenness would be a brief psychotic episode." Such a condition, he said, is frequently associated with becoming angry, "which most of us do from time to time. The condition is such that it could interfere with the ability to respond to the demands of an ordinary environment. And in that sense we all experience micro-psychotic episodes from time to time."

When asked by Kunkle if a person suffering from these episodes would be excused from criminal behavior, Heston replied no.

On cross, Amirante asked Heston if Gacy's numerous contradictory statements weren't a symptom of some mental condition. "Not necessarily," Heston said. "We all tend to make socially approved comments, or construe our actions in the best light, when in fact our actual conduct may be quite the opposite. This is an ordinary human experience."

"If I told you," Amirante said, "that Dr. Freedman's reports state that Mr. Gacy is a complex combination of manic compulsivity and obsessiveness with a paranoid personality, extraordinary disassociation between the most violent action and idea and the appropriate responsive emotion—what does that indicate to you?"

"Sir, that, I'm afraid, means nothing to me," Heston answered. "There are six or eight diagnostic terms there that are all thrown in a pudding. . . ."

On redirect, to attack what he considered to be the defense doctors' Freudian bias, Kunkle asked Heston to explain the basic problem with psychoanalytic theory, in regard to diagnostic criteria.

It is a theoretical assumption, Heston said, about how the mind or brain works, and its basic problem is always this fact: "That one cannot test what is going on in the mind or brain of another person. There's no way to test these postulated mechanisms."

The witness who undoubtedly shocked the jury more than any other was Robert Donnelly. Testifying on the following day, the twenty-one-year-old college student recounted his night of terror after being abducted at gunpoint by Gacy late on December 30, 1977. Donnelly stuttered, and he frequently expressed his anguish over reliving his hours of torment, but he continued on, even through a merciless cross-examination, relating the details of the attack step by step. Throughout his testimony, Gacy scoffed and smirked, shaking his head as if in disbelief.

Although I had prepared Donnelly extensively, some of his recollections brought him close to breakdown. *"Please, please, please!"* he exclaimed when I showed him a picture of Gacy's recreation room. In the midst of describing how Gacy had raped him, he cried out: "This is hell! This is hell!" and Garippo called a recess. After reconvening, in the well of the courtroom, Donnelly showed the jurors how Gacy had seated himself and put his foot into Donnelly's stomach while playing Russian roulette.

Donnelly told of going to the police, then having a subsequent meeting with them and an assistant state's attorney. He testified that they would not allow him to sign any complaints against Gacy and that they weren't going to do anything about it. I asked Donnelly if Gacy had told him, when he let him off in the alley at Marshall Field's, not to go to the police "because they won't believe you."

He had, Donnelly said. "They *didn't* believe me."

Motta came on very hard in an attempt to discredit Donnelly's testimony, and there were several times when I feared that the witness might buckle under the stress. He fought back, however, and Motta's heartless questioning seemed to me very damaging to the defense's case. By taking Donnelly through the ordeal all over again he was doing little more than burning the horrible images into the minds of the jurors.

We were able to bring Donnelly in on rebuttal because the defense had used Jeffrey Rignall. We had been planning to call Arthur Winzel as well, but after Donnelly's appearance, there wasn't much need for his testimony. We were sure the jury had had enough.

Our second medical witness was Dr. Arthur Hartman, chief psychologist of the Psychiatric Institute of the Cook County Circuit Court. The Psychiatric Institute serves the court by examining several thousand patients referred to it each year. Almost a third of these cases involve felonies. Thus, in dealing with the Institute and its people, we had the benefit of working with doctors who had a track record in forensic psychiatry. They were accustomed to relating their findings to the facts of the case, using terminology that had meaning in the eyes of the law, and testifying in language the jurors could understand.

Hartman said he had found in Gacy no indication of any mental distrubance or mental disease. Hartman concluded that Gacy was a "psychopathic or antisocial personality with sexual deviation" who showed minor symptoms of paranoid hysterical reactions. Nor, in twelve interviews, had he found any evidence that Gacy had ever had a mental disease that could be considered a psychotic condition. Nor was Gacy's sexual deviation indicative of any mental defect, he said. In their examination of sexual offenders, Hartman said, the doctors had found that "almost any possible range of sexual deviant behavior seems to be consistent or compatible with otherwise normal or even good adjustment from the usual social considerations." In his opinion Gacy could appreciate the criminality of his actions and could conform his conduct to the requirements of the law. Hartman said he had asked Gacy to give three wishes. The defendant's response was: "To know myself better, to do good for others," and "I wish I was never in the mess I'm in."

Hartman's colleague and director of the Institute, Dr. Robert Reifman, testifying next, told the jury that he didn't believe you can have thirty-three cases of temporary insanity. The psychiatrist said that in his opinion, Gacy suffered a personality disorder, "specifically narcissistic type," which is not considered a mental disease. Reifman said he rejected the diagnosis of antisocial personality, a subtype of narcissistic, because it excluded things in which Gacy was well accomplished. Nor did he think Gacy had the chaotic symptoms of the borderline type. Gacy, he said, was a very efficient, functional person—as a businessman, politician, and clown.

At no time, he said, was Gacy out of touch with reality. He conned people into handcuffs. Had he been angry or disturbed, Reifman said, "it would have been unlikely that anybody would have gone along with him."

In closing, Kunkle asked Riefman why the thirty-three murders were not a product of thirty-three irresistible impulses. "I don't believe Mr. Gacy ever struggled against doing that," Reifman replied. Considering the testimony of Gray and Walsh as to digging graves in the crawl space, Reifman said, "I don't think that a person who *plans* to have an irresistible impulse in the future could be considered *having* irresistible impulses."

On cross, Amirante asked Reifman if Gacy's contradictory statements showed logical thinking. "I think that's lying," the psychiatrist said flatly. "I think he doesn't remember what he says from one day to the next because he lies."

Amirante asked if it was consistent for a person with a

logical mind to tell the truth, then turn around and lie about it. "A person who lies in what thing is [in] their best interest," Reifman said, "may be functioning logically." How, Amirante asked, would Gacy help himself by lying about not remembering some of the victims he killed?

"I think Mr. Gacy wants to be famous," Reifman said. "And I think he talks and talks and talks. As a matter of fact, I think Mr. Gacy talks too much."

"When he says he is not a homosexual," Amirante asked, "is he lying about that?"

"Well," Reifman replied, "it's like Bruce Sutter saying he is not a ballplayer—because he is."

Amirante pursued the question of Gacy's motivation to lie. How could it possibly help him to lie about stuffing underpants in the throats of some of his victims? the lawyer asked.

"I don't think thirty-three murders helps him. I don't think Mr. Gacy helps himself at all," Reifman replied.

"Assuming it was not a lie," Amirante said, "let's just assume for a minute that he forgot. Okay? Now when he forgets, what would that be, repression?"

"I don't know," Reifman said, "because this is your fantasy, not mine. I think he remembers."

Phillip Hardiman, executive director of the Cook County Department of Corrections, was the first witness on Thursday, the final day of our rebuttal case. Hardiman explained the rules under which Gacy lived at Cermak and gave his opinion that Gacy was "a very well behaved inmate" who adapted quite well.

Richard Rogers, a clinical psychologist, testified that he had diagnosed Gacy as having obsessive-compulsive and hypomanic disorders. He noted that in the past Gacy also had possibly experienced "sexual sadism, a psychosexual disorder in which the person intentionally inflicts either physical or psychological suffering on another person against their will for the sake of sexual arousal." But in Rogers's opinion, Gacy appreciated the criminality of his behavior and had the ability to conform his conduct.

In the afternoon, Dr. James Cavanaugh, Jr., testified, and we got into an imbroglio that made the headlines. As medical

director of the Isaac Ray Center, part of Chicago's Rush–
Presbyterian–St. Luke's Medical Center, Cavanaugh super-
vised a program of diagnosis, evaluation, and treatment of
mentally ill offenders. He testified that when Gacy had
required him and the psychiatrist's team to guarantee in writing
they would not release their notes to either the lawyers or the
court, the defendant was showing "a degree of sophistication,
awareness and concern about the criminal forensic psychiatric
process." He observed Gacy to be well organized and said that
he had forged a kind of "quasi-celebrity" status in Cermak. He
diagnosed Gacy as having a "mixed personality disorder,"
whose major features were a pervasive narcissism, and
obsessive-compulsive, antisocial, and hypomanic qualities. He
said he found no evidence that Gacy was a paranoid schizophrenic, that the sum total of his life didn't fit the basic
elements of the illness, a common downhill deteriorative
course impairing cognitive, thinking, and emotional ability.
Gacy, he said, does not meet the state's insanity defense
standard.

"Is it possible," Kunkle asked, "to guarantee a person
found not guilty by reason of insanity, and then committed to a
mental hospital, Department of Mental Health in Illinois, will
remain there for the rest of his life?"

"Absolutely impossible," Cavanaugh said. "We find it very
difficult to keep people in hospitals who in fact need to be there
because of concern, which I can understand, that to hospitalize
is a deprivation of civil rights. . . ."

Motta objected and called for a side bar.

Cavanaugh's answer, of course, had spelled out for the jury
exactly why an insanity defense was unacceptable to us. But
the other side had not objected in time. Now in side bar
Amirante called for a mistrial, asserting that Cavanaugh's
statement had created an inference in the jurors' minds that
might or might not be true. The judge denied his motion, and
Kunkle finished his direct examination.

Motta pressed the issue on cross, asking Cavanaugh if he
thought Gacy needed to be in a mental hospital. The psychiatrist said he did not. Motta asked him to describe the procedure
for commitment after a finding of not guilty by reason of
insanity.

"The individual must demonstrate imminent danger to himself or others, or be adjudged essentially unable to care for himself," Cavanaugh said.

Motta asked Cavanaugh if he thought Gacy presented an imminent danger to others. The psychiatrist said he did not.

"I believe if he was found not guilty by reason of insanity," Cavanaugh said, "he would not meet the state's involuntary commitment standards."

"Would you say that Mr. Gacy would be released?"

"If the law were followed, I believe he would have to be released."

Kunkle objected after Motta further questioned, then interrupted the witness, and the judge called a side bar. Garippo said he objected to a person who was not a lawyer trying to define the law and instructing the jury. Amirante and Kunkle, meanwhile, snapped at each other ("Come here"; "I don't have to come there"). The judge sustained Kunkle's objection.

Motta forged on, If Gacy were found not guilty by reason of insanity, he asked Cavanaugh, would the psychiatrist testify that Gacy did not need mental treatment? Again Kunkle objected, and Garippo struggled to put the lid on the pot. He told the jury that the question of what happens to a defendant after such a finding involves a legal hearing by the court that he would conduct himself. He suggested we move on.

Motta now asked Cavanaugh if, were Gacy committed and Cavanaugh the examining doctor, he would release the defendant, Garippo told the jury to step out and excused Cavanaugh.

"The issue before the jury is whether or not the defendant is sane or insane," Garippo said, by now somewhat exasperated. "Now, the defense in their opening statement said, 'We want him hospitalized for the rest of his life.'" The state, he continued, had brought up the question of commitment, but the defense hadn't objected until after the answer was in. He said both sides had created an issue that was not before the jury.

After thinking it over in recess, Garippo decided he would give the jury instructions on the matter. "Both sides," he said to us before the jury was called back in, "felt that there was probably some tactical advantage in going into this area. The defense wanted to go into it from the standpoint of softening the blow of the not guilty by reason of insanity. The state

wanted to go into it to show the unpredictability of it."
Accordingly, Garippo said he would instruct the jury to
disregard any comment by attorneys or witness regarding
Gacy's fate should he be found not guilty by reason of insanity.

Motta said he would not acquiesce in the instruction and
again called for a mistrial. Garippo denied it. There the matter
ended but, as Gacy would later say, the seed had been planted.
On the evening news more than one anchorman, eyebrows
raised, conjured up the image of John Gacy footloose on the
streets of Chicago.

Before the jury was called in on Friday for the defense's
surrebutter, Judge Garippo made an announcement: "Over two
weeks ago, Mr. Gacy wrote me a letter with a few complaints. I
gave that letter to his attorneys and was assured that there was
no problem. Today I have received another letter from Mr.
Gacy. Mr. Gacy, if you will step forward."

The judge asked the defendant if he wished to say anything
in respect to the letter. Gacy didn't. Garippo then read the letter
into the record.

"Over two weeks ago," Gacy had written, "I asked that my
trial be stopped and I haven't heard from you. When I asked
my attorneys as to why we are not putting on more witnesses, I
am told that we don't have money to bring in experts.

"I also ask for a mistrial, as never before has this court
allowed a professional witness plants a seed in the Jury head
like it was done yesterday.

"I think that you can give them instructions until you blue in
the face and you won't take that out of their heads.

"When Cavanaugh said, 'John Gacy would not qualify for
commitment to a mental institution and would have to be set
free if he were found not guilty by reason of insanity.'

"As you know, other than so-called statements made by me,
and given in a self-serving manner by officers for the
prosecution, there is only evidence that I owned the house that
was used for (bodies), their safe-keeping.

"Until something is done to correct this injustice, I will no
longer have anything to do with my attorneys. And I am taking
back my word in regards to not saying anything in the
courtroom. The prosecution continued to tries to make me mad

while the trial is going on with the taking of my PDM Contractor labels and putting them all over the place. That's receiving of stolen properties, as I have never given permission. And when yesterday Greg Bedoe came up to me in open court and told me that I should stop smiling, and swore at me, I don't have to take that. I don't think anyone should come forward to the prosecution tables until I am out of the courtroom.

"I await to hear from you and will abide with your word."

Garippo told Gacy that at no time had he been denied the opportunity to bring in experts, that the court had allowed all those the defense had requested and had provided for their compensation. He then asked Gacy if he still intended not to deal with his attorneys.

"That's correct," Gacy said.

"Why?" the judge asked.

"Because I'm not running the trial," Gacy said.

"Are there any tactics your attorneys are using that you don't agree with?"

"I was against the insanity defense from the beginning," Gacy replied.

Garippo told Gacy to be seated and asked his counsel for comment. Amirante said that neither he nor Motta had ever felt that Gacy could fully cooperate with them because of the inconsistencies produced by a "deep and penetrating mental illness." He said he felt the fitness standard, as it exists in Illinois, was unconstitutional as applied to Gacy. "I did not commit the crimes," Gacy interjected.

Garippo asked if either side had any evidence to present as to Gacy's fitness to stand trial. Amirante said the only evidence the defense could conceive of would be to allow Gacy himself to testify. The judge decided to conduct an immediate hearing to determine his fitness, but the two defense lawyers said they had no further evidence to present.

"Based on my observations of the defendant in the courtroom, his demeanor, and all of the evidence in the trial," Garippo said, citing the Illinois statute governing his decision, "I would enter a finding that the defendant is in fact fit to stand trial."

He asked Amirante and Motta if they had anything to say

regarding Gacy's dispute with them. They didn't, and he told Gacy to step forward. "Do you stand by your statements relative to your disagreement with your attorneys?" he asked.

After a long pause, Gacy said he didn't know. Garippo told him to be seated.

"Between now and the time your attorneys rest your case," Garippo said, "you have to decide whether or not you wish to testify before this jury. Do you understand that?"

Gacy said he did, and the judge ordered the jury called in.

The defense brought in Dr. Tobias Brocher, a psychiatrist associated with the Menninger Foundation in Kansas. They used Brocher, who had examined Gacy for one day, to try to rebut the testimony of Cavanaugh and Reifman. Brocher diagnosed Gacy as borderline towards a schizophrenic process. During his interview he had noted anger and grandiosity and observed that Gacy's conscience function "looks like a Swiss cheese with big holes in it."

When court resumed in the afternoon, Garippo was told that Gacy wanted to make a statement, and he delayed bringing in the jury.

During the lunch break, Gacy apparently had heard news broadcasts reporting his earlier statements. "Everything I seem to say," Gacy now told the court, "has been misconstrued by the press. And I would like to set the record straight that I did not fire my attorneys. It's just that I do not understand everything that is going on, and I am against the insanity defense because I don't truly understand it myself.

"All the statements, in retrospect, that I have given," he continued, "are confusing enough to me, that at the time I made the statement, I believe I would have confessed to the St. Valentine's Day Massacre, if it was put to me."

Gacy accused the press of taking everything out of context. He said he would like to know if he had committed the crimes, but despite three hundred hours of doctor visits, he said he was still confused. "While I am not denying the commission of the crime, I don't understand it . . . why it happened, and that is why I don't understand the proceedings. I have been called every name under the sun in this courtroom, and half the time I leave not even knowing who I am—from an onion to a piece of

Swiss cheese, to somebody that is sane and somebody that is crazy."

Police officers from various departments, he said, had all made self-serving statements. The news media, he charged, had already tried and convicted him. "Nowhere in this land can I get fair trial," Gacy exclaimed.

"I think you have got some of the finest lawyers here in the country," he continued. "I can see why Bernard Carey is not here—because he is not qualified. But be that as it may, everybody is going to twist eveything to their own liking. And to me, it's just like they're playing a chess game."

Gacy's earlier cockiness had vanished, and now he was acting out of desperation. His statement to the court was just as self-serving as any he had made before, and in spots just as untruthful. In a gratuitous slap, he even disavowed that he had ever been friends with Ron Rohde—an absurd statement, considering his tearful farewell on the Rohde doorstep and the communication they had had while Gacy was in Cermak.

The incident concerning Greg Bedoe that Gacy had mentioned in today's letter to the judge was similarly twisted. Gacy generally waited with appropriate deference while the jury filed out of the courtroom at the close of each session. Once they were gone, however, his ebullience would return, and he would laugh and joke with his attorneys or the bailiffs, or pull out a cigar, light it, and casually discard the match on the courtroom floor. The previous day, looking over at Gacy in disgust at these antics, Greg had gritted his teeth and said to the defendant, "Keep smiling, John," as if to suggest his judgment was soon coming.

When testimony resumed Kunkle began his cross-examination and asked Brocher to define the Illinois standard for the insanity defense.

"The Illinois defense of insanity," Brocher responded, "is somebody that has not the capacity to follow the insight of his wrongdoing because of—" Garippo interrupted, saying he would instruct the jury as to the definition. Kunkle asked Brocher if he agreed with a conclusion that Dr. Karl Menninger had reached in his book *The Crime of Punishment*, that psychiatrists don't belong in the courtroom—"It is not our sphere of action," Menninger had written.

Brocher said he disagreed, that his experience convinced him the opposite was true, "that most people in the legal profession don't understand psychiatry." Kunkle rested.

After Jack and Elaine Shields, two of Gacy's clown associates, testified to his character, Amirante put on Anthony De Blase, whom Gacy knew through the Democratic organization. De Blase told of Gacy's meticulous bookkeeping while serving as secretary-treasurer of the Norwood Park Township Lighting District and said he thought Gacy must have put in twenty-three-hour work days. The two men had discussed going into business together at one time, to open a disco, De Blase said, but the plans had fallen through. On cross, De Blase said he thought Gacy was sane.

In a session on Saturday, March 8, Dr. Helen Morrison, a psychiatrist, concluded the defense's surrebuttal testimony. She diagnosed Gacy as having mixed or atypical psychosis. Despite his high IQ, she said, Gacy had not developed emotionally; his entire emotional makeup was that of an infant. She concluded that Gacy suffered from mixed psychosis at least since 1958.

On cross by Egan, Morrison said that Gacy was psychotic when he killed Rob Piest. She said she would not change her opinion even in the light of Gacy's conducting business on the phone immediately after the killing or of his storing the body and later throwing it into the Des Plaines River.

"Do you think that under the circumstances," Egan asked, "John Gacy would have killed Robert Piest if there was a uniformed police officer in the home with him at the time?"

"Yes, I do," Dr. Morrison replied.

Outside the presence of the jury, Gacy made a brief statement to the court. "I don't feel I could add anything to something that I don't understand myself," he told the judge, thereby waiving his right to testify before the jury.

The Sixth Week

Dr. Jan Fawcett, chairman of the Department of Psychiatry at Rush–Presbyterian–St. Luke's, was our final medical witness, whom we brought in on Monday, March 10, to rebut the testimony of Drs. Brocher and Morrison. "Amnesia could not be ruled out by what he told me," Fawcett said, "but it was my impression that he was remembering more than he was telling me." In his opinion Gacy was not suffering from a mental disease, nor did he fit the Illinois insanity defense standards. Fawcett testified that even if he accepted Brocher's diagnosis, he found no "causal relationship between his diagnostic theory and any possible inability of the defendant at the time of the crimes to either not appreciate the criminality of his conduct or not being able to control his conduct."

Asked by Kunkle if he saw any factual basis to support Morrison's diagnosis of atypical psychosis, Fawcett replied, "No, he didn't meet the characteristics of a psychosis, so he can't meet the characteristics of a mixed or atypical psychosis." He said that he did not believe Morrison's inferences justified the conclusion that Gacy wasn't able to appreciate the criminality of his conduct and conform it to the requirements of the law.

On cross, Amirante brought up the fact that Fawcett had been initially approached by the defense lawyers to do a psychiatric evaluation of Gacy. Fawcett had declined to act as an agent of the defense, but had said he was willing to make the examination if appointed by the court.

Amirante tried to suggest that Fawcett had rejected the lawyers' request because the connection with Gacy's defense would be bad for the hospital's image, especially when it came to fund-raising. Kunkle was able to bring out the real reason on redirect.

Kunkle asked Fawcett what significant difference he saw between being a "friend of the court" and a defense-retained psychiatrist. Fawcett said that as a friend of the court he would avoid having to take an adversarial position because his report would go to both sides.

Q. Mr. Amirante didn't want that, did he?

A. Well, he wanted me to be a private witness, which, as he said, would mean that he didn't have to use my report if he didn't want it.

Q. In other words, if it didn't come out the way he wanted it, nobody else but he would know.

AMIRANTE AND MOTTA: Objection.

Our last witness was a Chicago police officer who had had absolutely nothing to do with the Gacy investigation; all along he had been working quietly in the hit and run unit just north of the Loop. This was Officer James Hanley, the man whose name Gacy had often dropped as "Jack Hanley" in his cruising, in case any of his victims suspected his cop masquerade and bothered to check. When they learned that there was indeed a Hanley on the force, very few would have pursued the matter further, doubting their chance of successfully prosecuting a kinky cop.

I was convinced that Gacy's Hanley alias was taken from a real cop, and we had had investigators looking for Hanley for more than a year, but somehow the police computer didn't turn up his name. In the closing days of the trial I was determined to find him. And luckily I did.

James Hanley testified that he had worked in plain clothes since the late 1960s. He had met Gacy, whom he knew only as John, in the summer or fall of 1971, in Bruno's, where Hanley sometimes went with his fellow officers. Normally, Hanley talked with them, but sometimes Gacy, who was working at

Bruno's as a chef, came up to the bar and initiated a conversation with him.

I asked how Hanley was known at the tavern.

"By my last name," he replied.

"Officer Hanley," I continued, "to your knowledge, did the defendant ever know your first name?"

"He never knew my first name." Hanley said that after Gacy quit Bruno's, he just dropped out of sight.

On cross, Amirante questioned the policeman. "You don't go cruising around Bughouse Square, do you?"

"No, sir," Hanley replied.

"You're not John Gacy, are you?"

"No, sir."

"Nothing further."

After the witness was excused, Kunkle addressed the court. "Judge, pending the acceptance of certain items in evidence, the People of the State of Illinois rest."

After a brief side bar, Amirante announced that the defense, too, would rest.

We had heard the testimony of more than a hundred witnesses, which ran to more than 5,000 pages of court transcript, but now we had finished in what many observers considered record time. Tomorrow we would argue the case, and I would be the lead-off man. Right now I had a case of the butterflies. I have John Gacy to thank for curing me.

Just after court was adjourned, he swaggered up to me, waving a newspaper clipping that advertised a St. Patrick's Day party at some tavern.

"I'll see you at this party, Terry," he said. "And don't forget to bring my present. St. Patrick's Day, you know, is my birthday."

I could have bashed him with my shillelagh on the spot, but in the interest of due process of the law, I retired to hone the edge of my closing argument.

Although the closing arguments don't come until both sides have rested, the preparation for them is long, because the whole trial itself is the basis from which you work. I would open for the prosecution, and my main task was to explode the insanity defense. Early in the trial, Kunkle and I had worked up a list of things that would be the foundation of our attack. Throughout the proceedings I had gone through the transcripts as soon as they were available, marking passages of testimony, especially those that concerned Gacy's character and behavior. At my request, Larry Finder had compiled large charts for each category, keyed to the transcripts. Thus we had composites, from many sources, that documented various facets of Gacy's personality and habits: credibility/boastfulness, memory, strength, manipulation, intelligence, sanity, work-sleep-recreation pattern, drug/alcohol usage, consciousness of choice, emotion/affect, self-control/discipline, and, of course, some of his memorable quotes.

Over the weekend I had worked on what seemed to be my one hundredth outline, and Sunday night Larry had come by and listened to my rehearsal. When I arrived at 26th and California on Monday morning, I was convinced my closing argument was no good, and I sat in a little windowless cubicle totally depressed as I began revising it even more. Larry stopped by and reassured me that it was good, but I didn't take him seriously. I appreciated his gesture, but Larry had never tried a jury case, and I didn't really believe him.

"Listen," he said, "Beethoven didn't like his fifth Symphony either." I don't know if his remark was off the wall or not, but it brought me to my senses. I was too close to it, and maybe I'd already made too many revisions. Larry's encouragement put me back on track.

"Today is March 11, 1980," I told the jurors in the crowded but hushed courtroom. "On Thursday, March 13, two days from now, John Mowery would have been twenty-three years old, if he had been allowed to live. Instead, his body was uncovered from John Gacy's crawl space.

"On Sunday, March 16, Robert Piest would have celebrated his seventeenth birthday. Instead, his body was recovered from the Des Plaines River, the very river that he had volunteered to clean to become an Eagle Scout.

"On Monday, March 17, John Gacy will celebrate his thirty-eighth birthday . . . Before that, you will decide whether or not he is allowed to tell a friend, such as Ron Rohde, on the telephone, 'Ron, didn't I tell you I'd be out? I beat the system again.' Or you will be the ones to tell John Gacy, in a loud and clear tone, a message that says, 'John Gacy, your cruising days are over. Young boys need fear you no more.' "

I had to make it clear that although we were denying the insanity defense we were not saying Gacy was normal. "There have been other mass-murders," I said, "but seldom, if ever, has anyone been so cold, so cunning, so calculated over such a long period of time as John Gacy has. Now, I am not going to stand here for one minute and tell you that he is normal. I wouldn't expect you to believe it. I'm going to tell you, right up front, that we consider him to be abnormal. But because he is abnormal doesn't mean that he doesn't know the difference between right and wrong. If he does, he is legally responsible. There is quite a difference between being abnormal and legally insane." We had proved beyond a reasonable doubt, I said, that John Gacy was guilty of thirty-three murders and that he was legally responsible. I called Gacy's insanity defense a fraud, pure and simple.

I cited Gacy's self-admitted stalking of the victims as an example of his intent, contrary to the picture of helplessness the defense psychiatrists had attempted to paint. Against Motta's assertion in his opening statement that his client's memory was sketchy, I tossed out Gacy's former wife's statement that he had a memory like an elephant, his pinpointing the precise upright on the bridge from which he had dumped the bodies, the detailed recollections offered in his statements. Calling his defense one of convenience, I pointed to Rappaport's "audacity to expect you people to believe the theory that John Gacy was insane thirty-three times over some seven or eight or nine years, but *never* any other time. He *just happened* to slip into it."

Iowa, I said, was very important: "The pattern he used in Iowa was later to be used back here in Illinois." And Iowa told us about his good behavior: "Remember this much—John Gacy could conform when he had to. The penitentiary is a good example of that."

" 'Clarence,' he told his friend, 'I'm never going back' when he got out of the penitentiary. Yes, folks, he had learned well from his experiences in Iowa. He was now a cunning ex-con about to go back into society, but little had changed about him except one thing: his resolve to make sure that he never got in that type of bind again. John Gacy was to make sure of that." Gacy, I said, emerged well aware of his legal rights.

Of the trenches in the crawl space, I pointed out, "Gacy later said, 'I had them dig those for graves.' If that isn't premeditation, there exists none anywhere. I ask you, does anyone dig holes in anticipation of having an unconscious rage?" When Gacy thought his crawl space was full, he went all the way down to the Des Plaines River bridge on I-55, sixty-five miles away. "These were conscious acts to avoid detection—acts of a sane man."

Gacy, I said, was like a spider caught in his own web as the Piest investigation progressed. On the first day, he manipulated the police. When he called to see if they still wanted him to come in, "he wanted to find out whether or not they were still sitting at his house. And since they were in the police station, he knew now is the chance for him to get rid of the body. Is that a calculating mind? Remember their doctors saying he was in a rage during all this time? Please!" I emphasized Gacy's continued manipulation, his lies, and finally, when confronted with a search warrant to his house, his calling his attorney. The web was now tightening. But the manipulation continued, in the relationships he tried to establish with the surveillance officers. Then he threatened a lawsuit, threatened the policemen with death; still the web tightened. To the end he was manipulating and lying until he saw that the game was over and he said, "Dave, I want to clear the air."

Even at the statement table, Gacy was planning when he said there are four Johns. "This was the start of his fake, planned insanity defense of multiple personality. Little did he know that later all the psychiatrists would come in and reject that theory."

What did all that show? I asked the jury. "It shows beyond a reasonable doubt a man who knew what he was doing. He knew what he was doing was wrong and he nevertheless did it and then, furthermore, covered it up." I reminded the jurors of what Gacy had said when Finder asked him why he had let Donnelly go after inflicting such horrible torture on him. "'Larry,' he said, 'had I known he was going to beef to the police, Donnelly would have gotten the rope trick.'"

I was now in my fourth hour, and I could tell that the jury, although attentive, was waiting for me to sum it all up.

Besides, they were probably getting hungry. I went into my final argument, pointing to Gacy's path of destruction. "Thirty-three boys were dead and the lives of parents, brothers, sisters, fiancées, grandmothers, friends were left shattered. Even though technically he left some of the surviving victims, they were little more than void shells—you saw them—and perhaps described best as 'living dead.' John Gacy has accounted for more human devastation than many earthly catastrophes, but one must tremble—tremble when thinking just how close he came to getting away with it all.

"John Gacy caused misery and suffering—enough to last a century—thank God he's been stopped," I said.

I turned towards him. "John Gacy, you are the worst of all murderers, for your victims were the young, the unassuming, the naive. You truly are a predator."

Gacy greeted my statement by smiling and chuckling at me. I went on, turning to him each time I used his name. "John Gacy, you have pilfered the most precious thing that parents can give: that of human life. . . . finally, John Gacy, you have snuffed out those lives like they were just candles. You have snuffed out the very existence of those thirty-three young boys—*forever*. Those candles can't be lit again . . . for all eternity."

Now I did not ignore his behavior. "You saw him laugh at me," I told the jurors. "You are the only ones who can tell him—loud and clear—'We refuse to be used or manipulated by you, John Gacy.' . . . If you find him not guilty, then do so, remembering that eleven unidentified male bodies are still in the Cook County morgue." I stopped and picked up the sheaf of twenty-two eight-by-ten color photos and walked over to the display board bearing the names of each identified victim.

"If you do so, do so in spite of Body No. 2, Medical Examiner No. 1065 found with a clothlike material on his throat. Male white, five-nine, 150 pounds. Last seen July 29, 1975, Chicago, Illinois. Identified December 29, 1978, as John Butkovich." I placed the photo of Butkovich in its slot.

"If you find him not guilty, do so in spite of Body No. 29, Medical Examiner No. 494. Clothlike material in throat. Male white, five foot five, 140 pounds. Last seen April 6, 1976, at

Chicago, Illinois. Identified November 18, 1979, as Darrell Sampson, age eighteen.

And so I continued, with Stapleton, Reffett, Bonnin, Rick Johnston, William Carroll, Gregory Godzik, and the others, until twenty-one pictures were posted. During my presentation, frequent sobs broke the silence, and several members of victims' families got up and hurriedly left.

Finally I came to the last victim. "And, ladies and gentlemen, if you find him not guilty, do so over Body No. 30, Medical Examiner No. 231. Paper-like material in the throat. Male white, five foot eight inches tall, a hundred forty pounds. Last seen alive December 11, 1978, in Des Plaines, Illinois, identified April 9, 1979, as Robert Piest. Student. Birthday is Sunday."

With Piest's photo, the "Gallery of Grief" was complete; the faces of twenty-two young men, some smiling, others simply caught in a moment of anticipation, peered down at the jury, frozen in time.

John Gacy, I said, was criminally responsible, and he had committed the crimes charged. That much we had proved beyond a reasonable doubt. I gestured toward the photographs, then walked up to the board and pointed to each victim, individually. *"This* was murder. *This* was murder. *This* was murder. *This* was murder. Murder. Murder. Murder . . . and *this* was murder. Justice implores you to find John Gacy guilty of murder . . . murder in the worst degree!"

Sam Amirante gave an impassioned, sometimes eloquent and sometimes rambling, closing argument for the defense. He began by thanking the jury, then graciously commended me for giving "a fantastic and brilliant, persuasive closing argument." That done, he got down to the business of rebutting my statement and our case.

Mr. Sullivan, he said, had drawn a lot of inferences, speculated a lot, and rarely talked about the evidence. He accused me of trying to arouse the jurors' sympathy by manipulation, getting them to hate his client.

"Mr. Gacy is not an evil man," Amirante said. "He has done some evil things. Yet he tried so hard to be good. He tried to please his father, and he kept doing it throughout the course of his life."

Amirante cited the example of a woman accused of being a witch who was tried in Salem, Massachusetts, in 1692. After the jury found her not guilty, the courtroom spectators were enraged, just as the judge was, and he sent the jury back to reconsider. They came back and found her guilty after all, and she was hanged. "They decided it on emotion," Amirante said, "and everybody was pleased." Avoid anger, he counseled, avoid vengeance, in the interest of learning what the defendant is all about so that his victims did not die in vain. "If revenge, if sympathy would bring back one of those boys, Mr. Motta and I would join hands with you in putting Mr. Gacy to death or trundling him off to the side."

Amirante interpreted Gacy's dealings with the Des Plaines police force as the acts "of a man who wants to get caught." "He wasn't in any police web—he was in his own web," Amirante said. "He was tangled in that web of his mind, encased in his flesh for so many years, and the killing had to stop."

He scoffed at the idea that Gacy had planned Piest's murder, considering that Gacy didn't even know the youth's name. "That is the drive of a madman," he said, "a man driven by perverted obsessions and compulsions he could not control. Why Robert Piest?"

He spoke of what the doctors had called lack of appropriate affect. "Did you see what he did when Mr. Sullivan was calling him a murderer, murderer, murderer? He was laughing. Laughing. Put yourself in that chair over there. Somebody calling you a murderer, somebody asking the jury to find you guilty of this crime—are you going to laugh?"

Amirante attacked the idea that digging the crawl space graves was an example of planning. He accused me of glossing over Stein's testimony that in thirteen cases the cause of death was not strangulation, but suffocation caused by something stuffed in the victims' throats. Either Gacy did not remember, Amirante said, or he did not do it—because that's not part of his pattern, that's not the rope trick. Why, Amirante asked rhetorically, were these inconsistencies in his statement?

Amirante traced his client's early history, his medical

difficulties, his relationship with his family and friends, the perception that many people had of him as a good man. "The man wanted to be good," Amirante said. "He tried so hard to consume all of his time because he knew that there was this raging disease inside of his mind, something he could not control."

The defense lawyer turned to the testimony of the surviving victims, attempting to discredit some, like Antonucci, for not reporting Gacy's attack "until all this stuff was in the newspaper." He then focused on the psychiatrists, who "found that [Gacy] was a deeply distrubed man suffering from severe and deep obsessions and unconscious compulsions." Amirante conceded that "none of them could look back in the past to the time and place of the act itself and tell you exactly what happened. I don't even know if Mr. Gacy himself could tell you that. Obviously, he can't. His statements are so inconsistent . . . a ritual of tying a rope around somebody's neck, yet that is inconsistent with the physical evidence found by the medical examiner. I don't think even Mr. Gacy can tell you. The point is, none of them has a crystal ball." The jurors, he said, "are the only ones who can decide."

"If Dr. Heston had done his job in 1968," Amirante said, "if he had looked at those psychiatric signs, then we wouldn't be here today, and those twenty-two boys there would still be alive. Heston is here because he didn't do his job in 1968. . . . If my children, or your children or grandchildren, ever fall victim to the kind of disease Mr. Gacy has, then we should hang our heads in shame because what we have done is to ignore the facts, that this man has a deep and profound mental illness. If we look away, we will never find out. We will look back and say that we did not do our jobs in this courtroom. The man should have been studied.

"Use your common sense. If he could control his conduct, and if he was so afraid of going [to jail], why did he not stop it? I suggest he did not stop it because he could not stop it.

"A man does not have to be a bulging-eyed monster to be insane or to be mentally ill. He can walk around, and that is the most dangerous kind." Amirante suggested that fifteen months earlier, Gacy might have been the foreman on another jury.

"It is frightening: a neighbor, a brother, a friend, a man with such a deep, dark, hidden, sick, pervasive disease, and nobody can see it."

Why, Amirante asked, did Gacy go to Nisson Pharmacy? "To get his book—and he winds up killing Robert Piest. Is that premeditation, or is that compulsion?" A man who collected bodies, lived with them, showed no nervousness when the police were there—"Is that a sane man?"

Amirante began reading passages from Robert Louis Stevenson's *The Strange Case of Dr. Jekyll and Mr. Hyde,* interspersing words that Jeffrey Rignall had used to describe Gacy. The names Jekyll and Hyde had been heard frequently in testimony, "the words that were used so often in John Gacy's house [when he was] a child." Amirante quoted Dr. Jekyll: "'If I am the chief of sinners, I am the chief of sufferers also. Both sides of me were in dead earnest.'"

"John Gacy is truly a Jekyll and Hyde," Amirante said, "despite what psychiatric terms you put on it. He is the personification of this novel written in 1886—he was so good and he was so bad, and the bad side of him is the personification of evil."

A man who kills thirty-three people, Amirante said, is insanely evil. Gacy, however, "did not want to do it. He could not control himself. What do you do? Do you hold him responsible for that, or do you take the first step of having him studied to try to prevent something like this from happening again?

"My God, take that first step, ladies and gentlemen of the jury, do it! Do the right thing. Don't decide this case with hate, revenge, passion and fear. Commit yourselves to your laws.

"When you look at the whole picture, you will find that the state has not met their burden of proving Mr. Gacy sane beyond a reasonable doubt. We expect you to return a verdict of not guilty by reason of insanity. Our work is now on the verge of being over, and your work is just beginning."

Bill Kunkle made only two promises in his closing argument on Wednesday morning: "I won't speak as long as Mr. Sullivan—perhaps not as well, either. Hopefully, I won't be as loud as Mr. Amirante.

"Mr. Amirante asked you not to consider sympathy,"

Kunkle continued. "You should not consider sympathy. Don't consider sympathy for this defendant, either."

Gacy killed, and he knew he was killing. Kunkle called Gacy's defense a sham: "There is no evidence to support insanity in this defendant at the time of the crime, other than the crimes themselves." The core of psychoanalytic theories, as offered by the defense, he said, was the idea of predetermination. "When you turn that around, what it really means is that no one is responsible for his actions. We can't run society that way."

Kunkle turned to the medical witnesses. "Dr. Rappaport. You get a day and a half lecture in Psychology 101. But what did he say about causality? What did Dr. Rappaport ever say about the facts of these killings that led him to support his theory? No answers." Freedman, he said, used terms that were nonexistent in the standard reference used in the courts and gave no opinion as to sanity. Dr. Brocher didn't know the Illinois definition of the insanity defense. He called Dr. Morrison the champ in "stringing together paragraphs and sentences and long words."

"She tells you that John Gacy would kill with a policeman at his shoulder. If that were true, then why didn't Gacy kill Piest right in the middle of Nisson Pharmacy?" Kunkle asked. "If that were true, why didn't he run over Butkovich on the street with his car? He didn't do those things. He took them through force or guile to his home, and he killed them in that private and hellish place. And then he proceeded to cover up the evidence. And that is what he did thirty-three times. He never killed anyone in public. How convenient that he would only have these compulsions in the secrecy of his home at two and three o'clock in the morning."

Kunkle defended the testimony of Dr. Heston, who had had the rare opportunity to observe the defendant back in Iowa before the murders were committed. He pointed to the insulting comment Amirante had made, that had Heston done his work Gacy's victims would be alive today. "Dr. Heston made a thorough examination, and he found this defendant to be just what he is today, an antisocial personality, a psychopath, a person who commits crimes without remorse. And he said this guy is not going to improve with either social or psychiatric treatment. What you had better do is lock him up, and you had better keep him there. Heston did his job. He told them what would happen. And it did. But they let him out."

Why, Kunkle asked, if the defense admitted there were no neurological problems, did they keep talking about Gacy's getting hit in the head with a swing, about blackouts, and supposed epileptic seizures and fits? That, he said, was "nothing but a smokescreen." There was no evidence of any such troubles after 1963. "Can you picture the defendant in an epileptic seizure writhing around on the floor tying the three knots in the rope?"

As for Amirante's plea to study, not kill, John Gacy, Kunkle said that there would be plenty of time for that, years to do so while the appeals were going through. "If you want to study him, study him. It has got nothing to do with this verdict."

Kunkle called the defense's contention that Gacy wanted to be stopped "absolute nonsense. If he was a person having a brief psychotic episode, to come back to reality and find bodies on his floor, all he had to do is call the police, a hospital, a psychiatrist, the Department of Mental Health, a friend, Ron Rohde, his wife. He didn't do any of those things. He didn't want to be caught. If he wanted Kozenczak to catch him on the 12th, why not lead him up to the attic and show him the body? When he invited the police officers in to sit and talk, why didn't he give them a shovel?

"Why does the defendant finally clear the air? He knows what they are going to find. He doesn't have amnesia. He knows where all those bodies are. He drew a map." But Gacy never played anymore cards than he had to. "He told [the police] what they already knew, what they wanted to hear, just as much as he wanted to tell, and no more."

Kunkle conceded that Gacy probably hadn't returned to Nisson's specifically to pick up Piest, but when the boy came out, it was "an opportunity. John never passed up an opportunity, except maybe when the trunk of his car was already full on the way to the river."

Kunkle gave a detailed exposition of the location of the graves and the sequence in which the victims were killed. Then, picking up the Jekyll and Hyde theme introduced by Amirante, he reminded the jury how Stevenson's protagonist grew to enjoy the power that taking the potion and turning into Mr. Hyde gave him, "the power of playing God, the power of deciding who will live and who will die." Gacy, too, sought that ultimate power, he said. "He could torture victims to within seconds of their death and still maintain that Godlike power to let them live.

"We are not asking you to show sympathy," Kunkle said, stepping to the display board. He began removing the pictures of Gacy's victims one by one. "No matter what you do, you can't bring back these lives," he said, waving the pictures in his hand. Kunkle was now flushed as he worked up to the climax of his argument.

"Don't show sympathy," he roared. "Don't show sympathy! Show justice! Show justice! Show the same sympathy and pity that *this* man showed when he took *these* lives and put them *there!*"

And Kunkle flung the stack of photographs into the gaping maw of the trap door to the crawl space that was set up in the well of the courtroom. From the gasps heard round the room, we were sure that Bill had unequivocally stated our case.

After Kunkle ended his arugment by imploring the jurors to fulfill their oath as "the conscience" of the people of Illinois, Judge Garippo ordered the courtroom locked during his instructions to the jury. This recitation ensures that the jury follows the law in its deliberations, and ranges from restatements of constitutional principles to guidelines about handling the required paperwork. He explained such matters as the credibility of witnesses, the burden of proof, the insanity standard, the crime of murder and deviate sexual conduct, and the signing of verdicts. Because of the large number of exhibits, the jury's deliberations would take place in the closed courtroom, where the evidence would be displayed. Garippo recessed the court in the early afternoon, and the twelve regular jurors were left to make their decision. The verdict on each of the thirty-five indictments had to be unanimous, and there were only three possibilities: guilty, not guilty, or not guilty by reason of insanity.

As we walked back to our offices in the adjacent administration building, we were besieged by reporters, but there was little to tell them; now it was out of our hands. I thought we had presented an effective case, but a jury is subject to too many variable factors to be predictable. I just was relieved that it was over, and I was grateful to have a respite that might last several days while the jury deliberated.

That afternoon we went down the street to a little saloon that is a hangout for courthouse regulars, a place where after lunch hours you have to knock at the back door to be admitted. The bar was jammed with reporters and spectators, and Gacy's lawyers were there. Counsel from both sides congratulated one another for doing a nice job, in the normal post-adversarial ritual. I was just finishing my first beer when the bartender announced, "The jury's back."

My first reaction was, What's gone wrong? The jury had deliberated less than two hours—at least it was clear that they had had no trouble with holdouts. After all our work, maybe they had bought the psychiatric defense, just as we had feared at the start of the trial when most people were saying, "This guy's gotta be nuts."

The crowd in the courtroom was silent and tense. Before the jury returned, Garippo warned the hushed section of spectators that any visible reactions could impair the functioning of the jury in the event it had to be reconvened. Gacy, apparently emotionless, sat with his lawyers. The jurors filed back in and took their seats.

"Mr. Foreman," Garippo asked, "has the jury signed thirty-five verdicts?"

"Yes, we have," juror Ronald Geaver replied.

"Would you pass them to the bailiff, who will pass them to the clerk," the judge said. "Each verdict is in order. Will you read them please?"

The clerk, standing to the right of the judge and facing the packed courtroom, began the recitation:

"We, the jury, find the defendant, John Wayne Gacy, guilty of the murder of Robert Piest." The suspense was over. All of us at the prosecutors' table reached for one another's hands and rejoiced. Thank God, I thought.

"We, the jury, find the defendant, John Wayne Gacy, guilty of indecent liberties with a child upon Robert Piest.

"We, the jury, find the defendant, John Wayne Gacy, guilty of the murder of John Butkovich."

The clerk's reading of the verdicts continued for thirty-two more indictments. Some of the victims were named, others designated simply by the Cook County sheriff's numbers. The jury had found John Gacy guilty on all counts.

Garippo turned to the jury foreman. "Ronald Geaver," he asked, "did you hear all the verdicts as read by the clerk?"

"Yes," Geaver responded.

"Were they your verdicts?"

"Yes."

"Are they now your verdicts?"

"Yes."

Similarly, he questioned in turn jurors Mabel Loudenback, Dean Johnson, Bernard Lindberg, Lorraine Haavisto, David Osborn, Glenn A. Seiverston, Melvin Schmall, Pearl Christiansen, Charles Hansen, Evelyn Gustafson, and Rose Putnam.

John Gacy now had the singular notoriety of having been convicted of more murders than anyone else in American history. Yet even now he was not broken. As he was led from the courtroom, he winked at a deputy sheriff. No matter. Now we would begin final work on our case for the death penalty.

We reconvened at 1:30 Thursday afternoon, March 13, for the purpose of sentencing John Gacy. We requested a death sentence in twelve of the cases, those murders that had taken place since the new Illinois statute on capital punishment went into effect in 1977. The defense immediately offered two motions to declare the statute unconstitutional, but the judge denied them. Amirante argued that the killings had started before the statute went into effect and went on "ritually" as if one continuous transaction. Garippo replied that the basis on which he had decided to consolidate all the charges had nothing to do with any finding of his that the killings were "one continuous transaction." Then Amirante argued that Gacy had been "effectively precluded from his civil right to be committed prior to trial." Garippo persisted in his denial of the defense motions.

Next, the defense moved to discharge the jury, which, Amirante argued, "was obviously predisposed to their finding of guilty." He said that it was "incomprehensible" that the jurors could have gone through all the evidence and discussed the merits of the case in the short time they were out. If their minds were made up on the question of guilt, he said, so might they already have decided to administer the death penalty. Garippo denied the motion for failure to show good cause. Had he allowed it, the jury would have been dismissed, another one chosen, and the lengthy process of presenting evidence would have had to begin anew. We were relieved not to have to face that.

The defense could now choose to go before the jury again in the death penalty hearing, or leave sentencing solely in the hands of the judge. They opted for the jury, a proper move because only one dissenter out of the group of twelve would be sufficient to spare John Gacy from the electric chair. The judge ordered the jury brought in.

Garippo instructed the twelve jurors on the death penalty statute and told them they had two considerations to deal with. The first was whether the state had proved beyond a reasonable doubt the existence of an aggravating factor, and the judge explained that we were offering the twelve murder convictions involving intentional killings as evidence of that. Next, he said, "if you unanimously agree that there are not sufficient mitigating factors to preclude the imposition of the death penalty, you will then sign a verdict directing the court to fix punishment at death."

I gave the opening statement at the hearing. "During the trial," I told the jurors, "you sat there face to face with an accused murderer, an alleged murderer. Today you sit face to face with a convicted murderer. That veil of innocence that surrounded John Gacy has been torn asunder by your verdicts.

"The evidence will show that John Gacy is plainly and simply an antisocial person. That only means that he will murder and murder and murder again and again, if you allow him to do so.

"The evidence will likewise show that Robert Donnelly pled for his life. I ask you to please remember the torture, the terrifying acts of a sadistic animal, and remember, please, his bringing Robert Donnelly to the very edge of life and causing him to plead, 'Go ahead and kill me, get it over with.'

"Think about Robert Piest, remembering what Robert Donnelly said. The terrible anguish that ran through his mind when he realized, standing there, that he was immobilized by those handcuffs. When in those few brief moments he actually knew he was going to die, and when that terrible fear rushed up through his body to his head, and tears began flowing, and then he openly cried as he saw that rope in front of his wide, glassy eyes, and that convicted murderer of thirty-two [others] ruthlessly strangled the very last breath from an innocent fifteen-year-old. Can't you just hear those thirty-three young boys pleading one by one for their lives? For whom is the death penalty more appropriate?"

In his opening statement, Motta said that he did not look upon the guilty verdict as a rejection of the fact of an extreme mental or emotional disturbance. "Whether or not this emotional disturbance is sufficient for you to find him not guilty by reason of insanity is really at this point not in question. The question is whether or not those conditions are sufficient to impose less than the death penalty."

Motta warned the jurors of the consequences of putting their names on "the verdict that will put him in the electric chair and fry him, because when you put your name on the verdict, you pull the switch." Kunkle objected, and Garippo sustained the objection.

"Is there not one among you that does not believe in that cruel and barbaric custom . . . (Objection/Sustained) . . . and I ask you as ladies and gentlemen of the jury to stop it. I ask you to let him live. I ask you to let him exist in a six-by-ten cell for the rest of his life."

Bob Egan attempted to reassure the jurors after Motta's challenge. He told them that they were simply one cog in the wheel of the criminal justice system. And, he said, "let's not forget the man in the green suit over here, because a long time ago, before you or I knew about this case or knew that it even existed, John Gacy set the wheels in motion, whereby he would sentence himself to death. By his actions, he earned the death penalty. You are simply allowing him to follow through on what he has already done."

In closing, Amirante told the jury that they had followed the law up to now and that he hoped they continued to do so. He had two young sons, he said, and he didn't want them falling prey to the same kind of person as his client.

"Our whole case, from the very beginning, has been what you would call aggravation and mitigation," Amirante said. "We didn't feel [Gacy] should be free. We feel he belongs in a mental institution for the rest of his life." He asked his client to stand.

"Look at John Gacy. You have heard him described a lot of ways, both good and bad," he said. "All those things do not put aside the fact that he is still and always will be a human being. He was born the same way you and I were born. He had a mother and father. He grew up. Somewhere, somehow, something went wrong. Only God can judge his blackened soul.

"They are asking you to put him to death. Does that make any sense at all? How could, on one hand, we condemn a man for putting somebody to death, and then just turn right around and do it ourselves? Are we collectively John Gacys?" Amirante said that mass-murderers could not be deterred, pleading for a sentence of imprisonment. "There will be others out there—mark my words."

"Do you think," Kunkle asked the jurors in his rebuttal, "that the emotional disturbance that this defendant demonstrated when he left Robert Piest choking to death and went to answer the telephone and conducted business—do you think that is sufficient to preclude the imposition of the death penalty? Particularly when he was the thirty-third of thirty-three murders?

"'Spare his life . . . he is a human being . . . we are asking you to do the same thing to John Gacy that he did to his victims.' How absurd, how absurd. Are we asking you to take an innocent man, torture him with your hands, ropes, with instruments of sexual perversion and torture? We are asking you to follow the law of Illinois. John Gacy is not an innocent man. He is not a human being like you or like Mr. Amirante. He is a convicted killer.

"I will be frank with you, ladies and gentlemen, as a citizen of the State of Illinois myself, I don't want to pay this guy's rent for the rest of his life."

"Objection, Judge," Motta said angrily. "Then let Mr. Kunkle pull the switch."

"What will his motivation be," Kunkle asked, "when he knows he will not get an early parole? Who is the victim going to be next, an inmate, a young boy inmate, a guard?

"If this is not an appropriate case for the death penalty," Kunkle concluded, "then there is no death penalty in Illinois. This is a case that cries out, not only with the voices of thirty-three dead, but the voices of thirty-three families, but yes, the voices of every single citizen of this state, and that voice says, 'John Gacy, enough! Enough!'"

Then the judge instructed the jury, explaining that if the verdict were imprisonment, Gacy would be sentenced to a fixed term of not less than twenty years or more than forty for each offense. He added that a prisoner usually serves approximately half the number of years specified.

Once again the jury deliberated. It was now just a week before the vernal equinox, and the setting sun shone in a blaze of golden-orange out the west windows of our administrative offices. Below, the shadows lengthened over the courtyards and revetments of the Cook County penal complex. In the marble corridors of the courthouse, the press and throngs of spectators waited.

At 6:30 P.M., after slightly more than two hours of recess, we were called back. The jury had reached a verdict.

Standing before the bench, flanked by his two lawyers, John Gacy listened to the reading by the clerk.

"We, the jury, unanimously conclude that the defendant, John Wayne Gacy, attained the age of eighteen years at the time of the murders and has been convicted of intentionally murdering the following individuals:

"Matthew H. Bowman, Robert Gilroy, John Mowery, Russell O. Nelson, Robert Winch, Tommy Bolin, David Paul Talsma, William Kindred, Timothy O'Rourke, Frank Landingin, James Mazzara, and Robert Piest.

"That these murders occurred after June 21, 1977.

"We, the jury, unanimously conclude that the court shall sentence the defendant, John Wayne Gacy, to death." A rush of sound, held breaths released, swept through the courtroom.

The judge polled the jurors to confirm their written verdict, then sat back and began to talk gently to them, expressing his gratitude and commending them for their contributions. He explained why he had gone to Rockford to choose them and complimented them and their community on the way they had helped solve our problems. He called their willingness to make personal sacrifices to do so "inspiring."

"A couple of months ago," Garippo continued, "a group of prosecutors from another country came and couldn't understand how in the United States you could try a person who was arrested in this type of situation. A lot has been said about how much this case has cost, and I don't know what it cost. But whatever the cost was . . . it's a small price . . ." Garippo's voice choked. He lowered his head for a moment, then dabbed his eyes before going on: "My voice is cracking because I really, truly, feel it's a small price that we paid for our freedom.

"What we do for the John Gacys," he said, his voice now strong, his tone resolute, "we'll do for everyone."